ADVANCE PRAISE FOR *9/11 CO*

"When the smoke finally cleared from the pile of rubble on September 11, 2001, we were left with a host of burning questions. The 9/11 Commission did not provide the answers, despite their extensive mandate. *9/11 Contradictions* is a work that needed to be written. With characteristic clarity and focus, David Ray Griffin masterfully lays out the most critical of these questions. Now the challenge is to finally get real answers."

—Lorie Van Auken, widow of Kenneth Van Auken, who was killed at WTC 1 on 9/11/01, and member of the Family Steering Committee for the 9/11 Commission

"So who cares that the 9/11 Commission chose to believe that Dick Cheney did not enter the White House bunker until 'shortly before 10:00, perhaps at 9:58,' twenty minutes after the strike on the Pentagon. Surely the vice president would not fib, so the Commission threw out the testimony of several eyewitnesses, including Norman Mineta, the transportation secretary. Mineta must have been making it all up when he testified that he joined Cheney in the bunker at about 9:20 and heard Cheney reaffirm an apparent stand-down order just before the Pentagon was struck. Such conflicting testimony is typical of the many serious '9/11 Contradictions' documented in David Ray Griffin's highly readable book. We need a truly independent investigation to put Cheney and Mineta under oath, along with the still unidentified 'young man' who, Mineta reported, kept coming into the bunker and, after telling Cheney 'the plane is ten miles out,' asked Cheney whether 'the orders still stand'—about 12 minutes before 125 people in the Pentagon were killed. What were those orders?"

—Ray McGovern, former CIA analyst and presidential briefer

"Because the 9/11 attacks became the excuse for myriad disastrous changes in US foreign and domestic policy, unraveling the true history of those events is the paramount exigency of our times. By virtue of pointing out an astonishing number of irreconcilable contradictions in the official story of 9/11, David Ray Griffin's *9/11 Contradictions* is a must read, not only for the Congress and the press, but also for anyone concerned about the truth, because those contradictions suggest that we have not yet been told the truth about 9/11."

—David L. Griscom, research physicist, Fellow of the American Physical Society, retired from the Naval Research Laboratory

9/11 CONTRADICTIONS

AN OPEN LETTER TO CONGRESS AND THE PRESS

by David Ray Griffin

OLIVE
BRANCH
PRESS

An imprint of Interlink Publishing Group, Inc.
www.interlinkbooks.com

First published in 2008 by

OLIVE BRANCH PRESS
An imprint of Interlink Publishing Group, Inc.
46 Crosby Street, Northampton, Massachusetts 01060
www.interlinkbooks.com

Library of Congress Cataloging-in-Publication Data
Griffin, David Ray, 1939–
9/11 contradictions : an open letter to Congress and the press / by David Ray Griffin. —
1st ed.
p. cm.
Includes bibliographical references and index.
ISBN 978-1-56656-716-9 (pbk.)
1. September 11 Terrorist Attacks, 2001. 2. United States—Politics and government—
2001–3. Conspiracies. I. Title. II. Title: Nine eleven contradictions.
HV6432.7.G7455 2008
973.931—dc22
2007046494

Printed and bound in the United States of America

10 9 8 7 6 5 4 3 2

Cover image © AP Photos

To request our complete 40-page full-color catalog,
please call us toll free at 1-800-238-LINK, visit our
website at www.interlinkbooks.com, or write to
Interlink Publishing
46 Crosby Street, Northampton, MA 01060
e-mail: info@interlinkbooks.com

TABLE OF CONTENTS

PREFACE

The title of this book, *9/11 Contradictions*, refers entirely to *internal* contradictions within the public story about 9/11. The book deals, in other words, with issues on which one person, agency, institution, or official body that has helped articulate the public story about 9/11 has contradicted another such person, agency, institution, or official body. In some cases, the contradiction is a *self*-contradiction, in which people contradict what they had said at an earlier time.

To give a few examples: In Chapter 1, we see that the White House has told two radically different stories about President Bush's behavior in the classroom in Florida. The second and third chapters show that Secretary of Transportation Norman Mineta's testimony about Vice President Cheney's whereabouts that morning contradicts the account given by the 9/11 Commission. In Chapter 7, the contradiction is between Richard Clarke, on the one hand, and Donald Rumsfeld and the 9/11 Commission, on the other. In Chapters 8 and 17, we see that two of the government's claims—about Barbara Olson's calls to Ted Olson and about evidence of Osama bin Laden's responsibility for 9/11— are contradicted by one of its own agencies, the FBI. Chapters 12 and 13 show that the 9/11 Commission's main claims about United Flight 93, made in 2004, are contradicted by statements made in previous years by many US military officers. In Chapters 21 and 22, we see that statements made by the National Institute of Standards and Technology (NIST), which was given the task of explaining the destruction of the World Trade Center, are contradicted by numerous statements made by members of the Fire Department of New York.

In several chapters, the contradictions involve the mainstream media. (These contradictions are considered "internal" because the mainstream media, while perhaps challenging this or that detail of the story told by government officials, have supported all this story's main elements.) Chapter 16, for example, shows that stories about cell phone calls from the flights, which have appeared in the media from the beginning, were contradicted by the FBI's report on phone calls from the four flights, which was presented at the Moussaoui trial in 2006.

As its subtitle indicates, this book is addressed to Congress and the press. It is especially suitable for them for two reasons.

In the first place, most reporters and members of Congress are busy people, with little time to study complex issues. This book, besides being easy to read, requires no technical expertise in order to form a judgment about the issues involved.

Most other books about 9/11 revolve around various matters—such as FAA and military procedures, the conditions needed to cause steel-frame buildings to collapse, and the kind of damage that would be caused by an airliner striking the Pentagon—about which most people do not feel equipped to make a judgment.

In the present book, by contrast, no judgments requiring expertise are required, because each chapter revolves around a simple contradiction, which anyone can recognize. If Jones says "P" and Smith says "not P," we can all recognize that something must be wrong, because both statements cannot be true.

In the second place, many members of Congress and the press have been reluctant to look into any possible difficulties about the public story for fear of being labeled "conspiracy theorists." Although this may be unfortunate, it is understandable, because the most important asset of both journalists and politicians is their credibility. If they lose that, they lose their effectiveness, even their jobs. We can understand, therefore, that they are unwilling to risk being saddled with the dreaded "conspiracy theorist" label—one of the surest ways to lose credibility—by showing sympathy with people questioning the official account of what happened on 9/11.

Why is this—that anyone questioning the official story is almost automatically labeled a conspiracy theorist? It is because in most critical treatments of 9/11, the official account is rejected in favor of an alternative theory, which usually involves the idea that the 9/11 attacks resulted from a conspiracy within our own government.

The present book, however, contains no theory about what really happened. It provides simply an exposition of various facts. If Mineta said "P," that is a fact. If the 9/11 Commission said "not P," that is a fact. And it is a fact that "P" and "not P" cannot both be true.

Here, then, is the point of this book: 9/11 has clearly been the most important event in recent history. The accepted story about 9/11 has been used to increase military spending, justify wars, restrict civil liberties, and exalt the executive branch of the government. And yet there are serious contradictions within this accepted story: this book documents 25 of them. The existence of so many contradictions within such an important story is intolerable. Congress and the press are the two principal institutions with the power and the responsibility for looking into such matters.

This book is intended as a tool to help them fulfill this responsibility.

In doing the research for this book, I relied most heavily on the Complete 911 Timeline produced by Cooperative Research. This timeline, drawn entirely from stories in the mainstream press, aspires to identify and, when possible, provide links to all reports dealing with events related to the attacks of 9/11. This timeline, which is surely one of the greatest journalistic feats of all time, is an indispensable resource for serious discussions of 9/11. Many of the chapters in this book would have been simply impossible without it.

I also relied heavily on the help of three wonderfully unselfish people: Matthew Everett of England, who is one of the managers of the Complete 9/11 Timeline; Elizabeth Woodworth of British Columbia, a writer and former research librarian; and Tod Fletcher of California, who would regularly spot problems the rest of us had overlooked. These three individuals, besides improving this book immensely with their good advice and proofreading skills, alerted me to the existence of dozens of reports I would have otherwise missed. Insofar as this book is easy to read and its references are useful to other researchers by virtue of being complete and up to date, gratitude should be directed primarily toward them.

Enormous additional thanks go to Elizabeth: after serving as my virtual assistant in the production of this book, she did most of the work for the preparation of the index.

I also wish to thank Hilary Plum of Interlink Books, for excellent work in editing this book, and my wife, Ann Jaqua, making it possible, in so many ways, for me to engage in the research and writing required for this book.

PART I

Questions about Bush Administration and Pentagon Leaders

1

How Long Did George Bush
Remain in the Classroom?

O n September 11, 2001, President Bush was at an elementary school in Sarasota, Florida, to publicize his education policy (No Child Left Behind) by being photographed listening to students read. He arrived at the school at 8:55AM, at which time he reportedly first learned that a plane had flown into the WTC. Dismissing the crash as an accident,[1] Bush, according to the school's principal, said that "a commercial plane has hit the World Trade Center and we're going to go ahead and... do the reading thing anyway."[2] Bush entered the second-grade classroom of teacher Sandra Kay Daniels at about 9:03. At about 9:06 or 9:07—after the children had started reading aloud—the president's chief of staff, Andrew Card, came in and whispered in Bush's ear, telling him, Card has reported, "A second plane hit the second Tower. America is under attack."[3]

Up to that point, all accounts of the events at the school essentially agree. With regard to what happened next, however, we have been given two drastically different accounts.

The White House's First Anniversary Account
One account, put forth on the first anniversary of 9/11, was told primarily by Andrew Card. In an article in the *San Francisco Chronicle* on September 11, 2002, Card said that, after he had informed President Bush about the second attack, the president "looked up—it was only a matter of seconds, but it seemed like minutes.... And he just excused himself very politely to the

teacher and to the students and he left."[4] Two days earlier, Card had told Brian Williams of NBC News: "I pulled away from the president, and not that many seconds later, the president excused himself from the classroom, and we gathered in the holding room and talked about the situation."[5] Card similarly told ABC News: "The president waited for a moment for the students to finish, then said, 'Thank you all so very much for showing me your reading skills,' and headed for the empty classroom next door."[6]

Card, moreover, was not the only member of the White House giving this account. During an NBC interview aired on the first anniversary of 9/11, Karl Rove described the incident in the following words:

> Andy Card walked in to tell the President, and you can remember the famous photograph of him whispering in the President's ear. And the President was a little—you know, he didn't want to alarm the children. He knew the drill was coming to a close. So he waited for a few moments just to—literally—not very long at all before he came to the close, and he came into the staff room.[7]

Card and Rove got ABC News, during another program that aired on the first anniversary of 9/11, to endorse this account. This program contained the following segment:

> *Andrew Card*: I think there was a, a moment of shock and he did stare off maybe for just a second.
>
> *Charles Gibson*: The President stays calm and lets the students finish.
>
> *Karl Rove*: The President thought for a second or two about getting up and walking out of the room. But the drill was coming to a close and he didn't want to alarm the children.
>
> *Gibson*: Instead Bush pauses, thanks the children... and heads for the empty classroom next door.[8]

However, this account, given by Card, Rove, and even ABC one year after the events, disagreed with all prior accounts and with a videotape.

Prior Accounts and the Videotape

According to all these prior accounts, Bush remained in the room until about 9:16. In a *Tampa Tribune* article published September 1, 2002, Jennifer Barrs said that Bush remained silent for about 30 seconds after Card whispered in his ear, then picked up his book and read with the children "for eight or nine minutes."[9] Various reports indicate, moreover, that after the reading lesson was over, Bush continued to talk. Besides advising the children to stay in school and be good citizens,[10] he discussed his education policy.[11] In fact, Bill Sammon, the White House correspondent for the *Washington Times*, wrote—in a book that otherwise presents a sympathetic account of the president—that Bush was "openly stretching out the moment." Even referring to Bush as "the dawdler in chief," Sammon reported that "Bush lingered until the press was gone."[12]

Besides being contradicted by these and many other press reports, the Card–Rove account is disproved by a videotape of the event. As the *Wall Street Journal* reported in March 2004, this videotape shows that Bush "followed along for five minutes as children read aloud a story about a pet goat."[13] With the appearance in June 2004 of Michael Moore's film *Fahrenheit 9/11*, that videotape became widely known. But it had been available on the Internet since June 2003, and a shorter version, showing Bush remaining in the classroom for over two minutes, had been available since June 2002.[14] Although it is not clear exactly when the White House gave up trying to defend its revisionist account, this may have been after it realized that this video had become publicly available.

Dealing with the Contradiction

In any case, when the White House was contacted by the *Wall Street Journal* for a March 2004 article, it did not try to defend the revisionist version of Bush's behavior. Instead, spokesperson Dan Bartlett confirmed that the president remained in the classroom for at least seven minutes. Bush did not leave immediately after receiving the news of the second crash, Bartlett told the *Journal*, because his "instinct was not to frighten the children by rushing out of the room."[15]

However, even if Bartlett's statement is accepted as an explanation of why Bush did not do what Card and Rove had claimed he did, the real question, which should have been asked by the *Wall Street Journal*, was why the White House, through Card and Rove, had given a false account. Surely this is a question that the press in general should have explored. At least ABC News, NBC News, the *San Francisco Chronicle*, and other media that had been used to spread the White House's false account should have demanded that the White House explain why it put out an account that was demonstrably false. ABC News, which had itself endorsed this false account, especially owed its viewers a correction and an attempt to find out why the White House had used it to spread a lie.

The importance the White House put on covering up what really happened is underscored by the fact that it had enlisted someone else to spread its false account. Sandra Kay Daniels, the teacher of the second grade class at the Sarasota school, said in a *Los Angeles Times* story on the first anniversary of 9/11: "I knew something was up when President Bush didn't pick up the book and participate in the lesson…. He said, 'Mrs. Daniels, I have to leave now. I am going to leave Lt. Gov. Frank Brogan here to do the speech for me.' Looking at his face, you knew something was wrong. I said a little prayer for him. He shook my hand and left."[16]

On the next day, Daniels was quoted in a *New York Post* article as having given—in an interview on September 11, 2002—a quite different account. In this version, it was a Secret Service agent (not Andrew Card) who came into the room to inform the president, and this agent asked, "Where can we get to a television?" At that moment, Daniels reportedly said: "The president bolted right out of here and told me: 'Take over.' I knew something serious had happened, and then a short while later he came back and said, 'What we thought was an airline accident turned out to be a terrorist hijack.'" She then reportedly added: "My kids were so happy that morning—imagine the president of the United States sitting there shooting the breeze, and then poof, suddenly he's gone."[17]

Although Daniels—who says she received a letter from President Bush a week after 9/11, the contents of which she will not reveal[18]—gave two different accounts of what happened, they both supported the main point of the White House's first-anniversary version of Bush's response to learning about the second attack: He left very quickly.

Besides being different from each other, moreover, these two accounts by Daniels were radically different from what she had reportedly said while being interviewed for the aforementioned article by Jennifer Barrs, which had been published in the *Tampa Tribune* only ten days earlier. That article, besides saying that Bush "read with the students for eight or nine minutes," also reported that, after Card whispered in the president's ear, "Bush grimaced and, obviously lost in thought, forgot about the book in his lap." The article then quoted Daniels as saying: "I couldn't gently kick him.... I couldn't say, 'OK, Mr. President. Pick up your book, sir. The whole world is watching.'"[19]

Daniels should be asked what happened between September 1, 2002, when she gave this accurate account, and ten days later, when she gave two versions of a false account.

In any case, the fact that the White House seems to have enlisted Daniels in its effort to obscure the truth about Bush's behavior should have made the press suspect that something very important was at stake, giving it even more reason to try to learn the White House's motive for putting out a false account.

A Possible Motive

A possible motive is not hard to imagine. On the one hand, the Secret Service, which is responsible for protecting the president from any possible threat to his life, should have assumed, once it was clear that terrorists were going after high-value targets, that the president might have been one of those targets. As one article put it, "Bush's presence made... the planned reading event a perceived target," because "the well-publicized event at the school assured Bush's location that day was no secret."[20] On the other hand, people observed that the Secret Service had not acted accordingly. The day after 9/11, the *Globe and Mail*, one of

Canada's leading newspapers, commented: "For some reason, Secret Service agents did not bustle him [Bush] away."[21]

The background for this comment was explained by Philip Melanson, the author of a book about the Secret Service.[22] "With an unfolding terrorist attack," Melanson said, "the procedure should have been to get the president to the closest secure location as quickly as possible."[23] That this indeed would have been standard operating procedure is illustrated by the fact that, as soon as the second strike on the World Trade Center was seen on television, a marine carrying the president's phone said to Sarasota County Sheriff Bill Balkwill: "We're out of here. Can you get everybody ready?"[24]

But this marine's decision was obviously overridden by some higher-level Secret Service agent, as Bush was allowed not only to remain in the classroom for seven or more minutes, but also to remain at the school for another twenty minutes. He was even allowed to deliver a television address to the nation, thereby letting everyone know that he was still at the school.

This behavior seemed especially reckless in light of reports, issued at the time, that as many as eleven planes had been hijacked.[25] Should not the Secret Service have feared that one of those planes might be bearing down on the school?

The Secret Service was not, it is important to note, failing to protect the president from other types of threats to his life: "Police and Secret Service agents were on the roof, on horseback and in every hallway." They were even "lying in the trusses above the [class]room."[26] The night before, moreover, while Bush was staying at the Colony Beach and Tennis Resort:

> Snipers kept watch over the president from the roofs of the Colony and adjacent structures. The Coast Guard and the Longboat Key Police Department manned boats that patrolled the surf in front of the resort all night. Security trucks with enough men and arms to stop a small army parked right on the beach. An Airborne Warning and Control System (AWACS) plane circled high overhead in the clear night sky.[27]

In light of these protective measures against merely possible attacks, the Secret Service's behavior at the school, at a time where terrorist attacks were known to be going on, was very strange, suggesting that the Secret Service had no fear of an attack from a hijacked airliner.

That lack of fear contrasted strongly with the response, two months earlier, to a report that Islamic terrorists might crash an airliner into the summit of industrialized nations in Genoa, Italy, in an effort to kill President Bush. The Italian government closed the airspace above Genoa and installed anti-aircraft missiles at the airport.[28] Even with all this protection, Bush stayed overnight on an aircraft carrier, instead of staying, like the other leaders, on a luxury ship.[29] Why so much concern about a merely possible airplane attack in Genoa in July but no such concern in Sarasota in September, when such attacks were actually in progress?

The Secret Service's failure to hustle Bush away seemed even stranger in light of the reports that Dick Cheney, Condoleezza Rice, and several congressional leaders were quickly taken to safe locations.[30] Should not have protecting President Bush been an even higher priority? As Susan Taylor Martin of the *St. Petersburg Times* put it: "One of the many unanswered questions about that day is why the Secret Service did not immediately hustle Bush to a secure location, as it apparently did with Vice President Dick Cheney."[31]

The fact that this question was raised immediately after 9/11, then continued to be raised, could well have been perceived by the White House as dangerous. This question did, in fact, have dangerous implications, because it could—and in some circles did—lead to the inference that Bush was not evacuated from the school because the Secret Service knew that he would not be targeted. Could the desire to stop this kind of speculation have been behind the White House's attempts at getting a revisionist account of Bush's behavior instilled into the public consciousness?

That this might indeed be the case is suggested by the fact that, at the same time White House spokespersons were giving their revisionist account of Bush's behavior, they were also claiming that the presidential party had been fearful of an attack. Ari Fleischer, the White House press secretary, told ABC News:

The fear ran so deep that a... Cold War concept that I had never heard of actually came into play that day. The fear was this was an attack whose intent was to decapitate the government, in other words to take out the Congressional leaders, to take out the President, to take out the Vice President, so our government cannot function, decapitation.[32]

Karl Rove, telling ABC about the take-off of Air Force One from the Sarasota airport, said:

[B]efore [President Bush and I] could sit down and put on our seatbelts they were rolling the plane. And they stood that 747 on its tail and got it to about 45,000 feet as quick as I think you can get a big thing like that up in the air.[33]

Bob Woodward gave a similar account, writing:

The President's motorcade raced to the Sarasota Bradenton International Airport. He dashed up the steps and into his private front cabin and office on Air Force One.... "Mr. President," one of the agents said nervously, "we need you to get seated as soon as possible." Bush strapped in, and the plane accelerated down the runway, almost standing on its tail as it climbed rapidly.[34]

The 9/11 Commission Report, however, did not endorse this account. It instead said:

The President's motorcade departed at 9:35, and arrived at the airport between 9:42 and 9:45.... He boarded the aircraft, asked the Secret Service about the safety of his family, and called the Vice President.... About this time, Card, the lead Secret Service agent, the President's military aide, and the pilot were conferring on a possible destination for Air Force One.... Air Force One departed at approximately 9:54, without any fixed destination. The objective was to get up in the air—as fast and as high as possible—and then decide where to go.[35]

So, although the 9/11 Commission's final sentence suggested a sense of urgency, its account had the plane remaining on the ground for about ten minutes. There is no corroboration of Rove's and Woodward's tales of haste, in which the plane began rolling as soon as everyone was on board.

It would, in fact, have been difficult for the Commission to square the Rove and Woodward accounts with the public record, because this record has the presidential motorcade arriving at the airport before 9:45 and Air Force One not taking off until almost 9:55. It would appear, therefore, that the stories of extreme haste were later inventions, created to suggest that the Secret Service agents, in spite of their apparent complacency at the school, really did have an appropriate degree of fear.

Conclusion

These stories suggesting fear at the airport did not, in any case, solve the problem. Indeed, they arguably made it worse. If such fear existed at that time, so that there was concern to get the presidential plane into the air as quickly as possible, why was there apparently no such fear while the presidential party was at the school? (Sandra Kay Daniels and the school's principal, Gwendolyn Tosé-Rigell, according to a local newspaper, were "convinced that Booker Elementary was actually one of the safest places in the world on Sept. 11, 2001."[36]) Why was the president allowed to linger a full half-hour at the school after it was known that America was, as Card put it, "under attack"?

This question was of great concern to families of the 9/11 victims. One of the central questions raised by the Family Steering Committee for the 9/11 Commission—as Thomas Kean and Lee Hamilton, the chair and vice-chair of the Commission admit—was: "Why was President Bush permitted by the Secret Service to remain in the Sarasota elementary school where he was reading to children?"[37] Kean and Hamilton's 9/11 Commission, however, provided no answer. Its only response to this question was to say: "The Secret Service told us they were anxious to move the President to a safer location, but did not think it imperative for him to run out the door."[38] That response implied that the president's options were limited to (a) running out the door or (b) remaining at the school another half hour. But there was a third option: The Secret Service could have simply walked the president out of the room, put him in the limo, and whisked him away.

We have here, in fact, an implicit contradiction within the official story: The claim by Fleischer and Rove that the presidential party feared an attack on the president's life is contradicted by the Secret Service's indication by its statement to the 9/11 Commission—as well as by its behavior at the school—that no such fear existed.

In any case, we are still left with the central contradiction documented in this chapter: the contradiction between the actual behavior of the president at the school that morning and the account of that behavior given by the White House—through Andrew Card and Karl Rove—on the first anniversary of 9/11. The fact that the White House later admitted the falsity of this account does not lessen the importance of the question to which Congress and the press should demand an answer: Why was that false account put out?

2

WHEN DID DICK CHENEY ENTER THE UNDERGROUND BUNKER?

Everyone agrees that at some time after 9:03AM, when the South Tower of the World Trade Center was struck, and before 10:00, Vice President Dick Cheney went down to the Presidential Emergency Operations Center (PEOC), which is under the east wing of the White House (and is sometimes called the "shelter conference room," the "bomb shelter," or simply the "bunker"). Everyone also agrees that Cheney, once there, was in charge—that he was either making decisions or relaying decisions made by President Bush. Indeed, Cheney himself said on *Meet the Press* five days after 9/11: "I was in a position to be able to see all the stuff coming in, receive reports and then make decisions in terms of acting with it."[1] But there is enormous disagreement as to exactly when Cheney entered the PEOC.

According to *The 9/11 Commission Report*, Cheney arrived "shortly before 10:00, perhaps at 9:58."[2] This official time, however, contradicts almost all previous reports, some of which had him there before 9:20. This difference is important because, if the 9/11 Commission's time is correct, Cheney was not in charge in the PEOC when the Pentagon was struck or for most of the period during which United Flight 93 was approaching Washington. But if the reports that have him there by 9:20 are correct, he *was* in charge in the PEOC all that time.

Mineta's Report of Cheney's Early Arrival

The most well-known statement contradicting the 9/11 Commission is that of Secretary of Transportation Norman Mineta, given in his public testimony to the 9/11 Commission on May 23, 2003. Reporting that he "arrived at the PEOC at about 9:20AM," Mineta said that he shortly thereafter overheard an ongoing conversation between a young man, who came into the room three times, and Vice President Cheney. In the third exchange, the young man asked, "Do the orders still stand?" Cheney replied that they did. When Mineta was later asked by Commissioner Timothy Roemer how long it was after he arrived that this conversation between Cheney and the young man occurred, Mineta replied: "Probably about five or six minutes." This would mean, Roemer pointed out, "about 9:25 or 9:26."[3]

This is a remarkable contradiction. Given the fact that Cheney, according to Mineta, was engaged in an ongoing exchange in which he had, before Mineta's 9:20 arrival, given "orders," he must have been in the PEOC for several minutes before Mineta's 9:20 arrival. If Cheney had been there since 9:15, for example, there would be a 43-minute contradiction between Mineta's testimony and *The 9/11 Commission Report*. Why would such an enormous contradiction exist?

One explanation would be that Mineta was wrong.[4] His story, however, is in line with that of many other witnesses.

Other Reports Supporting Cheney's Early Arrival

Richard Clarke, in his book *Against All Enemies*, reported that he, Cheney, and Condoleezza Rice had a brief meeting shortly after 9:03, following which the Secret Service wanted Cheney and Rice to go down to the PEOC. Rice, however, first went with Clarke to the White House's Video Teleconferencing Center, where Clarke was to set up a video conference, which, Clarke's statements suggest, began at about 9:10.[5] After spending a few minutes there, Rice said, according to Clarke: "You're going to need some decisions quickly. I'm going to the PEOC to be with the Vice President. Tell us what you need." Clarke replied: "What I need is an open line to Cheney and you."[6] Some minutes later, evidently at about 9:15, Norman

Mineta arrived and Clarke, after receiving him in the Situation Room, "suggested he join the Vice President."[7] Clarke thereby implied that Cheney was in the PEOC several minutes prior to 9:15.

Cheney's own White House photographer, David Bohrer, reportedly supported the early descent time. Describing an episode that ABC reported as happening "just after 9AM," Bohrer said: "[Two or three Secret Service] agents came inside [Cheney's] office and said, 'Sir, you have to come with us.'"[8]

ABC also, like Clarke, reported that Rice supported Cheney's early descent. After describing Bohrer's account of the Secret Service agents and Cheney's trip down to the PEOC, ABC's Charles Gibson said: "Up above, National Security Adviser Condoleezza Rice is trying to find the rest of the President's team," after which Rice said: "As I was trying to find all of the principals, the Secret Service came in and said, 'You have to leave now for the bunker. The Vice President's already there. There may be a plane headed for the White House.'" Gibson then added: "In the bunker, the Vice President is joined by Rice and Transportation Secretary Norman Mineta."[9] So although the accounts of Rice and Clarke differed somewhat, they agreed that Mineta went down to the PEOC quite early and that Cheney was already there.

Cheney's early descent was also described by White House strategist Karl Rove. As we saw in the previous chapter, he told NBC News that after Andrew Card came into the classroom shortly after 9:03 to tell President Bush about the second strike on the World Trade Center, Bush "waited for a few moments… literally—not very long at all," before getting up to leave. According to Rove, Bush then came into the staff room and watched the replay of the second plane flying into the building, then said: "We're at war. Give me the Vice President." But, Rove then said:

> The Vice President, we didn't get because at this moment, the Vice President was being moved literally, grabbed by his belt, lifted off the floor and grabbed by a Secret Service agent and moved to the bunker because the plane was approaching the White House.[10]

Given Rove's account of how quickly Bush left the classroom, we can infer that, according to Rove, Cheney was taken to the PEOC some time between 9:10 and 9:15.

Mineta's account was also supported by a BBC program entitled "Clear the Skies," which aired in September 2002. This program, after telling of Cheney's being rushed to the underground bunker, showed Mineta telling the story about the young man asking Cheney, prior to the Pentagon strike, if the orders about the incoming plane still stood.[11]

Mineta's account was also supported in advance by a *Wall Street Journal* article, published about a month after 9/11, that told the story of that morning from the perspective of the two airlines, American and United. Discussing the actions of Gerard Arpey and Jim Goodwin, top executives of AA and UA, respectively, this article says:

> Mr. Carty and Mr. Goodwin… were talking on the phone with Secretary of Transportation Norman Mineta, who was in a government command bunker with Vice President Dick Cheney. Mr. Carty told Mr. Mineta that American was ordering all 162 of its planes out of the sky; United already had ordered its 122 planes down. About five minutes later, the FAA shut down the skies over the U.S. completely to all but military aircraft.… Soon, reports began pouring in that a plane had crashed into the Pentagon.[12]

This WSJ article, therefore, said that Cheney was in the PEOC with Mineta at about 9:21 (approximately five minutes before Mineta, as will be discussed in Chapter 4, had the FAA order a national ground stop).

Mineta's statement that Cheney was in the PEOC before 9:20 was anticipated, therefore, by David Bohrer, Karl Rove, ABC News, the BBC, the *Wall Street Journal*, and, after Mineta gave his testimony, by Richard Clarke.

The 9/11 Commission's Late-Arrival Claim
The 9/11 Commission agreed that the vice president was hustled down to the PEOC after word was received that a plane was headed toward the White House. It claimed, however, that this word was not received until 9:33, when a tower supervisor at Reagan National Airport told the Secret Service that "an aircraft [is] coming at you and not talking with us." Even then, however,

the Commission said that the Secret Service agents immediately received another message, telling them that the aircraft had turned away, so "[n]o move was made to evacuate the Vice President at this time." It was not until "just before 9:36" that the Secret Service ordered Cheney to go below and not until 9:37 that he entered the underground corridor leading to the PEOC.[13]

The 9/11 Commission's claim was based primarily on a timeline in a Secret Service report. The Commission admitted, however, that the Secret Service said that "the 9:37 entry time in their timeline was based on alarm data, which is no longer retrievable."[14] The claim that Cheney entered the corridor at 9:37 is, in other words, not documented. Should this undocumented claim really be considered evidence sufficiently strong to overrule the combined testimony of Bohrer, Clarke, Mineta, Rice, Rove, ABC, the BBC, and the *Wall Street Journal*?

In any case, the Commission then claimed that even after entering the corridor at 9:37, Cheney did not immediately go to the PEOC at the other end. Rather:

> Once inside, Vice President Cheney and the agents paused in an area of the tunnel that had a secure phone, a bench, and television. The Vice President asked to speak to the President, but it took time for the call to be connected. He learned in the tunnel that the Pentagon had been hit, and he saw television coverage of the smoke coming from the building.[15]

The Commission then, after saying that Lynne Cheney "joined her husband in the tunnel," claimed that "Mrs. Cheney and the Vice President moved from the tunnel to the shelter conference room" after the call ended, which was not until after 9:55. This was the Commission's basis for concluding that "the Vice President arrived in the room shortly before 10:00, perhaps at 9:58." As for Condoleezza Rice, she "entered the conference room shortly after the Vice President."[16]

The contradiction could not be clearer. According to the Commission, Cheney, far from entering the PEOC before 9:20, as Mineta and others said, did not arrive there until about 9:58, 20 minutes after the 9:38 strike on the Pentagon, about which he had learned in the corridor. Why does this contradiction exist?

Accounts Giving a Middle Position

Besides this contradiction between stories supporting a very early arrival (before 9:20) and those supporting a very late arrival (about 9:58), there were stories supporting a middle position. In these accounts, Cheney was not taken downstairs until after 9:33, but, unlike what the 9/11 Commission claimed, most of these accounts said that he went directly to the PEOC, rather than lingering in the corridor. These accounts, which were given by the *New York Times*,[17] NBC,[18] and the BBC,[19] agreed with Mineta's account that Cheney was already in the bunker when the Pentagon was struck. But by saying that Cheney arrived in the PEOC at about 9:36 instead of prior to 9:20, they held that he arrived only very shortly before the Pentagon strike.

In addition to these stories, which took an early-middle position, there was a *Washington Post* story by Dan Balz and Bob Woodward that came closer to the 9/11 Commission's position by taking a late-middle position. That is, although Balz and Woodward did not have the very late PEOC arrival time for Cheney, they did have him stop in the corridor: "Cheney stopped to watch a television showing the smoke billowing out of the World Trade Center towers, heard the report about the plane hitting the Pentagon, and called Bush again."[20]

Nevertheless, according to Balz and Woodward, Cheney would have entered the PEOC before 9:45. Without any indication of the exact time, Balz and Woodward had Cheney in the PEOC when Norman Mineta ordered that all planes be landed. After quoting Mineta as saying "Get those goddamn planes down," they wrote: "Sitting at the other end of the table, Cheney snapped his head up, looked squarely at Mineta and nodded in agreement." This order was reportedly issued at 9:45, so Balz and Woodward's account would have Cheney enter the PEOC no later than 9:43, hence about 15 minutes earlier than did *The 9/11 Commission Report*. On the crucial issue of where Cheney was when the Pentagon was struck, however, the position of the 9/11 Commission, articulated in 2004, was foreshadowed in the 2002 Balz–Woodward story, according to which the Pentagon was hit while Cheney was still in the corridor.[21]

What did Cheney himself say? It would appear that he, during various interviews, supported *all* the positions summarized here (except the view that he entered before 9:20). In his earliest public statement, however, he supported the early-middle position, according to which he arrived in the PEOC shortly before the Pentagon strike. Speaking to Tim Russert on NBC's *Meet the Press* only five days after 9/11, Cheney said: "[A]fter I talked to the president, ... I went down into... the Presidential Emergency Operations Center.... [W]hen I arrived there within a short order, we had word the Pentagon's been hit."[22]

Dealing with the Contradictions

How did the 9/11 Commission deal with the fact that its claim about the time of Cheney's arrival in the PEOC had been contradicted by Bohrer, Clarke, Mineta, Rice, several news reports, and even Cheney himself? It simply omitted any mention of these contradictory reports. For example, the Commission cited a Cheney interview with *Newsweek* that reportedly took place on November 19, 2001,[23] which resulted in a story by Evan Thomas in the December 31, 2001, issue. Thomas's story said: "Shortly before 10AM, the Cheneys were led into the PEOC conference room.... [T]hey looked up at the TV screens. It was 9:58AM."[24]

This *Newsweek* story was evidently the *only* early story that supported the position later taken in *The 9/11 Commission Report*. The Commission simply ignored all other accounts of Cheney's descent to the PEOC. One of those accounts was, interestingly enough, by Evan Thomas himself. Published only two weeks after 9/11, this story said: "Vice President Dick Cheney had already been hustled into a bunker designed to withstand the shock of a nuclear blast when, at about 9:30AM, Secret Service men told staffers leaving the West Wing to run, not walk, as far away as possible."[25] The Commission, however, did not mention this Evan Thomas story, which, like Mineta's testimony, had Cheney in the PEOC before 9:30. The Commission did not even mention Cheney's well-known interview with Tim Russert on September 16, 2001, in which Cheney said that he had arrived in the PEOC *before* learning about the attack on the Pentagon—even though this interview, unlike the one said to have taken place with *Newsweek* on November 19, appears on the vice president's list of "Speeches and News Releases."[26]

But the Commission's most important omission involved Norman Mineta's testimony. Although this testimony was given to the Commission in an open hearing, in response to questions from Commissioners Lee Hamilton and Timothy Roemer, and although it can be read in the transcript of that session,[27] Mineta's testimony that Cheney was already in the PEOC before 9:20 was not mentioned in *The 9/11 Commission Report* (although the Commission perhaps alludes to it by admitting the existence of "conflicting evidence about when the Vice President arrived in the shelter conference room"[28]). Moreover, this portion of Mineta's testimony is not contained in the official version of the video record of the 9/11 Commission hearings, which is in the 9/11 Commission archives.[29] (There can be no doubt that this portion of Mineta's testimony was taped, incidentally, because it can be viewed on the Internet.[30])

During an interview for the Canadian Broadcasting Corporation in 2006, Lee Hamilton was asked what "Mineta told the Commission about where Dick Cheney was prior to 10AM?" Hamilton replied: "I do not recall."[31] It was surprising that Hamilton could not recall, because he had been the one doing the questioning when Mineta told the story of the young man who came in repeatedly to tell Cheney that an aircraft was approaching. Hamilton, moreover, had begun his questioning by saying to Mineta: "You were there [in the PEOC] for a good part of the day. I think you were there with the Vice President." And Mineta's exchange with Timothy Roemer, during which it was established that Mineta had arrived at about 9:20, came immediately after Hamilton's interrogation. And yet Hamilton, not being able to recall any of this, simply said, "we think that Vice President Cheney entered the bunker shortly before 10 o'clock."[32]

In any case, Mineta himself repeated his assertion about Cheney during an interview in 2006. He said that right after the second WTC strike, he had his driver take him from the Department of Transportation to the White House. After saying that he was told that he had to be briefed by Clarke in the Situation Room, Mineta stated:

So I went in there, he talked to me for four or five minutes, and he said, "You have got to go to the PEOC." ... [A] Secret Service agent standing there, says, "I will take you." ... I got to the PEOC and the Vice President was already there.[33]

This statement by Mineta, besides reaffirming his assertion that when he arrived in the PEOC Cheney was "already there," also provides the basis for what we can consider a Clarke–Mineta statement about the time of Cheney's arrival in the PEOC. If Mineta arrived there, as he had previously said, at "about 9:20," following a conversation with Clarke that lasted "four or five minutes," then Mineta must have arrived at the Situation Room at about 9:15. So if Cheney had gone down to the PEOC about five minutes before Mineta's arrival at the Situation Room, as Clarke's account implied, then Cheney must have gone to the PEOC by about 9:10.

In repeating his testimony about Cheney in 2006, incidentally, Mineta was evidently, as can be seen during an informal interview in 2007, not aware that he was challenging *The 9/11 Commission Report*. Asked if Cheney was already in the PEOC when he arrived at 9:20, Mineta said "absolutely," adding that Mrs. Cheney was also there. When told that the Commission had claimed that Cheney did not arrive until 9:58, Mineta expressed surprise and said: "Oh no, no, no; I don't know how that came about." Although Mineta said that he "might have been mistaken on the 9:25" (he had said, to recall, that Cheney's discussion with the young man had occurred at about 9:25 or 9:26), Cheney was clearly there, he said, before the Pentagon was struck.[34]

Conclusion

Why did *The 9/11 Commission Report* contradict the combined testimony of David Bohrer, Richard Clarke, Norman Mineta, Condoleezza Rice, Karl Rove, ABC, the BBC, the *Wall Street Journal*, and even Dick Cheney himself (in at least one interview) with regard to the time of Cheney's arrival in the PEOC? Why was the testimony of the most important of these witnesses, Secretary of Transportation Norman Mineta, not mentioned in the Commission's report and not contained in its archived videotape? And why do we have four different answers—about 9:10, about 9:36, about 9:43, and about 9:58—to the question as to when Cheney arrived? Given the central role that Dick Cheney had on the morning of 9/11, Congress and the press should have resolved these questions long ago. They should, in any case, do so now.

CHAPTER 2

3

WAS CHENEY OBSERVED CONFIRMING
A STAND-DOWN ORDER?

As we saw in the previous chapter, in Norman Mineta's testimony before the 9/11 Commission on May 23, 2003, he said that he arrived in the PEOC, where Vice President Cheney was in charge, at "about 9:20." During this testimony, he recounted an episode that could reasonably be interpreted as Cheney's confirmation of an order to stand down air defenses.

Mineta's Testimony

In his testimony to the Commission, Mineta described the following episode:

> During the time that the airplane was coming in to the Pentagon, there was a young man who would come in and say to the Vice President, "The plane is 50 miles out." "The plane is 30 miles out." And when it got down to "the plane is 10 miles out," the young man also said to the Vice President, "Do the orders still stand?" And the Vice President turned and whipped his neck around and said, "Of course the orders still stand. Have you heard anything to the contrary?"[1]

When asked by Commissioner Timothy Roemer how long this conversation occurred after he arrived, Mineta said, as we saw in the prior chapter, "Probably about five or six minutes." That, as Roemer pointed out, would have been "about 9:25 or 9:26."

One problem created by Mineta's testimony was that it implied that Cheney and members of the military knew that an aircraft was approaching Washington about twelve minutes before the Pentagon was struck. This directly contradicted the official account, according to which the military did not know that an aircraft was approaching the Pentagon until 9:36, so that it, in the words of the 9/11 Commission, "had at most one or two minutes to react to the unidentified plane approaching Washington."[2] That claim was essential for explaining, among other things, why the Pentagon had not been evacuated before it was struck—a fact that resulted in 125 deaths. Rumsfeld's spokesperson, when asked why this evacuation did not occur, said: "The Pentagon was simply not aware that this aircraft was coming our way."[3]

Even more problematic was the question of the nature of "the orders." Mineta assumed, he said, that they were orders to have the plane shot down. But no plane approaching Washington was shot down arguably. Another problem with Mineta's interpretation was that it made the episode unintelligible. Had Cheney given the expected order—to have an aircraft approaching the ultra-restricted airspace over Washington shot down—there would have been, critics argued, no reason for the young man to ask if the orders still stood. His question made sense only if the orders were to do something unusual—*not* to shoot it down. It was suggested, accordingly, that Mineta inadvertently reported having observed Cheney confirm stand-down orders, meaning orders to suspend the standard policy.

Removing the Suspicion

The grounds for this suspicion were removed by the accounts given of Cheney's actions that morning by most mainstream media stories and, subsequently, the 9/11 Commission. The mainstream media stories in question all aired before Mineta testified to the 9/11 Commission in 2003. But Mineta had given this account of Cheney and the young man on a BBC program, "Clear the Skies,"[4] which appeared on the first anniversary of 9/11. And he may have been telling it even earlier. Accordingly, insofar as several mainstream stories removed the grounds for suspicion that Mineta observed Cheney's confirmation of a stand-down order, they could have been responses to Mineta's story, even though they appeared before his 2003 testimony to the 9/11 Commission.

Revising the Descent Time

One way to remove this suspicion involved simply portraying Cheney as not entering the PEOC until later. Three prominent television shows on the first anniversary of 9/11—one by CNN and two by ABC[5]—did portray Cheney as entering the PEOC early enough for the episode recounted by Mineta to have occurred. The two ABC shows even contained Mineta's account. But most television and newsprint accounts portrayed Cheney as arriving too late for the episode to have occurred—whether just before the Pentagon attack,[6] just after it,[7] or, as Evan Thomas's story in the December 31, 2001, issue of *Newsweek* had it (see the previous chapter), not until 9:58.[8] Although each of these three types of accounts contradicted the other two, they all ruled out the possible occurrence of Cheney's being asked, after being told that a plane was approaching the Pentagon about twelve minutes before it was attacked, whether "the orders" still stood.

The 9/11 Commission then turned Evan Thomas's *Newsweek* account into the official position. According to this account, Mrs. Cheney arrived to meet the vice president in the corridor just after he had "learned that the Pentagon had been hit," while he was speaking on the phone to the president. And then, Thomas said: "Shortly before 10AM, the Cheneys were led into the PEOC conference room…. [T]hey looked up at the TV screens. It was 9:58AM." *The 9/11 Commission Report* said: "There is conflicting evidence about when the Vice President arrived in the shelter conference room. We have concluded, from the available evidence, that the Vice President arrived in the room shortly before 10:00, perhaps at 9:58."[9]

There is, interestingly, little correlation between the dates of the various news stories and the times at which they portray Cheney's entry into the PEOC. On the assumption that most of the stories were based on interviews with and/or other statements made by Cheney himself, one might suspect that the descent time would have gotten progressively later, so that the later the story, the closer it would correspond to the position taken in 2004 by the 9/11 Commission. That, however, was not the case.

In his November 19, 2001, interview with Evan Thomas for

the *Newsweek* story, to be sure, Cheney gave a later time for his entry into the PEOC than he had given during his September 16 interview on *Meet the Press*, in which he indicated that he learned about the Pentagon attack *after* entering the PEOC, not before. Otherwise, however, there is little correlation. In fact, the two stories that came the closest to the final position were two of the earliest ones.

The only story that got all the main points of the final position—descending to the corridor late, learning about the Pentagon strike while in the corridor, and not entering the PEOC until shortly before 10:00—was Evan Thomas's *Newsweek* story, which appeared on December 31, 2001.

The story that was the next closest to anticipating the final position was the *Washington Post* article by Dan Balz and Bob Woodward, mentioned in the previous chapter, which appeared January 27, 2002, less than a month after Thomas's *Newsweek* story. The Balz–Woodward story, unlike the Thomas story, had Cheney in the PEOC by 9:45. But it, like the Thomas story, had Cheney learn about the Pentagon strike while still in the corridor. It also added an element of the final position not contained in the Thomas story: Cheney watching television while in the corridor.

In any case, although these two stories anticipated the position that would be adopted by the 9/11 Commission, most of the other news reports—for example, an October 16, 2001, story in the *New York Times*[10]—said that Cheney arrived in the PEOC shortly *before* the Pentagon was struck. These stories included an NBC program on the first anniversary of 9/11 and a BBC program aired three days earlier.[11] These shows, in ignoring the claims made in the Thomas and Balz–Woodward stories, would appear to have taken their cue directly from Cheney's September 16 statement on *Meet the Press*.

Moreover, the two ABC shows appearing during the week of the first anniversary of 9/11, which were based on interviews by Peter Jennings, ignored Cheney's *Meet the Press* position in favor of Mineta's position, according to which Cheney entered the PEOC at about 9:15. These stories even contained Mineta's account of the conversation between Cheney and the young man.

It would be interesting to learn why ABC, which in those shows endorsed Andrew Card's revisionist account of when President Bush left the Sarasota classroom (as we saw in Chapter 1), was not persuaded to endorse either of Cheney's revisionist accounts of his entry into the PEOC. Perhaps it was because Peter Jennings, having interviewed Mineta directly, found his story credible.

In any case, these two accounts—Mineta's account and Cheney's *Meet the Press* account—were swept into oblivion by the 9/11 Commission's decision to endorse the account given by Cheney to *Newsweek*'s Evan Thomas. Although that account contradicted Norman Mineta's account, as given in public testimony to the 9/11 Commission, and even Cheney's own earlier account, as stated to Tim Russert on "Meet the Press," it became the official account simply by virtue of being endorsed by the 9/11 Commission, even though it had been, up to that time, very much a minority view. In fact, as pointed out in the previous chapter, the transcript of Cheney's interview with *Newsweek* was the only document to which the 9/11 Commission could refer to support its claim that Cheney did not enter the PEOC until shortly before 10:00.

Nevertheless, in this way, the 9/11 Commission ruled out the possible truth of Mineta's dangerous story, the most natural interpretation of which was that Mineta inadvertently gave witness to Cheney's confirmation of a stand-down order.

Alternative Versions of the Incoming Airplane Story

A second way in which news stories and the 9/11 Commission avoided this interpretation was to provide an alternative version of the story of an incoming aircraft. At least four such versions appeared.

One version, which involved the least amount of divergence from Mineta's story, was contained in the Balz–Woodward *Washington Post* article. Like Mineta's own story, this variation mentioned the reports about the incoming plane and connected them to Mineta:

> Secretary Norman Y. Mineta... was on an open line to the Federal Aviation Administration operations center, monitoring Flight 77 as it hurtled toward Washington, with radar tracks

coming every seven seconds. Reports came that the plane was 50 miles out, 30 miles out, 10 miles out—until word reached the bunker that there had been an explosion at the Pentagon.[12]

But although this story connected these reports to Mineta, it distanced them from Cheney, who, according to Balz and Woodward, was still out in the corridor at this time. Balz and Woodward also said nothing about any "orders." Furthermore, they portrayed these reports as coming so late—just before the strike on the Pentagon—that there would have been no time for any "orders" to have been either canceled or confirmed.

A second alternative version of the incoming airplane story was told on the CNN program that aired on the first anniversary of 9/11. As mentioned earlier, this program's account, like Clarke's and Mineta's accounts, said that Cheney was taken down to the PEOC shortly after the second tower was hit. This program was, in fact, entitled "Cheney Recalls Taking Charge from Bunker." It did not, however, mention either Mineta or his story of an airplane approaching before the Pentagon was struck. It instead contained a similar story about the approach of United Flight 93, told, with a little help from Cheney, by Josh Bolten, who at the time was the White House deputy chief of staff. This story went like this:

> After the planes struck the twin towers, a third took a chunk out of the Pentagon. Cheney then heard a report that a plane over Pennsylvania was heading for Washington. A military assistant asked Cheney twice for authority to shoot it down.
>
> "The vice president said yes again," remembered Josh Bolton, deputy White House chief of staff. "And the aide then asked a third time. He said, 'Just confirming, sir, authority to engage?' And the vice president—his voice got a little annoyed then—said, 'I said yes.'"
>
> It was a rare flash of anger from a man who knew he was setting the tone at a White House in crisis.
>
> "I think there was an undertone of anger there. But it's more a matter of determination. You don't want to let your anger overwhelm your judgment in a moment like this," Cheney said.

This story has two of the main elements of the Mineta account: three exchanges between Cheney and a military aide followed by Cheney's affirmative but angry response in the third one.

But there were also three crucial differences: The exchanges came *after*, not before, the Pentagon strike; the orders, rather than being open to more than one interpretation, were clearly to shoot a plane down; and the plane in question was United 93, not American 77. This story could, therefore, serve as a "corrective" to the Mineta story, informing people who had heard the Mineta story that, although such an incident really occurred, it referred to Cheney's orders to shoot down United 93, not his orders *not* to shoot down the plane approaching the Pentagon.

However, although this CNN version completely separated the incoming aircraft story from both Cheney and the Pentagon strike, it would not be usable by the 9/11 Commission, because of the Commission's endorsement of the view that Cheney did not enter the PEOC until almost 10:00 and did not, as discussed in the following chapter, issue any shootdown authorization until after 10:10.

A third alternative version of the incoming aircraft story was told, interestingly, by Balz and Woodward. That is, after giving the account discussed above, which described an episode that occurred before the Pentagon strike and involved Mineta but not Cheney, they then offered another variation on the episode, which is said to have occurred after 9:55, at which time Cheney had just received shootdown authorization from the president. This Balz–Woodward story, which can be viewed as a synthesis of the Mineta account with the Bolten–CNN account, went like this:

> In the White House bunker, a military aide approached the vice president.
>
> "There is a plane 80 miles out," he said. "There is a fighter in the area. Should we engage?"
>
> "Yes," Cheney replied without hesitation.
>
> Around the vice president, Rice, deputy White House chief of staff Joshua Bolten and I. Lewis "Scooter" Libby, Cheney's chief of staff, tensed as the military aide repeated the

question, this time with even more urgency. The plane was now 60 miles out. "Should we engage?" Cheney was asked.

"Yes," he replied again.

As the plane came closer, the aide repeated the question. Does the order still stand?

"Of course it does," Cheney snapped.

Accordingly, after having taken Cheney out of Mineta's story and reduced it down to one sentence ("Reports came that the plane was 50 miles out, 30 miles out, 10 miles out"), Balz and Woodward put several elements of that story into an episode that happened 30 minutes later, when United 93 was approaching Washington: a military aide updating Cheney three times; the question, "Does the order still stand?" (almost word for word with Mineta's "Do the orders still stand?"); and Cheney's angry reply, "Of course it does" (very similar to Mineta's "Of course the orders still stand"). As a result, central elements of the Mineta story, which referred to a plane approaching the Pentagon, were now contained in a story referring to United 93.

Even this third alternative version of the incoming flight story, however, could not simply be taken over by the 9/11 Commission, given its claims that Cheney did not enter the PEOC until almost 10:00 and that (as discussed in the next chapter) the military did not know about the hijacking of United 93 until after it had crashed.

Accordingly, *The 9/11 Commission Report* provided a fourth alternative version of the incoming flight story, which was heavily based on notes provided by Lynne Cheney and Lewis "Scooter" Libby.[13] This version had the episode occurring still later:

> At 10:02, the communicators in the shelter began receiving reports from the Secret Service of an inbound aircraft.... At some time between 10:10 and 10:15, a military aide told the Vice President and others that the aircraft was 80 miles out. Vice President Cheney was asked for authority to engage the aircraft.... The Vice President authorized fighter aircraft to engage the inbound plane.... The military aide returned a few minutes later, probably between 10:12 and 10:18, and said the aircraft was 60 miles out. He again asked for authorization to

engage. The Vice President again said yes…. White House
Deputy Chief of Staff Joshua Bolten… watched the exchanges
and… suggested that the Vice President get in touch with the
President and confirm the engage order…. The Vice President
was logged calling the President at 10:18 for a two-minute
conversation that obtained the confirmation.[14]

In providing this story, the 9/11 Commission said that Cheney did
indeed interact with a military aide who repeatedly informed him
of an incoming plane. In the Commission's version, however, the
episode could not possibly be interpreted as involving either a
stand-down order for a plane approaching the Pentagon or a
shootdown order that might have resulted in the downing of
United 93. The dangerous Mineta story had been replaced by a
completely harmless version of the incoming flight story.[15]

Conclusion

Obviously, all the alternative accounts cannot be true. And even
if the Commission's incoming flight story is the only alternative
account taken into consideration, it and Mineta's account cannot
both be true.

There are, moreover, three reasons to suspect that the most
accurate account is the one given by Mineta. First, he had no
obvious motive to lie. Second, he has recently, as pointed out in
the previous chapter, reaffirmed his account, stating that the vice
president (along with Mrs. Cheney) was already there when he
arrived in the PEOC at about 9:20, and stating that the exchange
between Cheney and the young man definitely occurred before
the attack on the Pentagon. Third, the various alternative accounts
appear to have been created primarily for the purpose of over-
coming the impression, sure to be given by the episode reported
by Mineta, that Cheney had confirmed orders not to shoot down
an aircraft approaching the Pentagon.

Congress and the press need to determine if Mineta's account
is indeed true and, if it is, why and by whom the false accounts
were created.

4

DID CHENEY OBSERVE THE
LAND-ALL-PLANES ORDER?

nother contradiction between the accounts of Mineta and
the 9/11 Commission, beyond those discussed in Chapters 2 and 3, involves the question of who gave the order
to have all civilian planes brought down. According to Mineta, he
gave this order. The 9/11 Commission, however, said it was given
by Ben Sliney, the FAA's national operations manager at its
Command Center in Herndon, Virginia.[1] This discrepancy
appears to be related to the question of the time of Cheney's
arrival in the PEOC.

Reports that Mineta Gave the Order
Mineta consistently stated that he gave this order. On September
20, 2001, he told a Senate committee:

> On the morning of September 11th, on first word of the attack,
> I moved directly to the Presidential Emergency Operations
> Center in the White House. As soon as I was aware of the
> nature and scale of the attack, I called from the White House
> to order the air traffic system to land all aircraft, immediately
> and without exception.[2]

Jane Garvey, the administrator of the FAA, testifying the next
day to a different congressional committee, backed up Mineta's
account, saying:

> As soon as Secretary Mineta was aware of the nature and scale
> of the terrorist attack on New York and Washington... the
> Secretary ordered the air traffic system shut down for all civil
> operations.... At 9:26AM, before either American Airlines
> Flight 77 or United Airlines Flight 93 had crashed, a national

ground stop was issued that prevented any aircraft from taking off. At 9:45AM all airborne aircraft were told to land at the nearest airport.[3]

According to Richard Clarke, incidentally, he and Garvey had talked about bringing all planes down before Mineta arrived at the Situation Room (from which Clarke's video conference was run) and hence shortly before 9:15. After Clarke had suggested that they needed to "clear the airspace around Washington and New York," Garvey reportedly said: "We may have to do a lot more than that, Dick. I already put a hold on all takeoffs and landings in New York and Washington, but we have reports of eleven aircraft off course or out of communications, maybe hijacked." Clarke responded: "Okay, Jane, how long will it take to get all aircraft now aloft onto the ground somewhere?" Garvey replied that she did not know, adding that it was the first day on the job for the FAA's new national operations manager, Ben Sliney. Clarke then asked whether Garvey was prepared to issue the order and she responded in the affirmative. Shortly thereafter, Mineta called in from his car and then arrived at the Situation Room, after which Clarke suggested that "he join the Vice President."[4]

Accordingly, although Clarke said that the idea of bringing all planes down was discussed with Garvey before Mineta's arrival, his account does not contradict the statements by Garvey and Mineta, according to which the order to stop all civilian air traffic in the country—not only in certain regions—was given by Mineta.

Garvey's above-quoted congressional testimony, in any case, contained an important distinction. At 9:26, the order was issued for a "national ground stop," meaning that no more planes could take off. At 9:45, all planes already in the air were ordered to land.

The distinction between ordering a national ground stop (at 9:26) and ordering all planes to land (at 9:45) was reflected during Mineta's testimony to the 9/11 Commission on May 23, 2003. After getting to the PEOC (at "about 9:20"), Mineta said,

> I established contact with two lines—one with my Chief of Staff at the Department of Transportation and the second with Monte Belger, the acting Deputy Administrator of the FAA, and Jane Garvey, both of whom were in the FAA Operations Center....

The FAA began to restrict air travel in the Northeast United States by a combination of actions... [a]nd ultimately, a nation-wide ground stop of all aircraft regardless of destination.

Within a few minutes, American Flight 77 crashed into the Pentagon.... It was clear that we had to clear the airspace as soon as possible to stop any further attacks and ensure domestic airspace was available for emergency and defensive use. And so at approximately 9:45AM..., I gave the FAA a final order for all civil aircraft to land at the nearest airport as soon as possible.[5]

Mineta's account was also partially supported by the 2002 *Washington Post* article by Dan Balz and Bob Woodward, discussed in Chapters 2 and 3. This article, reflecting the view that Cheney did not enter the PEOC until about 9:45, did not deal with the period prior to 9:30, during which Mineta, he said, ordered the national ground stop in Cheney's presence. But Balz and Woodward did support the view that Mineta gave the order in Cheney's presence for all planes to be immediately landed. Reporting that, after the Pentagon strike, Mineta was on the phone with Monte Belger, the FAA's acting deputy administrator, they wrote: "Mineta shouted into the phone...: 'Monte, bring all the planes down.'" After Belger said that the FAA was "bringing them down per pilot discretion," Mineta yelled: "[Expletive] pilot discretion. Get those goddamn planes down."[6] Balz and Woodward then added: "Sitting at the other end of the table, Cheney snapped his head up, looked squarely at Mineta and nodded in agreement."

Reports that Sliney Gave the Order

By contrast, the 9/11 Commission said that, after the FAA's Command Center learned that a plane had struck the Pentagon, the "Command Center's national operations manager, Ben Sliney, ordered all FAA facilities to instruct all aircraft to land at the nearest airport."[7]

The claim that Sliney had given this order, as well as the order for the national ground stop, had already been made on August 2, 2002, by a *USA Today* story, which said:

At 9:25AM..., Sliney issues [an] order that no one has ever given: full groundstop. No commercial or private flight in the country is allowed to take off.... [At 9:38, after the Pentagon was hit, Sliney] has no time to consult with FAA officials in Washington.... "Order everyone to land! Regardless of destination!" Sliney shouts. Twenty feet away, his boss, Linda Schuessler, simply nods.... "OK, let's get them on the ground!" Sliney booms. Within seconds, specialists pass the order on to facilities across the country.[8]

There are, it must be said, some problematic elements in this *USA Today* story. One problem is that September 11, 2001, was Sliney's first day as the FAA's national operations manager, and yet he supposedly issued this unprecedented order without consulting any superior. *USA Today* said that he had "no time to consult with FAA officials in Washington," but such consultation could have been carried out in fifteen seconds or so. Sliney also supposedly did not even consult with his immediate superior, Linda Schuessler (manager of tactical operations at the FAA's Command Center in Herndon), who was only twenty feet away. And she, upon hearing him give this unprecedented order without consulting her or any other superior, simply nodded.

The *USA Today* writers, evidently trying to make all this seem less implausible, said:

> In Washington, FAA Administrator Jane Garvey and her deputy, Monte Belger, have been moving back and forth between a secret operations center and their offices. Throughout the morning, staffers have kept Garvey and Belger apprised of Sliney's decisions. Now, they tell them of the order to clear the skies. With little discussion, the FAA leaders approve.

Apparently Garvey and Belger, like Schuessler, were devoid of both ego and any concern that their subordinates follow the chain of command. They were happy just to be informed about, and then to approve, "Sliney's decisions."

In any case, the *USA Today* story next explained the conversation between Mineta and Belger in a way that made Mineta simply concur with a decision that had already been made, except for one detail.

> Minutes later, Transportation Secretary Norman Mineta calls
> from a bunker beneath the White House, where he has joined
> Vice President Cheney. Belger explains that the FAA plans to
> land each plane at the closest airport, regardless of its destina-
> tion. Mineta concurs.... Then... Mineta asks exactly what the
> order means. Belger says pilots will retain some discretion....
> "F—— pilot discretion," Mineta says. "Monte, bring down all
> the planes."

According to this account, Mineta simply approved an order that
had already been made, except for insisting that pilots not be
given any discretion.

The idea that Mineta simply approved the previously made
decision to land all planes had already been argued several
months earlier in an article in *Slate* entitled "The Mineta Myth:
How Bob Woodward Made the Secretary of Transportation a False
Hero." As this title suggested, the author, Joshua Green, sought
to undermine the "folk-hero status" that had been accorded to
Mineta, who, Green complained, had been "canonized in the
opening paragraphs of Bob Woodward and Dan Balz's six-part
Washington Post epic, '10 Days in September.'" According to
Green, who claimed to be reporting what had been revealed by
"insiders"—especially *Washington Post* transportation reporter
Don Phillips—the real hero was Monte Belger, the number two
official at the FAA, who "ordered flights grounded 15 minutes
before Mineta was even notified of the attacks."[9]

This account by Green was most likely inaccurate, because
Mineta, according to both himself and Richard Clarke, knew of
the attacks in time to arrive at the White House by 9:15, and the
order to land all planes in the country was clearly not given before
9:00. Green, who evidently did not know about Mineta's early
arrival at the PEOC, was perhaps misled by the Balz–Woodward
article, which could have been read as implying that Mineta had
arrived only minutes before the Pentagon strike (said to have
occurred at about 9:38). So Green, in speaking of a decision that
had been made fifteen minutes before Mineta knew what was
going on, was perhaps referring to the 9:26 decision to institute a
national ground stop, preventing any more take-offs. Green

perhaps assumed that this decision had been made before Mineta arrived in the PEOC.

Be that as it may, Green's article, while not saying that Sliney made the decision to have all (civilian) planes brought down—indeed, Sliney was not even mentioned—did dispute the claim that it was Mineta who first gave the order.

Dealing with the Contradiction

For our purposes, the question of whether the decision was made by Mineta and then implemented by Sliney, or made by Sliney—or perhaps Belger, or perhaps Linda Schuessler, or perhaps collaboratively by a number of people[10]—and then approved by Mineta, is unimportant. Indeed, it may largely be a non-issue, because if Mineta, rather than initiating the idea of bringing all planes down, simply approved a decision that had already been made by FAA officials, he could still reasonably regard the moment at which he, as their superior, approved this decision, rather than overriding it, as the moment at which the "order" was really given. So the contradiction between the two interpretations may be more apparent than real.

What *is* important, for our purposes, is the fact that the Commission did not mention this apparent contradiction and, in fact, did not mention Mineta whatsoever in relation to this episode. It simply made the statement, quoted earlier, that Ben Sliney "ordered all FAA facilities to instruct all aircraft to land at the nearest airport."[11] The Commission's treatment of this issue raises some questions.

One question is why the 9/11 Commission endorsed the view that it was Sliney who gave the order, thereby contradicting Mineta, the secretary of transportation, and Garvey, the head of the FAA. Of course, if the Commission had good evidence that it was Sliney who made the decision, rather than Mineta, that would explain its decision. But it presented no such evidence. It provided no reason, therefore, for endorsing the claim that Sliney, a subordinate on the first day of his new job, unilaterally made this key decision.

A second question is why, if it really believed that Mineta had merely confirmed a decision already made and implemented by

Sliney, the Commission did not point out that, although it was somewhat unusual for a person of Sliney's rank to have made such an
enormous decision, it was soon ratified by Mineta. After all, the
Commission did do this, as we will see in the next chapter, with
Cheney's shootdown authorization, saying that he called President
Bush to get confirmation. Why did the Commission, in relation to
the land-all-planes order, avoid any mention of Mineta whatsoever?

A third question is why, if it was for some reason important to
the Commissioners to say that Sliney rather than Mineta made
the decision, they did not appeal to the *Slate* and *USA Today*
stories to refute the impression, given by Balz and Woodward as
well as Garvey and Mineta, that it had been Mineta who gave the
order. The Commissioners could have cited the *Slate* story to
undermine the "Mineta Myth" and then cited the *USA Today* story
to add a further correction: that the decision had been made by
Sliney, not Belger. But they did not mention either story.

However, the question of whether it was Mineta or Sliney (or
Belger) who gave the order was probably not considered intrinsi-
cally important. What was important to the 9/11 Commission, as
we saw in the previous chapters, was its claim that Cheney did not
enter the PEOC until "shortly before 10:00, at perhaps 9:58."
And from that perspective, the Balz–Woodward story was not
helpful, because after quoting Mineta as saying, "Get those
goddamn planes down," it said: "Sitting at the other end of the
table, Cheney snapped his head up, looked squarely at Mineta
and nodded in agreement." This exchange, Balz and Woodward
said, occurred shortly after the Pentagon strike, which would fit
with the fact that the order to land all planes was issued at 9:45.
The Balz–Woodward story, accordingly, had Cheney in the PEOC
prior to 9:45, hence at least thirteen minutes prior to 9:58, the
time the Commission claimed he entered the PEOC.

This difference is perhaps relevant to the question of why,
besides not citing Balz and Woodward's *Washington Post* story,
the Commission avoided all mention of Mineta with regard to the
order to bring down all planes. Because of the Balz–Woodward
story, the idea that Mineta gave that order was associated with the
idea that Cheney was in the PEOC by 9:45. At one time, this had

been an orthodox idea: As we saw in Chapters 2 and 3, Cheney himself, five days after 9/11, told Tim Russert that he had gotten there even before the attack on the Pentagon. By the time *The 9/11 Commission Report* was written, however, this story had been superseded. It had become important to rule out not only the idea that Cheney might have confirmed a stand-down order in relation to the Pentagon, but also the possibility that Cheney's shootdown authorization had led to the downing of United 93 (as discussed in the next chapter). The Commission perhaps decided to bury both of those ideas by replacing all previous accounts with the idea that Cheney had not entered the PEOC until almost 10:00. Accordingly, given the association of the tradition that Mineta issued the order to land all planes with Cheney's 9:45 presence in the PEOC, the 9/11 Commission might have decided that this tradition needed to be replaced with the idea that someone else gave that order.

The idea that this someone was Belger had existed since at least April 2002, when Joshua Green's *Slate* article was published. But the Commission could not cite Green's article, because it referred to the Balz–Woodward article, and because Belger, in any case, was widely associated—due to the Balz–Woodward article—with the idea that Mineta made the decision, in Cheney's presence, to clear the skies.

The idea that it was Sliney who made this decision had existed since August 2002, when the *USA Today* article was published. The Commission could not refer to this article to back up its claim, however, because this article had said, in describing events that occurred at about 9:45: "Transportation Secretary Norman Mineta calls from a bunker beneath the White House, where he has joined Vice President Cheney." But although the Commission did not refer to this article, the fact that it had identified Sliney as the decision-maker meant that, in spreading this idea, the Commission did not have to start from scratch.

The identification of Sliney as the decision-maker has, in fact, been amazingly successful. A *USA Today* article in 2006 began: "Ben Sliney is the man who closed down the sky on Sept. 11, 2001…. [H]e gave the unprecedented order to ground all planes across the nation." The article went on to say: "He's a central figure in the film *United 93*…. And in another unprecedented move, Sliney plays himself in the movie." The article ended by saying: "When Sliney grounded the planes, … he didn't wait for approval."[12] Accordingly, this account, that Sliney made the decision without consulting any superiors, has become the accepted truth.

Conclusion

We can perhaps understand that Hollywood would take *The 9/11 Commission Report* as definitive, especially given the fact that Ben Sliney would make a better central figure for a movie than would Norman Mineta. But surely Congress and the press should be more critical, asking why, if both Mineta and Garvey said that the decision was made by Mineta, the Commission simply attributed it to Sliney, without even mentioning Mineta—just as it also obliterated Mineta's testimony about the events that occurred in the PEOC at about 9:25 or 9:26. If both of these omissions, along with the Commission's replacement stories, were due to the Commission's decision to falsify the truth about Cheney's presence in the PEOC, then getting the truth of the matter revealed would seem to be of prime importance. Congress and the press need to do this.

5

WHEN DID CHENEY ISSUE
SHOOTDOWN AUTHORIZATION?

E veryone agrees that Vice President Cheney issued authorization that morning to shoot down any civilian airliner threatening to cause damage on the ground. Disagreement exists, to be sure, on whether Cheney issued this authorization on his own or, as he claimed, was simply transmitting authorization he had received from President Bush. Even the 9/11 Commission has questioned this claim.[1] But everyone agrees that it was Cheney from whom others received the authorization. With regard to the time at which this authorization was given, however, there is a significant disagreement. *The 9/11 Commission Report* evidently disagreed, in fact, with all prior reports.

The 9/11 Commission Report's Account
According to the 9/11 Commission, as we have seen, Vice President Cheney did not reach the PEOC until "shortly before 10:00, perhaps at 9:58." Then at 10:02, Cheney "began receiving reports from the Secret Service of an inbound aircraft—presumably hijacked—heading towards Washington."[2] Although this aircraft turned out to be United 93, the Commission said, this was not known at the time (because no one except the FAA knew, according to the Commission, that this plane had been hijacked until after it crashed[3]). The Commission's account of what happened next was its version of the incoming aircraft story, which was already summarized in Chapter 3.

According to this account, as we saw, Cheney gave the shootdown authorization to the military aide at "some time between 10:10 and 10:15," and again "probably some time between 10:12

and 10:18," then obtained confirmation from President Bush by 10:20.[4] The Commission also, reporting that Richard Clarke had "ask[ed] the President for authority to shoot down aircraft," said: "Confirmation of that authority came at 10:25."[5]

Richard Clarke's Account

Richard Clarke himself, however, gave a very different account, saying that he received the authorization over 30 minutes earlier.

According to Clarke, he called down to the PEOC shortly after 9:30. Reaching Major Michael Fenzel, his liaison to Cheney, Clarke told him to request authorization for "the Air Force to shoot down any aircraft—including a hijacked passenger flight— that looks like it is threatening to attack and cause large-scale death on the ground."[6] Although Clarke said that he expected the decision to be slow in coming, Fenzel called back after the Pentagon had been struck and while Air Force One was still "getting ready to take off"—which it finally did at about 9:55—to say: "Tell the Pentagon they have authority from the President to shoot down hostile aircraft, repeat, they have authority to shoot down hostile aircraft." Clarke reported that he then, while still running his video conference, said: "DOD, DOD, ... the President has ordered the use of force against aircraft deemed to be hostile."[7]

Clarke wrote that he was "amazed at the speed of the decisions coming from Cheney and through him, from Bush."[8] As to the exact time that he received the authorization, Clarke indicated that it was shortly after the Secret Service's "order to evacuate [the White House] was going into effect,"[9] which would have been about 9:45. (Clarke clearly had in mind the *rushed* phase of the evacuation—he said that Secret Service guards were yelling at the women, "If you're in high heels, take off your shoes and run— run!"—not the slower evacuation that had started some twenty minutes earlier.[10]) Clarke's narrative, therefore, indicated that he received the shootdown authorization between 9:45 and 9:55, perhaps about 9:50.

Accounts by Military Officers

The 9/11 Commission's account was also contradicted by the statements of several military officers. A *US News and World Report* article in 2003, discussing "President Bush's unprecedented order to shoot down any hijacked civilian airplane," stated: "Pentagon sources say Bush communicated the order to Cheney almost immediately after Flight 77 hit the Pentagon and the FAA, for the first time ever, ordered all domestic flights grounded."[11] This would put the shootdown authorization shortly after 9:45. These "Pentagon sources" were perhaps the same officers who had earlier been quoted to this effect.

For example, Brigadier General Montague Winfield, the deputy director of operations at the National Military Command Center in the Pentagon, said that he received the authorization prior to the crash of United Flight 93. After "[t]he decision was made to try to go intercept Flight 93," Winfield told ABC News on the first anniversary of 9/11, "The Vice President [said] that the President had given us permission to shoot down innocent civilian aircraft that threatened Washington, DC."[12]

Winfield's account was, moreover, endorsed on a CNN show that same week. In recounting the events, Barbara Starr, CNN's Pentagon correspondent, said: "It is now 9:40, and one very big problem is out there: United Airlines Flight 93 has turned off its transponder. Officials believe it is headed for Washington, D.C." Winfield then said on screen: "That is almost the exact same scenario that the other three hijackings had followed." Then Starr stated: "Fighter aircraft begin searching frantically. On a secure phone line, Vice President Cheney tells the military it has permission to shoot down any airliners threatening Washington."[13]

General Larry Arnold, who was the commander of NORAD within the continental United States, said: "I had every intention of shooting down United 93 if it continued to progress toward Washington, D.C."[14]

Colonel Robert Marr, the head of NEADS, confirmed that he had received the shootdown order while United 93 was still aloft, saying: "we received the clearance to kill if need be."[15] He also stated that he "passed that on to the pilots," adding: "United

Airlines Flight 93 will not be allowed to reach Washington, DC."[16]

A pilot who was in the air confirmed that these orders were received. Lt. Anthony Kuczynski reported that while his E-3 Sentry and two F-16s from Langley Air Force Base were flying toward Pittsburgh, they were "given direct orders to shoot down an airliner."[17]

Additional testimony has been given by Lt. Col. Marc Sasseville, the director of operations for the 121st Fighter Squadron, which is stationed at Andrews Air Force Base just outside Washington. Shortly after the strike on the Pentagon, reported an article in *Aviation Week and Space Technology*, the Secret Service told Andrews Air Force Base, "Get in the air now!" At about the same time, someone from the White House declared the Washington area a "free-fire zone." Sasseville, explaining that expression, added: "That meant we were given authority to use force, if the situation required it, in defense of the nation's capital, its property and people."[18]

That the Secret Service was issuing such orders at this time was also stated by Major General Mike Haugen, adjutant general of the North Dakota National Guard. He said that just after the attack on the Pentagon, the Secret Service had told the Langley F-16s to "protect the White House at all costs."[19]

According to all of these military officers, in other words, Richard Clarke's account was much closer to the truth than that of the 9/11 Commission.

Dealing with the Contradiction

How did the 9/11 Commission deal with the fact that its account was contradicted by Clarke and all these military officers? In four ways.

One way was its insistence, discussed in previous chapters, that Cheney, who was known to have issued the shootdown authorization from the PEOC, did not even enter that room until almost 10:00.

The Commission's second method was to produce its own alternative version of the incoming flight episode, recounted in Chapter 3, which did not begin until 10:02 and did not lead to shootdown authorization until 10:18.

The Commission's third method of dealing with the contradictory accounts was simply to ignore them. It did not cite the statements by Arnold, Marr, Sasseville, Winfield, or the pilots. With regard to Clarke's account—according to which he received the authorization from Cheney while Air Force One was waiting to take off and hence before 9:55—the Commission simply stated: "Confirmation of [shootdown] authority came [to Clarke] at 10:25."[20]

The Commission's fourth method of replacing Clarke's narrative with its own was to provide an alternative account of the response (at about 9:50) to a threefold request made by Clarke. According to Clarke, he, after getting the response, reported to Secretary of Defense Rumsfeld and General Richard Myers, the two representatives from the Department of Defense participating in his videoconference: "Three decisions: One, the President has ordered the use of force against aircraft deemed to be hostile. Two, the White House is also requesting fighter escort of Air Force one. Three, ... we are initiating COG [Continuity of Government]."[21]

The 9/11 Commission, while agreeing that the White House had made a threefold request, gave an alternative version, in which Clarke had *not* requested shootdown authorization. In giving this alternative version, the Commission cited the transcript for the teleconference that was organized by the National Military Command Center in the Pentagon. According to this transcript, the Commission said, "The White House requested (1) the implementation of continuity of government measures, (2) fighter escorts for Air Force One, and (3) a fighter combat air patrol over Washington, D.C."[22] It is true, to be sure, that Clarke, on the same page, had reported that he wanted "Combat Patrol over every major city in the country."[23] But whereas for Clarke this was a fourth request, the 9/11 Commission said that it was the third request, thereby implying that the request for shootdown authorization had not been made at that time.

Through these four methods, the 9/11 Commission replaced the earlier account, which was more or less agreed upon by Arnold, Marr, Sasseville, Winfield, Clarke, and two fighter pilots, with its own version of events, in which shootdown authorization was not issued until long after United 93 had crashed. This version was then spread among the populace by the film *United 93*, which ended with words on the screen saying that at 10:18, the president authorized the military to engage.

It remains the case, however, that this account is strongly contradicted by the testimonies of Richard Clarke and several military officers. Congress and the press need to investigate to see which, if any, of these accounts is true. Congress could, for one thing, subpoena the tapes of Clarke's video conference, to see if they support the story he gave in his book.

Conclusion

The 9/11 Commission's account of when Vice President Cheney issued the shootdown authorization has been contradicted by Richard Clarke and several military officers, including Colonel Marr (the head of NEADS), General Larry Arnold (the head of NORAD within the continental United States), and Brigadier General Montague Winfield (deputy director of operations at the NMCC)—three officers in especially good position to know. Congress and the press need to investigate to see who has given a false account and why.

6

WHERE WAS GENERAL RICHARD MYERS?

On 9/11, General Richard B. Myers was the acting chairman of the Joint Chiefs of Staff, because General Hugh Shelton, who was still the chairman—Myers had been nominated to succeed him but had not yet had his confirmation hearing—was on his way to Europe. As the acting chairman, Myers was the highest ranking military officer at the Pentagon. Dozens of people, accordingly, would surely know where he was that morning. And yet, strangely, we have been given two radically different accounts of his whereabouts.

The Account by General Myers and the 9/11 Commission
Myers himself said that he was on Capitol Hill from roughly 8:40 until 9:40AM, visiting Senator Max Cleland (in preparation for Myers's upcoming confirmation hearing). Just before he went into Cleland's office, Myers said, he learned from a television report about the first strike on the World Trade Center. Gathering from this report that the aircraft was thought to be "a small plane or something like that," he went ahead and had the meeting with Cleland. While this meeting was going on, the second tower was struck, but "[n]obody informed us of that." Then when they came out of the office and saw that the second tower had been hit, "right at that time somebody said the Pentagon has been hit." After which:

> [I]mmediately, somebody handed me a cell phone, and it was General [Ralph] Eberhart out at NORAD in Colorado Springs talking about what was happening and what actions he was going to take. We immediately, after talking to him, jumped in the car, ran back to the Pentagon.[1]

The 9/11 Commission endorsed this account, saying: "Myers was on Capitol Hill when the Pentagon was struck, ... saw smoke as his car made its way back to the building,"[2] and returned to the Pentagon's National Military Command Center (NMCC) "shortly before 10:00."[3]

Myers's account, it must be said, raises some problems of plausibility, because it entails that after the first airplane strike on the World Trade Center, Air Force General Myers, the acting chairman of the Joint Chiefs of Staff, simply went ahead with a scheduled meeting without checking to see what had really happened; that after the second strike, which everyone reportedly took as evidence that the country was under attack, neither Cleland's secretary nor anyone from the Pentagon or the military in general called him; and that no one from the Pentagon called him even after it was struck.

For our purposes, however, the main problem is that the account given by Myers and the 9/11 Commission was completely contradicted by Richard Clarke.

Richard Clarke's Account

Clarke, as we have seen, ran a video conference that morning from the White House Video Teleconference Center. His account — according to which this conference began as soon as his brief meeting with Cheney and Rice, which took place upon his arrival at the White House shortly after 9:03, was over —suggested that this video conference began about 9:10. This starting time was further supported by his statement that this conference had been going on several minutes before Norman Mineta arrived, combined with Mineta's statement that, after he arrived, he spent "four or five minutes" talking with Clarke before going down to the PEOC, which he reached "about 9:20."[4]

Myers's account was contradicted by Clarke's description of what he saw in the moments before his video conference began.

> As I entered the Video Center, ... I could see people rushing into studios around the city: Donald Rumsfeld at Defense and George Tenet at CIA.... Air Force four-star General Dick Myers was filling in for the Chairman of the Joint Chiefs, Hugh

Shelton, who was over the Atlantic. Bob Mueller was at the FBI....[5]

Whereas according to Myers's own account, he would at this time—about 9:15—have been in Cleland's office, he was, according to Clarke's account, in the Pentagon, taking part in this video conference.

According to Clarke's account, his first actual exchange with Myers occurred shortly before 9:28. Prior to that, Clarke reported, he had a discussion with Jane Garvey, the head of the FAA, who said: "The two aircraft that went in [to the World Trade Center towers] were American flight 11, a 767, and United 175, also a 767. Hijacked." She also said, Clarke recounted, that the FAA had "reports of eleven aircraft off course or out of communications, maybe hijacked."[6] Following Clarke's description of that exchange and of the arrival of Norman Mineta, he gave the following account of his conversation with Myers.

"JCS [Joint Chiefs of Staff], JCS. I assume NORAD has scrambled fighters and AWACS. How many? Where?"

"Not a pretty picture Dick.... We are in the midst of Vigilant Warrior, a NORAD exercise, but... Otis has launched two birds toward New York. Langley is trying to get two up now." ...

"Okay, how long to CAP over D.C.?" ....

"Fast as we can. Fifteen minutes?" Myers asked, looking at the generals and colonels around him. It was now 9:28.[7]

This account, incidentally, matched NORAD's timeline of September 18, 2001, according to which Langley had received a scramble order at 9:24 but the fighters were not airborne until 9:30. At 9:28, therefore, Langley would have still been trying to get the fighters up.

Clarke's narrative, in any case, contrasted drastically with Myers's story, according to which he, while waiting to go into Cleland's office, learned about the first crash but believed that "it was a small plane or something like that"; then did not learn about the second crash until he came out of Cleland's office; and then made it back to the Pentagon shortly before 10:00. In

Clarke's narrative, Myers was at the Pentagon all along, with "generals and colonels around him," knew no later than 9:25 that two hijacked airliners had crashed into the World Trade Center, and knew that the military had scrambled four fighters to guard against further attacks.

Clarke's narrative next told about a pause for the president's address, Clarke's telephone call to the PEOC to request shoot-down authorization, Jane Garvey's report that the "potential hijacks" included "United 93 over Pennsylvania," the report that an aircraft was headed toward Washington, the Secret Service's decision to evacuate the White House, the report that "[a] plane just hit the Pentagon," the report that Air Force One was getting ready to take off, and the report that the Pentagon had "authority from the President to shoot down hostile aircraft"—after which Clarke said: "I was amazed at the speed of the decisions coming from Cheney and, through him, from Bush."

After that, according to Clarke, "General Myers asked, 'Okay, shoot down aircraft, but what are the ROE [Rules of Engagement]?'"[8]

Clarke then recounted the Secret Service's report of a "hostile aircraft ten minutes out," the completion of the evacuation of the White House ("except for the group with Cheney in the East Wing bomb shelter and the team with me [Clarke] in the West Wing Situation Room"), and a brief break, after which Clarke wrote:

> We resumed the video conference. "DOD, DOD, go." I asked the Pentagon for an update on the fighter cover.
>
> Dick Myers had a status report. "We have three F-16s from Langley over the Pentagon. Andrews is launching fighters from the D.C. Air National Guard. We have fighters aloft from the Michigan Air National Guard, moving east toward a potential hostile over Pennsylvania."[9]

Two pages later, Clarke described seeing on the monitor the collapse of WTC 2, which occurred at 9:59. This status report from Myers, accordingly, would have occurred some minutes before 10:00.

Testimony from the Secretary of the Army

Clarke's account, according to which Myers was in the Pentagon all along, was bolstered by a comment from then Secretary of the Army Thomas White, in reference to an 8:00 o'clock breakfast meeting that Secretary of Defense Donald Rumsfeld had held in his private dining room in the Pentagon that morning.[10] White, who attended, later said this about the meeting:

> Don Rumsfeld had a breakfast, and virtually every one of the senior officials of the Department of Defense—service chiefs, secretary, deputy, everybody, chairman of the Joint Chiefs of Staff. And as that breakfast was breaking up, the first plane had hit the World Trade tower.[11]

By "chairman of the Joint Chiefs of Staff," White had to mean Myers, the acting and soon-to-be-confirmed chairman, because General Hugh Shelton, the outgoing chairman, was on his way to Europe. According to White's testimony, therefore, Myers was in that meeting in the Pentagon, not in Senator Cleland's office on Capitol Hill, when the first strike on the World Trade Center occurred—unless Myers left the meeting, which had started at 8:00, early enough to get to Capitol Hill before 8:46. If he did not, he would have been available to participate, as Clarke said he did, in the White House video conference.

Dealing with the Contradiction

The contradiction between the two accounts could not be starker. In the account given by Clarke, Myers was fully aware of what was going on, was participating in Clarke's video conference from about 9:15 to 10:00, and was, as befitting his status as acting chairman of the Joint Chiefs of Staff, involved in making decisions. In the account given by Myers and the 9/11 Commission, by contrast, he was completely out of the loop and did not even get to the Pentagon until almost 10:00.

The difference is vital, because if Myers was indeed participating in Clarke's video conference and Clarke's account of that conference is substantively correct, Myers would have learned many important things that were discussed: He would have heard Jane Garvey's statement at about 9:15 that the two planes that struck the World Trade Center had been hijacked and that the FAA, moreover, had "reports of eleven aircraft off course or out of communications, maybe hijacked." He would have heard Garvey's report of "United 93 over Pennsylvania" as a "potential hijack." He would have known that Clarke had received shootdown authorization from Cheney at about 9:50. And he would have known that he himself then said: "Okay, shoot down aircraft, but what are the ROE [Rules of Engagement]?" But if Myers was not there, it could be assumed that he was unaware of all those things.

The Commission's Treatment of Clarke's Book: In early March of 2004, while the 9/11 Commission's hearings were still going on, Clarke's book, *Against All Enemies*, came out. This was four months before the publication of *The 9/11 Commission Report.* How did the 9/11 Commission deal with the fact that Clarke's account completely contradicted Myers's account, which the Commission endorsed? By simply ignoring Clarke's account. Clarke's book was a national bestseller, read by millions, and yet the 9/11 Commission published an account of Myers's activities that morning that completely contradicted Clarke's account without mentioning this fact. Why would it do this?

The Commission did, to be sure, refer to Clarke's video conference. But it acted as if Clarke's book did not exist, mentioning it neither in the text of *The 9/11 Commission Report* nor in its notes.

By thus ignoring Clarke's book, the Commission could contradict it without needing to argue against it. For example, Clarke's account indicated that his video conference began at about 9:10. But the 9/11 Commission simply said that it "began at 9:25." The Commission even added: "Indeed, it is not clear to us that the video teleconference was fully under way before 9:37, when the Pentagon was struck."[12]

With regard to the location of General Myers from 9:15 until 10:00, the Commission, by not acknowledging the existence of Clarke's book, did not need to dispute Clarke's claim that Myers was in the Pentagon participating in the White House video conference. The Commission knew, of course, that someone from the Pentagon must have been participating. But it avoided explicitly challenging Clarke's account, while still implying its falsity, by saying: "We do not know who from Defense participated, but we know that in the first hour none of the personnel involved in managing the crisis did."

This, it must be said, is a very strange claim, for two reasons.

First, the commissioners were familiar with Richard Clarke and his book. They could have easily found out who from the Pentagon participated in his video conference by reading his book or simply asking him. Or, if they distrusted his account, they could have obtained a copy of the videotape. For the Commissioners to claim that they could not find out this information is to claim an extreme degree of incompetence.

A second problem: If the Commissioners did not know who from the Pentagon participated, how could they know that "in the first hour none of the personnel involved in managing the crisis did"? To be sure, the commissioners could have pointed out one way in which they *could* have deduced this: If they, without knowing who did participate, knew that everyone in the Pentagon who was involved in managing the crisis did *not* participate, they could have intelligibly made the claim. With regard to Myers, the Commission could have known that he did not participate during the first hour if it knew that he, as it claimed, was elsewhere until almost 10:00 and then, when he did get to the Pentagon's NMCC, was occupied with its own teleconference.[13] However, if this was the Commission's implicit claim, its failure to make it explicit, especially when combined with its failure to deal with Clarke's proffered information, seems strange.

Despite the strangeness of the Commission's claim of ignorance, this claim served its purposes. The Commission, as we will see in later chapters, argued that the military was not informed about the hijacking of either American Flight 77 or United Flight 93 prior to their crashes. By stating that Clarke's video conference did not involve Myers—or any other Pentagon personnel "involved in managing the crisis"—the Commission could claim that this conference did not provide a means by which the military could have learned about the hijackings of these two flights.

Making this claim was especially vital with regard to United 93, because, as we saw, Clarke reported that Jane Garvey, the head of the FAA, had reported at about 9:35 that the "potential hijacks" included "United 93 over Pennsylvania."[14] If the Commission had accepted Clarke's account, according to which Myers was participating in that conference and Garvey made that report, it could not have maintained its claim that no one in the military, at least no one "involved in managing the crisis," knew that United 93 had shown signs of being hijacked. If it had even acknowledged Clarke's account, it would have had to argue against it, thereby raising doubts about Myers's claim.

Clarke's account was also a threat with regard to the Commission's account of the damage to the Pentagon, according to which this damage was caused by American Flight 77, about which, according to the Commission, the military knew neither that it was headed back toward Washington nor even that it had been hijacked. Although Clarke did not report that any discussion of Flight 77 occurred during his video conference, the FAA told the Commission that it had been keeping the military informed about "all the flights of interest, including Flight 77."[15] By endorsing Myers's claim that he was on Capitol Hill during that crucial period and thereby implicitly rejecting Clarke's claim about Myers's participation in the video conference, the Commission ruled out the possibility that Myers could have learned anything about Flight 77 from FAA head Jane Garvey's contributions to that conference. By completely ignoring Clarke's book, the Commission did not even have to argue the point.

Myers vs. Myers

Besides being contradicted by Clarke's account, the account that Myers gave on October 17, 2001, also contradicted some of his other accounts of what he experienced between 9:00 and 10:00 that morning.

Myers gave the first of several versions while testifying at his confirmation hearing on September 13, 2001. During this testimony, he said: "I was with Senator Cleland when this happened [the Pentagon was struck]." This was consistent with his October

17 account. But then, having been asked about the military's response to the awareness that airliners had gone off course, he said: "I spoke, after the second tower was hit, I spoke to the commander of NORAD, General Eberhart."[16] This account, by stating that he spoke to Eberhart after the second tower was struck, appears to contradict his October 17 account, according to which the call from Eberhart came only after Myers had learned about the strike on the Pentagon. But perhaps the contradiction is only apparent, because, it could be argued, he simply forgot to add, in his confirmation hearing, that the call from Eberhart came after the Pentagon strike as well as after the second WTC strike.

Be that as it may, Myers's October 17 account was more clearly contradicted by his testimony to the 9/11 Commission in 2004, in which he said:

> The first call I got when I left Capitol Hill after a meeting with Senator Cleland was from General Eberhart saying, "We've had these crashes and we're going to take certain actions." And it was shortly thereafter that the Pentagon was hit as we were on our way back to the Pentagon.[17]

In his October 17 statement, he said that he received the call from Eberhart while he was still on Capitol Hill, not after he had left. In his previous statements, moreover, he had said that he learned about the Pentagon attack while he was still on the Hill with Senator Cleland, and before he heard from Eberhart, not while he was on his way back to the Pentagon and after he had heard from Eberhart.

Finally, a 2006 DOD story, based on quotations from Myers, provided yet a different sequence of events:

> [General Myers] was visiting with Georgia Sen. Max Cleland when the second plane hit the World Trade Center. "I was called out by Gen. (Ralph) Eberhart... and my executive assistant," he said. Myers immediately got into his car and rushed back to the Pentagon. "Before we even got to the 14th Street Bridge, the Pentagon was hit," he said. "The scene coming across the bridge was the Pentagon with black smoke rolling out of it."[18]

In this 2006 version, Myers agreed with his statement to the 9/11 Commission that he received the call from Eberhart before the

Pentagon was struck and that the attack on the Pentagon occurred while he was driving back toward it (which means that he disagreed with his statements from 2001 on both of these points). But he contradicted all his previous statements by suggesting that his phone call from Eberhart came right after the second tower was hit, while he was still in Cleland's office ("I was called out")—not after he came out of the office, as he said in his October 17 account, and certainly not after he had already left Capitol Hill, as he told 9/11 Commission in 2004.

Still another problem with this 2006 account arises from Myers's statement that the Pentagon was hit before his car "got to the 14th Street Bridge." If he left Capitol Hill "immediately" after being phoned by Eberhart following the second WTC crash and hence by, say, 9:10, he should have reached this bridge long before 9:38, the time of the Pentagon strike.

Be that as it may, Myers's various accounts are, when compared with each other, full of contradictions. One would think that, if Myers had really lived through these events, the location and the order in which he had the various experiences would have been seared indelibly into his memory. One would especially assume this with regard to the strike on the Pentagon, where Myers and many of his colleagues had their offices. If he, for example, really learned about the Pentagon strike while he was still on Capitol Hill, could he later have come to imagine that he had learned about it only as his car was approaching the 14th Street Bridge? By contrast, we can imagine that if his story about being on Capitol Hill was an invention, he would sometimes forget, in telling this tale, what he had said in previous tellings. The contradictions in Myers's accounts, therefore, can raise reasonable doubts that he really was, contrary to Richard Clarke's account, on Capitol Hill that morning.

Max Cleland's Endorsement

Myers's account is bolstered, however, by the fact that it was supported by Senator Cleland himself, a Democrat who later became a member of the 9/11 Commission but subsequently resigned, after becoming critical of decisions made by its leaders to accommodate White House wishes.[19]

Cleland's first public expression of support came during Myers's confirmation hearing with the Senate Armed Services Committee. During his testimony, as we saw above, Myers had said: "I was with Senator Cleland when [the Pentagon was struck]." When it was Cleland's turn to raise questions, he began by saying:

> General, it's a good thing that, as I look back at that morning, that you and I were meeting. It's a good thing we were meeting here and not us meeting in the Pentagon because about the time you and I were having our visit, discussing the need to boost our conventional forces, to look at the question of terrorism and attacks on the United States, at just about that very moment, the Pentagon was being hit.[20]

By supporting Myers's statement to the Senate Armed Services Committee that the two of them were meeting while the Pentagon was struck, Cleland, of course, contradicted Myers's later statements, according to which he was in his car heading back toward the Pentagon when it was struck.

Another problem with Cleland's endorsement of Myers's early story arises from the fact that two years later, while he was a member of the 9/11 Commission, Cleland gave an account of the episode that introduced still more contradictions. In a lecture delivered in 2003, Cleland said:

> I was in my office in the Senate discussing the future of American defenses, particularly against worldwide terrorism, with the new Chairman of the Joint Chiefs of Staff, Gen. Myers. The first plane had already hit the World Trade Center and Gen. Myers bolted from his seat. We rushed into an adjoining office as we saw on TV the second plane slam into the second tower. Gen. Myers rushed out of my office, headed for the Pentagon. At that moment, the Pentagon was hit.[21]

Although it is clear that Cleland's new account is more supportive of Myers's later (2004 and 2006) accounts regarding the Pentagon strike than was his statement at Myers's 2001 confirmation hearing, it is otherwise difficult to tell exactly what Cleland was saying. One possible reading would be that Myers was already in Cleland's office when the first plane struck the WTC, after which

Myers "bolted from his seat" and they both rushed into the adjoining office. If so, that would, besides contradicting all of Myers's accounts, imply that the two crashes were only seconds apart (whereras in reality they were seventeen minutes apart).

Probably, however, Cleland meant that, as Myers said, the first plane had hit the WTC before their meeting started. But if so, what caused Myers to bolt from his seat and caused the two of them to rush into the adjoining room (which was where, apparently, they saw the second strike on TV)? Perhaps it was the phone call from General Eberhart. Cleland said, in any case, that after seeing the second crash, Myers rushed out and left for the Pentagon, which was hit "[a]t that moment."

But this account made the timeline problem even worse than did Myers's 2006 account, because Cleland's story implied that the Pentagon was hit even before Myers would have had time to reach the 14th Street Bridge. Cleland's account, in other words, appeared to reduce the 35-minute interval between the South Tower attack (9:03) and the Pentagon attack (9:38) to 5 or 10 minutes.

All in all, therefore, Senator Cleland's statements, rather than resolving the internal contradictions in General Myers's account, add to them.

Conclusion

Congress and the press should question General Myers and Senator Cleland about the internal contradictions in their accounts of Myers's actions on the morning of 9/11. Even more should Congress and the press explore the stark contradictions between Richard Clarke's account and that given by Myers and the 9/11 Commission. Obviously not all of these accounts can be true. And by finding out which accounts are false and why they were told, Congress and the press might discover something quite important.

7

WHERE WAS DONALD RUMSFELD?

As we have seen, Richard Clarke wrote that the Pentagon was represented in his video conference not only by General Myers but also by Secretary of Defense Donald Rumsfeld. Just as Clarke's account of this conference contradicted Myers's own account of his activities, so too did it contradict Rumsfeld's account of *his* activities.

Richard Clarke's Account

As we saw earlier, Clarke's account of his video conference began thus:

> As I entered the Video Center, ... I could see people rushing into studios around the city: Donald Rumsfeld at Defense and George Tenet at CIA.[1]

This would have been about 9:10AM.[2] Later in Clarke's narrative, after word was received about the strike on the Pentagon (and hence presumably just after 9:38), Clarke said: "I can still see Rumsfeld on the screen."[3] Then after getting the shootdown authorization at about 9:50, Clarke wrote that he, "tr[ying] to get the attention of those still on the screen in the Pentagon," said: "DOD, DOD." Clarke then added:

> Rumsfeld said that smoke was getting into the Pentagon secure teleconferencing studio. Franklin Miller urged him to helicopter to DOD's alternate site. "I am too goddamn old to go to an alternate site," the Secretary answered. Rumsfeld moved to another studio in the Pentagon and sent his deputy, Paul Wolfowitz, to the remote site.[4]

Although Clarke did not mention any further exchange with Rumsfeld until about 3:30 that afternoon,[5] his statement that

Rumsfeld "moved to another studio" implied that his participation in Clarke's conference did not cease at that point.

According to Clarke, in sum, when the Pentagon attack occurred, Rumsfeld was in the teleconferencing studio (which is in the Pentagon's Executive Support Center, close to Rumsfeld's office). He then moved to another studio.

The Rumsfeld–9/11 Commission Account

Rumsfeld himself, in his testimony to the 9/11 Commission on March 23, 2004, gave the following account:

> I was in my office with a CIA briefer and I was told that a second plane had hit the other tower. Shortly thereafter, at 9:38, the Pentagon shook with an explosion of then unknown origin. I went outside to determine what had happened. I was not there long because I was back in the Pentagon with a crisis action team shortly before or after 10:00AM.
>
> On my return from the crash site and before going to the Executive Support Center, I had one or more calls in my office, one of which was with the president.
>
> I went to the National Military Command Center where General Myers… had just returned from Capitol Hill…. I joined the air threat telephone conference call that was already in progress.[6]

Whereas Clarke's account had Rumsfeld in the "Pentagon secure teleconferencing studio" (in the Executive Support Center) when the Pentagon was hit, Rumsfeld's own account had him in his own office. And whereas Clarke's account suggested that smoke in the teleconferencing studio caused Rumsfeld to go to another studio, Rumsfeld himself said that curiosity caused him to go down to the attack site.

Although in this account, Rumsfeld seemed to say that he stayed at the attack site just long enough to "determine what had happened," he had claimed, in more extensive accounts, that he stayed at the attack site for a while to help rescue the wounded (a claim that is supported by some Pentagon photos).[7] For example, during an interview given one month after 9/11, he said:

I was sitting here [in my office] and the building was struck, and you could feel the impact of it very clearly.... I looked out the window, saw nothing here, and then went down the hall until the smoke was too bad, then to a stairwell down and went outside and saw what had happened.... I saw people on the grass, and we just, we tried to put them in stretchers and then move them out across the grass towards the road and lifted them over a jersey wall so the people on that side could stick them into the ambulances. I was out there for awhile.... Then at some moment I decided I should be in here figuring out what to do.... I came back in here, came into this office.[8]

Rumsfeld's story about going down to the attack site does not, it should be pointed out, necessarily contradict the account given by Clarke, who simply said that Rumsfeld, after the smoke got too bad, went to another studio. Clarke did not specify how long Rumsfeld remained visible there and did not mention him again until about 3:30. So, if Rumsfeld did participate in Clarke's video conference from about 9:10 until shortly after the Pentagon attack, he could also have spent some time at the attack site.

However, although that portion of Rumsfeld's testimony is not necessarily in tension with Clarke's book, there is a complete contradiction between the two accounts of what Rumsfeld was doing during the half hour from 9:10 to 9:40, and the 9/11 Commission failed to acknowledge this fact. Rather, it simply endorsed Rumsfeld's account, saying:

Rumsfeld was having breakfast at the Pentagon with a group of members of Congress. He then returned to his office for his daily intelligence briefing. The Secretary was informed of the second strike in New York during the briefing; he resumed the briefing while awaiting more information. After the Pentagon was struck, Secretary Rumsfeld went to the parking lot to assist with rescue efforts.[9]

The Commission later added:

[Rumsfeld] went from the parking lot to his office (where he spoke to the President [shortly after 10:00]), then to the Executive Support Center, where he participated in the White House video teleconference. He moved to the NMCC shortly before 10:30, in order to join Vice Chairman Myers.[10]

The Commission thereby endorsed the account given in Rumsfeld's testimony to it, without mentioning the contradictions between this account and Richard Clarke's.

The Commission also failed to point out that the Rumsfeld story it endorsed contains several elements that disagree with earlier versions given by Rumsfeld, to which we now turn.

Did Rumsfeld Go to the ESC or the NMCC?

In his statement to the Commission, as we saw, Rumsfeld said that, before going to the National Military Command Center (NMCC) after returning from the attack site, he first went to his office and then the Executive Support Center (ESC). The ESC, which is next to the NMCC, contains the secure teleconferencing studio to which Richard Clarke referred. This statement, however, differed from statements made earlier by Rumsfeld and his spokesperson, Torie Clarke, who was the assistant secretary of defense for public affairs.

In an interview only five days after 9/11, Torie Clarke said that after the second tower was hit, she went into Rumsfeld's office to inform him of this fact and also to tell him that "the crisis management process was starting up." She then gave this account of Rumsfeld's activities:

> He wanted to make a few phone calls. So a few of us headed across the hallway to an area called the National Military Command Center. He stayed in his office. We were in these rooms maybe 200 feet away where we felt the concussion.... When he came back in the building about half an hour later, he was the first one that told us he was quite sure it was a plane.[11]

Whereas the Commission, following Rumsfeld's own account to it, said that when he went back into the building, he went to his office briefly and then to the ESC, Torie Clarke implied that he went to the NMCC, where she and others were involved in the crisis management process.

That this was indeed the earlier story is shown by an interview Rumsfeld granted to John McWethy of ABC News in August 2002. When asked what he did while at the attack site, Rumsfeld said:

Oh, I was there for a relatively short period of time and tried to help some folks in the stretchers. Decided I'd best get back into the Command Center, which I then did. We... were able to spend all that day and then that evening until quite late in the Command Center.[12]

In these early statements by Rumsfeld and Torie Clarke, there was no mention of the Executive Support Center, which houses the secure teleconference studio. Rumsfeld's assistants, and then he, are said to have gone directly to the NMCC.

As we saw earlier, however, Rumsfeld, in his testimony to the 9/11 Commission on March 23, 2004, said: "On my return from the crash site and before going to the Executive Support Center, I had one or more calls in my office."[13]

That Rumsfeld did not simply misspeak, but had changed his story, is confirmed by Torie Clarke's book, which appeared in 2006. Although she had earlier said that after giving Rumsfeld some information, "a few of us headed across the hallway to an area called the National Military Command Center," in her book she said that Rumsfeld told her and Larry Di Rita, his personal chief of staff, to go to the Executive Support Center (ESC) and wait for him there.[14]

What could account for this change? Just two weeks before Rumsfeld's testimony to the Commission, Richard Clarke's book had appeared, instantly becoming a national bestseller (the publication date was March 10, 2004). In the early pages of that book, as we saw, Clarke said that Rumsfeld was participating in his White House video conference from the "Pentagon secure teleconferencing studio" (which is in the Executive Support Center). Had Rumsfeld told his earlier story to the Commission, his account would have been completely at odds with the account given by Clarke.

Thanks to Rumsfeld's new story, however, the Commission was able to soften the contradiction. It said, as we saw above:

> [Rumsfeld] went from the parking lot to his office..., then to the Executive Support Center, where he participated in the White House video teleconference. He moved to the NMCC shortly before 10:30, in order to join Vice Chairman Myers.[15]

The Commission thereby stated that Rumsfeld did participate in Clarke's video conference. But by saying that this participation did not begin until after 10:00, it maintained its claim, discussed in the previous chapter, that "none of the [Pentagon's] personnel involved in managing the crisis" participated in Clarke's video conference "in the first hour."[16] Given the fact that it was well established that Rumsfeld had arrived in the NMCC at about 10:30, his participation in Clarke's video conference had to be, in the Commission's account, quite brief, limited to about fifteen minutes. Nevertheless, the Commission, by stating that Rumsfeld did participate in that conference, was able to incorporate this idea while still shielding Rumsfeld from participation in that conference during the crucial period from 9:15 until 10:00.

By not being there during that period, Rumsfeld would have missed hearing the same things, if Clarke's account is historically accurate, that General Myers would also have missed if he was not there (as discussed in the previous chapter): Jane Garvey's statement at about 9:15 that the two planes that struck the World Trade Center had been hijacked; that the FAA had reports of eleven other aircraft that were "maybe hijacked"; that one of those was "United 93 over Pennsylvania"; and that Clarke had received shootdown authorization at about 9:50. Furthermore, if Rumsfeld had not been participating in the video conference but Myers had been, then Rumsfeld would have missed the fact—again, if Clarke's account is basically correct—that Myers at this time had asked that the rules of engagement be clarified.

When Did Rumsfeld Discuss Rules of Engagement?

In Rumsfeld's testimony to the 9/11 Commission, in which he described what happened after he had been in the Executive Support Center (from about 10:15 to about 10:30), he said:

> I went to the National Military Command Center where General Myers... had just returned from Capitol Hill.... I joined the air threat telephone conference call that was already in progress. And one of the first exchanges was with the vice president. He informed me of the president's authorization to shoot down hostile aircraft coming to Washington D.C. My thoughts went to

the pilots of the military aircraft who might be called upon to execute such an order. It was clear that they needed rules of engagement telling them what they could and could not do. They needed clarity. There were standing rules of engagement, but not rules of engagement that were appropriate for this first-time situation where civilian aircraft were seized and being used as missiles to attack inside the United States.... We went to work to refine the standing rules of engagement. I spent the remainder of the morning and the afternoon participating in the air threat conference.[17]

The 9/11 Commission, which endorsed this account, wrote: "At 10:39, the Vice President updated the Secretary [of Defense] on the air threat conference." The Commission then quoted some dialogue, said to be from the transcript of their conversation at that time, in which Cheney told Rumsfeld:

> There's been at least three instances here where we've had reports of aircraft approaching Washington—a couple were confirmed hijack. And, pursuant to the President's instructions I gave authorization for them to be taken out.[18]

After quoting some more dialogue, the Commission continued:

> As this exchange shows, Secretary Rumsfeld was not in the NMCC when the shootdown order [which had been given some time between 10:10 and 10:18[19]] was first conveyed.... He moved to the NMCC shortly before 10:30.... Secretary Rumsfeld told us he was just gaining situational awareness when he spoke with the Vice President at 10:39. His primary concern was ensuring that the pilots had a clear understanding of their rules of engagement.[20]

"DOD did not circulate written rules of engagement," the Commission added, "until sometime after 1:00PM."[21]

The Commission and Rumsfeld agreed, therefore, that Rumsfeld was not in the NMCC when the shootdown authorization was given, that his discussion of "rules of engagement" did not begin until after 10:39, and that the process of formulating these rules was a slow one.

This account is, however, in tension with what Rumsfeld told ABC's John McWethy in August 2002. With regard to his trip to the Pentagon attack site, Rumsfeld said that after being there "for a relatively short period of time," he decided that he should "get back into the Command Center." McWethy then asked:

> So you went into the NMCC, the National Military Command Center, and you had a series of decisions to make in those first early minutes. Do you remember what some of those decisions were? There was a DefCon [Defense Condition] decision, there was a shoot-at-the-plane decision, those sorts of things?

Rumsfeld replied:

> Yes, it's correct. I did make a decision with respect to changing the DefCon status and we rapidly developed some rules of engagement for what our military aircraft might do in the event another aircraft appeared to be heading into a large civilian structure or population.[22]

We will return below to the question of the order to go to DEFCON 3 (as it is usually written). For now, the point to notice is Rumsfeld's assertion that, after getting to the NMCC following his presence at the attack site for only "a relatively short period of time," he and others—he was on the telephone, he said, with "the President, the Vice President, a whole host of people"—developed the rules of engagement "rapidly." Then, in explaining why this discussion was needed, he said:

> It was a totally different circumstance for our country. The thought of having to shoot down one of our own civilian aircraft ... As a result we developed a rule of engagement that we decided was appropriate and then we decided the appropriate levels going up.

With regard to the time at which this had occurred, McWethy and Rumsfeld had the following exchange:

> *McWethy:* Had the Shanksville plane already gone into the ground at that point?
>
> *Rumsfeld:* No.
>
> *McWethy:* So you were still deliberating this early on in that process and there was that plane in particular that was the major—

Rumsfeld: You mean the one in Pennsylvania?

McWethy: The Pennsylvania plane.

Rumsfeld: I'd have to look at, some of the people who were with me, they have notes. I don't. I was pretty busy.

Rumsfeld's initial response, as can be seen, was that this discussion about rules of engagement occurred before the crash of United Flight 93. But then, after clarifying that McWethy meant "the [plane] in Pennsylvania," Rumsfeld drew back, saying he would have to check the notes of the meeting. He suggested, in other words, that when he had quickly said "No," he had been unclear that the plane that went down in Pennsylvania was the one to which McWethy was referring. McWethy's question, however, had been: "Had the Shanksville plane already gone into the ground at that point?" No other plane had "gone into the ground." How could Rumsfeld possibly have been confused about the plane to which McWethy was referring?

It would seem, therefore, that in August of 2002, Rumsfeld said that his conversation about rules of engagement occurred prior to 10:00 (not after 10:39, as the 9/11 Commission said on the basis of Rumsfeld's 2004 testimony). That version would, moreover, correspond with Clarke's account of when this issue came up.

The January 2002 *Washington Post* story by Dan Balz and Bob Woodward, which was mentioned earlier, also supported the idea that the rules of engagement were settled before United 93 crashed. In their account, Bush and Rumsfeld clarified the procedures shortly after Air Force One took off from Sarasota at 9:55 and before word was received that a plane had crashed in Pennsylvania. Balz and Woodward also say that there was concern that this plane had been shot down—which in itself suggests that the shootdown authorization, complete with rules of engagement, had already been given.[23]

Strangely, however, in the interview that Rumsfeld granted to Balz and Woodward on January 9, 2002, which was presumably the basis for their article, Rumsfeld put the time later. According to the transcript of this interview, the rules of engagement were settled "sometime between [10:15] and 11:15."[24] It is hard to know what to make of this discrepancy. Did Balz and Woodward give a distorted account? Or did they have a follow-up interview, perhaps by telephone, in which they elicited further statements from Rumsfeld (a possibility that is suggested by the fact that some other statements attributed to Rumsfeld in this article are also not found in the transcript of the interview)?[25]

Closely related, in any case, is the question of the time that the military was put on DEFCON 3, meaning Defense Condition 3 (also called "Condition Delta"). These two issues are closely related because Rumsfeld indicated in 2002 that the DEFCON 3 order was given at roughly the same time that the rules of engagement were rapidly worked out. Determining when the military was put on DEFCON 3, therefore, should further help determine the time at which Rumsfeld's discussion of the rules of engagement occurred.

The 9/11 Commission, in line with its claim that Rumsfeld did not begin discussing rules of engagement until after 10:39, said: "The secretary of defense directed the nation's armed forces to Defense Condition 3.... The Secretary's decision was broadcast on the air threat conference call at 10:43."[26] By contrast, Richard Clarke, right after referring to the crash of United 93 (which occurred at 10:03 or 10:06—see Chapter 13), wrote: "Frank Miller reported that DOD had gone on a global alert, DEFCON 3."[27]

Clarke's timeline, moreover, seems to be supported by all previous reports. One such report was included in the ABC program on the first anniversary of 9/11, which was based on interviews that Peter Jennings had with several government leaders, including Rumsfeld. This program, while discussing the Pentagon Command Center's conference call shortly after the Pentagon strike, said: "Rumsfeld orders US forces to Defcon Three. The highest alert for the nuclear arsenal in 30 years."[28] During that same week, CNN had a program on the NMCC put together by Barbara Starr, CNN's correspondent at the Pentagon. After mentioning the crash of United Flight 93, Starr said: "10:10, all U.S. military forces ordered to Condition Delta, highest level."[29]

The true time when the DEFCON 3 order was given should not be hard for Congress and the press to determine. So if, as everyone seems to agree, this order was closely connected to

Rumsfeld's discussion of rules of engagement, then the time of that discussion should also be easy to determine. If it did indeed occur prior to 10:00, as all the early reports indicate, then Rumsfeld clearly had "situational awareness" long before 10:39. Congress and the press need to determine whether Rumsfeld and the 9/11 Commission changed the time of that discussion and, if so, why.

Why Did Rumsfeld Go to the Attack Site?

The main question the press has raised regarding Rumsfeld's story about his behavior that morning is whether his decision to go to the attack site was justified.

As we saw earlier, Torie Clarke reported that, after she told Rumsfeld about the second WTC strike and informed him that the crisis management process was beginning, he replied that he wanted to stay in his office, make some phone calls, and complete his CIA briefing. This briefing was still going on when the Pentagon was attacked.

This part of Rumsfeld's story raised some eyebrows in the press. John McWethy, for example, asked: "So you did not alter, after the second building had been hit in New York, you did not alter your routine. You continued with your intelligence briefing?"[30]

McWethy was right to express surprise. There had already been two attacks by hijacked airliners. Rumsfeld was the head of the Defense Department. As such, he and President Bush constituted the National Command Authority, which has the power to authorize military pilots to shoot down civilian aircraft, and Bush was in a classroom in Florida. Accordingly, if there had been more hijacked planes, so that an order would need to be given to shoot them down before they hit their targets, Rumsfeld would have been the key figure. Moreover, a document recently promulgated by the chairman of the Joint Chiefs of Staff could be understood—if mistakenly—to mean that all FAA requests to the military to respond to a hijacking had to be approved by the Secretary of Defense.[31] Some people in the chain of command might have held that mistaken interpretation. It was important, for all these reasons, that Rumsfeld be immediately involved in the crisis management process. His delay, even for a few minutes, at such a time demonstrates irresponsibility of the highest order, bordering on criminal negligence.

Even worse was the fact that, after the Pentagon strike, he went down to the strike zone. He was then evidently out of touch for quite a period. The 9/11 Commission, while offering no criticism of Rumsfeld's behavior, did say that the NMCC, immediately after the strike on the Pentagon, began trying to get Rumsfeld added to its air threat conference call, but that Rumsfeld did not join in until 10:30.[32] It also reported that at 9:44, NORAD was "still trying to locate Secretary Rumsfeld and Vice Chairman Myers."[33] Furthermore, a senior White House official, who was in its Situation Room that morning, has said:

> What was Rumsfeld doing on 9/11? He deserted his post. He disappeared. The country was under attack. Where was the guy who controls America's defense? Out of touch! How long does it take for something bad to happen? No one knew what was happening. What if this had been the opening shot of a coordinated attack by a hostile power? Outrageous, to abandon your responsibilities and go off and do what you don't need to be doing, grandstanding.[34]

The seriousness of this issue, as emphasized by this White House figure, forces the question: Why indeed did Rumsfeld go to the attack zone? Put otherwise, was Rumsfeld's behavior justifiable? Rumsfeld appears to have given contradictory answers.

Rumsfeld at times suggested that his action was justifiable, fully logical. In his interview with John McWethy, he said: "I was going, which seemed to me perfectly logically, towards the scene of the accident to see what could be done and what had happened."[35] This was a logical thing to do, Rumsfeld appears to have said, because he wanted to see (a) what happened and (b) what he could do to help. He gave this same twofold response to CNN's Larry King, saying: "I wanted to see what had happened. I wanted to see if people needed help. I went downstairs and helped for a bit with some people on stretchers."[36]

But Rumsfeld was not just an ordinary citizen. He was the head of the Department of Defense. Besides the fact that he could have satisfied his curiosity about what happened by sending some young assistant down to investigate and then report back to him, Rumsfeld could have been most helpful not by using his 69-year-old body to help people onto stretchers but by taking steps, as the head of the US military, to ensure that no other attacks on America succeeded. His answers to McWethy and King seemed to suggest that he did not understand that he should have acted as if the danger were not over.

Later in the interview with McWethy, however, he showed that he did. McWethy asked: "Did you have a concern that the U.S. was about to be hit again in those early moments, those early hours?" Rumsfeld replied: "Sure. There's no question about it. Once you take the three airplanes into three buildings…, you can't help but be very attentive to the possibility of another attack."

Rumsfeld's answers to the two questions raised by his reported behavior—why he did not immediately go to the ESC or NMCC to get involved in the crisis management process, and why he then spent twenty or more minutes going to the attack site—are clearly inadequate, suggesting that they are not the real reasons. When this problem is added to the contradiction between Rumsfeld's account of his behavior and Richard Clarke's account, it is clear that Congress and the press need to find out what Rumsfeld was really doing and, if he has given a false account, why.

Conclusion

As we have seen, Richard Clarke's account of Rumsfeld's participation in the White House video conference contradicted the account that Rumsfeld had, prior to 2004, been giving of his own activities. It is not immediately obvious which account is closer to the truth. A desideratum in favor of Clarke's account is provided, however, by the fact that, after Clarke's account was published, Rumsfeld and the Commission presented a new account of Rumsfeld's behavior that, while still maintaining most of the elements of his previous story, incorporated into it a new element: his participation in Clarke's video conference. Also the times assigned to some of his activities by the Rumsfeld–9/11

Commission account are significantly different from the times given in Rumsfeld's earlier statements. Finally, Rumsfeld, by implicitly giving contradictory answers to the question of whether his trek to the attack site was justifiable, has provided grounds for doubting that he has provided the real reason for this trek. Clues to the answer to this question might be found if the various contradictions exposed in this chapter were to be explored.

The main question, however, remains that of whether Rumsfeld was participating in Clarke's video conference from 9:10 to 9:40, as Clarke says. If he was, and if Clarke's account is essentially correct, then Rumsfeld would have known by 9:15 that the two planes that struck the World Trade Center had been hijacked and that eleven more aircraft were "maybe hijacked"; and he would have learned before the Pentagon attack that "United 93 over Pennsylvania" was a "potential hijack." He would, accordingly, have had "situational awareness" more than a hour earlier than 10:39, the time at which he later, according to the 9/11 Commission, said he reached that state. If that is true, then his self-reported behavior over the next hour would have clearly constituted criminal negligence, if not worse.

On the other hand, if Clarke's account is false, then we have quite a different question to explore: Why did Richard Clarke give a false account of Rumsfeld's behavior during that period?

In any case, whatever be the truth of the matter, it is clear that Clarke's account and the account given by Rumsfeld and the 9/11 Commission cannot both be true. Congress and the press need to find out who gave a false account and why. As with the contradiction in the previous chapter, Congress could resolve this question quite easily, it would seem, by acquiring, by means of a subpoena, the videotape of Clarke's video conference.

8

DID TED OLSON RECEIVE CALLS FROM BARBARA OLSON?

Ted Olson was the US solicitor general during the first term of the Bush–Cheney administration. (He had previously represented candidates Bush and Cheney successfully in the Supreme Court case, *Bush v. Gore*, which brought them to power.) As such, he represented the administration in cases before the Supreme Court, such as Cheney's successful fight to keep secret the documents of his National Energy Policy Development Group.

On the afternoon of 9/11, CNN put out a story that began: "Barbara Olson, a conservative commentator and attorney, alerted her husband, Solicitor General Ted Olson, that the plane she was on was being hijacked Tuesday morning, Ted Olson told CNN." According to this story, Olson reported that his wife had "called him twice on a cell phone from American Airlines Flight 77," saying that "all passengers and flight personnel, including the pilots, were herded to the back of the plane by armed hijackers. The only weapons she mentioned were knives and cardboard cutters."[1]

Although this report was instrumental in the creation of the official story about 9/11, according to which the planes had been hijacked by terrorists armed with knives and box cutters,[2] this report was contradicted, strangely, by Ted Olson himself, American Airlines, and the FBI.

Olson's Self-Contradictions

Olson's own accounts contain self-contradictions. The main contradiction concerns the type of phone used by his wife. According to

CNN, as we have seen, he said on September 11 that she had "called him twice on a cell phone." On September 14, however, Olson told Fox News's *Hannity & Colmes* that she had reached him by calling the Department of Justice *collect*. She must, therefore, have been using the "airplane phone"—because, he surmised, "she somehow didn't have access to her credit cards."[3]

On CNN's *Larry King Show* later that same day, Olson returned to his first story. After saying that the second call from her suddenly went dead, he surmised that this was "because the signals from cell phones coming from airplanes don't work that well."[4]

Two months later, however, Ted Olson went back to his second story. In the "Barbara K. Olson Memorial Lecture" delivered to the Federalist Society, he said that she used "a telephone in the airplane to [make] those two telephone [calls]."[5] This story was then repeated in March 2002. "[C]alling collect," he told the London *Daily Telegraph*, his wife "us[ed] the phone in the passengers' seats." She called collect, he again surmised, because "she didn't have her purse" and hence her credit card.[6]

This revised version of his story evidently went virtually unnoticed in the American press. A year after 9/11, for example, CNN was still reporting that Barbara Olson had used a cell phone.[7] Nevertheless, Ted Olson's statement to the Federalist Society and the *Telegraph*—that she called collect using a passenger-seat phone—was apparently his final word on the matter.

That, however, was a self-contradictory claim, because it takes a credit card to activate an onboard phone.[8] If she did not have a credit card, she could not have used a passenger-seat phone, whether to call collect or otherwise. Some people have suggested that she reversed the charges because she had borrowed someone else's credit card. In that situation, however, speed would have been far more important than saving a few dollars.

The credibility of Ted Olson's story is challenged, therefore, by this self-contradictory claim and also by the fact that the first version of his story, according to which his wife had used a cell phone, was contradicted by his final version.

Olson's Final Version Contradicted by American Airlines

By settling on the assertion that his wife had used a passenger-seat phone, nevertheless, Olson avoided having his story challenged by the assertion that, given the cell phone technology in 2001, cell phone calls from airliners were generally possible only if they were flying at a low altitude.[9] For example, a story in *Travel Technologist*, published one week after 9/11, said:

> [W]ireless communications networks weren't designed for ground-to-air communication. Cellular experts privately admit that they're surprised the calls were able to be placed from the hijacked planes.... They speculate that the only reason that the calls went through in the first place is that the aircraft were flying so close to the ground.[10]

This assumption, that the planes from which cell phone calls were made on 9/11 must have been flying at very low altitudes, was also stated by Brenda Raney, a Verizon Wireless spokesperson, who said: "the planes were flying low when people started using their phones."[11]

However, Barbara Olson's first call, according to the 9/11 Commission (which endorsed Ted Olson's story), occurred "[a]t some point between 9:16 and 9:26."[12] According to the Flight Data Recorder information released by the National Transportation Safety Board, Flight 77 would at those two times have been at about 25,000 feet and 14,000 feet, respectively.[13]

But although the final version of Olson's story avoided this problem, American Flight 77 was a Boeing 757 and, according to American Airlines itself, this plane did not have onboard phones. One indication that this might have been the case is provided by the AA website, which, while informing travelers that telephone calls are possible on AA's Boeing 767 and 777, does not mention its 757.[14]

In 2004, two UK researchers asked American Airlines whether "757s [are] fitted with phones that passengers can use." An AA spokesperson replied: "American Airlines 757s do not have onboard phones for passenger use." The researchers then asked: "[A]re there any onboard phones at all on AA 757s, i.e., that could be used either by passengers or cabin crew?" The response was: "AA 757s do not have any onboard phones, either for passenger or crew use. Crew have other means of communication available."[15]

It was possible, however, that although this was true in 2004, when the question was asked, it had not been true in September 2001. But in February of 2006, a German researcher sent American Airlines an email asking a more specific question:

> [O]n your website... there is mentioned that there are no seatback satellite phones on a Boeing 757. Is that info correct? Were there any such seatback satellite phones on any Boeing 757 before or on September 11, 2001 and if so, when were these phones ripped out?

Here is the reply (except that the researcher's name has been crossed out):

> Dear Mr. XXXXXXX:
>
> Thank you for contacting Customer Relations. I am pleased to have the opportunity to assist you.
>
> That is correct we do not have phones on our Boeing 757. The passengers on flight 77 used their own personal cellular phones to make out calls during the terrorist attack. However, the pilots are able to stay in constant contact with the Air Traffic Control tower.
>
> Mr. XXXXXXX, I hope this information is helpful. It is a privilege to serve you.
>
> Sincerely,
>
> —Chad W. Kinder
> Customer Relations, American Airlines[16]

On May 31, 2007, another researcher was able to reach Chad Kinder by telephone to ask if he had indeed written the reply. Kinder answered that he could not specifically recall having written that letter, which was sent over a year earlier. But, he said: "That sounds like an accurate statement." Kinder indicated, in other words, that it was a letter he might well have written, because what it said—that AA 757s in 2001 did not have onboard phones, so the passengers on American 77 had to use cell phones—was, to the best of his present knowledge, accurate.

Accordingly, the final version of Ted Olson's story, according to which his wife called him from American 77 using an onboard telephone, was contradicted by a representative of American Airlines itself.[17]

Olson's Story Contradicted by the FBI

The 9/11 Commission Report endorsed Ted Olson's story.[18] The Commission did not specify whether the calls were made from a cell phone or an onboard phone. But it did cite an FBI report entitled "American Airlines Airphone Usage," dated September 20, 2001.[19] According to this FBI report as cited by the Commission, however, there was apparently no reference to any calls from Barbara Olson or to the Department of Justice (DOJ). Instead, it referred merely to four "connected calls to unknown numbers." The 9/11 Commission then said:

> The records available for the phone calls from American 77 do not allow for a determination of which of [these four calls] represent the two between Barbara and Ted Olson, although the FBI and DOJ believe that all four represent communications between Barbara Olson and her husband's office.[20]

That was a strange conclusion: If Ted Olson reported receiving only two calls, why would the Commission conclude that the DOJ had received *four* connected calls from his wife?

That conclusion, in any case, was starkly contradicted by the evidence about phone calls from the four hijacked airliners presented by the US government in 2006 at the trial of Zacarias Moussaoui. Far from attributing all four of the "connected calls to unknown numbers" to Barbara Olson, as the 9/11 Commission suggested, this government document attributed *none* of them to her, saying instead that each one was from an "unknown caller." The only call attributed to Barbara Olson was an "unconnected call" to the Department of Justice, which was said to have been attempted at "9:18:58" and to have lasted "0 seconds."[21]

According to the US government in 2006, in other words, Barbara Olson attempted a call to the DOJ, but it did not go through.[22] The federal government itself presented evidence in a court of law, accordingly, that contradicted Ted Olson's story—

regardless of whether the calls were supposedly made from a cell phone or an onboard phone.

This government report was surely provided by the FBI in particular. For one thing, the 2001 FBI document cited earlier, "American Airlines Airphone Usage," appears to be simply one portion of the complete report on telephone calls from all four flights, which was made available at the Moussaoui trial. According to a reporter at the Moussaoui trial, moreover, the government's testimony about the number of phone calls made from United Flight 93 was given by "a member of an FBI Joint Terrorism Task Force."[23]

Therefore, although the FBI is part of the Department of Justice, it presented evidence in 2006 that contradicted the testimony of Ted Olson, the DOJ's former solicitor general.

This FBI report also contradicted statements still being made by other branches of government. For example, a US Department of State document on the Pentagon attack, after saying that "several passengers from American Airlines flight 77 made phone calls reporting that their plane had been hijacked," stated: "Passenger Barbara Olson called her husband Ted Olson, the solicitor general of the United States, ... reporting that the flight had been hijacked, and that the hijackers had knives and box cutters."[24] The FBI's report at the Moussaoui trial implied that this was not true.

It would appear, moreover, that the FBI had prepared this report long before 2006. According to the 9/11 Commission, the 2001 FBI report entitled "American Airlines Airphone Usage" said, in reference to the four "connected calls to unknown numbers," that they "were at 9:15:34 for 1 minute, 42 seconds; 9:20:15 for 4 minutes, 34 seconds; 9:25:48 for 2 minutes, 34 seconds; and 9:30:56 for 4 minutes, 20 seconds."[25] By comparing this summary with the report entitled "American Airlines Flight #77 Telephone Calls" that was part of the government's report presented at the Moussaoui trial in 2006, we can see that they are identical.[26] This fact suggests that the government's report on telephone calls from this flight submitted to the Moussaoui trial in 2006 was simply the FBI report that was originally dated September 20, 2001.

If so, this would mean that the FBI knew since at least September 20, 2001, that Ted Olson's claim—that his wife had talked to him twice on phone calls from this flight—was untrue, and yet it allowed the press to continue reporting these calls without issuing any correction. Even in 2006, the FBI did not issue its report in a press release or even make it available in written form. Rather, it is publicly available only on the Internet in an interactive computer presentation. At least partly for this reason, perhaps, this report has thus far not been widely reported.

Conclusion

It is certainly strange that Ted Olson's initial story, that he received two cell phone calls from his wife, was later contradicted by Olson himself; that his later story, according to which she had used an onboard phone to make these calls, was implicitly contradicted by American Airlines; and that both versions of his story were implicitly contradicted by the FBI, which is part of the very governmental department for which Olson formerly worked. Whatever be the explanation for these strange contradictions, however, they cry out for investigation by Congress and the press, as does the FBI's failure to make public its report, which contradicted the widely held view that cell phone calls had been made from American Flight 77.

PART II

Questions about the US Military

9

WHEN WAS THE MILITARY ALERTED
ABOUT FLIGHT 11?

O n September 18, 2001, NORAD (North American Aero-
space Defense Command) put out a document entitled
"NORAD's Response Times."[1] It stated, among other
things, the times at which the FAA, after learning about each of
the four hijacked airliners, notified the military—the notification
in each case going to NORAD's northeast sector, known as
NEADS (Northeast Air Defense Sector). This document, along
with hundreds of news stories consistent with it, provided the official account of the notification times from September 18, 2001,
until the final 9/11 Commission hearing, on June 17, 2004. At
this session, the Commission began providing a new account,
which was then fully developed in *The 9/11 Commission Report,*
published that July.

This new account contradicted NORAD's earlier statement of
the times at which the FAA had notified NEADS about the four
airliners. These contradictions are quite severe with regard to
United Flight 175, American Flight 77, and United Flight 93,
which were the second, third, and fourth airliners, respectively,
involved on 9/11. These contradictions are so severe because the
9/11 Commission changed the notification times for these flights
radically, saying that the FAA had notified the military much later
than NORAD had indicated in "NORAD's Response Times."
Indeed, the Commission said, the military received "no advance
notice on the second [plane], no advance notice on the third, and
no advance notice on the fourth."[2]

However, the Commission left NORAD's account of the first
plane—American 11, which struck the WTC's North Tower—

virtually unchanged. In dealing with this flight, the Commission was, in fact, slightly kinder to the FAA than NORAD had been, saying that the FAA had notified the military at 8:38, rather than at 8:40. This meant that the notification was made only seventeen minutes later than it should have been, rather than nineteen minutes. There was, accordingly, no serious contradiction between *The 9/11 Commission Report* and the military's earlier account of American Flight 11. The change meant merely that the notification came about nine, rather than about seven, minutes before Flight 11 struck the North Tower.

There are, nevertheless, some contradictions in the accounts of this flight. These contradictions constitute implicit challenges, by some federal employees who were involved that day, to the Commission's notification time of 8:38—8:37:52, to be precise.

Contradictions Regarding Joe Cooper's Call

According to the 9/11 Commission, the military was first notified about Flight 11 by a phone call to NEADS from the FAA's Boston Center at 8:37:52. The call was answered by Jeremy Powell, a technical sergeant at NEADS, who heard the caller say:

> Hi. Boston Center TMU [Traffic Management Unit], we have a problem here. We have a hijacked aircraft headed towards New York, and we need you guys to, we need someone to scramble some F-16s or something up there, help us out.

The caller was Joe Cooper, an air traffic management specialist at Boston Center.[3] Powell then transferred the call to Colonel Dawne Deskins.[4]

According to the ABC program "Moments of Crisis," which was broadcast a few days after the first anniversary of 9/11, Deskins, after identifying herself to the Boston Center caller (Cooper), heard him say: "Uh, we have a hijacked aircraft and I need you to get some sort of fighters out here to help us out." The time of this call, according to this program, was "shortly after 8:30 AM."[5] Another ABC show, "9/11: Interviews by Peter Jennings," which was broadcast on the first anniversary, specified the time at which this call was received as "8:31."[6] These two ABC programs were based on interviews with many of the principals involved in the military response on 9/11, including General Larry Arnold, the commander of NORAD's Continental Region, and Colonel Robert Marr, the battle commander at NEADS, as well as Dawne Deskins. At least one of them must have endorsed the idea that the FAA first contacted NEADS at about 8:31, not 8:38, as the 9/11 Commission would later say.

An even earlier time for Joe Cooper's call has been implied by statements made by Colin Scoggins, Boston Center's military specialist, who made most of the calls to NEADS that morning and is cited and even quoted in *The 9/11 Commission Report*.[7] At 8:40, Scoggins told NEADS that AA 11 was "35 miles north of Kennedy now at 367 knots."[8] That point is not in dispute. However, Scoggins, who says that he "made about forty phone calls to NEADS" that day,[9] has indicated that this call at 8:40 was his third call.[10] In his *first* call to NEADS, which came after Joe Cooper's call, he says, he had reported that American 11 was "20 [nautical miles] South of Albany heading south at a high rate of speed, 600 knots."[11] By the time the plane was 35 miles north of JFK, therefore, it would have traveled about 90 miles. If we estimate the plane's average speed to have been about 500 knots and hence about 8.3 nautical miles per minute, almost eleven minutes would have been required for it to traverse that distance. Scoggins's account, therefore, implies that his first call to NEADS must have been at about 8:29.[12]

Scoggins says, moreover, that when he arrived on the floor that morning, Joe Cooper had already completed his call to NEADS.[13] When Cooper's call was made, Scoggins adds, American 11 was over Albany, which means that Cooper's call would have been made two minutes earlier than Scoggins's first call, at which time the plane was 20 nautical miles south of Albany. (At 600 knots, it would have taken the plane two minutes to travel 20 nautical miles.) This would mean that Cooper's call, in which the hijacking of American 11 was reported to NEADS, must have occurred at about 8:27.

Scoggins's testimony implies, in other words, that the FAA notified the military about the hijacking of American 11 about eleven minutes earlier than the time, 8:38, given by the 9/11

Commission. A hijack notification at 8:27 would, moreover, have been closer to what should have occurred, assuming that the controller for Flight 11 had obtained clear evidence of its hijacking at 8:25, as is claimed.[14]

An Approximately 8:20 Notification?

Although 8:27 is close to the time at which the FAA's Boston Center should have notified NEADS about the *hijacking* of Flight 11, it is many minutes later than the first notification whatsoever about this flight should have been made. This is because between 8:14 and 8:21, the controller for American 11 reportedly witnessed four of the classic signs of an in-flight emergency: the pilot failed to obey an order, radio contact was lost, the transponder signal was lost, and then the plane went radically off course. When controllers see such signs of an in-flight emergency, especially the last one, they are supposed to contact the military immediately, after which the military is to scramble two jet fighters from the nearest base with fighters on alert, which will then intercept the flight to see what is wrong and, if necessary, take appropriate action. If Boston Center had followed standard procedures, it would have contacted the military by 8:21.

This is the opinion of two men who have worked at Boston Center. One of these is Colin Scoggins, who has said that, if he had seen those signs, "I would have [called the military] almost immediately," which would have meant 8:21 or 8:22. The other man is former air traffic controller Robin Hordon, who believes the call should have occurred by 8:20.

Hordon, in fact, believes that it actually did occur then, because, he has said, he still knows someone at Boston Center who told him, emphatically, that "the FAA was not asleep and the controllers... followed their own protocols."[15]

These claims alone would not constitute a significant contradiction. There is a report, however, that an FAA official stated that the teleconference initiated by the Pentagon started at about 8:20.

The fact that the Pentagon's NMCC (National Military Command Center) organized a telephone conference that morning is well known. The 9/11 Commission mentioned it, pointing out that it began as a "significant event" conference call but was then upgraded to an "air threat" conference call.[16] The Commission claimed that this conference call did not begin until 9:29. That claim was, however, contradicted by Richard Clarke, who reported that, as he was getting ready to set up his White House video conference, the deputy director of the White House Situation Room told him: "We're on the line with NORAD, on an air threat conference call."[17] This would have been, as we saw in Chapter 2, at about 9:10AM. Clarke's account thereby clearly contradicted the Commission's claim that this conference call did not begin until 9:29.

Moreover, if this conference call had already been changed from a "significant event" to an "air threat" call by 9:10, it must have been going on for some time. Could it have been going on since 8:20?

Investigative journalist Tom Flocco reported that at the 9/11 Commission hearing in Washington on May 22, 2003, he talked with Laura Brown, the deputy in public affairs at FAA headquarters. She told him, he reported, that the NMCC's conference call had begun at about 8:20 or 8:25. "After returning to her office and conferring with superiors," Flocco added, Brown sent an email to him, revising her estimate of the commencement time to "around 8:45 am." Flocco, however, put more stock in her original statement, before her memory had been "refreshed" by her superiors.[18]

Unlike our previous cases of contradictions, we have here merely a secondhand report of someone who contradicted the 9/11 Commission's account. The credibility of this report is strengthened, however, by the fact that Richard Clarke's book, while not directly addressing this issue, did contradict the 9/11 Commission's claim that the NMCC teleconference did not begin until 9:29 and by the fact that both Hordon and Scoggins have said that, if FAA protocol had been followed, 8:20 is roughly the time at which the military *would* have been notified—with Hordon adding that, according to his source within the Boston Center, protocol was indeed followed. This combination of reports, therefore, can be said to constitute a claim that contradicts that of the 9/11 Commission, according to which the military did not learn anything about Flight 11's troubles until 8:38.

Conclusion

The 9/11 Commission, adjusting only slightly the time given by NORAD on September 18, 2001, claimed that the FAA's first notification about American Flight 11 was about its hijacking and that this notification did not occur until a few seconds before 8:38. This claim has been indirectly challenged by a report that the FAA's Laura Brown had originally stated that the NMCC's teleconference had begun at or shortly after 8:20 (which would suggest the military had learned about this flight's troubles before its controller had clear evidence of a hijacking but after he had seen multiple signs of an in-flight emergency). The Commission's claim was more directly contradicted by ABC programs in 2002 that, drawing on interviews with some military officials involved in the event, placed Joe Cooper's call about the hijacking at 8:31. It has also been contradicted by Colin Scoggins's testimony about his own calls to NEADS, which imply that Cooper's call must have occurred at about 8:27. Congress and the press should ask why the 9/11 Commission's claim is contradicted by these other testimonies.

10

WHEN WAS THE MILITARY ALERTED
ABOUT FLIGHT 175?

A ccording to *The 9/11 Commission Report*, the "nine minutes' notice" that NEADS received about Flight 11 before it struck the North Tower "was the most the military would receive of any of the four hijackings."[1] Indeed, the Commission claimed, the military received "no advance notice on the second [plane], no advance notice on the third, and no advance notice on the fourth."[2] In this chapter, we will examine the Commission's claim about the second plane: United Flight 175, which struck the World Trade Center's South Tower at 9:03.

NORAD's Early Position

A *Washington Post* timeline, published the day after 9/11, contained this item: "8:43AM: The FAA notified military authorities of a second hijacking."[3] A CNN timeline, put out five days later, likewise said: "8:43AM: FAA notified NORAD that United Airlines flight 175 has been hijacked."[4] That notification time became official one day later, September 18, when NORAD put out its document, "NORAD Response Times," which also stated that the FAA had notified NORAD about United 175 at 8:43.[5]

This notification time, while widely acknowledged, created problems: If the military was notified about this flight 20 minutes before it struck the South Tower, why was this flight not intercepted? The military's answer was that although the F-15 fighter jets, which were launched from Otis Air National Guard Base in Cape Cod, tried to get there in time, they were still 71 miles away at 9:03, when United 175 slammed into the South Tower.

That answer, however, raised further questions. For example, the F-15s were reportedly airborne at 8:52 and one of the pilots, Lieutenant Colonel Timothy Duffy, was quoted as saying that he "was in full-blower all the way."[6] That would probably mean that the fighters were going about 1,300 mph and hence about 22 miles a minute.[7] At that speed, they would have covered the 180 miles from Otis to Manhattan in ten minutes (allowing two minutes to get up to speed and to slow down). Rather than being 71 miles away at 9:03, therefore, they should have already been there for a minute.

These problems would no longer exist in the position taken by the 9/11 Commission.

The 9/11 Commission's Position

According to *The 9/11 Commission Report*: "The first indication that the NORAD air defenders had of the second hijacked aircraft, United 175, came in a phone call from New York Center to NEADS at 9:03," which was "at about the time the plane was hitting the South Tower."[8]

The notification came so late, the Commission explained, because of inattentiveness and failure to communicate by FAA officials. "United 175 turned southwest without clearance from air traffic control" at about 8:44 and then its transponder code was changed twice at 8:47. However, even though a "suspicious transmission" had been reported to the New York Center controller at 8:42, this controller did not notice the course and code changes until 8:51. Moreover, although the New York Center manager knew by 8:48 that American 11 had been hijacked, the controller, once he had noticed Flight 175's course and code changes, made no effort to contact the military. Beginning at 8:53, controllers and other FAA personnel began discussing the fact that United 175 was probably hijacked, but no one called the military. Even between 9:01 and 9:02, when word of the probable hijacking reached the FAA's Command Center in Herndon, Virginia, the military was not called. Finally, at 9:03, someone at New York Center called NEADS.[9]

Although this account by the 9/11 Commission may seem highly implausible, our focus here is solely on the question of whether there were reports that contradicted this account. The answer is: quite a few.

Reports to the Contrary

One such report was, of course, "NORAD's Response Times," which had said that NORAD was notified at 8:43. Accordingly, the 9/11 Commission, in stating that the notification did not occur until 9:03, contradicted the position that NORAD had been stating for almost three years.

NORAD's notification time was supported by several news reports (beyond the two timelines by CNN and the *Washington Post* cited above). For example, after saying that the FAA had notified NORAD about the possible hijacking of American 11 at 8:40, Leslie Miller, writing for the Associated Press in 2002, said: "[T]hree minutes after that, NORAD was told United Airlines 175 had been hijacked."[10]

NBC likewise endorsed the idea that the military learned about the hijacking of UA 175 before it crashed. In a first-anniversary program, "America Remembers: The Skies over America," Tom Brokaw, the host, said:

> 8:52AM: It has been six minutes since American 11 hit the north tower. And NORAD—responsible for the defense of north American airspace—is now alerted to a second hijacking. It scrambles two F-15 fighter jets from Otis air force base [*sic*] in Massachusetts to potentially intercept the United plane.[11]

According to NBC, therefore, the military not only knew about the hijacking of United 175 but also, at 8:52—eleven minutes before the South Tower was struck—sent fighters to intercept it.

In 2006, to be sure, MSNBC provided an "updated" version of this program, in which Brokaw's statement was changed to say:

> 8:53AM: It has been just over six minutes since American 11 hit the north tower. By now, NORAD—responsible for the defense of north American airspace—has scrambled two F-15 fighter jets from Otis air force base in Massachusetts.[12]

In this new version, NORAD was *not* told about "a second hijacking" and the Otis F-15s were no longer scrambled in order to "intercept the United plane." Brokaw's narration was, in other words, modified to fit the 9/11 Commission's new story, according to which the military did not know anything about United 175's troubles until after it had crashed. The fact remains, however, that the original version of this program, which aired in September 2002,[13] contradicted the Commission's claim.

Whereas Brokaw's NBC program was told from the perspective of FAA controllers, ABC's first anniversary special, which was based on interviews by Peter Jennings, presented the perspective of military officers. One officer was Brigadier General Montague Winfield, the deputy director of operations at the Pentagon's NMCC. The program contained footage of Winfield saying:

> When the second aircraft flew into the second tower, it was at that point that we realized that the seemingly unrelated hijackings that the FAA was dealing with were in fact a part of a coordinated terrorist attack on the United States.[14]

Although the Commission later claimed that the military was aware of only one hijacking—that of AA 11, which had already crashed—Winfield, in speaking of the military's awareness prior to 9:03, referred in the plural to the "seemingly unrelated *hijackings*." He also said that it was at that point—when the second plane hit the second tower—that he and others in the NMCC realized that those hijackings, which up to that moment they had assumed to be unrelated, were part of a coordinated attack.

This statement constitutes a very strong contradiction to the Commission's claim about United 175, because Winfield was evidently, one year after the events, stating his own memory of what had gone through his mind on 9/11.

Further military testimony that the military knew about United 175 before it crashed came from Captain Michael Jellinek, a Canadian who was overseeing NORAD headquarters in Colorado on 9/11. According to a story in the *Toronto Star*, Jellinek was on the line with people at NEADS while they watched United 175 crash into the South Tower. Jellinek then asked: "Was that the hijacked aircraft you were dealing with?" They replied: "Yes, it was."[15] NEADS could hardly have been "dealing with" United 175 if it had not known about its troubles before it crashed.

Another report of prior notification was provided in a 2003 book by Pamela Freni entitled *Ground Stop: An Inside Look at the*

Federal Aviation Administration on September 11, 2001. Although Freni did not support the 8:43 notification time, she did say that in "the minutes between the first crash and the second," Mike McCormick, the air traffic manager at the New York Center, called NORAD to ask for assistance.[16] She also said that after the Otis pilots had taken off (at 8:52), "Word of the hijacking of UA175 was passed up to them."[17]

A phone call from the FAA's New York Center was, moreover, not the only possible way the military could have learned about this flight. According to a Newhouse News Service story by Hart Seely published four months after 9/11, technicians at NEADS learned about it by overhearing a conversation: "At 8:43AM, [Master Sergeant Maureen] Dooley's technicians, their headsets linked to Boston Center, heard of a second plane, United Flight 175, that also was not responding. It, too, was moving to New York."[18] According to this story, in other words, NEADS learned about the hijacking at the same moment that controllers at the FAA's Boston Center did.

That story from January of 2002 is in strong tension with an episode in a 2006 article by Michael Bronner in *Vanity Fair*, which was oriented around the same women: Sergeant Maureen Dooley and her two technicians, Stacia Rountree and Shelley Watson. According to Bronner—who based his account on tapes that, after being used by the 9/11 Commission in 2004, were provided to him by the military—Rountree fielded a call from the FAA's New York Center at 9:03, which informed her that United 175 was descending into Manhattan, after which she exclaimed: "They have a second possible hijack!" This exclamation implied that Rountree and the others had previously had no idea that this flight was in trouble. According to Hart Seely's 2002 story, however, they knew already by 8:43 that Flight 175, besides not responding, was heading toward New York. We can, without knowing which story is true, see that they cannot both be.

The 9/11 Commission's claim about United 175—that the military was not informed about it in advance of its crash—is also in tension with a memo, "FAA Communications with NORAD on September 11, 2001," which was sent to the 9/11 Commission in

May of 2003 by Laura Brown, the deputy in public affairs at FAA headquarters. This memo, in seeking to clarify how the FAA responded to the events of 9/11, said:

> Within minutes after the first aircraft hit the World Trade Center, the FAA immediately established several phone bridges [teleconferences] that included FAA field facilities, the FAA Command Center, FAA headquarters, DOD [meaning the NMCC in the Department of Defense], the Secret Service.... The US Air Force liaison to the FAA immediately joined the FAA headquarters phone bridge and established contact with NORAD.... The FAA shared real-time information on the phone bridges about the unfolding events, including information about loss of communication with aircraft, loss of transponder signals, unauthorized changes in course, and other actions being taken by all the flights of interest.[19]

"Within minutes" after the first attack would mean about 8:50, and "all flights of interest" at that time would have definitely included United 175, because if FAA headquarters did not already know about its situation, it would have quickly learned about them from the Boston and New York "field facilities." This memo implied, therefore, that NORAD and the NMCC, if they did not already know that United 175 was in trouble, would have learned this from the FAA-initiated teleconference.

In sending this memo in May 2003, incidentally, Laura Brown and other FAA personnel would not have thought of themselves as doing anything subversive: As we have seen, it was generally assumed in those days that the military had been notified about UA 175 before it crashed. Indeed, the 9/11 Commission itself evidently still assumed this in 2003. In its hearing on May 22 of that year, Commissioner Richard Ben-Veniste, in discussing what transpired at 8:55AM, mentioned in passing that "United Airlines Flight 175 [had been] declared to be hijacked."[20]

That position, to be sure, created the problem discussed earlier—that Flight 175 should have been intercepted before it got to Manhattan. The 8:43 notification time, accordingly, gave rise to suspicions that there had been a stand-down order, canceling standard procedures.

Dealing with the Contradiction

By saying that the military was not notified about United 175's hijacking at 8:43—not notified, in fact, until after this plane had hit the South Tower—the Commission overcame that basis for suspicion. But this solution left the Commission with the contradiction between its claim and all those previous reports. How did it deal with this contradiction? By simply ignoring those previous reports.

For example, just as *The 9/11 Commission Report* failed to mention Norman Mineta's testimony about Vice President Cheney's early presence in the PEOC, even though this testimony had been given at one of the Commission's open hearings (as discussed in Chapters 2 and 3), it also failed to mention the FAA memo sent by Laura Brown, even though it too had been discussed in one of the Commission's hearings.

This discussion, which occurred at the hearing on May 23, 2003, had been initiated by Commissioner Richard Ben-Veniste during his interrogation of General Craig McKinley. After saying that "we are advised that there was… essentially an ongoing conference where under, in real time, FAA was providing information as it received it, immediately after the first crash into the Towers," Ben-Veniste asked McKinley whether NORAD "did not have an open line with the FAA at that time." McKinley replied: "It is my understanding from talking with both FAA and our supervisors at the Northeast Air Defense Sector [NEADS] in Rome, that those lines were open and that they were discussing these issues."[21] McKinley, therefore, attested to the accuracy of the FAA's memo.

When *The 9/11 Commission Report* appeared, however, it contained no reference to this FAA memo. Indeed, even though Ben-Veniste had mentioned the memo's statement as to when the FAA's conference had begun—"immediately after the first crash into the Towers" (and hence about 8:50)—the Commission made a contradictory claim: "At about 9:20," *The 9/11 Commission Report* stated, "security personnel at FAA headquarters set up a hijacking teleconference with several agencies, including the Defense Department."[22]

So whereas the Commission had seemingly acknowledged in 2003 that the FAA-initiated conference had begun at about 8:50, its final report asserted that it did not begin until a half-hour later. Given this later starting time, the military could not possibly have learned about United 175 from the FAA-initiated teleconference.[23]

Accordingly, just as *The 9/11 Commission Report* contradicted, without mentioning it, Richard Clarke's account as to when his conference began (see Chapter 6), it also contradicted, without mentioning it, the FAA's statement as to when *its* conference began.

The Commission dealt in the same way with the other reports that contradicted its position. It did not mention the CNN and *Washington Post* timelines, published immediately after 9/11, that said that NEADS was notified at 8:43. It did not mention the fact that "NORAD's Response Times" had made that statement official. It did not mention the Associated Press story that affirmed the truth of that statement. It did not mention the 2002 NBC program in which Tom Brokaw reported that NORAD, after being alerted to "a second hijacking," scrambled two F-15s "to potentially intercept the United plane." It did not mention the fact that in Peter Jennings's ABC program, General Winfield reported that the crash into the second tower revealed to him and others in the NMCC the true nature of the "seemingly unrelated hijackings" with which the FAA had been dealing. Nor did the Commission mention the *Toronto Star*'s report about Captain Jellinek's conversation with people at NEADS as they watched United 175 hit the South Tower.

The Commission simply told a different story, without refuting any of those prior reports. The contradictions, therefore, remain.

Conclusion

The 9/11 Commission's claim as to when the military was alerted about United 175 is contradicted by NORAD's 2001 statement, by several news reports, and by a memo sent to the Commission by the FAA in 2003. The Commission, besides ignoring the FAA memo, also contradicts the FAA's statement as to when its telephone conference began. Congress and the press need to ask why these contradictions exist.

11

WHEN WAS THE MILITARY ALERTED ABOUT FLIGHT 77?

The 9/11 Commission's story about Flight 175 is challenged by more contradictions, as we have seen, than is its story about Flight 11. Its story about American Flight 77 involves even more contradictions. My discussion of this flight is more complex than my discussions of the previous flights, partly because the 9/11 Commission explicitly contradicted NORAD's 2001 position on Flight 77, and partly because that position was already deeply problematic.

NORAD's Position from September 2001 to May 2004

In its news release of September 18, 2001, NORAD said that at 9:24AM, which was thirteen or fourteen minutes before the Pentagon was hit, it had been notified by the FAA about American Flight 77. This news release also indicated that NORAD immediately—at 9:24—gave Langley Air Force Base in Virginia an order to scramble fighters.[1] According to CNN, unnamed "senior Defense Department officials" specifically said that the Langley fighters were scrambled to go after Flight 77.[2] CNN also reported that, according to "informed defense officials," the FAA had stated at 9:25 that American 77 may have been hijacked and appeared to be heading back toward Washington.[3]

According to the story being reported in the press at that time, radio contact with American 77 was lost at 8:50.[4] At 8:55, the plane made a U-turn over southern Ohio and headed back east, but this U-turn was not noticed—at least according to most reports[5]—by the controller handling the flight. This controller noticed a problem only when the plane's transponder quit sending a signal a minute later.[6] "By 8:56AM," a *New York Times* story said, "it was evident that Flight 77 was lost."[7] And yet the FAA, according to NORAD's timeline, did not notify the military about this flight until 9:24.

Reports Contradicting NORAD's First Position

NORAD's timeline raised several questions, the three most serious being: Why did the FAA wait until 9:24 to notify NEADS?[8] Why, once it was reported that this flight was headed back toward Washington, was the Pentagon not evacuated?[9] And why were the F-16s from Langley Air Force Base, about 130 miles away, not able to get to the Pentagon in time to prevent the attack?[10] Besides being challenged by such questions, NORAD's account was, to come to our concern here, contradicted by other reports.

Wald's *New York Times* Story: Even before NORAD's timeline was put out on September 18, its statement about Flight 77 had been contradicted in advance by a *New York Times* story that appeared four days after 9/11. This story, written by Matthew Wald, said:

> During the hour or so that American Airlines Flight 77 was under the control of hijackers, up to the moment it struck the west side of the Pentagon, military officials in a command center on the east side of the building were urgently talking to law enforcement and air traffic control officials about what to do.
>
> But despite elaborate plans that link civilian and military efforts to control the nation's airspace in defense of the country, and despite two other jetliners' having already hit the World Trade Center in New York, the fighter planes that scrambled into protective orbits around Washington did not arrive until 15 minutes after Flight 77 hit the Pentagon.[11]

The "command center on the east side" is the NMCC, of course, and the "air traffic control officials" are FAA personnel. In speaking of a discussion between these parties that lasted approximately an hour, Wald was presumably referring to a conference call. If this was the NMCC's air threat conference call, Wald's story lends support to Laura Brown's reported statement that it had begun by 8:45.[12] If it was the FAA's conference call, his story supports the account presented in the FAA memo of May 2003, according to which the call began right after the first attack on the WTC, hence at about 8:50. Wald's story, in any case, contradicted NORAD's claim that it first learned about Flight 77's hijacking at 9:24.

The FAA Memo Sent by Laura Brown: This claim by NORAD was most fully and explicitly contradicted by the FAA memo sent to the 9/11 Commission by Laura Brown. This memo was written on May 22, 2003, following an embarrassing performance by Jane Garvey, the FAA administrator, at the 9/11 Commission earlier that day, while she was being questioned about American 77 by Commissioner Richard Ben-Veniste. Here is part of that exchange:

> MR. BEN-VENISTE: I want to focus on Flight 77, American 77, which, according to the timelines that we have, indicate that at 8:55 in the morning, the FAA received information that Flight 77 turned off its course. By that time the fate of American Airlines 11 was known, and United Airlines Flight 175 was declared to be hijacked and crashed shortly thereafter. Why was it… that Flight 77 was not immediately declared to be hijacked? According to our information, NORAD was not notified until 9:24….

> MS. GARVEY: Commissioner, I would like to go back and look at those records more carefully, because that is not consistent with… the timeline that I remember. [It] had a notification of NORAD twice before the time that you mention, … with the first notification being at 8:34.

> MR. BEN-VENISTE: At 8:34?

> MS. GARVEY: At 8:34 from a controller at the Boston office….

> MR. BEN-VENISTE: We are talking about American Airlines Flight 77, the plane that ultimately crashed into the Pentagon.

> MS. GARVEY: Yes…. [T]he information that I have is that the first notification was at 8:34 from an individual controller in Boston… to NORAD at Otis….

> MR. BEN-VENISTE: Are you not confusing Flight 11 with Flight 77?

MS. GARVEY: Sorry. I may be.... [I]t's been a while since I have looked at that chronology.... My belief is that we did notify them in a timely fashion.

MR. BEN-VENISTE: Mr. Chairman, may I simply for purposes of perhaps refreshing our witness's recollection read from the testimony of General Eberhart, [who testified that] the first documented notification that he had [was at 9:24]. And then, [in answer to the question] "Well, why was the delay?" General Eberhart said, "You'll have to ask the FAA." So we are asking.

MS. GARVEY: Right... [M]y recollection is not quite the same, so I'd like to double-check it before I say it here....

MR. KEAN: It would be useful if you could get back to staff this evening.[13]

It was in response to this request that the memo, "FAA Communications with NORAD on September 11, 2001," was sent to the Commission on May 22, 2003, by Laura Brown, the deputy in public affairs at FAA headquarters, who was also the senior career person in the FAA.[14] Being aware of this context helps us see that the memo was written primarily to answer the question of when the FAA told the military about Flight 77. Here, now, is that memo in its entirety.

> Within minutes after the first aircraft hit the World Trade Center, the FAA immediately established several phone bridges that included FAA field facilities, the FAA Command Center, FAA headquarters, DOD, the Secret Service, and other government agencies. The U.S. Air Force liaison to the FAA immediately joined the FAA headquarters phone bridge and established contact with NORAD on a separate line. The FAA shared real-time information on the phone bridges about the unfolding events, including information about loss of communication with aircraft, loss of transponder signals, unauthorized changes in course, and other actions being taken by all the flights of interest, including Flight 77. Other parties on the phone bridges, in turn, shared information about actions they were taking. NORAD logs indicate that the FAA made formal notification about American Flight 77 at 9:24 AM, but information about the flight was conveyed continuously during the phone bridges before the formal notification.[15]

As this memo shows, the FAA explicitly took issue with the claim, made by General Eberhart, that the FAA did not notify NORAD about Flight 77 until 9:24. Eberhart's statement, it should be noted, was that 9:24 was the first "documented notification," which would refer to the formal notification. Responding to that qualification, the FAA memo said that although the formal notification may have occurred at 9:24, *"information about the flight was conveyed continuously during the phone bridges before the formal notification."*

During a telephone conversation I had with Laura Brown in 2004, she emphasized the importance of this distinction. The time of the formal notification was irrelevant to the question of when the military first became aware of Flight 77. The important point was that military officials were receiving "real-time information" about Flight 77 on an ongoing basis by means of the phone bridges that were established at about 8:50.[16]

At the hearing on May 23, 2003, the day after the memo was written, it appeared to have made an impression on the Commission. After NORAD's General Craig McKinley had testified that the FAA had reported "a possible hijack of 77" at 9:24, Ben-Veniste asked: "Is it in fact correct, sir, that the first notification of any type that NORAD received was not until 9:24 with respect to Flight 77?" McKinley then asked General Larry Arnold, who was "on floor that morning," to address the question. The following exchange ensued:

> GEN. ARNOLD: The simple answer to your question is I believe that to be a fact: that 9:24 was the first time that we had been advised of American 77 as a possible hijacked airplane.
>
> MR. BEN-VENISTE: Well, is it not the case, General Arnold, that there was an open line established between FAA, NORAD and other agencies, including CIA and FBI, that morning?
>
> GEN. ARNOLD: … We did not have an open line at that time with the FAA. That is not accurate.
>
> MR. BEN-VENISTE: You did not. You were not—NORAD was not in contact—

GEN. ARNOLD: The continental United States NORAD region, my headquarters, responsible for the continental United States air defense, did not have an open line with the FAA at that time.

MR. BEN-VENISTE: Was there some NORAD office that had an open line with the FAA—

GEN. ARNOLD: Our—

MR. BEN-VENISTE: Excuse me. Let me finish my question, please. Was there some NORAD office.... [W]e are advised that there was indeed an open line... essentially an ongoing conference where under, in real time, FAA was providing information as it received it, immediately after the first crash into the Towers, we were told, with respect to each of the events that were ongoing of any remarkable nature? I see General McKinley is nodding.

GEN. MCKINLEY: It's my understanding that the FAA was in contact with our Northeast Air Defense Sector at Rome, New York. Understanding the relationship of how we defend North America from threats, NORAD located in Peterson Air Force Base, Colorado Springs, our continental NORAD region, our air operations center located at Tyndall[17] Air Force Base in Florida.... And then we have three sectors based on the size and volume of our country that handle that. It is my understanding from talking with both FAA and our supervisors at the Northeast Air Defense Sector in Rome, that those lines were open and that they were discussing these issues.[18]

So, after Ben-Veniste pressed the point made in the FAA memo, General McKinley confirmed its claim that the FAA and the military had open lines on which they were "discussing these issues."

Ben-Veniste then asked General Arnold: "You don't have anything further to shed light on when you first learned—you, NORAD—first learned of Flight 77's probable hijack status prior to 9:24?" Arnold replied: "I do not have any further knowledge at this time."[19]

Later in that session, while General Mike Canavan, the former associate administrator of Civil Aviation Security, was testifying, Ben-Veniste brought the discussion back to Flight 77. Saying that the previous evening the Commission had been "provided a statement which comes from the FAA," he read the memo, which, as we saw earlier, ended by saying that "information about [Flight 77] was conveyed continuously during the phone bridges before the formal notification."

After reading this memo into the record, Ben-Veniste commented: "So now we have in question whether there was an informal real-time communication of the situation, including Flight 77's situation, to personnel at NORAD." He then asked General Canavan "whether it is likely in view of this communication we have just received, that there was some informal communication of the distress of Flight 77?" After Canavan described how a phone bridge works, Ben-Veniste asked:

> So if the military were apprised, as FAA is now telling us, in real time of what FAA is seeing on its radars, and now focusing specifically on Flight 77, that would mean that someone at NORAD was advised of the deviation from course, which is substantially earlier than the formal notification of hijacking. Would it have been expected that receiving that information the military personnel or NORAD personnel on that phone bridge, would communicate with other NORAD facilities, apprising them of the information he or she was learning in real time?

Canavan replied: "I would think that they would pass it to someone within the NORAD command center."[20]

Given the direction that Ben-Veniste was taking the discussion, it might have seemed that the Commission, when it issued its final report in July of the following year, would conclude that the military had been notified about Flight 77 prior to 9:24. This, however, was not to be.

The 9/11 Commission's Position

The 9/11 Commission Report did, in fact, reject the 9:24 notification time for Flight 77. But its modification was in the opposite direction from that suggested by the FAA memo. Rather than saying that the FAA talked to the military about this flight *before* 9:24, the Commission declared: "NEADS never received notice that American 77 was hijacked."[21]

Making this assertion required stating that the military officers had given false testimony to the Commission:

> In public testimony before this Commission in May 2003, ... NORAD officials stated that at 9:24, NEADS received notification of the hijacking of American 77. This statement was incorrect.... In their testimony and in other public accounts, NORAD officials also stated that the Langley fighters were scrambled to respond to the notification about American 77.... These statements were incorrect as well.[22]

By rejecting the 9:24 notification time, the Commission then pointed out, it had overcome one of the main problems that had plagued the official account:

> More than the actual events, inaccurate government accounts of those events made it appear that the military was notified in time to respond, raising questions about the adequacy of the response. Those accounts... overstated the FAA's ability to provide the military with timely and useful information that morning.... Thus the military did not have 14 minutes to respond to American 77, as testimony to the Commission in May 2003 suggested.[23]

Dealing with the Contradictions

By saying that the military had not been notified about Flight 77, the Commission had overcome the basis for questions about "the adequacy of the [military's] response." But how did it deal with the fact that its new account contradicted all previous accounts? Except for declaring the May 2003 testimony of the NORAD officials "incorrect," it simply ignored the contradictions between its new story and previous accounts, which were numerous.

Norman Mineta's Account: As we saw in Chapter 3, Norman Mineta testified to the 9/11 Commission that Vice President Cheney was informed about an unauthorized flight approaching Washington shortly before the Pentagon was struck, probably at about 9:25. If the Pentagon was, as the Commission says, struck by Flight 77, then it would seem that Mineta's account contradicted the claim that no one in charge knew that Flight 77 was approaching the

Pentagon. *The 9/11 Commission Report*, as we saw, handled this problem by omitting any mention of Mineta's testimony.

The FAA Memo: In rejecting the 9:24 notification time for Flight 77, *The 9/11 Commission Report* said: "The notice NEADS received at 9:24 was that American 11 had not hit the World Trade Center and was heading for Washington, D.C."[24] But that claim, even if accepted, provided no response to the point made in the FAA memo sent by Laura Brown—that the 9:24 notification time was wrong by being too late, not too early. The Commission dealt with this point by simply ignoring it.

Although Richard Ben-Veniste had read the FAA memo into the record at the hearing on May 23, 2003, this memo was not mentioned in *The 9/11 Commission Report*. Ben-Veniste had, as we saw, doggedly raised the memo's claim—that the FAA was talking about Flight 77 with military officials well before the official notification time of 9:24. He also obtained General McKinley's concurrence on the existence of a teleconference in which the FAA and the military were discussing the issues. And yet when *The 9/11 Commission Report* appeared, it contained Ben-Veniste's signature, even though it contained no mention of the FAA memo. Should not Ben-Veniste and the rest of the Commission be required to explain why their final report contradicted what the FAA memo said without offering any rebuttal to it?

Although the Commission did not rebut that memo, it said, in effect, that the memo's account could not be true, because the FAA-initiated conference did not begin at approximately 8:50, as the FAA's memo indicated, but at 9:20.[25] The Commission thereby implied that Laura Brown and the other FAA officials who approved the memo were lying or at least seriously confused. The Commission did not have to defend this charge, however, by virtue of not mentioning the memo.

The FAA's position, that its teleconference had begun long before 9:20, was supported by Pamela Freni's account of the actions of Bill Peacock, the FAA's director of air traffic services, and his deputy, Jeff Griffith, who served as the acting air traffic manager on that day while Peacock was away in New Orleans.

After the first tower was struck, Freni reported, Griffith had a subordinate put into motion what became a "never-ending tele-conference."[26] Concurrently, after Peacock had learned about the attack on the first tower and gotten to his New Orleans hotel room:

> He flipped through the channels and found CNN just in time to join the world in viewing the attack on the second tower. He determinedly dialed the phone, trying to connect with his staff. His call was routed to the phone in the conference room next door to his office at headquarters, into the never-ending teleconference.[27]

According to Freni's account, therefore, Peacock joined the FAA's telephone conference about fifteen minutes before the time at which the 9/11 Commission claimed it began.

The account given in the FAA's memo of May 2003 was, therefore, supported by Freni's book, which appeared later that year. However, by not mentioning the FAA memo, the 9/11 Commission avoided any need to defend its implicit charge that this memo had given a false account.

The NYT, the FBI, and American Airlines: The Commission also did not rebut the previously mentioned *New York Times* story, published four days after 9/11, which said that in the hour during which Flight 77 was controlled by the hijackers, "military officials in a command center on the east side of the [Pentagon] were urgently talking to law enforcement and air traffic control officials about what to do." The later claim that the military was unaware of a flight coming its way was, in fact, contradicted by this story's title: "Pentagon Tracked Deadly Jet but Found No Way to Stop It."[28]

The 9/11 Commission's claim, according to which the military did not know that Flight 77 was hijacked prior to the strike on the Pentagon, was also in strong tension with a statement by the FBI in the *Arlington County After-Action Report*, which said:

> At about 9:20AM, the [FBI's] WFO [Washington Field Office] Command Center was notified that American Airlines Flight #77 had been hijacked shortly after takeoff from Washington Dulles International Airport. [The FBI special agent in charge] dispatched a team of 50 agents to investigate the Dulles hijacking and provide additional security to prevent another.[29]

Had the 9/11 Commission mentioned this report, it would have had to ask its readers to believe that although the FBI in Washington, DC, knew about the hijacking of AA 77 by 9:20, the military did not know about it until almost 20 minutes later. The Commission avoided this demand on readers by not citing this report.

Another report in tension with the Commission's claim, one which *The 9/11 Commission Report* did mention, came from officials at American Airlines headquarters in Fort Worth, Texas. These officials said that they knew by 9:00 that communications with AA 77 had been lost and that by 9:10 they suspected that it had been hijacked.[30] This report, if taken together with *The 9/11 Commission Report*, requires us to believe that although American Airlines believed its Flight 77 to have been hijacked by 9:10, the US military remained clueless until almost 25 minutes later, when NEADS learned about it by chance during a conversation with the FAA's Washington Center at 9:34AM.[31]

Indianapolis Ignorance: One of the essential elements in the 9/11 Commission's new story about American 77 was its explanation as to why the FAA's air traffic control center in Indianapolis, which was handling the flight when it started showing signs of being in trouble, did not immediately notify the military. At 8:56, we are told, the controller in Indianapolis lost this flight's transponder signal, its radar track, and its radio. The controller did not contact the military, the Commission claimed, because he concluded that "American 77 had experienced serious electrical or mechanical failure," after which it had crashed.[32]

Why would the controller have made this inference at this time, when it was known that two planes had already been hijacked, one of which had crashed into the World Trade Center and the other of which was also headed toward New York? Because, the Commission claimed, this controller "did not know that other aircraft had been hijacked." Indeed, according to the Commission, no one at the Indianapolis center "had any knowledge of the situation in New York." And so, although Indianapolis started calling various agencies to see if they had reports of a downed aircraft, it did not contact the military. Only at 9:20, the Commission wrote, did Indianapolis begin to doubt its initial assumption that American 77 had crashed, because at that time it "learned that there were other hijacked aircraft." If the officials in Indianapolis had known earlier about the other hijackings, the point is, they would have inferred, having seen all those danger signals, that Flight 77 had probably also been hijacked. But they did not yet know about the other hijackings.[33]

This story, it must be said, strains credulity. Television networks had started broadcasting images of the World Trade Center at 8:48. These images included, at 9:03, the crash of the second airliner into the South Tower. Millions of people knew about these events. And yet no one at the Indianapolis center "had any knowledge of the situation in New York" until 9:20?

Former air traffic controller Robin Hordon finds this claim extremely improbable, saying: "The system would be notified about a hijacked aircraft.... This would be the *hottest news in a decade*. It would fly around the ATC [Air Traffic Control] community."[34] The same view of standard procedures was expressed by General Mike Canavan, some of whose testimony to the 9/11 Commission was quoted above. While being questioned by Richard Ben-Veniste, Canavan said: "[A]s soon as you know you had a hijacked aircraft, you notify everyone.... [The notification] gets broadcast out to all the regions.... [T]hose things happen."[35]

Our concern here, however, is not with whether the 9/11 Commission's account is plausible but whether it was contradicted by other reports. According to the Commission's account, as we saw, the Indianapolis controller could assume that Flight 77 had simply crashed because of electrical or mechanical failure because, at that time, he "did not know that other aircraft had been hijacked." It was not until 9:20, when he "learned that there were other hijacked aircraft," that he realized that that might also be the explanation for Flight 77's disappearance.

According to several reports, however, the various FAA centers had been notified of the hijacking of AA 11 long before 9:20. A timeline in the *Guardian*, published about a month after 9/11, said that at 8:25, "The [Boston Center] control tower notifies several air traffic control centres that a hijack is taking place."[36] In NBC's first-anniversary program, narrated by Tom Brokaw, viewers were told that at 8:30, "Boston Center supervisors notify the FAA and other air traffic centers about the hijacking of American Flight 11."[37] In *Ground Stop*, Pamela Freni wrote:

> At 9:07AM a message was sent from the Air Traffic Control System Command Center in northern Virginia to every air traffic facility in the nation, announcing the first hijacking.[38]

These reports explicitly contradicted the Commission's claim that the Indianapolis center had not been informed about the hijackings until 9:20. And if the controller in Indianapolis did already know about the other hijackings, then the Commission's contention—that he did not call the military because he believed that American 77 had crashed because of an electrical or mechanical failure—would become implausible. The Commission avoided this consequence by simply not mentioning these reports.

Secret Service Secret: One poorly kept secret about 9/11 was that even if the FAA had failed to notify the military about Flight 77, the Secret Service would have known everything the FAA knew. Dick Cheney came close to revealing this fact during his interview on *Meet the Press* five days after 9/11. He said: "The Secret Service has an arrangement with the FAA. They had open lines after the World Trade Center was…"—at which point Cheney stopped himself before finishing the sentence.[39]

In his book *Against All Enemies*, Richard Clarke added another detail. After saying that Brian Stafford, the director of the Secret Service, had slipped him a note that said, "Radar shows aircraft headed this way," Clarke added, by way of explanation: "Secret Service had a system that allowed them to see what FAA's radar was seeing."[40]

In 2006, Barbara Riggs, who had just retired as the Secret Service's deputy director, referred explicitly to the Secret Service's awareness of Flight 77. Riggs, who was in the Washington headquarters on the morning of 9/11,[41] said: "Thru monitoring radar and activating an open line with the FAA, the Secret Service was able to receive real time information about… hijacked aircraft. We were tracking two hijacked aircraft as they approached Washington, D.C."[42] One of the two aircraft to which she referred would have been American 77. Her statement made explicit, therefore, a point that was already implicit in the statements by Cheney and Clarke.

If people had been widely aware of this fact, the 9/11 Commission would have had to claim that although the Secret Service knew that Flight 77 was heading back toward Washington, it did not inform the military. The Commission did not need to make this case, however, because it did not mention the Secret Service's real-time awareness of the flights.

Military Liaisons: Another difficulty for the Commission's account arises from the presence of military liaisons at the FAA's headquarters in Washington and its Command Center in Herndon. According to the Commission, although the fact that Flight 77 was lost was known at Herndon by 9:20 and at FAA headquarters by 9:25, this knowledge did not get passed to the military. However, Ben Sliney, the operations manager at the Command Center, had provided the 9/11 Commission with the following information:

> Available to us at the Command Center of course is the military cell, which was our liaison with the military services. They were present at all of the events that occurred on 9/11.... If you tell the military you've told the military. They have their own communication web.... [I]n my mind everyone who needed to be notified about the events transpiring was notified, including the military.[43]

Monte Belger, the FAA's acting deputy administrator on 9/11, had reinforced the point, telling the Commission:

> [I]t is a fact—there were military people on duty at the FAA Command Center, as Mr. Sliney said. They were participating in what was going on. There were military people in the FAA's Air Traffic Organization in a situation room. They were participating in what was going on.[44]

The presence of a military liaison at FAA headquarters was also mentioned by Pamela Freni, who referred to "the onsite Department of Defense (DoD) liaison to the FAA."[45]

These testimonies to the existence of military liaisons contradict the 9/11 Commission's claim about Flight 77—that although Flight 77's troubles were known at Herndon and FAA headquarters, they were not known by the military. The 9/11 Commission dealt with this contradiction by ignoring it. Like the FAA memo sent by Laura Brown, the testimonies given by Sliney and Belger about military liaisons were not mentioned in *The 9/11 Commission Report*.

Conclusion

The 9/11 Commission's claim about American Flight 77, according to which the military did not know of its hijacking until after the Pentagon was struck, was contradicted by a number of reports: a *New York Times* story of September 15, 2001; NORAD's timeline of September 18, 2001; the FAA's memo of May 22, 2003, which was discussed the next day by 9/11 Commissioner Richard Ben-Veniste and at least partially confirmed by General Craig McKinley of NORAD; the *Arlington County After-Action Report*; Secret Service statements; and reports of the presence of military liaisons at the FAA. Its claim that Indianapolis controllers did not know about any prior hijacking until 9:20 was contradicted by the *Guardian*, NBC News, and Pamela Freni's book. Congress and the press need to ask why such contradictions exist.

12

WHEN WAS THE MILITARY ALERTED ABOUT FLIGHT 93?

The questions about United Flight 93 are different from those about the first three flights. The overarching issue about those prior flights was: How were they able to reach their targets? Flight 93, however, crashed in Pennsylvania, without reaching a target. The overarching question about this flight has been: What happened to it? Officials first said that heroic passengers brought it down after storming the cabin and wresting the controls from the hijackers. It was later said that the hijackers, fearing that the passengers would gain control of the plane, brought it down themselves. But there have been, from the first, rumors that the plane was shot down by the US military.

In this chapter and the next, we will look at contradictions regarding two questions relevant to this issue. In the next chapter, we will examine whether the military was in position to shoot down United 93. The present chapter deals with a prior question: When was the military first alerted about this flight?

A CNN timeline published on September 17, 2001, stated: "9:16AM: FAA informs NORAD that United Airlines flight 93 may have been hijacked." The same story, however, also said: "Officials at the Pentagon... said that they were never made aware of the threat from hijacked United Airlines flight 93 until after it crashed in Pennsylvania."[1] In addition to those two extreme positions, a middle position would emerge.

NORAD's Early Position

"NORAD's Response Times," put out on September 18, 2001, did not list a specific time at which the FAA notified NEADS about United Flight 93. It instead simply had "N/A," meaning "Not Applicable," followed by five asterisks. A note at the beginning of the document, explaining the meaning of the five asterisks, said: "The FAA and NEADS established a line of open communication discussing AA Flt 77 and UA Flt 93."[2] Accordingly, instead of there being a formal notification, at which time NEADS was telephoned by someone from the FAA, NEADS would have learned about United 93 informally through the ongoing conversation on this open line (conference call).

This NORAD document did not indicate exactly when this "line of open communication" was established. As we saw in the previous chapter, however, this same document indicated that NORAD had been notified by the FAA about American Flight 77 at 9:24, so the meaning might have been that this open line between the FAA and NEADS had been established at about that time. The implication would seem to be that the military would have learned about the hijacking of UA 93 as soon as the FAA did.

In any case, when NORAD officials testified before the 9/11 Commission on May 23, 2003, they affirmed the 9:16 notification time, which had been reported by CNN on September 17, the day before "NORAD's Response Times" had appeared. Colonel Alan Scott, while giving NORAD's timeline to the 9/11 Commission, said: "At... 9:16, now FAA reports a possible hijack of United Flight 93, which is out in the Ohio area."[3]

General Larry Arnold then added a twist that further contradicted "NORAD's Response Times." That document stated, with regard to the scramble order: "Langley F-16s already airborne for AA Flt 77." That statement reflected NORAD's early position, as we saw in the previous chapter, that the Langley fighters had been scrambled to go after American Flight 77. Arnold, however, told the Commission: "[W]e launched the aircraft out of Langley to put them over top of Washington, DC, not in response to American Airline 77, but really to put them in position in case United 93 were to head that way."[4]

The Position of the 9/11 Commission

The 9/11 Commission rejected all three claims that had previously been made—the claim that the military knew about United 93's hijacking by 9:16, the claim that it knew by 9:24, and the more general claim that the military knew about United 93's hijacking before it crashed. With regard to the first claim, the Commission said:

> In public testimony before this Commission in May 2003, NORAD officials stated that at 9:16, NEADS received hijack notification of United 93 from the FAA. This statement was incorrect. There was no hijack to report at 9:16. United 93 was proceeding normally at that time [because the hijack did not begin until 9:28].... The military [did not] have 47 minutes to respond to American 93, as would be implied by the account that it received notice of the flight's hijacking at 9:16. By the time the military learned about the flight, it had crashed.[5]

With regard to the second claim, the Commission said: "[General Arnold's statement that] the Langley fighters were scrambled to respond to the notification about... United 93... [was] incorrect."[6]

Regarding the more general claim—that the military did know about United 93 before it crashed—the Commission said: "By 10:03, when United 93 crashed in Pennsylvania, there had been no mention of its hijacking [to the military]."[7] Being more precise, the Commission added: "NEADS first received a call about United 93 from the military liaison at Cleveland Center at 10:07," at which time the FAA's Cleveland Center had been "[u]naware that the aircraft had already crashed."[8]

To make this position seem plausible, the Commission had to explain why the FAA had failed to notify the military about Flight 93, even though its controller in Cleveland had begun detecting signs of the hijacking at 9:28.

Here is the Commission's explanation: At 9:28, the Cleveland controller heard "sounds of possible screaming" and noticed that Flight 93 had descended 700 feet. At 9:32, after hearing a voice saying, "We have a bomb on board," he reported the hijacking to his supervisor, who in turn notified the FAA's Herndon Command Center, which then notified FAA headquarters. But four minutes later, at approximately 9:36 (the Commission claimed):

Cleveland advised the Command Center that it was still track-ing United 93 and specifically inquired whether someone had requested the military to launch fighter aircraft to intercept the aircraft. Cleveland even told the Command Center it was prepared to contact a nearby military base to make the request. The Command Center told Cleveland that FAA personnel well above them in the chain of command had to make the decision to seek military assistance and were working on the issue.[9]

A seemingly inconsistent feature appeared in the Commis-sion's story at this point. It said that, after the Pentagon strike, "Boston Center called NEADS at 9:41 and identified Delta 1989... as a possible hijack. NEADS warned the FAA's Cleveland Center to watch Delta 1989."[10] So, just five minutes after Cleve-land had volunteered to notify the military about the hijacking of United 93, it was called by NEADS. And yet, while it was on the phone with NEADS, talking about Delta 1989, Cleveland did not take advantage of this opportunity to tell NEADS about United 93. The Commission did not explicitly say this, to be sure, but this is the implication of its statement that this call occurred combined with its assertion that NEADS first learned about Flight 93 when Cleveland called at 10:07. The authors of *The 9/11 Commission Report* apparently did not notice this problem.

In any case, the Commission said that Herndon at 9:46 told FAA headquarters that United 93 was "twenty-nine minutes out of Washington." At 9:49, the Commission then said, the following conversation occurred:

Command Center: Uh, do we want to think, uh, about scram-bling aircraft?

FAA Headquarters: Oh, God, I don't know.

Command Center: Uh, that's a decision somebody's gonna have to make probably in the next ten minutes.[11]

The FAA's decision, *The 9/11 Commission Report* implies, was that a hijacked airliner headed toward Washington—after three hijacked airliners had already caused great death and destruc-tion—was not important enough to disturb the military. The Commission's report implies this by telling us that fourteen minutes later, when Flight 93 reportedly crashed in Pennsylvania at 10:03, "no one from FAA headquarters [had yet] requested military assistance regarding United 93."[12]

Contrary Reports

Although this story of FAA stupidity and incompetence is implausible in the extreme, our concern is limited to the question of whether it was contradicted by other reports about Flight 93. And that is, indeed, the case.

White House Officials: ABC's first-anniversary program, based on interviews with Peter Jennings, had several individuals from the White House testifying that they had known about Flight 93 shortly after the Pentagon strike (at 9:38). Charles Gibson, the narrator, reported that Vice President Dick Cheney, in the bunker under the White House, was compiling a list of possible threats. David Bohrer, Cheney's photographer, then recalled: "Eventually it narrowed to Flight 93. That was the biggest threat at that point." Karl Rove said: "If you take the trajectory of the plane, of Flight 93 after it passes Pittsburgh and draw a straight line, it's gonna go to Washington, DC." Cheney himself, asked by Gibson "whether he had any thoughts at the time as to what the target of that airplane might be," replied: "I thought probably the White House or Capitol. We found out later... that... the fourth plane was intended for the White House."

As to when the military learned about this flight, Richard Clarke said that during his teleconference, at about 9:35, FAA Administrator Jane Garvey reported a number of "potential hijacks," which included "United 93 over Pennsylvania."[13] As we saw earlier, moreover, Clarke said that both Donald Rumsfeld and General Richard Myers were participating in this conference. According to Clarke, therefore, the secretary of defense and the acting chairman of the Joint Chiefs of Staff heard from the head of the FAA that Flight 93 was considered a potential hijack more than 25 minutes before it crashed.

Military Officers: The above-mentioned ABC program then described events in the Pentagon's National Military Command Center at the same time. Brigadier General Montague Winfield recalled: "We received the report from the FAA that Flight 93 had turned off its transponder, had turned, and was now heading towards Washington, DC."[14] In a CNN program that also aired near the first anniversary of 9/11, Barbara Starr, CNN's Pentagon correspondent, said: "It is now 9:40, and one very big problem is out there: United Airlines Flight 93 has turned off its transponder. Officials believe it is headed for Washington, D.C."[15]

Whereas Richard Clarke's account suggested that the military would have learned about Flight 93 by 9:35, General Larry Arnold, the commander of NORAD's US continental region, indicated that the military knew even earlier. In an interview that appeared in January 2002, he said, describing a time between the crash into the second tower and the attack on the Pentagon: "By this time, we were watching United Flight 93 wander around Ohio." Then, after seeing this flight heading toward Washington: "We wanted to go out and meet it. But we were not going to do anything until the airliner got closer to DC. The flight came within about 200 miles of the DC area [before it crashed]."[16] In the US Air Force book about 9/11, *Air War over America*, which appeared in 2003, Arnold repeated his statement about early awareness. Reporting that the military was tracking UA 93 even before it turned around—meaning before 9:36—he stated: "we watched the 93 track as it meandered around the Ohio-Pennsylvania area and started to turn south toward D.C."[17] During his appearance before the 9/11 Commission in May 2003, Arnold was asked what NORAD was doing at 9:24. He said: "Our focus was on United 93, which was being pointed out to us very aggressively I might say by the FAA."[18] This account strongly contradicted in advance the portrait that *The 9/11 Commission Report* would later paint of an FAA that could not bring itself to disturb the military.

According to the same book, NEADS Commander Colonel Robert Marr, after saying that he had at first thought Flight 93 was "headed towards Detroit or Chicago," stated that he had contacted a base in that area so that its fighters could "head off 93 at the pass."[19]

The FAA Memo: The account by *The 9/11 Commission Report,* according to which the military knew nothing about Flight 93's hijacking until after it crashed, is also challenged by the FAA memo sent to the Commission by Laura Brown and read into its record by Richard Ben-Veniste. According to this memo, as we saw in the previous chapter, the FAA, immediately after the first crash into the WTC, established phone bridges that included both the Pentagon and NORAD. And then:

> The FAA shared real-time information on the phone bridges about the unfolding events, including information about loss of communication with aircraft, loss of transponder signals, unauthorized changes in course, and other actions being taken by all the flights of interest.[20]

Even the 9/11 Commission agreed that UA 93 was a "flight of interest" for FAA headquarters by 9:34.[21] It, therefore, would have been one of the flights discussed by that time.

In May 2003, the idea that the FAA was talking to the military about United 93 for over a half hour before it crashed was not controversial. The FAA memo agreed with "NORAD's Response Times," which said, as we saw, that the FAA and NEADS were discussing United 93, as well as American 77, on "a line of open communication," evidently since about 9:24. The FAA memo was also consistent with General Arnold's portrait, according to which United 93 "was being pointed out to [the military] very aggressively... by the FAA."

Military Liaisons: The 9/11 Commission's claim that the military was unaware of this flight because the FAA had failed to contact it was also contradicted, of course, by the testimonies, quoted in the previous chapter, pointing to the existence of the military liaisons at the FAA Command Center. As we saw, Ben Sliney, the operations manager, said: "They were present at all of the events that occurred on 9/11."[22] Monte Belger, the FAA's acting deputy administrator, even spoke of them specifically in reference to United 93. Referring to this flight, Commissioner Bob Kerrey had said to Belger: "[A] plane was headed to Washington D.C. FAA Headquarters knew it and didn't let the military know." Belger replied:

I truly do not mean this to be defensive, but it is a fact—there
were military people on duty at the FAA Command Center, as
Mr. Sliney said. They were participating in what was going on.
There were military people in the FAA's Air Traffic Organization in a situation room. They were participating in what was
going on.[23]

Although these testimonies were given to the 9/11 Commission
in open hearings, they were ignored in the Commission's final
report.

Secret Service Knowledge: As we saw in the previous chapter, the
Secret Service was able to know everything the FAA knew about
flights. The 9/11 Commission may have even alluded to this fact
when it said: "At 10:02, the communicators in the shelter [the
PEOC] began receiving reports from the Secret Service of an
inbound aircraft—presumably hijacked—heading toward Washington. That aircraft was United 93. The Secret Service was
getting this information directly from the FAA."[24] According to
the account that was provided in *The 9/11 Commission Report*,
the Secret Service was very late in conveying this information.
(The main information was said to have come only after 10:10AM,
long after United 93 had already crashed—this being the
Commission's version of the incoming airplane story, which was
discussed in Chapter 3.) As we saw in the previous chapter,
however, Barbara Riggs, who in 2006 had just retired as deputy
director of the Secret Service, said that the Secret Service had
this information much earlier. Referring to Secret Service headquarters in Washington on the morning of 9/11, she said: "Thru
monitoring radar and activating an open line with the FAA, the
Secret Service was able to receive real time information about…
hijacked aircraft. We were tracking two hijacked aircraft as they
approached Washington, D.C."[25] One of those aircraft would have
been United 93.

FBI Knowledge: According to *New York Times* reporter Jere Longman's well-known book about United 93, Deena Burnett, the wife
of passenger Tom Burnett, received a phone call that she believed

to be from him. Being told that this flight had been hijacked, she was asked to call the authorities. By 9:34, she was talking to the FBI.[26] According to Longman, therefore, the FBI knew about the hijacking of Flight 93 at least a half hour before it went down.

This assertion was backed up by a flight controller. In the first anniversary NBC show with Tom Brokaw, flight controller Greg Callahan said:

> We were tracking United 93, and I was in conversation with the FBI agent, and he was relaying to me that, "We suspect that this aircraft has now been taken over by hostile forces," described the sharp turn it made over eastern Ohio and now was heading back along southwestern Pennsylvania. And I could tell just by giving it a visual track that it was obviously heading for the Washington, DC, area.[27]

Brokaw then said: "As Flight 93 speeds towards Washington, DC, the Federal Aviation Administration [begins] the grounding of every single civilian plane in the sky." That order to ground all planes was, as we saw in Chapter 4, given at 9:45. Brokaw thereby indicated that the FBI suspected a hijacking prior to 9:45.

In 2002, when this program aired, this idea was not problematic, because it was taken for granted that the military also knew about Flight 93's hijacking by this time. After the appearance of *The 9/11 Commission Report*, however, this idea, affirmed by both Longman and NBC, suggested a very strange situation: that the FBI—like the Secret Service and the FAA—knew about the hijacking, but did not inform the military.

Conclusion

In addition to these stories of FBI and Secret Service awareness about Flight 93, which are in strong tension with the 9/11 Commission's account, there is an enormous amount of evidence that even more directly contradicts it. The Commission's claim that the military was not informed by the FAA about this flight's troubles until after it crashed was contradicted by "NORAD's Response Times," put out one week after 9/11; by the FAA's 2003 memo to the Commission; and by the fact that there were military liaisons at FAA headquarters. There were also statements by three senior White House figures—Dick Cheney, Richard Clarke, and Karl Rove—and several military officers—including Brigadier General Montague Winfield, General Larry Arnold, and Colonel Robert Marr—that the military had been tracking United 93 before it crashed.

The 9/11 Commission, in defending its position that the military was unaware of Flight 93 until 10:07, directly challenged only the most extreme contrary claims, according to which the military learned at 9:16 or at least by 9:24. The Commission could rebut these claims by pointing out the lack of evidence that the flight had shown any signs of being hijacked by either of those times. But the Commission simply ignored all the testimonies pointing to the truth of a middle position, according to which the military learned about this flight's troubles shortly after those signs began to appear, at about 9:30.

The Commission's account and this set of earlier accounts cannot both be true. Congress and the press need to determine who gave a false account and why.

13

COULD THE MILITARY HAVE SHOT DOWN FLIGHT 93?

In addition to the contradictory reports about whether the military was aware of United 93's troubles before it crashed, discussed in the previous chapter, there have also been contradictory reports on the question of whether the military could have shot the flight down.

Rumors that the military *had* shot down Flight 93 existed from the start. Major Daniel Nash, one of the Otis pilots sent to fly over New York City that morning, reported that when he returned to base, he was told that a military F-16 had shot down an airliner in Pennsylvania.[1] This rumor became sufficiently widespread that it came up during General Richard Myers's interview with the Senate Armed Services Committee on September 13. Chairman Carl Levin, saying that "there have been statements that the aircraft that crashed in Pennsylvania was shot down," added: "Those stories continue to exist."[2]

The military insisted from the outset that those rumors were untrue. After Senator Levin asked whether the military did, in fact, take action against Flight 93, Myers replied:

> Mr. Chairman, the armed forces did not shoot down any aircraft. When it became clear what the threat was, we did scramble fighter aircraft, AWACS, radar aircraft and tanker aircraft to begin to establish orbits in case other aircraft showed up in the FAA system that were hijacked. But we never actually had to use force.[3]

Already the previous day (September 12), NORAD had issued a statement denying that United Flight 93 had been shot down by US military aircraft.[4] On the 13th, NORAD issued yet another denial, saying: "Contrary to media reports that speculate that United Airlines Flight 93 was 'downed' by a U.S. fighter aircraft, NORAD-allocated forces have not engaged with weapons any aircraft, including Flight 93."[5]

The FBI also denied that this plane had been shot down. In a story published September 14, FBI agent William Crowley, who was investigating the flight's crash, was quoted as saying: "There was no military involvement. I hope that ends that speculation."[6]

The speculation, however, did not end, partly because of further statements suggesting that the flight had indeed been shot down. In 2002, for example, Susan Mcelwain, who lived near the crash site, reported that within hours of the crash, she had received a call from a female friend who said that her husband, who was in the air force, had called and said: "I can't talk, but we've just shot a plane down."[7]

Even Donald Rumsfeld contributed to the speculation that the plane had been shot down. On Christmas Eve of 2004, during his surprise trip to Iraq, he referred to "the people who attacked the United States in New York, shot down the plane over Pennsylvania and attacked the Pentagon."[8] A few days later, a Pentagon spokesperson stated that "Rumsfeld simply misspoke."[9] But many people took Rumsfeld's statement as a *revealing* misstatement, in which he had inadvertently expressed his knowledge that United 93 had been shot down.

UA 93 Could Not Have Been Shot Down: The 9/11 Commission's Threefold Argument

Although the 9/11 Commission never directly mentioned this controversy, it had three indirect means for implying that United 93 had not been shot down. First, it gave a description of how the plane *was* brought down, namely, by al-Qaeda hijackers, who feared that the passengers were about to wrest control of the airplane from them.[10] Second, it gave an account of FAA actions and military awareness that ruled out any possibility that United 93 *could* have been shot down. Third, it claimed that the flight did not crash at 10:06, as previously reported, but at 10:03. This third element will be addressed at the end of this chapter.

Most of the chapter, however, deals with the second of these elements—the argument that the military could not possibly have shot down Flight 93. This argument contains three claims: that the military did not know about United 93's hijacking until after it had crashed; that the authorization to shoot down airliners was not given until after United 93 had crashed; and that, in any case, military jets had not been in position to shoot it down. Contradictory reports, as we will see, exist in relation to each of these claims.

When the Military Became Aware of the Hijacking of United 93

The 9/11 Commission's claim with regard to this question—the claim that the military did not know about the hijacking of United 93 until after it had crashed—was thoroughly discussed in the previous chapter, in which we saw that the Commission's claim was contradicted by earlier statements by several military figures. This question requires no further comment here.

When the Shootdown Authorization Was Given

The question of the time of the shootdown authorization, having been discussed in Chapter 5, can here be treated quite briefly.

The 9/11 Commission's Position: According to the 9/11 Commission, Vice President Cheney did not arrive in the PEOC until almost 10:00, did not give the shootdown authorization until some time after 10:10, and gave this authorization in response to a false report that United 93 was still aloft and headed toward Washington.[11] "At 10:10, the pilots over Washington were emphatically told, 'negative clearance to shoot.' Shootdown authority was first communicated to NEADS at 10:31."[12] Richard Clarke, who had asked for this authorization, did not receive confirmation that it had been given until 10:25.[13]

Contrary Statements: Clarke himself, however, indicated that he, after asking for the authorization shortly after 9:30 and then being "amazed at the speed of the decisions coming from Cheney," received the authorization at about 9:45.[14]

Shortly after 9/11, Cheney himself was quoted as apparently supporting this account. A *Newsday* story published two weeks after 9/11 said:

> Vice President Dick Cheney has disclosed that President George W. Bush authorized military jets to shoot down "as a last resort" a hijacked airliner, apparently Flight 93, that was heading for Washington. Officials said later that the decision wasn't made until after Flight 77 crashed into the Pentagon.[15]

This account, according to which it was given "after Flight 77 crashed into the Pentagon [at 9:38]," suggested that the authorization came at about the time Clarke suggested, hence much earlier than the 9/11 Commission would later claim.

Clarke's account also agreed with statements made by several military officers. In 2003, *US News and World Report* wrote: "Pentagon sources say Bush communicated the order [to shoot down any hijacked civilian airplane] to Cheney almost immediately after Flight 77 hit the Pentagon."[16]

One Pentagon officer who said the authorization came before United 93 crashed was Brigadier General Montague Winfield. Speaking of the time after the "decision was made to try to go intercept Flight 93," he said that according to the Cheney, "the President had given us permission to shoot down innocent civilian aircraft that threatened Washington, DC."[17]

ABC's first-anniversary program, which contained Winfield's statement, also portrayed Donald Rumsfeld as supporting this view. After Peter Jennings stated, "In the Pentagon command center, there was a report of another hijacked plane, United Airlines Flight 93, which apparently had switched off its transponder and turned toward Washington," Rumsfeld said: "We rapidly developed some rules of engagement for what our military aircraft might do."[18] This statement by Rumsfeld in 2002,[19] according to which these rules of engagement were developed "rapidly," contrasted sharply with the 9/11 Commission's later account (as discussed in Chapter 7), according to which it took Rumsfeld much of the day to develop these rules.

Colonel Robert Marr, the head of NEADS, clearly stated that shootdown authorization came before United 93 crashed. Speaking of a time when this plane was still aloft, Marr said, "we received the clearance to kill if need be."[20] He also stated that he had "passed that [order] on to the pilots" so that "United Airlines Flight 93 [would] not be allowed to reach Washington, DC."[21]

The position of the 9/11 Commission on the time of the shoot-down authorization was, therefore, contradicted by Richard Clarke, Colonel Marr, Brigadier General Winfield, ABC News, and *US News and World Report*.

Were Military Jets Ready to Shoot Down United 93?

If, as *The 9/11 Commission Report* claimed, the military did not know about Flight 93's troubles until after it crashed, then military fighter jets could not possibly have been ready to shoot it down. Many previous reports, however, contradicted this view.

On September 13, General Richard Myers said, "if my memory serves me, ... we had launched on the [airliner] that eventually crashed in Pennsylvania... [W]e had gotten somebody close to it, as I recall."[22]

That same day, a reporter for the *Telegraph* in Nashua, New Hampshire (where the Boston Air Traffic Control Center is actually located), wrote: "FAA air traffic controllers in Nashua have learned through discussions with other controllers that an F-16 fighter stayed in hot pursuit of another hijacked commercial airliner until it crashed in Pennsylvania." According to the journalist's source (an employee "who worked in the control center that fateful morning"), "an F-16 fighter closely pursued Flight 93" and even "made 360-degree turns to remain close to the commercial jet." Referring to Flight 93's crash, this employee said: "He [the F-16 pilot] must've seen the whole thing."[23]

The next day, September 14, Deputy Secretary of Defense Paul Wolfowitz, being interviewed on PBS's *NewsHour with Jim Lehrer*, said:

> We responded awfully quickly, I might say, on Tuesday, and, in fact, we were already tracking in on that plane that crashed in Pennsylvania. I think it was the heroism of the passengers on board that brought it down. But the Air Force was in a position to do so if we had had to.[24]

This portion of the Wolfowitz interview was noticed. A Reuters headline the following day declared: "Pentagon: Air Force Was in Position to Down Hijacked Jet." The story began: "The U.S. Air Force was tracking the hijacked plane that crashed in Pennsylvania… and had been in a position to bring it down if necessary, Deputy Secretary Paul Wolfowitz said on Friday."[25] Wolfowitz's statement was paraphrased that day by the *New York Times*.[26]

On September 16, a CBS story led with this incident, saying:

U.S. officials were considering shooting down the hijacked airliner that crashed in western Pennsylvania, but it crashed first.

"The president made the decision… that if the plane would not divert, if they wouldn't pay any attention to instructions to move away from the city, as a last resort, our pilots were authorized to take them out," Vice President Dick Cheney told NBC's "Meet the Press" program Sunday….

As the fourth hijacked plane was over Pennsylvania, seemingly headed for Washington, military commanders, the FAA, and White House officials were on a conference call discussing options.

At the time, there were two F-16s armed with air-to-air missiles within 60 miles of Flight 93. But the fighters were still out of missile range when the jetliner crashed, sources said.

No decision had to be made, but administration officials say that, had the jetliner continued toward Washington, the fighter jets would have shot it down. The rationale, say the sources, was that the government was willing to "kill 100 to save a thousand."[27]

In Chapter 5, we saw that while Lt. Anthony Kuczynski was flying towards Pittsburgh in an E-3 Sentry—which is an AWACS (Airborne Warning and Control System) airplane, with advanced radar and surveillance instruments useful for directing fighters to their targets—alongside two F-16s, Kuczynski said that they were "given direct orders to shoot down an airliner." According to the story about this episode in the newspaper of his alma mater, "Just as Kuczynski and his crew were about to intercept United Airlines Flight 93 on Sept. 11, passengers on the hijacked plane apparently rushed the terrorists, and the airliner crashed."[28]

We also saw in Chapter 5 that Major General Mike Haugen, the adjutant general of the North Dakota National Guard, said that right after the attack on the Pentagon, the Langley pilots were told by the Secret Service to "protect the White House at all costs." Only the crash of Flight 93, Haugen told the *New York Times*, "kept us from having to do the unthinkable." Haugen thereby confirmed that military jets were in position to have brought United 93 down.[29]

Several stories in 2002 and 2003 reflected the same view. Leslie Filson, the author of the air force's account of 9/11, quoted Colonel Robert Marr, the head of NEADS, saying that the military was ready to bring down United 93. Filson wrote:

> The North Dakota F-16s were loaded with missiles and hot guns and Marr was thinking about what these pilots might be expected to do. "United Airlines Flight 93 would not have hit Washington, D.C.," Marr says emphatically. "He would have been engaged and shot down before he got there."[30]

A story in *Aviation Week & Space Technology* said:

> Above Washington, F-16s flown by crews of the 119th FW [Fighter Wing] from Fargo, N.D.— which had been pulling NORAD alert duty at Langley AFB—were prepared to shoot down United 93, if it came toward the capital city. Instead, passengers rushed the terrorists, causing the Boeing 757 to crash in southwestern Pennsylvania.[31]

During ABC's first-anniversary program, Brigadier General Montague Winfield, while discussing United 93, stated:

> We started receiving reports from the fighters that were heading to, to intercept. The FAA kept us informed with their time estimates as the aircraft got closer and closer…. And at some point, the closure time came and went, and nothing had happened. So you can imagine everything was very tense in the NMCC. We had basically lost situational awareness of where this airplane was.

Winfield's statement referred to the time, according to ABC's Charles Gibson, when "Flight 93 [was] about 175 miles north and west of Washington."[32]

Pamela Freni's book *Ground Stop*, which was published in 2003, also supported this account. It stated that while Flight 93 was flying over the Pennsylvania countryside, "a fighter jet was positioning itself between UA93 and the District of Columbia. There would be no more buildings attacked today."[33] Prior to the publication of *The 9/11 Commission Report* in 2004, these reports show, it was widely accepted that the military knew about Flight 93 before it crashed, had received shootdown authorization, and was ready to shoot it down.

When Did United 93 Crash?

With the discussion of the three preceding issues, we have completed the examination of the Commission's claim that the military could not possibly have shot down United 93. That claim constituted an implicit argument that the flight was, in fact, *not* shot down. (The argument, if made explicit, would have run: The military could not have possibly shot down Flight 93; therefore, it did not.) Another implicit argument that the flight was not shot down was contained in the Commission's claim about the time that it crashed.

The Time Stated in Most Prior Reports: According to most reports prior to 2004, United 93 crashed at about 10:06AM.[34]

This time was given by several Pennsylvania newspapers in the days immediately following 9/11. For example, a September 12 story by Jonathan Silver in the *Pittsburgh Post-Gazette* said: "United Airlines Flight 93, a Boeing 757-200 en route from New Jersey to San Francisco, fell from the sky near Shanksville at 10:06AM, about two hours after it took off."[35] Another story by Silver the following day said:

> Early news reports put the crash time at 10:06. The Federal Aviation Administration said yesterday it turned over to the FBI a radar record of United Airlines Flight 93's route. The data traced the Boeing 757-200 from its takeoff from Newark, N.J., to its violent end at 10:06AM, just outside Shanksville.[36]

The 10:06 crash time continued to be affirmed in the following months. In October, Dennis Roddy, also writing for the *Pittsburgh Post-Gazette*, reported that Cleveland Air Traffic Control reported losing track of Flight 93 at 10:06.[37] In November, William Bunch, writing in the *Philadelphia Daily News*, reported that "people in Shanksville and the surrounding farm fields... saw or heard the jetliner go down at roughly 10:06."[38] In August 2002, a timeline provided by *USA Today* put the crash of United 93 at 10:06.[39]

In the spring of 2002, the 10:06 time was confirmed in a study by seismologists Won-Young Kim of Columbia University's Lamont-Doherty Earth Observatory and Gerald R. Baum of the Maryland Geological Survey. Their report put the exact time of the crash at 10:06:05.[40]

The Position of NORAD and the 9/11 Commission: In spite of the virtually unanimous agreement on the 10:06 crash time during the first week after 9/11, NORAD, in its timeline of September 18, 2001, put the time at 10:03.[41] Then in 2004, *The 9/11 Commission Report*, while admitting that "[t]he precise crash time has been the subject of some dispute," reaffirmed NORAD's crash time, refining it to exactly 10:03:11.[42]

This time helped support the official view, according to which United 93 was not shot down. How it did so was explained in an article by William Bunch in the *Philadelphia Daily News* entitled "Three-Minute Discrepancy in Tape: Cockpit Voice Recording Ends Before Flight 93's Official Time of Impact." According to all reports, Bunch pointed out, the flight's cockpit voice went completely silent at 10:03:11, with no sound of impact. If the plane did not crash until 10:06, there was a three-minute period between the end of the tape and the crash. "[T]he three-minute gap," Bunch wrote, "points to how little is really known about how and why Flight 93 crashed." He then added: "the three-minute gap is certain to fuel ongoing debates... over... whether the plane could have been shot down by military jet fighters."[43]

However, if the crash time was 10:03:11, as *The 9/11 Commission Report* claimed, there was no gap to fuel such speculation.

Dealing with the Contradiction: How did the 9/11 Commission deal with the fact that its crash time was contradicted by both the official seismic study and the initial news reports? *The 9/11 Commission Report* simply made no mention of those news reports. It did mention the seismic study by Kim and Baum, but dismissed it by saying that the seismic data on which they based their conclusion were "far too weak in signal-to-noise ratio and far too speculative in terms of signal source" to be considered definitive.[44]

But that claim contradicted what Kim and Baum, who had sought to determine the time for all four crashes, had said. According to their report, only the signal from the crash into the Pentagon was too weak for a definite time to be determined. Their conclusion about the crash time of UA 93 was based on the seismic records from three stations near the crash site. "Although seismic signals across the network are not as strong and clear as the WTC case," they said, "three component records... are quite clear."[45]

Kim and Baum's time has also been supported by seismologist Terry Wallace, who, according to Bunch, is widely considered the leading expert on the seismology of humanly caused events. Saying, "I don't know where the 10.03 time comes from," Wallace stated: "The seismic signals are consistent with impact at 10.06:05 plus or minus two seconds."[46]

According to the 9/11 Commission, "The 10:03:11 impact time is supported by previous National Transportation Safety Board analysis."[47] This claim, however, had been contradicted in advance by Mary Schiavo, former inspector general of the Department of Transportation. Commenting that NTSB officials "ordinarily dissect the timeline to the thousandth of a second," she said, alluding to the fact that the investigation was instead handled by the FBI: "We don't have an NTSB investigation here."[48] This statement was supported by Bunch's 2002 report that the "NTSB referred all questions [about the crash time] to the FBI."[49]

The Commission, besides ignoring all the early news reports that put the crash time at 10:06, also ignored a reported phone call from Flight 93 that contradicted the Commission's timeline. The Commission wrote: "At 9:57, the passenger assault began. Several passengers had terminated phone calls with loved ones in order to join the revolt."[50] Although that time for the beginning of the assault by the passengers was consistent with the Commission's crash time of 10:03, it did not fit with Lyz Glick's account of her phone conversation with her husband, Jeremy Glick, as

told to *New York Times* reporter Jere Longman (as well as elsewhere[51]). According to this account, Jeremy, reporting that
"passengers were hearing on their phones that planes were crashing into the world Trade Center," asked: "Was it true about the
Trade Center?" Longman then wrote:

> Lyz said, ... yes, it was true that two planes had crashed into the
> World Trade Center. By now, it was almost ten o'clock. At nine
> fifty-eight, the south tower collapsed.... Were they going to crash
> his plane into the World Trade Center? Jeremy wanted to know.
> "No," Lyz said.... "They are not going there." Why? Jeremy
> asked. One of the towers had just fallen. "They knocked it
> down," Lyz told him.... What should he do? Jeremy asked
> Lyz.... They were problem-solving. Lyz asked Jeremy about the
> United pilots. Were they alive? He didn't know. Had the real
> pilots said anything to the passengers over the public address
> system? No. Did the hijackers have any automatic weapons? Lyz
> asked.... No guns, Jeremy said. "They have knives." How could
> people have gotten on the plane with knives and a bomb? He
> wanted to know. And then he made a joke that was typical
> Jeremy. "We just had breakfast and we have our butter knives."
> He said that they were taking a vote. There were three other guys
> as big as him. They were thinking about attacking the hijackers.
> Was that a good idea? What should they do? .... "I think you
> need to do it," Lyz told Jeremy. "Okay," he said. "Stay on the
> phone, I'll be right back." ... They were going to jump on the
> hijackers and attack them, Jeremy said.... Put a picture of me
> and the baby in your head, Lyz said to Jeremy.... He went away,
> and it sounded as if he were talking to people.[52]

So although the Commission claimed that the passenger revolt
began at 9:57, Lyz Glick said that she was still talking to her
husband after the collapse of the South Tower, which occurred at
9:59 (Longman said 9:58, but it began at 9:58:59—essentially
9:59). She indicated, moreover, that they continued talking several
minutes more before the passengers took a vote and, furthermore,
that still more time passed before the assault actually began.

According to Lyz Glick's account, therefore, the passenger
assault would not have begun much, if at all, before 10:03,
making a crash time of 10:03:11 impossible. This impossibility

was further increased by Longman's account of what happened next.

> [Lyz] couldn't bear to listen and handed the phone to her father.... Richard Makely... took the phone.... For what seemed like more than a minute, he heard no background noise, only silence. Then came screams, a mass of shouting..., female screams more than male screams. Then another sixty seconds of silence, or ninety seconds, followed by another set of screams....[53]

According to the account given by Lyz Glick and her father, therefore, the plane could not have crashed much if any before 10:06.

Although the 9/11 Commission referred to Jere Longman's book and an interview with Lyz Glick,[54] it failed to mention the fact that their accounts contradicted the Commission's claim as to when the passenger revolt began and therefore when the plane went down.

Conclusion

Although the US military has consistently maintained that it did not shoot down United 93, rumors have existed from the first that it did. The 9/11 Commission supported the military's denial primarily by arguing that the military could not possibly have shot the flight down. Contradictions, however, exist in relation to all four of the main issues, namely: When did the military learn that United 93 was hijacked? When was the shootdown authorization given? Were military jets ready to shoot the flight down? And when did United 93 crash? Given the importance of the question as to what happened to United 93, such contradictions should never have existed. They certainly should not have been allowed to stand until this day. Congress and the press need to find out the truth.

14

HAD 9/11-TYPE ATTACKS
BEEN ENVISIONED?

M embers of the Bush administration repeatedly claimed that
the type of attacks that occurred on 9/11 could not reasonably have been anticipated and hence prevented. This
claim, however, was contradicted by numerous official reports, which
showed that such attacks had been envisioned and even simulated in
military exercises. This contradiction came to be perceived as less
important after July 2004, when the 9/11 Commission released its
report. As we saw in previous chapters, NORAD's original timeline,
according to which the FAA had notified it about all four flights, was
rejected by the Commission, which claimed that the military, after
having been notified about the first flight only nine minutes before it
crashed, did not even know about the latter three flights until after
they had crashed. This change meant that the question of whether
the military should have been able to prevent the attacks came to be
widely regarded as less important than it had seemed before. The
fact remains, however, that leading members of the Bush administration and its military made claims that were clearly contradicted by a
wide range of evidence coming from official sources.

Claims that 9/11-Type Attacks Were Not Anticipated

On September 16, President Bush declared: "Never [in] anybody's
thought process about how to protect America did we ever think
that the evil-doers would fly not one, but four commercial aircraft
into precious U.S. targets—never."[1]

On September 23, *Newsday* quoted an unnamed defense official
as saying: "I don't think any of us envisioned an internal air threat by
big aircraft. I don't know of anybody that ever thought through that."[2]

Two days later, FAA Administrator Jane Garvey said that, before 9/11, "No one could imagine someone being willing to commit suicide, being willing to use an airplane as a lethal weapon."[3]

On September 26, President Bush, in response to a question from the press as to whether someone needed to be held responsible for a massive intelligence failure, replied: "[T]he intelligence gathering capacity of the United States is doing a fine job.... These terrorists struck in a way that was unimaginable."[4]

On September 30, Tim Russert, while interviewing Donald Rumsfeld on *Meet the Press*, asked: "Did you ever imagine that, as the secretary of defense, that your building, the Pentagon, would be attacked by a terrorist using an American commercial airline?" Rumsfeld replied: "Oh goodness no! Never would have crossed anyone's mind."[5]

On October 17, General Richard Myers, the new chairman of the Joint Chiefs of Staff, told the Armed Forces Radio and Television Service: "You hate to admit it, but we hadn't thought about this."[6]

The same claims continued the following year, even becoming more emphatic after the revelation by CBS News on May 15, 2002, that President Bush's CIA briefing in August 2001 had warned that Osama bin Laden wanted to hijack aircraft. Responding that same day, White Press Secretary Ari Fleischer said that, although Bush had been warned of possible hijackings, "The president did not—not—receive information about the use of airplanes as missiles by suicide bombers."[7]

The emphatic nature of Fleischer's denial reflected the threat posed by this revelation, which was stated a few days later in the London *Guardian*: "'conspiracy' begins to take over from 'incompetence' as a likely explanation for the failure to heed—and then inform the public about—warnings that might have averted the worst disaster in the nation's history."[8]

The next day, May 16, 2002, Bush's national security advisor, Condoleezza Rice, made what turned out to be the most notorious denial on this subject. During a press briefing, in which she discussed the CIA briefing of August 6, 2001, she was asked, "Why shouldn't this be seen as an intelligence failure, that you were unable to predict something happening here?" She replied:

I don't think anybody could have predicted that these people would take an airplane and slam it into the World Trade Center, take another one and slam it into the Pentagon, that they would try to use... a hijacked airplane as a missile. All this reporting about hijacking was about traditional hijacking.[9]

That same day, Ari Fleischer, during his daily press briefing, said: "Never did we imagine what would take place on September 11th, where people use those airplanes as missiles and weapons."[10] The following day, Fleischer was quoted as saying: "Until the attack took place, I think it is fair to say that no one envisioned that as a possibility."[11]

That same day—May 17, 2002—Bush said in a speech: "The American people know this about me...: Had I known that the enemy was going to use airplanes to kill on that fateful morning, I would have done everything in my power to protect the American people."[12]

These claims, however, were contradicted by statements from other officials and reports of military exercises that had been conducted or at least planned before 9/11.

Some Contradictory Statements

On October 14, 2001, Paul Pillar, the former deputy director of the CIA's Counterterrorist Center, was quoted by the *Los Angeles Times* as saying: "The idea of commandeering an aircraft and crashing it into the ground and causing high casualties, sure we've thought of it."[13]

On May 17, 2002, CBS revealed that former CIA Deputy Director John Gannon said: "If you ask anybody could terrorists convert a plane into a missile, nobody would have ruled that out."[14]

On July 24, 2003, the Joint Congressional Inquiry into the Terrorist Attacks of September 11, 2001, issued its report. One of its findings was that in April 2001, the intelligence community learned that "bin Laden was interested in commercial pilots as potential terrorists."[15]

The Administration's Claim Continued in 2004

In spite of this evidence to the contrary, the Bush administration was still claiming in 2004 that it had had no idea that such attacks were possible. On March 23 of that year, Donald Rumsfeld told the 9/11 Commission: "I knew of no intelligence during the six-plus months leading up to September 11 to indicate terrorists would hijack commercial airlines, use them as missiles to fly into the Pentagon or the World Trade Center towers."[16]

On April 8, 2004, Condoleezza Rice, testifying under oath before the 9/11 Commission, said that the "kind of analysis about the use of airplanes as weapons actually was never briefed to us."[17]

On April 13, Bush said during a nationally televised press conference:

> [T]here was... nobody in our government... [who] could envision flying airplanes into buildings on such a massive scale.... Had I had any inkling whatsoever that the people were going to fly airplanes into buildings, we would have moved heaven and earth to save the country.[18]

Dealing with the Contradiction

In July 2004, the 9/11 Commission issued its final report. It endorsed, for the most part, the claim by the Bush administration and its military leaders that the attacks of 9/11 were of a type that had not been anticipated. The Commission wrote:

> The threat of terrorists hijacking commercial airliners within the United States—and using them as guided missiles—was not recognized by NORAD before 9/11.[19]

In saying this, the Commission was accepting General Richard Myers's claim that "our military posture on 9/11... was focused on responding to external threats, threats originating outside of our borders." This posture, he had added, had implications for radar coverage: "[W]e were clearly looking outward. We did not have the situational awareness inward because we did not have the radar coverage."[20] The Commission, endorsing Myers's claims, wrote:

> America's homeland defenders faced outward.... [NORAD's] planning scenarios occasionally considered the danger of hijacked aircraft being guided to American targets, but only aircraft that were coming from overseas.[21]

The Commission also accepted the military's claim that it had presumed that any hijacking of an American airliner would *not* be "a suicide hijacking designed to convert the aircraft into a guided missile." Because of that presumption, the Commission said, we had "a military unprepared for the transformation of commercial aircraft into weapons of mass destruction."[22]

However, the 9/11 Commission's claim, that "[t]he threat of terrorists hijacking commercial airliners within the United States—and using them as guided missiles—was not recognized by NORAD before 9/11," was challenged not only by the contradictory statements quoted above but also by some reports that the Commission itself mentioned. For example:

> [Richard] Clarke had been concerned about the danger posed by aircraft since at least the 1996 Atlanta Olympics.... In 1998, Clarke chaired an exercise [that] involved a scenario in which a group of terrorists commandeered a Learjet on the ground in Atlanta, loaded it with explosives, and flew it toward a target in Washington, D.C.[23]

The 9/11 Commission Report also said:

> After the 1999–2000 millennium alerts, ... Clarke held a meeting of his Counterterrorism Security Group devoted largely to the possibility of a possible airplane hijacking by al Qaeda.... [T]he possibility was imaginable, and imagined.[24]

Moreover, the Commission's report said:

> In early August 1999, the FAA's Civil Aviation Security intelligence office summarized the Bin Ladin hijacking threat.... [T]he paper identified a few principal scenarios, one of which was a "suicide hijacking operation."[25]

So although the 9/11 Commission endorsed the military's claim that "[t]he threat of terrorists hijacking commercial airlines within the United States—and using them as guided missiles—was not recognized by NORAD before 9/11," this claim was undermined by examples provided by the Commission itself.

For the most part, however, the Commission simply ignored evidence that contradicted its claim, even though that evidence was provided by official sources, mainstream news reports, and people giving information at Commission hearings.

Reports: In 1993, a panel of experts commissioned by the Pentagon suggested that airplanes could be used as missiles to bomb national landmarks. In 1994, one of these experts wrote: "Targets such as the World Trade Center not only provide the requisite casualties but, because of their symbolic nature, provide more bang for the buck. In order to maximize their odds for success, terrorist groups will likely consider mounting multiple, simultaneous operations."[26] (That same year, incidentally, Tom Clancy published a bestselling novel, *Debt of Honor*, in which a Japanese commercial airline pilot, during a short war between Japan and the United States, loads a Boeing 747 with explosives and crashes it into the US Capitol during a joint session of Congress.[27])

In 1995, *Time* magazine reported, in a cover story, that Senator Sam Nunn had described a scenario in which terrorists crash a radio-controlled airplane into the US Capitol.[28]

In 1999, the National Intelligence Council, which advises the president and US intelligence agencies on emerging threats, said in a special report on terrorism:

> Al-Qaeda's expected retaliation for the US cruise missile attack [of 1998]… could take several forms of terrorist attack in the nation's capitol. Suicide bombers belonging to al-Qaeda's Martyrdom Battalion could crash-land an aircraft packed with high explosives… into the Pentagon, the headquarters of the Central Intelligence Agency (CIA), or the White House.[29]

Military Exercises: Some of the evidence ignored by the Commission consisted of exercises planned by the US military—exercises that envisioned events similar to those that occurred on 9/11.

In October 2000, Pentagon officials carried out an emergency drill to prepare for the possibility that a commercial airliner might crash into the Pentagon.[30]

In May 2001, two medical clinics in the Pentagon held a training exercise involving a scenario in which an aircraft—a hijacked 757 according to some reports—was crashed into the Pentagon.[31]

In July 2001, NORAD planned an exercise, called Amalgam Virgo 02, that would simulate a scenario in which airliners hijacked within the United States would be used as weapons. As explained in a 2004 *USA Today* article ("NORAD Had Drills of Jets as Weapons"), this was part of a series of exercises planned by the military in the two years prior to 9/11 in which "hijacked airliners [were] used as weapons.... One of the imagined targets was the World Trade Center." Although NORAD claimed that "[t]he planes in the simulation were coming from a foreign country," *USA Today* noted that "there were exceptions..., including one operation, planned in July 2001 and conducted later, that involved planes from airports in Utah and Washington state that were 'hijacked.'"[32] As explained in a 2002 article by the American Forces Press Service, this particular exercise was called "Amalgam Virgo 02," because although it was "planned before the Sept. 11 attacks," it was scheduled to be carried out in 2002.[33]

About a month before 9/11, the Pentagon held a mass casualty exercise involving the evacuation of the building after it was hit by an airplane. General Lance Lord, head of US Air Force Space Command, later said that on 9/11, thanks to this practice just a month earlier, "our assembly points were fresh in our minds." He then added: "Purely a coincidence, the scenario for that exercise included a plane hitting the building."[34]

At 9:00AM on the morning of 9/11, the National Reconnaissance Office in Chantilly, Virginia, had planned to simulate the accidental crashing of an airplane into its headquarters, just 24 miles from the Pentagon.[35]

Information Provided at Commission Hearings: Besides ignoring all these reports, the 9/11 Commission even ignored, in issuing its final report, information that had been discussed in its own hearings.

During the hearing of May 23, 2003, when military leaders were testifying, Richard Ben-Veniste tried to extract information from General Craig McKinley and Colonel Alan Scott about the aforementioned exercise called Amalgam Virgo 02. This exercise, as we saw, was planned in July 2001 to take place in June 2002 and would have involved multiple hijackings. Pointing out that "[t]he concept of terrorists using airplanes as weapons was not something which was unknown to the U.S. intelligence community on September 10th, 2001," Ben-Veniste asked General McKinley: "[I]sn't it a fact, sir, that prior to September 11th, 2001, NORAD had already in the works plans to simulate in an exercise a simultaneous hijacking of two planes in the United States?… That was Operation Amalgam Virgo." After McKinley passed the question off to Scott, who said he knew nothing about it, McKinley read a prepared statement, which failed to address Ben-Veniste's question about simultaneous hijackings. At that point, Ben-Veniste, apparently realizing that he would not get an answer, moved on to another issue.[36]

In 2004, former FBI director Louis Freeh informed the Commission that in 2000 and 2001, planning for events designated "National Special Security Events" involved the possible use of "planes as weapons" and that "resources were actually designated to deal with that particular threat." The planning, he said, even included "the use of airplanes, either packed with explosives or otherwise, in suicide missions."[37]

When *The 9/11 Commission Report* appeared, it made no mention of Freeh's statement, the information about Amalgam Virgo 02, or most of the other evidence that contradicted the military's claim not to have envisaged 9/11-type attacks. So, although the 9/11 Commission mentioned a few reports that were in tension with this claim, its overall effect was to support the claims of the military and the Bush administration. This support was most clearly expressed in the following summary statements.

> In sum, the protocols in place on 9/11 for the FAA and NORAD to respond to a hijacking presumed that… the hijacking would take the traditional form: that is, it would not be a suicide hijacking designed to convert the aircraft into a guided missile…. NORAD and the FAA were unprepared for the type of attacks launched against the United States on September 11, 2001. They struggled, under difficult circumstances, to improvise a homeland defense against an unprecedented challenge they had never before encountered and had never trained to meet.[38]

In *Without Precedent*, a book billed as "the inside story of the 9/11 Commission," its chair and vice chair, Thomas Kean and Lee Hamilton, restated this claim, saying:

Why did NORAD fail to intercept any of the hijacked planes?.... [T]hose responding to the events... had not trained for the scenario they were facing. Before 9/11, NORAD's main focus had been repelling an air attack on America by foreign bombers or ballistic missiles, not by civilian aircraft.... [W]e had not imagined hijacked civilian airliners being used as guided missiles.[39]

Conclusion

The position of the Bush administration (including then Secretary of Defense Rumsfeld) and the 9/11 Commission is clearly contradicted by numerous reports issued by military and other official bodies. As mentioned at the outset of this chapter, this contradiction, involving the question of whether 9/11-type attacks had been envisioned, became perceived as less important after the publication of *The 9/11 Commission Report*, which claimed that the military had not even been notified about most of the flights until after they had crashed. The fact remains, however, that the Bush administration and the 9/11 Commission contradicted a great deal of publicly available evidence about this matter. Indeed, as we have just seen, Kean and Hamilton, in a book published two years after *The 9/11 Commission Report*, continued to state that the military had "not imagined hijacked civilian airliners being used as guided missiles," in spite of all the evidence to the contrary, including military exercises based around just such an eventuality. Congress and the press need to discover and report the reasons for this contradiction.[40]

PART III

Questions about Osama bin Laden and the Hijackers

15

WERE MOHAMED ATTA AND THE OTHER HIJACKERS DEVOUT MUSLIMS?

Accord ing to the official story of 9/11, the planes were hijacked by devout Muslims ready to meet their Maker. *The 9/11 Commission Report* supported this picture, saying of Mohamed Atta, the supposed ringleader, that he had become very religious, even "fanatically so."[1] This image of Atta and the other alleged hijackers as devout Muslims contributed to the Commission's characterization of them as a "cadre of trained operatives willing to die."[2] But there have been many stories in mainstream newspapers that contradict the claim that they were devout Muslims.

Reports of Illicit Sex and Heavy Drinking

Five days after 9/11, a story in London's *Daily Mail* contained this report:

> At the Palm Beach bar Sunrise 251, [Mohamed] Atta and [Marwan] Al Shehhi spent $1,000 in 45 minutes on Krug and Perrier-Jouet champagne.... Atta was with a 6ft busty brunette in her late twenties; the other man was with a shortish blonde. Both women were known locally as regular companions of high-rollers.[3]

One month after 9/11, a *Boston Herald* story, entitled "Terrorists Partied with Hooker at Hub-Area Hotel," said:

> A driver for a pair of local escort services told the *Herald* yesterday that he drove a call girl to the Park Inn in Chestnut Hill on Sept. 9 around 10:30PM where she bedded down with one of the mass murderers. It was her second trip to the terrorist's room

that day. Two of the hijackers aboard Flight 11 that crashed into the World Trade Center—Waleed M. Alshehri and Wail Alshehri—spent Sept. 9 in the Route 9 hotel, sources said.... The dirty Hub dalliances of the terrorists is just the latest link between the Koran-toting killers and America's seedy sex scene. In Florida, several of the hijackers—including reputed ringleader Mohamed Atta—spent $200 to $300 each on lap dances in the Pink Pony strip club.[4]

A week earlier, a *San Francisco Chronicle* article, "Agents of Terror Leave Their Mark on Sin City," reported that at least five of the "self-styled warriors for Allah," including Mohamed Atta, had "engaged in some decidedly un-Islamic sampling of prohibited pleasures [including lap dances] in America's reputed capital of moral corrosion," Las Vegas. The group, investigators said, had "made at least six trips here." The story then quoted Dr. Osama Haikal, president of the board of directors of the Islamic Foundation of Nevada, as saying: "True Muslims don't drink, don't gamble, don't go to strip clubs."[5]

On October 10, the *Wall Street Journal*, in an editorial entitled "Terrorist Stag Parties," summarized both of these stories.[6]

Whereas the *Journal*'s editorial pointed to the contradiction only implicitly, by means of its ironic title, the problem had already been drawn out explicitly, five days after 9/11, by a story in the *South Florida Sun-Sentinel* entitled "Suspects' Actions Don't Add Up," which said:

Three guys cavorting with lap dancers at the Pink Pony Nude Theater. Two others knocking back glasses of Stolichnaya and rum and Coke at a fish joint in Hollywood the weekend before committing suicide and mass murder. That might describe the behavior of several men who are suspects in Tuesday's terrorist attack, but it is not a picture of devout Muslims, experts say. Let alone that of religious zealots in their final days on Earth.... [A] devout Muslim [cannot] drink booze or party at a strip club and expect to reach heaven, said Mahmoud Mustafa Ayoub, a professor at Temple University in Philadelphia. The most basic tenets of the religion forbid alcohol and any sex outside marriage. "It is incomprehensible that a person could drink and go to a strip bar one night, then kill themselves the next day in the name of Islam," said Ayoub. "People who would kill themselves for their faith would come from very strict Islamic ideology. Something here does not add up."[7]

As this story pointed out, the behavior of these men seemed to contradict the idea that they were "devout Muslim[s]" ready to "kill themselves for their faith."

The Episode at Shuckums on September 7

One of the references in the just-quoted *Sun-Sentinel* story—about two of the hijackers "knocking back glasses of Stolichnaya and rum and Coke at a fish joint in Hollywood the weekend before [9/11]"—is worthy of special treatment, because early reports of this episode were contradicted by later ones. The episode occurred on Friday, September 7, at a restaurant called "Shuckums" in Hollywood, Florida (close to Miami).

According to early reports, Atta was drunk. On September 12, the Associated Press published a story by Ken Thomas based on an interview with the manager, Tony Amos. After reporting that Amos, having been shown photos of the two men, had identified the one signed "Mohamed," Thomas wrote:

> Amos said the two men had each consumed several drinks Friday night and had given the bartender a hard time.... "The guy Mohamed was drunk, his voice was slurred and he had a thick accent," Amos said. Bartender Patricia Idrissi said the men argued over the bill, and when she asked if there was a problem, "Mohamed said he worked for American Airlines and he could pay his bill."[8]

The next day, the *St. Petersburg Times* quoted the bartender to this effect, writing:

> Tony Amos, the night manager at Shuckums Bar in Hollywood, told the Palm Beach Post that Atta argued with him over his tab. When Amos asked Atta whether he could pay, Atta got offended and said, "I'm a pilot for American Airlines and I can pay my bill," bartender Patricia Idrissi said. "They were wasted," said Idrissi, who said she directed the two men to a Chinese restaurant a few doors down. They later returned and each ordered about five drinks, she said.[9]

That same day, September 13, a *New York Times* story by Dana Canedy and David Sanger said:

> Patricia Idrissi would not have noticed [Mohamed Atta] except that he drank Stolichnaya vodka for three hours [while Marwan al-Shehhi drank rum] and then seemed not to want to pay his $48 bar tab. The man's response when Ms. Idrissi called her manager [was], "Of course I can pay.... I'm a pilot."[10]

Three days later, Eric Bailey of London's *Daily Mail*, having identified Atta's companion as Marwan al-Shehhi, wrote:

> Atta and Al Shehhi went with another man to Shuckums bar in Hollywood, Florida. The man went off to play a video machine, while Atta and Al Shehhi ordered the first of five rounds of Stolichnaya vodka with orange juice.[11]

That same day, September 16, a story in Scotland's *Sunday Herald* gave an account in which Atta used quite colorful language. According to this story:

> Last Friday Atta... and two other Middle Eastern men were spotted at a bar in Hollywood in Florida called Shuckums. They ran up a bill and started rowing with waitress Patricia Idrissi over the cost of their vodkas and rums. Atta shouted at the manager: "You think I can't pay? I'm a pilot for American Airlines. I can pay my f***ing bill."[12]

A timeline published in the *Miami Herald* on September 22 still reflected this version of the story, saying:

> Sept. 7: ... Shuckums, a raw bar on Hollywood's Harrison Street. Al-Shehhi and Atta knocked back drinks—forbidden by the Islamic teachings they so zealously embraced. The men bickered with a bartender over a $48 tab.[13]

This version of the story also appeared in September 24 issue of *Time* magazine, which wrote:

> [A]t Shuckums, ... Mohamed Atta and Marwan Al-Shehhi did some pre-mass murder tippling. Atta drank vodka and orange juice, while Al-Shehhi preferred rum and cokes, five drinks apiece. "They were wasted," the bartender recalled, and Atta objected to the $48 bill.[14]

Newsweek, appearing the same day, gave a still more startling account, in which Atta blasphemed. Evan Thomas and Mark Hosenball, having noted that Atta "could knock back a vodka with his buddies," wrote:

> Last week Atta and two of his buddies seem to have gone out for a farewell bender at a seafood bar called Shuckums. Atta drank five Stoli-and-fruit-juices, while one of the others drank rum and Coke. For once, Atta and his friends became agitated, shouting curse words in Arabic, reportedly including a particularly blasphemous one that roughly translates as "F—k God."[15]

Thomas and Hosenball's account, with both the drinking and the blasphemous language, was in strong tension with their own characterization of the hijackers as "a small band of religious zealots."[16]

This tension was more or less completely overcome in a new version of the Shuckums story, which began to emerge quite early. According to a September 15 article in the *Toronto Star*, here is what happened at Shuckums:

> While Atta played video games the other two had about five drinks each and then argued about the $48 bill. Manager Tony Amos recalled this week that, when he inquired whether they could not afford their bill, Al-Shehhi "looked at me with an arrogant look." "He pulled out a wad of cash," Amos said, "and put it on the bar table and said 'There is no money issue. I am an airline pilot.'"[17]

In this version, therefore, Atta did not drink or swear or even speak in an arrogant manner. Apparently the first writer to articulate this new version within the United States was Joel Achenbach of the *Washington Post*, who on September 16 wrote:

> Atta played video Trivial Pursuit and blackjack with great determination.... Al-Shehhi and the other man had about five drinks each, [manager Tony Amos] said—Captain Morgan rum and Coke, and Stolichnaya vodka and orange juice.... "Al-Shehhi was definitely upset," Amos said. The bartender feared that Al-Shehhi might leave without paying his $48 tab. The manager intervened, asking if there was a problem. Al-Shehhi, glaring, ... said: "There is no money issue. I am an airline pilot."[18]

According to Achenbach, then, Atta, besides not drinking alcohol, did not get upset about the bill. On September 22, the Atta-does-not-drink part of this new version was told in another *Washington Post* article, "A Fanatics' Quiet Path to Terror," by Peter Finn. During the three-and-a-half hours that Atta and two other men spent at Shuckums, Finn wrote,

> Atta played video games, a pursuit out of line with fundamentalist beliefs. But the manager on duty that night has said that he doesn't recall seeing Atta drink alcohol.[19]

Five days later, on September 27, the *St. Petersburg Times*, which on September 13 had quoted the bartender as saying that Atta and his drinking companion "were wasted," told the new version, saying:

> Witnesses say Atta plays video games while al-Shehhi and another man sip vodka and orange juice at Shuckums Oyster Pub and Seafood Grill in Hollywood.[20]

Atta, of course, had to drink *something*. This detail was filled in by a *Los Angeles Times* story on September 27, which said:

> [Shuckums'] owner, Tony Amos, says Atta sat quietly by himself and drank cranberry juice and played a video game, while Al-Shehhi and the other customer tossed back mixed drinks and argued.[21]

That same week, the Atta-drank-cranberry-juice story appeared in *Time* magazine, which wrote:

> Atta, Al-Shehhi and another man visited Shuckums.... Contrary to earlier reports of his carousing, Atta was the only one of the three who didn't drink alcohol. Instead, he downed cranberry juice all night, sugary fuel for the pinball machine... that he played for 3 1/2 hours.[22]

In the new version, therefore, other hijackers may have drunk alcohol, but Atta did not. And he no longer swore. His behavior was consistent with that of a devout Muslim.

Dealing with the Contradictions involving Alcohol & Sex

How did the 9/11 Commission deal with stories about the hijackers having an appetite for alcohol and illicit sex? By ignoring them. In spite of the fact that several mainstream publications, including the *Wall Street Journal*, had carried such stories, the Commission wrote as if they did not exist. For example, referring to a trip to Las Vegas by Atta and two other hijackers roughly a month before 9/11, the Commission wrote: "Beyond Las Vegas's reputation for welcoming tourists, we have seen no credible evidence explaining why, on this occasion and others, the operatives flew to or met in Las Vegas."[23]

With regard to Atta in particular, the Commission simply asserted that by 1998, he had "adopted fundamentalism," becoming "fanatically [religious],"[24] without dealing with any of the stories that seemed to contradict this image. Even though the later version of the Shuckums episode, in which Atta drank cranberry juice, could have been employed, the Commission did not mention this episode. Indeed, the Commission even implicitly denied that it had occurred at all. In its description of Atta's activities in the week before the attacks:

> Atta was still busy coordinating the teams. On September 7, he flew from Fort Lauderdale to Baltimore, presumably to meet with the Flight 77 team in Laurel. On September 9, he flew from Baltimore to Boston.[25]

The Commission's ability to portray Atta as a fundamentalist Muslim could have certainly been made easier by the fact that the most well-known story about his drinking, the episode at Shuckums, had become modified in later renditions. According to the Commission, however, Atta on September 7 did not spend any time in a bar whatsoever. He instead was all business, flying north for a meeting on the Friday before the attacks rather than remaining in Florida. The Commission thereby contradicted one of the most widely reported stories about Atta.

However, although the Commission ignored all the stories about Atta's appetite for sex and alcohol, and even the cranberry-juice version of the Shuckums episode, these stories remain in the public record. These stories, moreover, were not the only ones that contradicted the Commission's profile of Mohamed Atta. There were also stories that had him living with a stripper in Venice, which is on the west coast of Florida, in 2001.

Reports that Atta Lived in Venice in 2001, Part of the Time with a Stripper

According to the 9/11 Commission, Atta never actually lived in Venice, Florida. He and his constant companion, Marwan al-Shehhi, did take flight training at Huffman Aviation, in Venice during most of the period from July to December 2000. While doing this, however, they lived in Nokomis, the town just north of Venice. And when they finished their training, in December of 2000, they moved to southeastern Florida, never to return.[26] The sole source cited by the Commission for this information was an FBI report entitled "Hijackers Timeline."[27]

This account is challenged, however, by stories that appeared in local newspapers immediately after 9/11 reporting that Atta had lived in Venice. According to a September 14 story by Christy Arnold in the *Charlotte Sun*:

> Paula Grapentine immediately recognized the face of a suspected terrorist who may have trained for the World Trade Center attacks at Huffman Aviation in Venice. He was her next-door neighbor. Postal Carrier Neil Patton also recollects the names and faces of Mohamed Atta, 33, Marwan Alshehhi, 23, and four other Middle Eastern flight school students. They lived at the Sandpiper Apartments, unit 26, in Venice until earlier this year [2001].[28]

Another story in the same paper that same day, written by Elaine Allen-Emrich and Jann Baty, was based on an interview with Tony and Vonnie LaConca of nearby North Port. They had rented a place to a man they knew as "Mohamed," who was 5 feet 10 inches tall, had "dark, perfect" skin, and was training at Huffman Aviation. According to this story,

> Mohamed was associated with a local woman believed to be Amanda Keller, a local restaurant manager, [Tony] LaConca said.... "Mohamed bailed her out of South County Jail," Vonnie LaConca said.... After meeting Mohamed and Keller on Feb. 21, [another young woman] joined the couple on an adventure to Key West the following day. "They were gone for three days.... They didn't sleep—it was a continuous party." LaConca said Mohamed footed the entire bill for the weekend

including buying Keller and the unnamed [woman] new clothes, alcohol, drugs and hotel stay.[29]

The account by the LaConcas contradicted the idea that Atta was on the other side of the state in February 2001. It also added some more information inconsistent with the 9/11 Commission's portrait of Atta as a devout, fundamentalist Muslim: He reportedly spent a drug-and-booze weekend with Amanda Keller, with whom he was "associated."

The nature of this association was further specified in a September 22 story in the *Sarasota Herald-Tribune* (which is owned by the *New York Times*). This story, written by Earle Kimel and two other reporters, stated:

> Atta may have been in Venice as recently as April [2001]. Charles Grapentine, the manager of Sandpiper Apartments on Airport Avenue in Venice, said he remembers seeing Atta at the complex for about three weeks in April. He said Atta was living in the apartment of Amanda Keller.[30]

So, besides living in Venice, when he was supposedly living on the other side of the state, Atta was living, not with five other men, but with Amanda Keller. Kimel's article then added:

> In a telephone interview late Friday, Keller said… authorities told her not to say anything at all about Atta. "I can't really discuss anything," she said. "I'm afraid I'll get in trouble." Keller's mother, Susan Payne of Lady Lake, remembered Atta. "I didn't like him; he just seemed strange," she said.[31]

According to Keller's mother, then, she had met Atta, and if what Keller herself told Kimel was true, "authorities" did not want her talking about Atta. That story appeared Saturday, September 22, 2001.

The very next day, a contradictory story appeared in the same paper, the *Sarasota Herald-Tribune*, by a different reporter, Chris Grier. It said:

> Investigators have identified a fifth man of Middle Eastern descent who trained to fly in Venice, but… they can't find him…. The man, known as Mohammed, stayed at Amanda Keller's unit in the Sandpiper Apartment complex on Airport Avenue in April. Authorities would not release the man's full

name and Keller would not divulge it, citing instructions from the Florida Department of Law Enforcement…. Keller said comments attributed to her in the *Herald-Tribune* on Saturday, saying that Atta lived in her apartment, were wrong. She said that it was this unidentified fifth man, also named Mohammed, that stayed in her home…. The fifth man being eyed by investigators was tall, lanky and quiet, according to Keller's mother…. Susan Payne, Keller's mother, said her daughter and then-boyfriend Garrett Metts often took in strangers at her apartment…. In an interview at her mother's house, Keller wouldn't talk about the man who stayed on her couch.[32]

Although this article was clearly intended to break the connection between Atta and Amanda Keller, it was unconvincing. According to Christy Arnold's article, both Paula Grapentine and the postal carrier had recognized Atta's picture. According to the article by Elaine Allen-Emrich and Jann Batty, the LaConcas had said that the Mohamed they knew, who was associated with Amanda Keller, was about 5 foot 10 inches, not "tall and lanky." This Mohamed, moreover, had taken Keller to Key West and then bailed her out of jail; he was not a stranger who had been invited to stay with her and her boyfriend. According to Earle Kimel's article, moreover, Charles Grapentine, the manager of the Sandpiper Apartments, had remembered Atta and said that he had been living in the apartment with Amanda Keller, not simply staying there a few days with her and her boyfriend.

Nevertheless, when the FBI put out a press release about the suspected hijackers on September 27, its list of Mohamed Atta's "possible residences" said: "Hollywood, Florida; Coral Springs, Florida; Hamburg, Germany." Venice, therefore, was not even a *possible* residence.[33]

In the following years, however, the original stories, which challenge the FBI's position, would be corroborated by an investigative reporter.

Daniel Hopsicker's Account of Atta and Amanda Keller

A couple of months after 9/11, investigative reporter Daniel Hopsicker went to Venice. On the basis of interviews with witnesses mentioned in the local newspaper accounts and finally with Amanda Keller herself (who had in the meantime moved to another state), he gave the following account of Atta's locations and his relationship with Keller.

After Atta completed flight training at Huffman Aviation in December 2000, he and several other men rented an "immense and beautiful" house in North Port until they were evicted at the end of February 2001. During the weekend of February 25–28, Amanda Keller, who had decided to leave her husband, agreed to go to Key West with Atta, whom she had met while she was managing Papa John's Pizza. They were accompanied by two German men, named Peter and Stephan, and a stripper named Linda.[34] While in Key West, the three men used cocaine. (Keller also reported that she saw Atta using cocaine—which he got from Huffman Aviation—on other occasions.)[35] Keller confirmed, moreover, that Atta also drank heavily. Hopsicker, referring to the later modification of the Shuckums episode, said: "it's not as if the Shuckums story was the only drinking incident: there were many." One day, Keller reported, "Mohamed and a bunch of his cronies, drunk and stoned out of their minds," came to the place where she worked, screaming to see her.[36]

In any case, somewhere during this period, she and Atta had decided to share an apartment, which would be in her name although he would pay the rent.[37] Upon their return from Key West, a fight between Keller and her husband led to her being arrested and put in jail, after which Atta bailed her out.[38] She then helped Atta move from the North Port house, from which he had been evicted, to a North Port rental unit owned by Tony and Vonnie LaConca, where Atta lived for a week in early March, while she was finding a place for them to live.[39] Keller and Atta then moved into unit 26 of the Sandpiper Apartments while Atta's friends took a downstairs unit.[40]

But things did not go well. Keller soon came to dislike Atta, but she had to put up with him because he was paying the rent (she admitted to Hopsicker that she was using Atta).[41] Soon, however, she took a job as a stripper and private dancer at a place called "Fantasies and Lingerie," where she started making $3,000 a week.[42] Some time after this, she met a much more attractive man, named Garrett Metts, whom she started inviting to sleep over. She forced Atta to sleep on the couch, which led him to become increasingly abusive. No longer needing Atta's money, she soon, with the support of the apartment manager, kicked him out.[43]

Contrary to Chris Grier's claim, therefore, the man sleeping on her couch was Mohamed Atta, not some other man with the same first name. Keller had recanted her original statement about having lived with Atta, she said, because of intimidation from the FBI (which was also experienced, Hopsicker learned, by Keller's neighbor at the Sandpiper Apartments, Stephanie Frederickson). Alluding to Kimel's article, she said: "The newspaper quote was accurate: 'I can't say anything because I'm afraid I'll get in trouble.'"[44]

With regard to Chris Grier himself, both Keller and Frederickson said that he, claiming that he worked for the *New York Times* (instead of merely the *Sarasota Herald-Tribune*, which is owned by the *Times*), tried to get them to change their stories. (Hopsicker reported, incidentally, that Grier was later fired from the *Tribune* for "snooping through other reporters' computers."[45])

In any case, although Hopsicker cited many people in the Venice area who could corroborate one or more elements in his account,[46] the *Sarasota Herald-Tribune*, on the fifth anniversary of 9/11, again claimed that Keller had recanted her statement that she had lived with Atta. In a story entitled "'Lover': Amanda Keller," the reporter, Heather Allen, claimed that Keller admitted that she had lied to Hopsicker. Allen wrote:

> For five years, Amanda Keller has been portrayed by conspiracy theorists as Mohamed Atta's lover. But the former Venice stripper now says her boyfriend was another flight student not connected to 9/11…. "There's nothing there to corroborate the relationship between the two," a New York-based FBI counterterrorism agent said recently after reviewing 9/11 case files. The agent got clearance to talk from the U.S. Attorney's Office and the FBI, but only agreed if his named [*sic*] was not used.[47]

It should be noted that this anonymous agent stated merely that there was nothing to corroborate the relationship between Atta and Keller *in the FBI files*. The question of whether there was anything to corroborate the relationship *in Venice*—such as the many witnesses cited by Hopsicker—went unaddressed.

Further Sightings of Atta in Venice

The FBI's timeline was contradicted, moreover, not only by Hopsicker and previous journalists insofar as they reported Atta's presence in Venice from January to May, during which he had an affair with Amanda Keller. They also reported that Atta's presence in Venice did not end in May, when he was kicked out of the Sandpiper Apartments, but that he was repeatedly seen in the area in July and August. On October 1, 2001, a CNN report said:

> In Punta Gorda, Florida, the owner of The Shipping Post told CNN that Atta and one unidentified associate came into her store several times between mid-July and mid-August and purchased money orders on at least two occasions. "He was very cold," said Jeanne Waldorf.... Atta attended an aviation school in Venice, Florida, which is just north of Punta Gorda.[48]

Waldorf's testimony was also reported by the Associated Press.[49]

Hopsicker, stating that after moving away, Atta and al-Shehhi returned to Venice three times in the six weeks before 9/11, quoted four additional witnesses: Betty Cover, a deli clerk at the Publix supermarket near the Venice airport; Tom and Rene Adorna, who own the Pelican Alley restaurant, near one of the places where Atta and al-Shehhi had lived; Brad Warrick, the owner of a car rental agency in Pompano Beach; and Bob Simpson, a Venice Yellow Cab driver. Both Warrick and Simpson said that they had reported their contacts with Atta to the FBI.[50] Simpson, moreover, stated that during at least one of Atta's last visits, he met with the owner of Huffman Aviation, Rudi Dekkers—contrary to Dekkers's testimony to a Congressional committee in 2002 that he never saw Atta in the eight months prior to 9/11.[51]

Dealing with the Contradictions about Atta's Whereabouts

There are clearly contradictions between the FBI's account, according to which Atta was not in the Venice area in 2001, and accounts provided by the local newspapers and—with regard to

July and August—CNN and the Associated Press, which were then corroborated by investigative reporter Daniel Hopsicker.

How did the 9/11 Commission deal with these contradictory accounts of Atta's whereabouts and activities? It simply ignored them. The Commission did not mention of any of those local news articles that spoke of Atta's presence in Venice in the early months of 2001, some of which referred to his relationship with Amanda Keller. Nor did it mention his visits in July and August, reported by CNN and the Associated Press. Rather, the Commission simply told a story based on the FBI's timeline. Reporting that both Atta and al-Shehhi took trips abroad early in January 2001, the Commission wrote:

> After returning to Florida from their trips, Atta and Shehhi visited Georgia.... By February 19, Atta and Shehhi were in Virginia... and then promptly returned to Georgia.... We have found no explanation for these travels. [This is the period during which, according to the local newspapers, Atta and al-Shehhi were living in North Port, near Venice.] In early April, Atta and Shehhi returned to Virginia Beach.... On April 11, they moved into an apartment in Coral Springs. [According to newspapers in the Venice area, Atta was then living with Amanda Keller.] ... [O]n May 2, ... Atta and [Ziad] Jarrah were together about 30 miles to the north [of Miami], visiting a Department of Motor Vehicles office in Lauderdale Lakes, Florida. [According to people in Venice, this was when Atta's relationship to Keller was about to end.][52]

The contradiction between these accounts could hardly be greater.

Hopsicker, moreover, brought out the subversive implications of the portrait of Atta that emerges from Amanda Keller's account of his activities in the early months of 2001: "The more we heard about Mohamed Atta, the more his image as an Islamic fundamentalist began to crumble."[53]

Although the national press did not pick up the story about Atta's relationship with Amanda Keller, including the *Charlotte Sun's* report of (in Hopsicker's words) the "very un-Islamic three-day drug-and-booze-fueled party in Key West,"[54] some members of the press did become aware of at least some of this reported behavior. According to a writer who was at the first hearing of the 9/11 Commission, in March of 2003, one member of the press asked Commissioner Richard Ben-Veniste: "If Atta belonged to the fundamentalist Muslim group, why was he snorting cocaine and frequenting strip bars?" Ben-Veniste reportedly replied, "You know, that's a heck of a question."[55] But it was a question that the 9/11 Commission, when it issued its report sixteen months later, did not address.

Conclusion

The contradiction between the Commission's portrayal of Mohamed Atta and the other supposed hijackers as devout Muslims, on the one hand, and their actual behavior as reported by a wide variety of sources, on the other, is an issue that does need to be addressed. Congress and the press need to ask why this contradiction exists and why the 9/11 Commission failed to address it.

16

WHERE DID AUTHORITIES FIND ATTA'S TREASURE TROVE OF INFORMATION?

On the first page of *The 9/11 Commission Report*, we read:

> Tuesday, September 11, 2001.... For those heading to an airport, weather conditions could not have been better.... Among the travelers were Mohamed Atta and Abdul Aziz al Omari, who arrived at the airport in Portland, Maine.... Atta and Omari boarded a 6:00AM flight from Portland to Boston's Logan International Airport.[1]

The note for this seemingly unproblematic statement said:

> No physical, documentary, or analytical evidence provides a convincing explanation of why Atta and Omari drove to Portland, Maine, from Boston on the morning of September 10, only to return to Logan on Flight 5930 on the morning of September 11.... Whatever their reason, the Portland Jetport was the nearest airport to Boston with a 9/11 flight that would have arrived at Logan in time for the passengers to transfer to American Airlines Flight 11, which had a scheduled departure time of 7:45AM.[2]

This admission by the Commission, that it could not explain why Atta would have taken this trip, had earlier been made by FBI Director Robert Mueller, during his testimony on September 26, 2002, to the Congressional Joint Inquiry into 9/11. Having stated that Marwan al-Shehhi, after flying from Florida to Boston, had taken a room at the Milner Hotel, Mueller said:

> On September 9, Mohamed Atta also checked into the Milner Hotel staying that night where he met with Marwan al-Shehhi. Shortly after noon on the day before the attacks, Mohamed Atta left the Milner Hotel, picked up Abdul Aziz al Omari at the Park

Inn, and drove to Portland, Maine. They checked into the Comfort Inn in South Portland. Atta and al Omari were seen together on several occasions in the Portland area later that evening but their reason for going there, to date, remains unclear.[3]

That same admission had been made two weeks earlier, on the first anniversary of 9/11, in a *New York Times* article, which said:

> There have been many theories [as to why Atta and Omari made the trip]: that they made contact with a confederate in Portland who gave them the final go-ahead, or more likely, that by arriving on a connecting flight, they would avoid the security check in Boston. None of those explanations seems entirely satisfactory, given the risk.[4]

Those final three words, "given the risk," explain why the trip has been so puzzling.

Two Mysteries: The Portland Trip and Atta's Luggage

The 9/11 Commission, after stating that on September 10 Atta and al-Omari "drove to Portland, Maine, for reasons that remain unknown," said: "In the early morning hours of September 11, they boarded a commuter flight to Boston to connect to American Airlines Flight 11."[5] This flight, as we saw above, left Portland at 6:00AM and arrived at the Boston airport at 6:45, enabling Atta and his companion to get on AA Flight 11, which was scheduled to depart at 7:45.

But if the commuter flight from Portland to Boston had been delayed by an hour, Atta and al-Omari would have missed the connection. This point was even made in a statement submitted by the 9/11 Commission staff on June 16, 2004. This statement said (in a sentence that did not make it into the Commission's final report): "The Portland detour almost prevented Atta and Omari from making Flight 11 out of Boston."[6] If this had happened, there would have been only three hijackers to take control of Flight 11. Atta, moreover, was reportedly the designated pilot for this flight and also the ringleader of the whole operation. After years of planning for this operation, he might have had to call it off. Why would Atta, after already being in Boston on September 10, have taken such an enormous risk? No satisfactory explanation had emerged one year later, as the *New York Times* observed, or even three years later, as the 9/11 Commission admitted.[7]

The Commission's story about this episode contained another unexplained element. Although Atta made the connection to Flight 11, his luggage did not—a fact that led to important discoveries. The above-quoted 9/11 Commission staff statement, just after saying that the Portland detour almost caused Atta and al-Omari to miss Flight 11, added:

> In fact, the luggage they checked in Portland failed to make it onto the plane. Seized after the September 11 crashes, Atta and Omari's luggage turned out to contain a number of telling items, including: correspondence from the university Atta attended in Egypt; Omari's international driver's license and passport; [and] a video cassette for a Boeing 757 flight simulator.[8]

Mueller, in his testimony to the Joint Inquiry in 2002, had also reported the discovery of this treasure trove of information, saying:

> Following the crash of Flight 11, authorities recovered two pieces of luggage in the name of Mohamed Atta that had not been loaded onto that flight. A search of this baggage revealed a three page letter handwritten in Arabic, which, upon translation, was found to contain instructions on how to prepare for a mission applicable, but not specific, to the September 11 operation.[9]

In 2006, *Newsday* would publish a story by Michael Dorman, entitled "Unraveling 9-11 was in the Bags," which elevated the importance of this discovery even further. Dorman reported that Warren Flagg, a former FBI agent, had said that one of Atta's bags contained far more than what had been previously reported, including the names of the hijackers. Although Flagg was already retired by September of 2001, he obtained this information, he said, from a young FBI agent whom he had helped train and who was working on the 9/11 investigation. According to Dorman, Flagg said:

> It had all these Arab-language papers that amounted to the Rosetta stone of the investigation. How do you think the government was able to identify all 19 hijackers almost immediately after the attacks? They were identified through those papers in the luggage. And that's how it was known so soon that al-Qaida was behind the hijackings.[10]

Whatever the historical accuracy of Flagg's statement, it served, by describing the treasure trove of information found in Atta's luggage as the investigation's "Rosetta stone," to bring out the importance of this reported discovery.

But why did Atta's luggage not get loaded onto Flight 11? The 9/11 Commission staff statement, quoted above, implied that it was a tight connection, with Atta and al-Omari just barely making it. That statement, however, was not included in *The 9/11 Commission Report*, which instead said: "Atta and Omari arrived in Boston at 6:45.... Between 6:45 and 7:40, Atta and Omari... checked in and boarded American Airlines Flight 11... scheduled to depart at 7:45."[11] There was, in other words, a full hour between the arrival of the commuter flight and the scheduled departure time of Flight 11. Also, the failure could not be explained by reference to a careless ground crew, because "Atta was the only passenger among the 81 aboard American Flight 11 whose luggage didn't make the flight, American sources confirm[ed]."[12]

We have, therefore, two mysteries. Why would Atta have risked the trip to Portland? And why did his luggage fail to get loaded onto Flight 11? This book, to be sure, is about contradictions, not mysteries. Clues to these mysteries, however, can be found by exploring a full-fledged contradiction in the Portland story. That is, the 9/11 Commission's story about Atta driving to Portland contradicts stories that appeared in the press in the first days after 9/11.

The Original Story: Boston and the Bukharis

According to all later news stories about the trip, Atta drove to Portland in a Nissan Altima that he had rented at Boston's Logan Airport. In the first few days after 9/11, however, the story was very different.

On September 12, Susan Candiotti of CNN gave this report from Vero Beach, Florida:

> Law enforcement sources say that two of the suspected hijackers... are brothers that lived here.... One of them is Adnan Bukhari. We have a photograph of him.... Also living in Vero

Beach, Bukhari's brother, Ameer.... Law enforcement sources... tell CNN that the Bukhari brothers were believed to have been on one of the two flights out of Boston.... Also we can report to you that a car impounded in Portland, Maine, according to law enforcement authorities, was rented at Boston Logan Airport and driven to Portland, Maine. Now the Maine state police confirm that two of the suspected hijackers were on a U.S. Air flight [to] Logan Airport.... The FBI is also looking at two more suspected hijackers..., Mohammad [sic] Atta and Marwan Yusef Alshehhi. Now they stayed for a few days at the home of Charlie Voss in Venice, Florida. And they took courses at Hoffman [sic] Aviation.[13]

This report seemed to suggest that two brothers named Adnan and Ameer Bukhari were the two hijackers who drove to Portland and then took a commuter flight back to Boston. Atta was mentioned, but not in connection with the rental car that was impounded in Portland.

The reason for Candiotti's reference to Charlie Voss, as a person with whom Atta and al-Shehhi had stayed, was spelled out in Christy Arnold's September 14 story in the *Charlotte Sun*, mentioned in the previous chapter, which said:

Atta and Alshehhi are suspected of helping crash airliners into the World Trade Center on Tuesday.... Authorities first recognized Atta's name on one of the flight's passenger manifests. They then found a car abandoned at Logan Airport in Boston which connected Atta's name to a South Venice address of Charles and Drucilla Voss. The two men stayed with the Vosses for a short time in July 2000.[14]

These two stories, therefore, seemed to say that the Bukharis left a rental car at the airport in Portland and that Atta left one at the airport in Boston.

On September 13, CNN—in a story that is no longer available on its website—gave a more complete account, which said:

Two of the men were brothers, ... Adnan Bukhari and Ameer Abbas Bukhari.... The two rented a car, a silver-blue Nissan Altima, from an Alamo car rental at Boston's Logan Airport and drove to an airport in Portland, Maine, where they got on US Airways Flight 5930 at 6AM Tuesday headed back to

Boston, the sources said…. Before CNN learned the identities of the two brothers, Portland Police Chief Mike Chitwood said, "I can tell you those two individuals did get on a plane and fly to Boston early yesterday morning… I can tell you that they are the focus of a federal investigation." …

Charles Voss, a bookkeeper for Huffman [Aviation], … confirmed he briefly allowed two students from the flight school to stay at his house…, Mohammed [*sic*] Atta and Marwan Yousef Alshehhi…. A Mitsubishi sedan impounded at Logan Airport was rented by Atta, sources said. The car contained materials, including flight manuals, written in Arabic that law enforcement sources called "helpful" to the investigation.[15]

According to the original story, therefore, the Bukharis left the Nissan Altima in Portland, whereas Atta had left a rented Mitsubishi at Logan Airport in Boston. It was in this Mitsubishi, moreover, that authorities found the treasure trove of information that was helpful to the investigation—not, as Mueller and the 9/11 Commission would later claim, in luggage that failed to get transferred to AA 11 from the Portland-to-Boston commuter flight.

This point—that the helpful material was found in a Mitsubishi left at Logan—was spelled out more explicitly in another CNN program that same day, September 13. Eileen O'Connor, reporting on CNN Live, said:

Federal law enforcement in the United States was led to the Hamburg connection by way of information linked to a car seized at Logan Airport. It was a Mitsubishi. It was rented by Mohammed [*sic*] Atta, who lived in an apartment in Hamburg…. Inside was a flight manual in Arabic language material that law enforcement investigators say was very helpful…. [Another car, found at the airport in Portland, Maine,] was rented at Logan, … and it was… documents… the FBI looked at or law enforcement looked at—that led them to these Bukhari brothers. Also, we know that those two men who took that car to Portland were on a U.S. Air flight from Portland to Logan right before the American and United planes took off. And [authorities] are convinced that those two men were at least some of the hijackers.[16]

So, it was the Mitsubishi left at Logan Airport in which authorities found documents that, besides leading them to Atta, were otherwise helpful to the investigation. The Nissan left at the airport in Portland contained documents indicating that the Bukharis, who took the early morning flight from Portland to Boston, were two of the hijackers.

BBC News, the same day, reported the same basic facts, albeit with much less detail, saying:

> A trail of evidence led investigators… from one abandoned rental car in Portland, Maine, to two houses in Vero Beach, Florida. A second hired car, found in Boston's Logan Airport, … led investigators to the Florida homes of two pilots: Mohammed [sic] Atta and Marwan Yousef Al-Shehhi.[17]

A Correction

However, that same day, September 13, CNN issued a correction, saying:

> We would like to correct a report that appeared on CNN. Based on information from multiple law enforcement sources, CNN reported that Adnan Bukhari and Ameer Bukhari of Vero Beach[,] Florida, were suspected to be two of the pilots who crashed planes into the World Trade Center. CNN later learned that Adnan Bukhari is still in Florida, where he was questioned by the FBI. We are sorry for the misinformation…. Ameer Bukhari died in a small plane crash last year.[18]

This discovery, that neither Adnan nor Ameer Bukhari had died on 9/11, meant that the original story had been wrong.

This discovery, however, did not lead immediately to a complete change of story. "Evidence found in a rental car left in Portland," that same CNN story continued, led investigators to the Bukharis, whereas materials found in a Mitsubishi sedan at Logan Airport in Boston "led investigators to two more men who were pilots: Mohammed [sic] Atta and Marwan Yousef Alshehhi." It also "contained materials written in Arabic, including flight manuals, that law enforcement sources called 'helpful' to the investigation."[19] Another CNN report the following day, September 14, still maintained this same correlation:

According to law enforcement sources, ... [a] Mitsubishi sedan [Atta] rented was found at Boston's Logan Airport. Arabic language materials were found in the car.... Federal sources initially identified Bukhari and Ameer Bukhari as possible hijackers who boarded one of the planes that originated in Boston.... Their names had been tied to a car found at an airport in Portland, Maine, but Adnan Bukhari's attorney said it appeared their identifications were stolen.[20]

Immediately after the correction, as can be seen, everything remained the same, except that the Bukharis, rather than being hijackers, were victims of identity theft. The treasure trove of helpful information was still said to have been found in a Mitsubishi at Boston's Logan Airport, which led authorities to Atta.

Still another CNN report, which gave an initial list of hijackers, said that "Atta rented a car that was later found at Boston's Logan Airport."[21]

In a story by Neil Mackay appearing in Scotland two days later (September 16), another slight change occurred: The Bukharis were no longer mentioned. But Atta was still said to have left a Mitsubishi sedan at Logan. Mackay's story even included another detail, saying that Atta and al-Shehhi had "argued with another driver over spaces" at the Logan Airport parking lot.[22]

The Emergence of the Final Story

Back in the United States, however, the story had begun to change more drastically. On September 14, an Associated Press report, discussing "two suspects in the terrorist attacks on the World Trade Center," said:

One of the two suspects who boarded a flight in Portland was Mohamed Atta, 33.... The 2001 Nissan Altima used by the men came from the same Boston rental location as another car used by additional suspects that contained incriminating materials when it was seized at Boston's Logan Airport.

Once in Maine, the suspects spent the night at the Comfort Inn in South Portland before boarding the plane the next morning, said Stephen McCausland, spokesman for the Maine Public Safety Department.[23]

Suddenly, the Nissan Altima had been driven to Portland by Atta and his companion, who then stayed there at the Comfort Inn that night. In this Associated Press version of the Portland story, however, the transition to what would become the accepted narrative was not yet complete. The incriminating materials were still found in a rental car left at Logan (although this car had been rented by unnamed "additional suspects," not by Atta).

The complete transition to the final official account was made on September 16,[24] in a *Washington Post* story by Joel Achenbach (the same reporter, interestingly, who apparently introduced, within the United States, the revised version of the Shuckums episode, discussed in the previous chapter, according to which Atta did not drink alcohol). Achenbach wrote:

> Among the 19 hijackers identified by authorities was Mohamed Atta…. Atta is thought to have piloted American Airlines Flight 11, the first to slam into the World Trade Center. A letter written by Atta, left in his luggage at Boston's Logan Airport, said he planned to kill himself so he could go to heaven as a martyr. It also contained a Saudi passport, an international driver's license, instructional videos for flying Boeing airliners and an Islamic prayer schedule. Officials believe that Atta and Alomari rented a car in Boston, drove to Portland, Maine, and took a room Monday night at the Comfort Inn…. They then flew on a short flight Tuesday morning from Portland to Boston, changing to Flight 11.[25]

Achenbach's *Washington Post* story not only had Atta and al-Omari, instead of the Bukharis, driving to Portland, staying overnight at the Comfort Inn, and then taking the commuter flight back to Boston. It also said that the incriminating evidence was found in Atta's luggage, which was found inside Logan Airport (not in a Mitsubishi sedan that Atta had rented and left in the Logan parking lot).

This new story, which evidently first appeared five days after 9/11, was soon fleshed out with various details, including physical evidence that Atta and al-Omari had been in Portland the night before the attacks. An article in the *Portland Press Herald* on October 5, for example, said:

> The FBI released a detailed chronology Thursday [October 4] showing that two of the suspected hijackers in the Sept. 11 attack on the World Trade Center spent their final hours in Greater Portland stopping at ATMs and visiting a pizza restaurant and Wal-Mart…. After checking in at the motel, Atta and Alomari were seen several times between 8PM and 9:30PM. Between 8 and 9PM, they were seen at Pizza Hut; at 8:31PM, they were videotaped by a KeyBank automatic teller machine, and videotaped again at 8:41PM at a Fast Green ATM next to Pizzeria Uno…. At 9:15PM, the two stopped at Jetport Gas on Western Avenue, where they asked for directions, and at 9:22PM, Atta was caught on videotape in the Wal-Mart in Scarborough. The FBI reports he spent about 20 minutes there…. On Tuesday morning, the two men checked out at 5:33AM; their rental car was recorded entering the airport parking lot at 5:40. The two checked in at the counter at 5:43; [and] passed through security, as shown on videotape, at 5:45.[26]

This new story solved a problem created by the discovery that the Bukharis had not died on 9/11— how to explain why a rental car left at the Portland airport could have led authorities to two of the hijackers. In the new version of the Portland story, the rental car led the authorities to Atta and al-Omari, because they were the ones who rented it and drove it to Portland.

The Mysteries and the Contradictions

This solution, however, created one of the afore-discussed mysteries: Why would Atta have taken this trip, thereby putting the whole operation at risk?

The Atta-to-Portland solution to the Bukhari problem also created another problem: how to explain the well-reported fact that incriminating materials, "helpful" to the investigation, had been found at Logan Airport. This problem was solved by saying that they were found in Atta's luggage, which did not make it onto Flight 11. But this solution created, in turn, the other mystery: Given the fact that the commuter flight from Portland was on time, arriving at Boston a full hour before the scheduled departure time of Flight 11, why did Atta's luggage fail to get loaded onto this flight?

The main problem facing the new story, however, is simply the fact that it is a new story, which is radically different from what the authorities had said the first few days. If the Nissan Altima was driven to Portland by Atta, why did authorities originally say that it had documents leading them to Adnan and Ameer Bukhari? If the treasure trove of materials that was so helpful to the investigation was really found in Atta's luggage, which was inside Logan Airport, why did authorities first say that those materials were found outside the airport, in a Mitsubishi? If Atta and al-Omari were really the ones who stayed overnight in the Comfort Inn in Portland, why did officials originally say that it was the Bukharis? If it was Atta and al-Shehhi who really took the commuter flight from Portland to Boston, why did authorities originally say that it was Adnan and Ameer Bukhari?

Although these problems are severe enough, there was yet another contradictory report.

Another Contradiction: Atta Reported in New York City September 10

On May 22, 2002, Susan Candiotti of CNN gave this startling report:

> The FBI has found credit card receipts that appear to place September 11 hijacker Mohamed Atta in Manhattan the day before the attacks, a source close to the investigation told CNN Wednesday…. The source also said investigators have determined Atta may have been accompanied to Manhattan on September 10 by Abdulaziz Alomari.[27]

Why might Atta have been there? "Officials speculate Atta may have been in New York… to make a final visit to the World Trade Center to program the towers' location into a global positioning system, the source said."[28]

That same day, a *New York Daily News* story gave basically the same information, saying:

> Mohamed Atta… was in New York on Sept. 10 and perhaps

Sept. 9, according to a law enforcement source familiar with the investigation…. The FBI found transactions that show Atta used a credit card in Manhattan the day before the planes crashed into the World Trade Center…. Sometime on Sept. 10, the FBI believes, Atta traveled to Boston and rented a blue Nissan sedan. He and Abdulaziz Alomari then drove to Portland, Maine.[29]

Although that statement seemed to leave open the means by which Atta "traveled" to Boston, one of the article's summary points states: "FBI believes he visited World Trade Center, then flew to Boston." It is, therefore, theoretically possible that Atta could have been in Manhattan in the morning and then, after rushing to an airport, arrived in Boston in time to rent a car and—assuming that, as the CNN story suggested, al-Omari was already with him—leave for Portland in time to check in at the Comfort Inn, as the FBI said he did, at 5:43PM.[30]

However, this story, even though it was evidently based on FBI-derived information, contradicted the FBI's account of what Atta actually did. In FBI Director Robert Mueller's testimony to the Congressional Joint Inquiry, cited earlier, he said:

Marwan al-Shehhi [was staying] at the Milner Hotel in Boston. On September 9, Mohamed Atta also checked into the Milner Hotel staying that night where he met with Marwan al-Shehhi. Shortly after noon on the day before the attacks, Mohamed Atta left the Milner Hotel, picked up Abdul Aziz al Omari at the Park Inn, and drove to Portland.[31]

There is simply no possibility, given this account, that Atta could have been in Manhattan during any part of September 10. So unless either the FBI or "the source" was mistaken,[32] we have another contradiction.

Dealing with the Contradictions

The 9/11 Commission dealt with these contradictions by ignoring them. It did not mention the early reports that the Nissan left at the Portland airport had documents leading the FBI to Adnan and Ameer Bukhari. It did not mention the early reports that the Bukharis had stayed at the Comfort Inn in Portland on September

10 and then taken the early morning flight from Portland to Boston. It did not mention the early reports that the FBI was led to Atta (along with Marwan al-Shehhi) by information found in a Mitsubishi left at Logan Airport. It also did not mention the fact that this Mitsubishi, according to the early reports, was where the treasure trove of information, which was so helpful to the investigation, was found. It instead simply told the new story as if it had been the story all along. The Commission also did not mention the 2002 story saying that, according to the FBI, Mohamed Atta had used his credit card in Manhattan on September 10.

Former FBI agent Warren Flagg's 2006 claim about the Atta's luggage raised an additional question. If this "Rosetta stone" contained, as Flagg claimed, the names of all nineteen hijackers, why did the authorities, after opening the luggage, claim that Adnan and Ameer Bukhari were two of the hijackers? Could Atta, as the ringleader of the operation, have included the names of two people who were not going to be involved—one of whom was already dead?

Conclusion

The treasure trove of information that was reportedly discovered in Atta's belongings played a central role in the process of placing blame on al-Qaeda for the 9/11 attacks. And yet the present version of the story about this treasure trove of information radically contradicts the version that was told in the first days after 9/11. Congress and the press need to ask why these contradictory stories emerged and why the 9/11 Commission ignored the existence of the original story.

17

WERE HIJACKERS REPORTED ON CELL PHONE CALLS?

A central element in the story of the hijackings of the four airliners, as it unfolded in the press and then was told in *The 9/11 Commission Report*, was that passengers had reported the presence of Middle Eastern hijackers on the planes by means of cell phone calls to family members and authorities. The hijackers' presence was also, in some cases, reported through the use of onboard phones. But cell phone calls were portrayed as a central—even the principal—means by which we had learned what happened on the planes. In a story that appeared in the *Washington Post* on September 13, for example, Charles Lane and John Mintz, wrote:

> [Passenger Jeremy] Glick's cell phone call from Flight 93 and others like it provide the most dramatic accounts so far of events aboard the four hijacked aircraft during the terrifying hours of Tuesday morning, and they offer clues about how the hijackings occurred.[1]

Cell phone calls also played a central role in the narrative provided by the 9/11 Commission, which presupposed these press reports.

For some reason, there were no reported cell phone calls from American Flight 11, the first plane to crash into the World Trade Center. But cell phone calls were reported from the other three flights. Most of this chapter consists of representative press reports, along with statements from *The 9/11 Commission Report*, about reported cell phone calls from these flights in which the callers mentioned the presence, appearance, and activities of hijackers. In at least some of these cases, as we will see, those who received the calls gave their reason for saying that the calls had been made on cell phones: either they had been told this by the caller or they had recognized the caller's cell phone number on their own phone's caller ID.

The final section of the chapter looks at a report provided in 2006 by the FBI at the trial of Zacarias Moussaoui, which, surprisingly enough, contradicted the prior reports. In the intervening years, however, the FBI had not discouraged the press or the 9/11 Commission from claiming that passengers had used cell phones to report the existence of hijackers on the planes.

United 175: Press Reports and the 9/11 Commission

On September 13, 2001, BBC News published a story entitled "Harrowing Final Phone Calls," which concluded with the following statement:

> Businessman Peter Hanson, who was with his wife and baby on the United Airlines flight 175 that hit the World Trade Center, called his father in Connecticut. Despite being cut off twice, he managed to report how men armed with knives were stabbing flight attendants, apparently in an attempt to force crew to unlock the doors to the cockpit. "A stewardess has been stabbed... the plane is going down," he said, before being cut off.[2]

The 9/11 Commission, after quoting the content of this reported call, said, "Lee Hanson received a second call from his son Peter," in which Lee Hanson heard the following:

> It's getting bad, Dad—A stewardess was stabbed—They seem to have knives and Mace—They said they have a bomb—It's getting very bad on the plane.... The plane is making jerky movements—I don't think the pilot is flying the plane.... I think they intend to go to Chicago or someplace and fly into a building.[3]

Although neither the BBC nor the 9/11 Commission specified the kind of phone used for these calls, an Associated Press story, reporting this call on 9/11 itself, said: "A minister [the Rev. Bonnie Bardot] confirmed the cell phone call to [Peter Hanson's] father, Lee Hanson."[4] Peter Hanson's sister, moreover, has stated that the calls were made on a cell phone.[5]

Another reported call from this flight, by passenger Brian Sweeney, was described as a cell phone call, five days after the event, by David Maraniss in a *Washington Post* article, which said:

> Brian Sweeney called his wife Julie: "Hi, Jules," Brian Sweeney was saying into his cell phone. "It's Brian. We've been hijacked, and it doesn't look too good." His wife, Julie, was not at their home in Barnstable, Mass., so he was talking into the answering machine. His voice sounded calm, but his message was fatalistic.... "Hopefully, I'll talk to you again, but if not, have a good life. I know I'll see you again some day."[6]

The 9/11 Commission, after mentioning that Sweeney had left a message for his wife, said: "He then called his mother, Louise Sweeney, told her the flight had been hijacked, and added that the passengers were thinking about storming the cockpit."[7] Although the Commission did not say that these were cell phone calls, it did not contradict press reports saying that they were.

American 77: Press Reports and the 9/11 Commission

Two phone calls were reportedly made from American 77, both of which have widely been understood as having been made from cell phones.

As we saw in Chapter 8, Ted Olson originally reported to CNN that his wife, Barbara Olson, had called him twice from this flight, using a cell phone. Although he went back and forth on the kind of phone she had used, the call was almost unanimously reported in the media as a cell phone call. For example, David Maraniss, in his September 16 *Washington Post* article, said: "By 9:25, one of the passengers, Barbara K. Olson, the television commentator, was on the cell phone with her husband, U.S. Solicitor General Theodore B. Olson."[8] In what was evidently his final word on the subject, to be sure, Ted Olson said that she had used an onboard phone.[9] But that statement, perhaps because it was made to a British newspaper, had little if any effect within the United States. On the first anniversary of 9/11, for example,

CNN said: "Unbeknown to the hijackers, passenger and political commentator Barbara Olson, 45, was able to call her husband—Solicitor General Ted Olson—on her cellular phone."[10]

The 9/11 Commission, without contradicting this widely held view, wrote:

> At some point between 9:16 and 9:26, Barbara Olson called her husband, Ted Olson, the solicitor general of the United States. She reported that the flight had been hijacked, and the hijackers had knives and box cutters. She further indicated that the hijackers... had put all the passengers in the back of the plane. About a minute into the conversation, the call was cut off....
>
> Shortly after the first call, Barbara Olson reached her husband again. She reported that the pilot had announced that the flight had been hijacked.... The Solicitor General then informed his wife of the two previous hijackings and crashes.[11]

The other reported call from this flight was by flight attendant Renee May. The Commission wrote:

> At 9:12, Renee May called her mother, Nancy May, in Las Vegas. She said her flight was being hijacked by six individuals who had moved them to the rear of the plane. She asked her mother to alert American Airlines. Nancy May and her husband promptly did so.[12]

Although the Commission again did not specify the kind of phone used, the call has generally been thought to have been a cell phone call, due to the fact it was thus characterized in stories from Las Vegas, including one entitled "Flight Attendant Made Call on Cell Phone to Mom in Las Vegas."[13]

United 93: Press Reports and the 9/11 Commission

It was passengers on United Flight 93 who were most explicitly said to have made cell phone calls. Even the 9/11 Commission, which had not specifically referred to any of the calls from other flights as cell phone calls, said, in discussing United 93: "Shortly [after 9:32], the passengers and flight crew began a series of calls from GTE airphones and cellular phones."[14]

It was also in relation to this flight that cell phone discussions of hijackers reportedly played the biggest role. For example, David Maraniss, in his September 16 *Washington Post* article, said:

> The plane was at once a lonesome vessel, the people aboard facing their singular fate, and yet somehow already attached to the larger drama, connected again by cell phones. People on the plane learned about what had happened in New York and sent word back the other way about what was happening to them.[15]

This point was illustrated by several calls reportedly made by passengers on cell phones.

Charles Lane and Charles Mintz, in their aforementioned *Washington Post* story of September 13, wrote:

> As United Airlines Flight 93 entered its last desperate moments in the sky, passenger Jeremy Glick used a cell phone to tell his wife, Lyzbeth, ... that the Boeing 757's cockpit had been taken over by three Middle Eastern-looking men wielding knives and a red box they claimed was a bomb. The terrorists, wearing red headbands, had ordered the pilots, flight attendants and passengers to the rear of the plane.... Lyzbeth Glick, in turn, informed her husband that another hijacked jet had already crashed into the World Trade Center.... Glick said he and others aboard the plane had decided to rush the cockpit and try to subdue the terrorists—a display of resistance that may have staved off a much worse catastrophe.[16]

A reported call from passenger Mark Bingham was also widely described as a cell phone call. For example, Lane and Mintz wrote:

> Kathy Hoglan of Los Gatos, California says her nephew, Mark Bingham, 31, did not specifically mention a plan to tackle the hijackers in his cell phone call to her at 9:44AM Eastern time. Bingham managed only to tell his aunt and mother, Alice Hoglan, that the plane had been hijacked and that he loved them before the phone "went dead," Kathy Hoglan said.[17]

Another reported caller widely said to have used a cell phone was Honor Elizabeth Wainio. A *Newsweek* story entitled "The Final Moments of United Flight 93," for example, said:

Crucial evidence, *Newsweek* has learned, may come from yet another phone call made by a passenger. Elizabeth Wainio, 27, was speaking to her stepmother in Maryland. Another passenger, she explains, had loaned her a cell phone and told her to call her family. "I have to go," Wainio says, cutting the call short. "They're about to storm the cockpit" referring to her fellow passengers.[18]

Still another female passenger, Marion Britton, reportedly made a cell phone call that provided information about the hijackers. According to a representative story in the *Pittsburgh Post-Gazette*:

> She called longtime friend Fred Fiumano, from whom she had borrowed a cell phone. She said the plane had been hijacked, they had slit the throats of two people and the plane had made a U-turn. Fiumano told her that the World Trade Center towers were in flames. She said, "I know, and we're going to go down." ... Fiumano heard a lot of yelling and screaming, and the line went dead.[19]

One of the flight attendants was also reported to have made a cell phone call. A story entitled "Flight Attendant Helped Fight Hijackers," discussing a "cellular phone conversation" between Sandra Bradshaw and her husband, said:

> Bradshaw said he took his wife's call about 9:30AM.... "Have you seen what's happening? Have you heard?" Sandy asked her husband in a calm voice. "We've been hijacked." ... She said the plane had been taken over by three men with knives. She had gotten a close look at one of the hijackers.... "He had an Islamic look," she told her husband. While Sandy talked, she and other flight attendants were boiling water to toss on the hijackers. Nearby, many passengers were making cell phone calls, a few were plotting an uprising.... Around Sandy, three men were whispering the 23rd Psalm.... Then one of the men apparently made the call to charge the hijackers. Phil Bradshaw heard the phone drop. "We're all running to first class," were her last words. "I've got to go. Bye."[20]

According to Phil Bradshaw, therefore, his wife had told him that "many passengers" besides herself were making cell phone calls.

Although many cell phone calls from United 93 were indeed reported, the most well-known were those that Deena Burnett reported receiving from her husband, Tom Burnett. In his *Washington Post* story of September 16, David Maraniss, after having said that people aboard the plane were "connected [to the larger drama] by cell phones," wrote:

> Thomas E. Burnett Jr., a California businessman, called his wife, Deena, four times. In the first call, he described the hijackers and said they had stabbed a passenger and that his wife should contact authorities. In the second call, he said the passenger had died and that he and some others on board were going to do something about it. She pleaded with him to remain unobtrusive, but he said no way.[21]

Deena Burnett explicitly and repeatedly stated that these calls were made from Tom Burnett's cell phone. She knew this, she said, because the caller ID identified his cell phone as the source.[22] Her testimony has been widely publicized in the media. For example, a special segment about her on CBS's *Early Show* said: "Tom Burnett made four cell phone calls from Flight 93 to Deena Burnett at home, telling her he and some other passengers were going to 'do something.'" In a letter published in the *National Review*, Tom's father, Thomas Burnett, Sr., spoke of "Tom's four cell-phone calls from Flight 93 to his wife, Deena."[23]

In addition to the six reported callers mentioned here— Jeremy Glick, Mark Bingham, Honor Elizabeth Wainio, Marion Britton, Sandy Bradshaw, and Tom Burnett (who reportedly made four calls)—there was one other passenger, Edward Felt, and one other flight attendant, CeeCee Lyles, who were widely reported to have made cell phone calls from United 93. With regard to Felt, a representative story in a Pittsburgh newspaper said:

> Investigators believe Edward Felt may have been in a group of passengers who were herded into the rear of the plane near the bathrooms. From there, at 9:58AM, he called 911 on his cell phone and reached an operator in Westmoreland County. "We're being hijacked. We're being hijacked," he told John Shaw.... Shaw spoke to Edward Felt for one minute and 10 seconds, learning that he'd locked himself in the bathroom to make the call.[24]

With regard to CeeCee Lyles, a story in a different Pittsburgh paper stated: "Moments before Flight 93 went down, CeeCee dialed home twice on a cell phone to tell [her husband] of the hijacking and of her love for him and their boys."[25]

It has been widely held, accordingly, that there were at least eleven cell phone calls from United Flight 93, through which passengers and crew members reported that the plane had been hijacked by men with knives. When these eleven reported calls are added to the calls reviewed above from the other flights—two each from UA 175 and AA 77—we can see that it has been widely believed that there were at least fifteen such cell phone calls.

In 2006, however, an FBI report contradicted this belief.

The FBI's 2006 Report on Phone Calls from the Flights

As we saw in Chapter 8, the FBI presented, as evidence at the Moussaoui trial, a report on phone calls from all four flights. As we also saw, this report did not back up the claim of Ted Olson, who at the time was the solicitor general at the Department of Justice, that his wife, Barbara Olson, had made two calls to him from American Flight 77, during which she reported the flight's hijacking. According to the FBI report, not even one connected call was attributed to Barbara Olson. The FBI report did mention her, but only to say that, although she attempted a call to the Department of Justice at "9:18:58," it was an "unconnected call," which lasted "0 seconds." According to the FBI in 2006, therefore, Barbara Olson did not make any completed calls from Flight 77 (on either a cell phone or an onboard phone).[26]

What about the reported call from this plane by flight attendant Renee May, which was widely understood to be a cell phone call? According to the FBI report, Renee May attempted one call to her parents at 9:11:24, which did not go through, and then another call at 9:12:18, which went through and, in fact, lasted 158 seconds. The report did not indicate, however, that a cell phone was used for either call.[27]

From examining only this portion of the FBI report, dealing with Flight 77, one might assume that when the FBI did not indicate that a particular call was made on a cell phone, it was leaving open the question of what kind of phone was used. However, an examination of the FBI's treatment of phone calls from United 93 shows that this would be an incorrect inference.

Greg Gordon of the McClatchy Newspapers covered the Moussaoui trial. In discussing the FBI's testimony about phone calls from United 93, he wrote:

> In the back of the plane, 13 of the terrified passengers and crew members made 35 air phone calls and two cell phone calls to family members and airline dispatchers, a member of an FBI Joint Terrorism Task Force testified Tuesday.[28]

Although, as we have seen, at least eleven of the reported calls from United 93 were widely thought to be cell phone calls, the FBI said that *only two* of them actually were.

Which two? According to the evidence presented at the Moussaoui trial, which is now publicly available in an interactive computer presentation, they were the call from passenger Edward Felt and one of the calls from flight attendant CeeCee Lyles. The graphic for a call by Lyles at 9:58 explicitly identifies it as a "cell phone call." The easily accessible graphic about the call from Felt, which was also said to have occurred at 9:58, says "call placed from bathroom," from which one can infer that it must have been made from a cell phone. We need not, however, rely on inference: There is also a less accessible graphic, which says: "9:58AM: Passenger Edward Felt, using his cell phone, (732) 241-XXXX, contacts John Shaw, a 911 Operator from Westmoreland County, PA."[29]

By reading this FBI report in conjunction with Greg Gordon's summary of the FBI's testimony at the trial, we can see that unless the FBI report specifically described a call as a *cell* phone call, it was indicating that the call was made from an onboard phone. By looking at the entire FBI report on phone calls from the hijacked airliners, moreover, we can see that those two 9:58 calls from CeeCee Lyles and Edward Felt are the only reported calls from all of the flights combined that were designated as cell phone calls. According to the FBI, therefore, there were no cell phone calls from United 175 or American 77.

In saying that only the two 9:58 calls from United 93 were cell phone calls, the FBI avoided a problem briefly mentioned in

Chapter 8, namely, skepticism about whether high-altitude cell phone calls from airliners are possible, especially calls that stay connected long enough for a conversation to occur. The FBI, when it had to present its evidence in a court of law, avoided this problem, because at 9:58, when the calls from Lyles and Felt were reportedly made, the plane, according to official reports, had descended to about 5,000 feet.

However, although the FBI's report at the Moussaoui trial avoided that problem, it created a new one: It implied that one of the chief elements in the story about 9/11 told by authorities and the press from the outset—that the presence of hijackers on the flights had been reported by means of cell phone calls from those flights—was untrue.

With regard to United 175, the FBI report implies that although the reported calls from Peter Hanson were understood by his family to have been made from his cell phone, they were not. The reports—by *Washington Post* reporter David Maraniss and others—that Brian Sweeney used a cell phone were also, according to the FBI report, wrong.

With regard to Flight 77, flight attendant Renee May's reported call to her parents was evidently understood by them to have been made on a cell phone. The FBI report entails, however, that it was not. And although Ted Olson, as we saw in Chapter 8, later changed his early claim that his wife had used a cell phone, saying instead that she had called collect using an onboard phone, the US media continued to say that she had used a cell phone. The FBI report, however, entails that she did not —indicating, in fact, that she did not reach her husband by means of *either* kind of phone.

By far the most extensive implications of the FBI report, however, concern the generally accepted story about United 93. Greg Gordon, part of whose report from the Moussaoui trial was quoted above, also wrote: "The struggle aboard Flight 93, America's most shining moment on one of its darkest days, has been the subject of at least four movies."[30] In these movies, the reported cell phone calls have played a central role. And yet the FBI report implies that all these movies, insofar as they portrayed several passengers making cell phone calls, were based on false information.

CHAPTER 17

When the FBI issued its report on phone calls in 2006, it also implied that hundreds of stories in the press had been wrong. Although Jeremy Glick, Mark Bingham, Honor Elizabeth Wainio, Marion Britton, Tom Burnett, and flight attendant Sandy Bradshaw have all been widely and repeatedly said to have made cell phone calls, the FBI report implied that none of them did, even though the recipients of the calls from at least two of them— Wainio and Britton—*evidently* reported that a cell phone had been used and one of them—Burnett—*publicly* reported this.

Of these three, the Burnett case is the most serious. Deena Burnett, as we saw, has repeatedly said that she knew that the calls came from her husband's cell phone, because she saw his caller ID. What are we to make of the fact that the FBI, several years after the event, issued a report entailing that her claim was false? What does the press do about the fact that it has repeatedly supported a claim that, according to the FBI, is false?

The FBI report also entails that *The 9/11 Commission Report* was wrong. While speaking of United Flight 93, the Commission, in a statement only partially quoted earlier, stated:

> Shortly [after 9:32], the passengers and flight crew began a series of calls from GTE airphones and cellular phones…. At least ten passengers and two crew members shared vital information with family, friends, colleagues, or others on the ground. All understood the plane had been hijacked. They said the hijackers wielded knives and claimed to have a bomb. The hijackers were wearing red bandanas, and they forced the passengers to the back of the aircraft. Callers reported that a passenger had been stabbed and that two people were lying on the floor of the cabin, injured or dead—possibly the captain and first officer. One caller reported that a flight attendant had been killed…. During at least five of the passengers' phone calls, information was shared about the attacks that had occurred earlier that morning at the World Trade Center. Five calls described the intent of passengers and surviving crew members to revolt against the hijackers. According to one call, they voted on whether to rush the terrorists in an attempt to retake the plane…. One of the callers ended her message as follows: "Everyone's running up to first class. I've got to go. Bye."[31]

Much of the information here summarized by the 9/11 Commission came, as we have seen, from calls widely said to have been made on cell phones. The Commission itself stated that some of these calls were cell phone calls.

These alleged cell phone calls have been widely used as evidence for the official story about United 93 against alternative views. For example, one journalist, after referring to the alternative view that this plane "was brought down not by the passengers struggling with the hijackers but by a U.S. missile," said: "But we know from cell phone conversations that passengers on board that plane planned on confronting the hijackers."[32]

In 2006, however, the FBI said that these alleged cell phone calls did not occur.

Some Questions for the FBI

The FBI's report about phone calls from the airliners for the Moussaoui trial has, as we have seen, created problems for the stories about phone calls from Barbara Olson, Tom Burnett, and various other passengers. But this report also raises questions about the FBI itself.

As we saw in Chapter 8, it would appear that the FBI's report on phone calls presented as evidence at the Moussaoui trial in 2006 was originally completed by September 20, 2001. If so, this would mean that the FBI, while knowing that its evidence did not support the belief that Tom Burnett or any of the others—except for CeeCee Lyles and Edward Felt—had made cell phone calls, it allowed the mass media to continue painting a false picture of what happened on United 93, when it could have set the record straight by simply issuing a press release.[33] The FBI needs to be asked why it did not do this.

Also, the FBI's statement about Barbara Olson, when taken in conjunction with the American Airlines statement reported in Chapter 8, is problematic. According to the FBI report, as we saw, although Barbara Olson did not, contrary to Ted Olson's claim, complete any calls from American 77, she did attempt a call to the Department of Justice at 9:18:58, which was "unconnected." The question arises, however, as to the type of phone from which this unconnected call was attempted. The FBI's report about United 93 showed, we saw, that all calls were understood to be calls from onboard phones unless they were specifically labeled cell phone calls. Because the FBI did not designate Barbara Olson's attempted call as an attempted cell phone call, the FBI report evidently meant that it had been attempted from an onboard phone. But according to a statement made by an AA representative in 2006, as we saw in Chapter 8, American 77 had no onboard phones.

Conclusion

The public has been led to believe, through press reports, films, and *The 9/11 Commission Report*, that passengers from three of the airliners—Flights 175, 77, and 93—used cell phones to report to loved ones that their plane had been hijacked. At least some of the people who reported receiving these calls gave a good reason for believing that the calls had been made on cell phones: either they had been told this or they recognized the cell phone number on their caller ID. According to the FBI report presented at the Moussaoui trial in 2006, however, no passenger on any of the flights used a cell phone to call a relative. Congress and the press need to find out why this contradiction exists.

Congress and the press also need to ask the FBI a number of questions: why it allowed the press to continue reporting that such calls had occurred; why it waited until 2006, when it had to present evidence in a court of law, to state publicly that there were only two cell phone calls from all the airliners combined; why even then it did not issue a press release to set the record straight; and how it concluded that Barbara Olson had attempted a call from Flight 77.

The central questions, however, involve the reported cell phone calls, which played a central role in establishing the claim that the planes were hijacked by al-Qaeda operatives. Congress and the press need to find out why the public was presented with a story that the FBI, five years later, quietly declared to be untrue.

18

IS THERE HARD EVIDENCE OF
BIN LADEN'S RESPONSIBILITY?

Nothing is more fundamental to the official story about 9/11 than the claim that Osama bin Laden was ultimately responsible for the attacks. This story is told by government officials and the press as if there were hard evidence proving his responsibility. The claim that such evidence exists is, in other words, at least implicitly made. And yet such evidence was never provided. Moreover, an FBI spokesperson has even contradicted the assumption that the FBI has such evidence.

The Position of the 9/11 Commission

The 9/11 Commission Report is entirely constructed around the idea that Osama bin Laden was responsible for the 9/11 attacks. Its second chapter, providing the historical background to the attacks, begins with a section entitled "A Declaration of War," which discusses a 1998 fatwa in which bin Laden "called for the murder of any American, anywhere on earth" as a duty for all Muslims.[1] Chapter 5, after describing Khalid Sheikh Mohammed—normally referred to in the report simply as KSM—as "the principal architect of the 9/11 attacks,"[2] presents a number of assertions, all said (in the notes[3]) to be based on statements of KSM, showing that KSM himself said that bin Laden had authorized the attacks.

> KSM arranged a meeting with Bin Ladin in Tora Bora [and] presented the al Qaeda leader with a menu of ideas for terrorist operations.... KSM also presented a proposal for an operation that would involve training pilots who would crash planes into buildings in the United States. This proposal eventually would

become the 9/11 operation…. Bin Ladin… finally decided to give the green light for the 9/11 operation sometime in late 1998 or early 1999…. KSM reasoned he could best influence U.S. policy by targeting the country's economy…. New York, which KSM considered the economic capital of the United States, therefore became the primary target…. Bin Ladin summoned KSM to Kandahar in March or April 1999 to tell him that al Qaeda would support his proposal…. Bin Ladin wanted to destroy the White House and the Pentagon, KSM wanted to strike the World Trade Center…. Bin Ladin also soon selected four individuals to serve as suicide operatives…. [Two of them] had already obtained U.S. visas…. KSM had not met them. His only guidance from Bin Ladin was that the two should eventually go to the United States for pilot training…. [Mohamed] Atta—whom Bin Ladin chose to lead the group— met with Bin Ladin several times to receive additional instructions, including a preliminary list of approved targets: the World Trade Center, the Pentagon, and the U.S. Capitol…. It is clear… that Bin Ladin and [Mohammed] Atef were very much in charge of the operation.[4]

The 9/11 Commission, then, wrote as if there were no doubt that the attacks were authorized and even partly planned by Osama bin Laden. Did that attitude reflect evidence provided by the Bush administration?

Did the Bush Administration Provide Hard Evidence?
On September 23, 2001, Secretary of State Colin Powell appeared on NBC's *Meet the Press*. The following exchange occurred between him and the moderator, Tim Russert.

> RUSSERT: Are you absolutely convinced that Osama bin Laden was responsible for this attack?

> POWELL: I am absolutely convinced that the al Qaeda network, which he heads, was responsible for this attack…. So what we have to do in the first phase of this campaign is to go after al Qaeda and to go after Osama bin Laden….

> RUSSERT: Will you release publicly a white paper which links him and his organization to this attack to put people at ease?

POWELL: We are hard at work bringing all the information together, intelligence information, law enforcement information. And I think in the near future we will be able to put out a paper, a document that will describe quite clearly the evidence that we have linking him to this attack.[5]

The following day, a *New York Times* story, referring to Powell's comments, said:

The Bush administration plans to make public evidence linking Osama bin Laden and Al Qaeda network to the terror attacks on the United States in an effort to persuade the world, and particularly Muslim nations, that a military response is justified.[6]

However, that same morning (September 24), Powell and President Bush, appearing together before the press in the White House Rose Garden, withdrew the pledge. Here is how the discussion went:

QUESTION: Mr. President, when will you publish the paper which Secretary Powell mentioned yesterday, outlining some of the proof that you have of the involvement of bin Laden and al Qaeda and others?

THE PRESIDENT: The Secretary said that he'd be glad to talk about the paper. Let me first tell you that I gave a speech to the nation last Thursday in which I spent a great deal of time talking about the al Qaeda organization as the first terrorist organization that we're going to deal with. And the reason I did is there is a lot of classified information that leads to one person, as well as one global terrorist organization. But for those of you looking for a legal peg, we've already indicted Osama bin Laden. He's under indictment for terrorist activity.... Mr. Secretary, if you'd like to make a comment on that.

SECRETARY POWELL: I just might point out that he has been under indictment for the bombings of our embassy. And as we gather information, and as we talk to our friends and allies around the world, and as we get more cooperation, more information is coming in with respect to his activities and the activities of this network. Most of it is classified, and as we look through it, we can find areas that are unclassified and it will allow us to share this information with the public, we will do so. That would be our intent. But most of it is classified. But there's no question that this network, with this gentleman at the head... is the one who is responsible. And as we are able to provide information that is not sensitive or classified, I think we will try to do that in every way.[7]

Accordingly, Powell, following Bush's lead, said that although there was a lot of information that pointed to bin Laden's responsibility, all such evidence available at the time was classified, but that they would try, some time in the future, to provide some unclassified evidence. Also, although Powell on Sunday had told Russert that he was "absolutely certain" of bin Laden's responsibility for 9/11, Bush and Powell on Monday emphasized that bin Laden had already been indicted for "terrorist activity" (Bush)— in particular, the "bombings of our embassy" (Powell).

Next, at a press briefing that afternoon with White House Press Secretary Ari Fleischer, the following exchange occurred:

QUESTION: Ari, yesterday Secretary Powell was very precise that he was going to put out a report on what we had on bin Laden that could be reported and not classified. Today, the president shot him down, and he's... indicating that he also retreated on the question of putting out a report....

FLEISCHER: No, I think that there was just a misinterpretation of the exact words the secretary used on the Sunday shows and the secretary talked about that in a period of time—I think his word was "soon"—there would be some type of document that could be made available. As you heard the secretary say today... , "As we are able, as it unclassifies" ....

QUESTION: Much more emphatic yesterday....

FLEISCHER: Well, I think he said the word "soon." As I was reminded today by a very knowledgeable official at the State Department, that's called State Department soon. And so it's fully consistent with what the president's been saying and the secretary said....

QUESTION: The American people thought soon meant soon....

FLEISCHER: ... As soon as the attack on our country took place the immediate reaction is that investigations begin.

They.... collect a whole series of information. Some of that information is going... to be classified and will [be] treated as such. Over the course of time, will there be changes to that that can lead to some type of declassified document over whatever period of time? That has historically been the pattern, and I think that's what the secretary is referring to....

QUESTION: ...[W]e're talking about a State Department white paper?

FLEISCHER: Well, I'm not aware of anybody who said white paper, and the secretary didn't say anything about a white paper yesterday.

QUESTION: Is this a sign then that allies, particularly Arab and Muslim allies, really want to see the evidence because... they want to be certain that we have the evidence?

FLEISCHER: ... It's not just the United States that collects information and knows that all roads lead to the Al Qaeda organization. Other nations have similar means of collecting information.

QUESTION: But, Ari, it does seem that across the board, on proving that... bin Laden is behind these acts, ... the answer is always "That's classified. Trust us." Does that really serve the democracy well if all this information on which the government is basing its actions is classified?

FLEISCHER: I think the American people get it. I think they understand that as the nation moves from a peacetime footing to a wartime footing, the government's need to hold certain pieces of information closer is an important need....

QUESTION: I realize you're saying that... you... share information privately. But is there any plan to present public evidence so that, you know, the average citizen, not just Americans, but people all over the world can understand the case against bin Laden?

FLEISCHER: Well, I think, as Secretary Powell said, there's hope to do that and to do so in a timely fashion over some course of time.... But I think the American people also understand that there are going to be times when that information cannot immediately be forthcoming.[8]

CHAPTER 18

A few days later, Seymour Hersh, in a *New Yorker* article, said that according to government officials to whom he had spoken, "the key factor behind the Bush Administration's decision last week not to issue a promised white paper listing the evidence linking Osama bin Laden's organization to the attacks" was, simply, a "lack of solid information." Citing "a Justice Department official," Hersh said:

> [Powell's] widely anticipated white paper could not be published, the Justice Department official said, for lack of hard facts. "There was not enough to make a sale."[9]

Hersh then, citing a CIA official, added:

> The Administration justified the delay by telling the press that most of the information was classified and could not yet be released. Last week, however, a senior C.I.A. official confirmed that the intelligence community had not yet developed a significant amount of solid information about the terrorists' operations, financing, and planning. "One day, we'll know, but at the moment we don't know," the official said.[10]

At the press conference with Ari Fleisher on the 24th, as we saw, a reporter asked whether allies, "particularly Arab and Muslim allies," wanted to see the evidence "to be certain that we have the evidence." Three days earlier, on September 21, a report on CNN had dealt with this issue. Saying that the United States had "labeled bin Laden a prime suspect" in the 9/11 attacks, it continued:

> President Bush demanded Thursday night that the Taliban surrender all leaders of bin Laden's al-Qaeda organization and close al-Qaeda's bases in the country. The Taliban have defied the U.S. demand, refusing to hand over bin Laden without proof or evidence that he was involved in last week's attacks on the United States.... The Taliban ambassador to Pakistan, Abdul Salam Zaeef, said Friday that deporting him without proof would amount to an "insult to Islam."[11]

This CNN story then provided further evidence that although the administration was claiming that it possessed proof, it was not proof of bin Laden's responsibility for 9/11.

> U.S. officials say evidence gathered in other attacks linked to al-Qaeda provide [*sic*] the proof needed. "There is already an

indictment for Osama bin Laden," Fleischer said. "There's an
indictment in the case of Tanzania, Kenya, the bombings in
East Africa, indications that the al Qaeda organization and
Osama bin Laden were involved in the bombing of the Cole.
The president last night made his conditions clear and he said
there would be no discussions and no negotiations."[12]

By saying "no discussions," Bush ruled out, therefore, providing
any evidence for bin Laden's responsibility for 9/11 in particular.
In any case, this CNN story then concluded by presenting the
Taliban's side of the argument:

Bin Laden himself has already denied he had anything to do
with the attacks, and Taliban officials repeatedly said he could
not have been involved in the attacks.... The Taliban told CNN
that Friday's press conference represented their final word on
the matter, and said President Bush's ultimatum posed great
danger for Muslims. "It has angered Muslims of the world and
can plunge the whole region into a crisis," Zaeef said. "We are
ready to cooperate if we are shown evidence. If American agencies are bent on putting the blame on bin Laden, then they
won't be able to catch the real culprits."[13]

The question of proof was again raised five weeks later in a
story by Kathy Gannon of the Associated Press, which said:

Four weeks into the US-led air campaign, a senior Taliban official said [they are] willing to negotiate an end to the conflict.
But he demanded proof of Osama bin Laden's involvement in
the September 11 terror attacks.... "We do not want to fight,"
Muttaqi told The Associated Press. "We will negotiate. But talk
to us like a sovereign country. We are not a province of the
United States, to be issued orders to. We have asked for proof
of Osama's involvement, but they have refused. Why?" State
Department spokesman Richard Boucher said the Taliban
already had plenty of proof. "All one has to do is watch television to find Osama bin Laden claiming responsibility for the
September 11 bombings. There is no question of responsibility."[14]

Early in November 2001, therefore, the Bush administration, still
not providing any hard evidence, was claiming that there was no
need to do so.

Did the Blair Government Provide Hard Evidence of Bin Laden's Responsibility?

The task of presenting public evidence was taken over by the British government. On October 4, Prime Minister Tony Blair presented a document entitled "Responsibility for the Terrorist Atrocities in the United States." Listing "clear conclusions reached by the government," it stated: "Osama Bin Laden and al-Qaeda, the terrorist network which he heads, planned and carried out the atrocities on 11 September 2001."[15]

The document, however, begins with this statement: "This document does not purport to provide a prosecutable case against Osama Bin Laden in a court of law." It begins, in other words, by saying that it provides no hard evidence.

The document does hint, to be sure, that such evidence exists. In its introductory statement, it says: "The document does not contain the totality of the material known to HMG, given the continuing and absolute need to protect intelligence sources." Later, after presenting various kinds of circumstantial evidence, the document says: "There is evidence of a very specific nature relating to the guilt of Bin Laden and his associates that is too sensitive to release."[16] But the document itself, by its own admission, does not provide evidence sufficient for "a prosecutable case against Osama Bin Laden in a court of law."

The weakness of the evidence was pointed out the following day by the BBC. In a report entitled "The Investigation and the Evidence," it said:

> There is no direct evidence in the public domain linking Osama Bin Laden to the 11 September attacks. At best the evidence is circumstantial.... The evidence is not being judged in a court of law. It only needs to persuade governments around the world to back the US-led war on terrorism and to a lesser extent to carry public opinion.[17]

The evidence might be good enough to go to war, the BBC seemed to be saying, but it would not be good enough to go to court.

In any case, the Blair government, like the Bush administration, did not provide hard evidence of bin Laden's responsibility for the attacks of 9/11.

The FBI: "No Hard Evidence"

The FBI has a website labeled "Most Wanted Terrorists." Its page for "Usama bin Laden" states at the top: "MURDER OF U.S. NATIONALS OUTSIDE THE UNITED STATES; CONSPIRACY TO MURDER U.S. NATIONALS OUTSIDE THE UNITED STATES; ATTACK ON A FEDERAL FACILITY RESULTING IN DEATH." Down below it says:

> Usama Bin Laden is wanted in connection with the August 7, 1998, bombings of the United States Embassies in Dar es Salaam, Tanzania, and Nairobi, Kenya. These attacks killed over 200 people. In addition, Bin Laden is a suspect in other terrorist attacks throughout the world.[18]

The FBI has another website labeled "The FBI's Ten Most Wanted Fugitives," which has the same page on "Usama bin Laden."[19] On neither site is there any mention of the attacks of 9/11.

On June 5, 2006, *Muckraker Report* editor Ed Haas, puzzled by this, contacted FBI headquarters to ask why. Rex Tomb, who was then the FBI's chief of investigative publicity, reportedly replied: "The reason why 9/11 is not mentioned on Usama Bin Laden's Most Wanted page is because the FBI has no *hard evidence* connecting Bin Laden to 9/11." When pressed to explain more fully, Tomb reportedly said:

> Bin Laden has not been formally charged in connection to 9/11.... The FBI gathers evidence. Once evidence is gathered, it is turned over to the Department of Justice. The Department of Justice then decides whether it has enough evidence to present to a federal grand jury. In the case of the 1998 United States Embassies being bombed, Bin Laden has been formally indicted and charged by a grand jury. He has not been formally indicted and charged in connection with 9/11 because the FBI has no *hard evidence* connecting Bin Laden to 9/11.[20]

From Tomb's statement, we can infer that the FBI—like Colin Powell and Ari Fleischer on September 24, 2001—suggests that there is hard evidence of bin Laden's responsibility only for the embassy bombings in East Africa (Tanzania and Kenya), not also for the 9/11 attacks. On the next day, June 6, 2006, in any case, Haas's *Muckraker Report* quoted Tomb's statements.[21]

The following day, Tomb's "no hard evidence" statement was quoted on a news program, the INN (International News Network) World Report, after editor Claire Brown, by calling Tomb, had confirmed the accuracy of the quotation.[22]

On August 20, 2006, Haas wrote a follow-up essay, in which he asked why the government "has yet to legally produce the evidence required to gain a federal indictment of Osama bin Laden," adding:

> After all, the evidence threshold for gaining a federal indict-ment is much lower than for gaining a conviction. Yet for reasons that remain obscure from the public record, the U.S. government... has not gained such an indictment of Osama bin Laden.[23]

Haas then, saying that he had "made many attempts... to get the DOJ Public Affairs Office to... explain why Osama bin Laden has not been indicted for 9/11," reported that on June 14, 2006, he asked Arthur Schwartz, a staff assistant in that office, several questions, including:

> Is the DOJ currently seeking an indictment by a federal grand jury of Osama bin Laden in connection with the events of September 11, 2001?
>
> Does the DOJ have any hard evidence connecting Osama bin Laden to the events of 9/11?[24]

In the following weeks, Haas reported, he emailed and telephoned Schwartz several times. Schwartz, however, "contend[ed] that he passed the questions onto 'others' but refuse[d] to give contact information that identifies exactly who these 'others' are."[25]

On August 15, 2006, deciding that he was not going to get a reply from Schwartz, Haas contacted another person at DOJ Public Affairs, Matt Lebaron. This time he asked only one ques-tion: "Why has Osama bin Laden not been indicted by a federal grand jury in connection with his alleged masterminding of 9/11?" Again he received no reply.[26]

However, Haas's two stories, along with the discussion they created on the Internet, may have evoked a story in the main-stream media. On August 28, 2006, Dan Eggen of the *Washington*

Post published a story entitled "Bin Laden, Most Wanted for Embassy Bombings?" It began:

> Al-Qaeda leader Osama bin Laden is a longtime and prominent member of the FBI's "Ten Most Wanted" list, which notes his role as the suspected mastermind of the deadly U.S. embassy bombings in East Africa on Aug. 7, 1998. But another more infamous date—Sept. 11, 2001—is nowhere to be found on the same FBI notice. The curious omission underscores the Justice Department's decision, so far, to not seek formal criminal charges against bin Laden for approving al-Qaeda's most notorious and successful terrorist attack.[27]

Although Eggen's story was in the portion of the paper devoted to reporting rather than editorializing, he took it upon himself to assure readers that this absence of any reference to 9/11 on the FBI's "Usama bin Laden" page has no significance, writing:

> The absence has... provided fodder for conspiracy theorists who think the U.S. government or another power was behind the Sept. 11 hijackings. From this point of view, the lack of a Sept. 11 reference suggests that the connection to al-Qaeda is uncertain. Exhaustive government and independent investigations have concluded otherwise, of course.... FBI officials say the wanted poster merely reflects the government's long-standing practice of relying on actual criminal charges in the notices.[28]

In his August 20 article, however, Haas had asked why the government had *not* made "actual criminal charges" against bin Laden for 9/11. Eggen replied to this question by quoting Rex Tomb:

> "There's no mystery here," said FBI spokesman Rex Tomb. "They could add 9/11 on there, but they have not because they don't need to at this point.... There is a logic to it."[29]

Aside from the question of whether that is a credible (or even intelligible) answer, it was definitely *not* the answer Tomb had given to Haas, which was: "[Osama bin Laden] has not been formally indicted and charged in connection with 9/11 because the FBI has no *hard evidence* connecting Bin Laden to 9/11."[30] That is a very different answer. It is an answer, moreover, that

Eggen, rather than pressing, ignored.

Eggen also sought to justify the absence of 9/11 from bin Laden's FBI page by quoting David N. Kelley, the former US attorney in New York, who said:

> It might seem a little strange from the outside, but it makes sense from a legal point of view…. If I were in government, I'd be troubled if I were asked to put up a wanted picture where no formal charges had been filed, no matter who it was.[31]

That, however, is to dodge the issue raised by Haas. Granting that the FBI would not put the 9/11 attacks on bin Laden's page unless he had been indicted for these attacks, Haas had asked: "Why has Osama bin Laden not been indicted by a federal grand jury in connection with his alleged masterminding of 9/11?" Does the *Washington Post* really consider this to be a question that the press should not ask?

Haas's writings about these issues have, in any case, served to reveal a rather startling contradiction: The idea that there is no question about Osama bin Laden's responsibility for 9/11, which has been expressed countless times by government officials, is contradicted by three facts: (1) Bin Laden is not listed by the FBI as wanted for 9/11. (2) He is not so listed because he has never been indicted for 9/11 by a grand jury. (3) "He has not been formally indicted and charged in connection with 9/11 because the FBI has no *hard evidence* connecting Bin Laden to 9/11."

Was Hard Evidence Provided by the 9/11 Commission?

What did the 9/11 Commission say about the fact that the FBI's websites for the Ten Most Wanted Fugitives and Most Wanted Terrorists do not mention 9/11 as something for which bin Laden is wanted? It might be thought that, because this fact did not become widely known until 2006, the Commission, which issued *The 9/11 Commission Report* in 2004, was simply unaware of it.

In February of 2004, however, the Family Steering Committee for the 9/11 Commission submitted a number of questions for the Commission to ask President Bush, one of which was: "Please comment on the fact that UBL's profile on the FBI's *Ten Most Wanted Fugitives* poster does not include the 9/11 attacks."[32]

There is no evidence that the Commission asked Bush to comment on this fact. The Commission itself, in any case, did not comment on this fact. It simply wrote as if there were no question about bin Laden's responsibility.

But perhaps the Commission could legitimately write with such confidence because it itself had provided hard evidence of bin Laden's responsibility for the 9/11 attacks. If so, the core of this evidence would have been the testimony of KSM (Khalid Sheikh Mohammed), discussed at the outset of this chapter. Citing "interrogation(s) of KSM,"[33] the Commission, as we saw earlier, said that it had learned many things about bin Laden, including the following.

> KSM... presented [to Bin Ladin] a proposal for an operation that... eventually would become the 9/11 operation.... Bin Ladin ... finally decided to give the green light for the 9/11 operation sometime in late 1998 or early 1999.... Bin Ladin also soon selected four individuals to serve as suicide operatives.... Atta—whom Bin Ladin chose to lead the group—met with Bin Ladin several times to receive additional instructions, including a preliminary list of approved targets: the World Trade Center, the Pentagon, and the U.S. Capitol.[34]

Does KSM's testimony not constitute hard evidence? Far from it.

In 2006, Thomas Kean and Lee Hamilton, the 9/11 Commission's chair and vice chair, respectively, published a book entitled *Without Precedent: The Inside Story of the 9/11 Commission.* In one of their "inside story" revelations, they said that the greatest difficulty they had was "obtaining access to star witnesses in custody..., most notably Khalid Sheikh Mohammed, a mastermind of the attacks, and [Ramzi] Binalshibh, who helped coordinate the attacks from Europe."[35] In explaining why getting such access was so important, they wrote:

> These and other detainees were the only possible source for inside information about the plot. If the commission was mandated to provide an authoritative account of the 9/11 attacks, it followed that our mandate afforded us the right to learn what these detainees had to say about 9/11.[36]

But they were not allowed to interrogate any of these detainees. Even their request to observe the interrogation of detainees through one-way glass, so that they "could at least observe the detainee[s'] demeanor and evaluate [their] credibility," was turned down, although they believed that without at least this much access, they "could not evaluate the credibility of the detainees' accounts."[37] The Commission, finally, "never even got to meet with the people conducting the interrogations."[38]

The closest they ever came to the detainees was a CIA "project manager," to whom they were allowed to submit questions to be asked, and through whom they would receive the answers. But this meant, Kean and Hamilton pointed out, that "they were receiving information thirdhand—passed from the detainee, to the interrogator, to the person who writes up the interrogation report, and finally to our staff in the form of reports, not even transcripts."[39] As a result, they say:

> We… had no way of evaluating the credibility of detainee information. How could we tell if someone such as Khalid Sheikh Mohammed… was telling us the truth?[40]

With that rhetorical question, Kean and Hamilton made clear that the 9/11 Commission—like the Blair government, the US State Department, the FBI, the Department of Justice, and the Bush administration more generally—had provided no hard evidence of the responsibility of Osama bin Laden for the attacks of 9/11.

Conclusion

This admission, made explicitly by the FBI and implicitly by the other agencies, contradicts the claim, which has been made explicitly and implicitly by government spokespersons countless times, that there is no question about bin Laden's responsibility for 9/11. Congress and the press need to ask why this contradiction exists and, in any case, whether there really is sufficient evidence of bin Laden's and al-Qaeda's responsibility for 9/11 to justify the policies that have been employed on the assumption that there is.[41]

PART IV

Questions about the Pentagon

19

COULD HANI HANJOUR HAVE FLOWN AMERICAN 77 INTO THE PENTAGON?

O ne of the central elements in the 9/11 story, as told by the government, the press, and the 9/11 Commission, is that American Flight 77, a Boeing 757, was piloted by a young Saudi named Hani Hanjour. This claim is challenged, however, by numerous reports in the press, some of which are even reflected in *The 9/11 Commission Report*, that imply Hanjour would have been incapable of flying a Boeing 757 through the trajectory reportedly taken by American 77. That trajectory, according to experts, would have required a very skillful pilot, and yet Hanjour, according to all reports, was a terrible pilot, even in a tiny plane.

The Reported Trajectory of Flight 77

The 9/11 Commission wrote:

> At 9:34, Ronald Reagan Washington National Airport advised the Secret Service of an unknown aircraft heading in the direction of the White House. American 77 was then 5 miles west-southwest of the Pentagon and began a 330-degree turn. At the end of the turn, it was descending through 2,200 feet, pointed toward the Pentagon and downtown Washington. The hijacker pilot then advanced the throttles to maximum power and dove toward the Pentagon.[1]

The Commission later identified this "hijacker pilot" as Hani Hanjour.[2]

An interesting but little known fact is that Hanjour's name was not included on the first FBI list of hijackers that was reported. That list, as stated orally by journalist Kelli Arena in a

CNN "Breaking News" report at about 10:00AM on September 14, included a name that, based on her pronunciation, was transcribed as "Mosear Caned."[3] On a list released by CNN at 2:00PM the same day, however, that name had been replaced by Hanjour's.[4] On September 19, a *Washington Post* story, seeking to explain why Hanjour's "name was not on the American Airlines manifest for the flight," suggested that "he may not have had a ticket"[5]—which would raise the question as to how he got on board. Be that as it may, Hanjour was quickly identified not only as one of the hijackers but also as the one who flew the plane back toward Washington and then into the Pentagon.

Prior to the time that Hanjour was identified as the pilot, Flight 77's trajectory in its final minutes had already been described as one requiring considerable skill. In a *Washington Post* story appearing on September 12, for example, Marc Fisher and Don Phillips wrote:

[J]ust as the plane seemed to be on a suicide mission into the White House, the unidentified pilot executed a pivot so tight that it reminded observers of a fighter jet maneuver. The plane circled 270 degrees to the right to approach the Pentagon from the west.... Aviation sources said the plane was flown with extraordinary skill, making it highly likely that a trained pilot was at the helm.[6]

The following day, September 13, a story by John Hanchette said:

Whoever flew at least three of the death planes seemed very skilled.... Investigators are particularly impressed with the pilot who slammed into the Pentagon and, just before impact, performed a tightly banked 270-degree turn at low altitude with almost military precision.[7]

The fact that this maneuver required great skill was reinforced by subsequent reports. Ten days after the attacks, a CBS report said that the "difficult high-speed descending turn" was "so smooth" that the hijackers' "flying skills" must have been very good.[8] Then in October, Barbara Walters interviewed Danielle O'Brien, an air traffic controller at Dulles International Airport who had been in the radar room on the morning of 9/11. Recounting how she had seen "an unidentified plane to the southwest of Dulles, moving at a very high rate of speed" toward the protected airspace over Washington, she said:

> The speed, the maneuverability, the way that he turned, we all thought in the radar room, all of us experienced air traffic controllers, that that was a military plane.[9]

Reports about Hanjour's Incompetence

But although the trajectory of the aircraft suggested that the pilot had extraordinary ability, stories making clear that Hani Hanjour was anything but a highly skilled pilot soon started appearing.

On September 19, Justin Paprocki of the Capital News Service published a story in the *Maryland Newsline* about the post-9/11 financial losses suffered by owners of small airfields in Maryland. This story contained a paragraph mentioning one of these airfields, Freeway Airport, near Bowie and Mitchellville:

> Freeway Airport evaluated suspected hijacker Hani Hanjour when he attempted to rent a plane. He took three flights with the instructors in the second week of August, but flew so poorly he was rejected for the rental, said Marcel Bernard, chief flight instructor at Freeway.[10]

On September 21, a story in a newspaper in Greenbelt, Maryland, gave more detail, saying:

> Marcel Bernard, the airport manager and chief flight instructor [at Freeway Airport in Mitchellville, Maryland], told FBI agents investigating last week's suicide attacks that [Hanjour] had flown with flight instructors [in single-engine Cessna 172s] on three occasions over the last six weeks. Hanjour had inquired recently about renting an airplane at Freeway to fly solo... but was declined after two different instructors questioned his flying ability. "His flying skills were so poor overall that [instructors] declined to rent a plane to him without future training," Bernard said.[11]

Two days later, on September 23, a story in *Newsday* made this information national. In "America's Ordeal: Tracing Trail of Hijackers," Thomas Frank wrote:

> At Freeway Airport in Bowie, Md., 20 miles west of Washington, flight instructor Sheri Baxter instantly recognized the name

of alleged hijacker Hani Hanjour when the FBI released a list of 19 suspects in the four hijackings. Hanjour, the only suspect on Flight 77 the FBI listed as a pilot, had come to the airport one month earlier seeking to rent a small plane. However, when Baxter and fellow instructor Ben Conner took the slender, soft-spoken Hanjour on three test runs during the second week of August, they found he had trouble controlling and landing the single-engine Cessna 172. Even though Hanjour showed a federal pilot's license and a log book cataloging 600 hours of flying experience, chief flight instructor Marcel Bernard declined to rent him a plane without more lessons.[12]

On October 15, the *Washington Post* lifted up the problem even further in a story entitled "Hanjour: A Study in Paradox." Besides mentioning several incidents in which instructors had "questioned his competence," including the refusal of Freeway Airport to rent a plane to Hanjour, this story said: "[H]ow and where [Hanjour obtained a commercial pilot's license] remains a lingering question that FAA officials refuse to discuss."[13]

The following year, reports of Hanjour's incompetence received even greater national exposure. On May 4, 2002, Jim Yardley, in a *New York Times* story entitled "A Trainee Noted for Incompetence," wrote:

> Hani Hanjour... was reported to the aviation agency in February 2001 after instructors at his flight school in Phoenix had found his piloting skills so shoddy and his grasp of English so inadequate that they questioned whether his pilot's license was genuine.[14]

Yardley's story ended with a quotation from a former employee of the flight school who was, he said, "amazed that [Hanjour] could have flown into the Pentagon" because "[h]e could not fly at all."[15]

A week later, CBS News put out a story entitled "FAA Was Alerted To Sept. 11 Hijacker," which said:

> [M]anagers at an Arizona flight school [called JetTech] reported [Hanjour] at least five times to the FAA... because his English and flying skills were so bad... they didn't think he should keep his pilot's license. "I couldn't believe he had a commercial license of any kind with the skills that he had," said Peggy Chevrette, the manager.[16]

(This was the same school reported in the *New York Times* article: JetTech was owned by Pan Am International Flight Academy.)

Whereas the contradiction on which this chapter is focused—between Hanjour's reported incompetence, on the one hand, and the skill that reportedly would have been required to fly American 77 into the Pentagon, on the other—was implicit in the aforementioned stories, it was made explicit by the *Washington Post* on the first anniversary of 9/11. In an article entitled "Mysterious Trip to Flight 77 Cockpit," Steve Fainaru and Alia Ibrahim wrote: "[N]o one has been able to offer a definitive portrait of Hanjour, leaving unreconciled a number of seemingly contradictory facts about his life." For their first example, they wrote:

> After the attacks, ... aviation experts concluded that the final maneuvers of American Airlines Flight 77—a tight turn followed by a steep, accurate descent into the Pentagon—was the work of "a great talent... virtually a textbook turn and landing," the law enforcement official said.... [B]ut months before the attacks [Hanjour] had failed to earn a rating to fly [an airliner]. His instructors became so alarmed by his crude skills and limited English they notified the FAA to determine whether his pilot's license was real.... [I]n the days that led up to Sept. 11[,] [f]light instructors at Freeway Airport in Bowie, where he tried unsuccessfully to rent a plane, questioned his piloting skills.[17]

As these articles illustrate, evidence of Hanjour's incompetence had received national publicity in 2001–2002, being reported by CBS, *Newsday*, the *New York Times,* and the *Washington Post*. The *Post*, moreover, had explicitly brought out the contradiction between Hanjour's reported incompetence and the skill reportedly required to pilot Flight 77 during its descent to the Pentagon. How did the 9/11 Commission deal with this contradiction?

Dealing with the Contradiction: The 9/11 Commission

On the one hand, the 9/11 Commission cited some of the stories that reported Hanjour's lack of flying ability. Besides pointing out that Hanjour had repeatedly been rejected by flight schools in Saudi Arabia, the Commission reported that after he started training on a Boeing 737 simulator at Pam Am International Flight Academy in December 2000, "An instructor there found his work well below standard and discouraged him from continuing."[18] The Commission also reported an incident in the summer of 2001, just months before 9/11. After Hanjour, with an instructor on board, had flown the Hudson Corridor in a small plane owned by Air Fleet Training Systems in Teterboro, New Jersey, the Commission wrote, "his instructor declined a second request because of what he considered Hanjour's poor piloting skills."[19] The Commission even admitted that a flight instructor in Arizona had described Hanjour as "a terrible pilot."[20]

On the other hand, the Commission made some comments suggesting that Hanjour was quite accomplished. In a note in which the Commission is citing a statement purportedly made by KSM (Khalid Sheikh Mohammed)—the problematic nature of all such citations was discussed in Chapter 17—it said: "KSM claims to have assigned the Pentagon specifically to Hanjour, the operation's most experienced pilot."[21] Although the Commission implied that it was not necessarily endorsing this statement by preceding it with "KSM claims," it did not ask how, if Hanjour had been a "terrible pilot"—so terrible that an instructor would not go up with him a second time in a single-engine airplane—KSM could have described him as the operation's "most experienced pilot." (The Commission could, to be sure, have reconciled these two statements by saying that the other three pilots were even worse, but it did not bring up this possibility.)

In another statement, which is irreconcilable with all previous assessments of Hanjour's abilities, the Commission wrote:

> Hanjour successfully conducted a challenging certification flight supervised by an instructor at Congressional Air Charters of Gaithersburg, Maryland, landing at a small airport with a difficult approach. The instructor thought Hanjour may have had training from a military pilot because he used a terrain recognition system for navigation.[22]

How could this instructor have had such a radically different view of Hanjour's abilities than all the others, right up through August of 2001? Who was this instructor? How could this report be verified?

The 9/11 Commission provided no answer to these questions. Its sole reference for its claim was: "Eddie Shalev interview (Apr. 9, 2004)." Extensive searches, however, turned up no record of Hanjour's having attended Congressional Air Charters and no one by the name of "Eddie Shalev" to whom the Commission could have been referring.[23]

The 9/11 Commission, in any case, did not deal with the contradiction—except by itself making contradictory statements. Although it mentioned that Flight 77 reportedly executed a 330-degree downward spiral, during which it descended several thousand feet in a few minutes, the Commission did *not* point out that, according to experts, this would have required a pilot "with extraordinary skill," who could fly with "almost military precision." It thus avoided the question of how a person of Hani Hanjour's incompetence could have been at the controls. It simply stated that he was.

The full problem, along with the Commission's failure to address it, was illustrated by a statement it made about President Bush. "As a former pilot," the Commission wrote, "the President was struck by the apparent sophistication of some of the piloting, especially Hanjour's high-speed dive into the Pentagon."[24] The Commission again failed to ask how Hani Hanjour could have been doing this sophisticated piloting.

Dealing with the Contradiction: Popular Mechanics

In 2006, *Popular Mechanics*, which had previously published an article intended to discredit alternative theories about 9/11, put out a somewhat revised and enlarged version of it as a book, entitled *Debunking 9/11 Myths*.[25] This book, besides having a foreword by Senator John McCain, has been endorsed by the US Department of State.[26] It can, therefore, be considered a quasi-official discussion of 9/11. How did this book deal with the contradiction?

On the one hand, it admitted that "none of the hijacker pilots had ever flown a commercial-size airline jet" and that their "flying skills were indeed rudimentary."[27]

On the other hand, it said that, although the pilots "may not have been highly skilled," they did not need to be, because the planes were already in flight when they took over. "All they had to do was pretty much point and go." The hijackers probably had portable GPS (Global Positioning System) units, *Popular Mechanics* claimed, so they would have needed "only to punch the destination coordinates into the flight management system and steer the planes while looking at the navigation screen."[28]

However, leaving aside the question of whether that might have been true about the flights aimed at the Twin Towers, it was certainly not true of the trajectory reportedly taken by Flight 77. How did the *Popular Mechanics* authors deal with the downward spiral, after which the plane came in at virtually ground level to strike the Pentagon between its first and second floors? They simply ignored it.

In their only statement about the final minutes of this flight, they wrote:

> The flight data recorder... of Flight 77 indicated that Hanjour input autopilot instructions to Reagan National Airport... He steered the plane manually for only the final eight minutes of the flight.[29]

It was, however, during those final eight minutes that the plane was reportedly "flown with extraordinary skill," with "almost military precision."

What did *Popular Mechanics* say about the downward spiral? Nothing. Referring to all the planes, it did acknowledge that they "made sharp turns of up to 330 degrees and at times dropped precipitously." But it did not point out that it was Flight 77 that executed the 330-degree turn in the "the final eight minutes of the flight," during which "Hanjour... steered the plane manually." More than one airline pilot has stated that it would have been impossible for an amateur pilot such as Hanjour to fly those final minutes. For example, former Pan American Airlines pilot Ted Muga, who had also been a pilot in the US Navy, has said:

> The maneuver at the Pentagon was... a tight spiral coming down out of 7,000 feet.... [I]t takes some very, very talented pilots to do that.... I just can't imagine an amateur even being able to come close to performing a maneuver of that nature.[30]

Conclusion

The claim that Hani Hanjour piloted American 77 into the Pentagon is inconsistent with all media reports about his piloting ability. Neither the 9/11 Commission nor *Popular Mechanics* has resolved this contradiction. Congress and the press need to ask why this contradiction exists and why the 9/11 Commission allowed it to go unresolved.

20

WHAT CAUSED THE HOLE IN THE
C RING?

A nother feature of the Pentagon strike concerning which a contradiction has emerged involves a round hole, about nine feet in diameter, that was created in the Pentagon's C ring in Wedge 2. This hole was at about the place a projectile continuing the attacking aircraft's reported trajectory would have hit, approximately 310 feet from the impact zone. What could have caused this hole?

The Original Explanation

The original explanation was that this hole was created by Flight 77's nose. Although the strike zone was in Wedge 1 of the Pentagon, Flight 77's reported trajectory was such that, by the time it reached the third of the Pentagon's five rings (the C ring), it would have been in Wedge 2. Two days after 9/11, Donald Rumsfeld, appearing on ABC's *Good Morning America*, said:

> [The plane] came in... between about the first and second floor.... And it went in through three rings. I'm told the nose is—is still in there, very close to the inner courtyard, about one ring away.[1]

Two days later, Lee Evey, the program manager for the Pentagon Renovation Project, said at a Pentagon news briefing:

> The plane actually penetrated through the... E ring, D ring, C ring.... The nose of the plane just barely broke through the inside of the C ring, so it was extending into A-E Drive a little bit.[2]

The press also gave this explanation. A *Newsweek* story on September 28, for example, said:

> The Boeing 757—American Airlines Flight 77—... crashed
> into the southwestern corner of the monolithic five-sided land-
> mark at speeds estimated at 450mph, cutting a 100-foot-wide
> wedge through the five floors of the outermost E-Ring, and
> penetrating into the D and C rings as well.[3]

Although this report did not specifically mention the nose, it did
say that the plane penetrated into the C ring, and the nose would
have presumably been leading the way.

A Problem

Although this explanation was generally accepted, it contained a
problem, which led critics to question it. The problem is that the
nose of a 757 is very fragile. Therefore, critics argued, the nose
of Flight 77 could not have gone through the outer (E ring) wall,
with its steel-reinforced concrete. And it certainly could not thereafter have punched out a large hole in the C-ring wall, with its
steel mesh and 8 inches of brick.

French critic Thierry Meyssan, for example, made this argument, writing:

> The nose of a plane... contains the electronic navigation
> system. In order to allow passage of the waves emitted by the
> apparatuses, it is not made of metal, but of carbon fibers. [It is]
> thus extremely fragile [and] would be crushed rather than
> piercing through.[4]

Meyssan used this as one of the arguments for his claim that the
Pentagon was instead struck by a missile—the type used to pierce
bunkers.[5] But the nose-cone theory was also questioned by critics
who did not share Meyssan's missile theory. Although Meyssan's
missile theory would be widely attacked, even by the US State
Department,[6] his negative claim—that the hole in the C ring
could not have been caused by the nose of a Boeing 757—would
eventually carry the day, as we will see below.

Official Reports

The first official report on the Pentagon was an "after-action
report" prepared by Arlington County, which came out in 2002.
Being focused on the response of local authorities to the attack on

the Pentagon, it had little to say about the damage to the building. But it did contain the following statement about the damage to the C ring:

> Flight #77 penetrated the outer wall of the Pentagon's E Ring and the damage extended all the way through the inner wall of the C Ring, a distance of approximately 285 feet.[7]

That statement could be read as supporting the original explanation, according to which the plane's nose went through the C ring. All that the statement actually says, however, is that the *damage* extended through the C ring. It might best be read, therefore, as pointing forward to the main official report on damage to the Pentagon.

This official report, the *Pentagon Building Performance Report*, appeared in 2003, having been prepared by the American Society of Civil Engineers (ASCE). In a statement about the damage to the C ring that could be read as supporting the original explanation, it said:

> The aircraft had entered the building at an angle.... The path of damage extended from the west exterior wall of the building in a north-easterly direction completely through Ring E, Ring D, Ring C.... There was a hole in the east wall of Ring C, emerging into AE Drive... in Wedge 2. The wall failure was approximately 310 ft from where the fuselage of the aircraft entered the west wall of the building. The path of the aircraft debris passed approximately 225 ft diagonally through Wedge 1 and approximately 85 ft diagonally through a portion of Ring C in Wedge 2.[8]

This statement, however, did not actually support the original explanation. Instead, it made only three claims: (1) the damage extended to the C ring; (2) there was a hole in the C ring; and (3) some of the aircraft debris passed through it. This statement did not say that the plane as such traveled to the C ring and caused the hole. It, in fact, said nothing whatsoever about what caused the hole.[9]

Moreover, whereas this statement merely failed to endorse the original explanation, that explanation was positively contradicted by other statements in the *Pentagon Building Performance Report*, especially the following one:

> At a depth of approximately 160 ft into the building, … it is highly unlikely that any significant portion of the fuselage could have retained structural integrity…. More likely, the fuselage was destroyed much earlier in its movement through the building. Therefore, the aircraft frame most certainly was destroyed before it had traveled a distance that approximately equaled the length of the aircraft.[10]

If the fuselage as a whole was destroyed before it got half the distance to the C ring, then the plane's nose certainly was not still being propelled forward.

This report did say, however, that some debris from the plane reached the C ring:

> The debris that traveled the farthest traveled approximately twice the length of the aircraft after entering the building… [coming] to rest at a point 310 ft from the area of impact.

As to the content of this debris, this report said:

> The remains of most of the passengers on the aircraft were found near the end of the travel of the aircraft debris. The front landing gear (a relatively solid and heavy object) and the flight data recorder (which had been located near the rear of the aircraft) were also found nearly 300 ft into the structure. By contrast, the remains of a few individuals (the hijacking suspects), who most likely were near the front of the aircraft, were found relatively close to the aircraft's point of impact with the building.[11]

This statement is certainly puzzling. It seems to suggest that the front landing gear made it so far because it is "a relatively solid and heavy object." But why, then, would "the remains of most of the passengers" have been propelled that far? And if they were indeed propelled that far, even though the passengers had reportedly been herded to the back of the plane, why would the remains of the hijackers, who were reportedly in the front of the plane, have been found way back near the point of impact?

Our concern, however, is not with such mysteries, but only with contradictions. And the original explanation of the hole in the C ring was clearly contradicted by this report's next sentence, which said:

These data suggest that the front of the aircraft disintegrated essentially upon impact but, in the process, opened up a hole allowing the trailing portions of the fuselage to pass into the building.[12]

"The front of the aircraft disintegrated essentially upon impact." This "front" would certainly include the fragile nose cone.

Accordingly, the ASCE's *Pentagon Building Performance Report*, without explicitly pointing it out, flatly contradicted the explanation that had been offered by Rumsfeld and Evey, according to which the hole in the C ring was punched out by Flight 77's nose.

Although the ASCE report did not offer an alternative explanation, *Popular Mechanics*—which, as we saw in the previous chapter, functions as a quasi-official organization with regard to 9/11—would soon proffer a new explanation.

Popular Mechanics' New Explanation

Popular Mechanics' 2005 article about 9/11 (which was mentioned in the previous chapter) contained only a brief statement about the hole: "The tidy hole in Ring C was 12 ft. wide.... ASCE concludes it was made by the jet's landing gear, not by the fusclage."[13]

As we saw, however, that is *not* what the ASCE report said. It did say that the front landing gear was found about 300 feet within the building, hence about 10 feet short of the wall with the hole in it. But that report did not suggest that the hole had been punched out by this landing gear.

To offer that theory, in fact, would have been to suggest a physical impossibility: If the landing gear had punched out a large hole in this steel-mesh-and-concrete wall, it could not then have bounced ten feet backwards. It is no cause for wonder, therefore, that the authors of the ASCE report did not make this causal suggestion.

For some reason, nevertheless, the authors of the *Popular Mechanics* article did. That this was not the result of some momentary lapse is shown, moreover, by the fact that in their book, *Debunking 9/11 Myths*, which they put out in 2006, these authors developed this claim at greater length.

Without mentioning the fact that the nose-cone explanation had been given by Rumsfeld and Evey, the *Popular Mechanics* authors explicitly rejected it, saying that "the hole was not made by... the nose of Flight 77 pushing through the building's interior." They then developed their own theory, saying:

> [Although] the less dense items, including the shell of the plane..., essentially disintegrated upon impact, [the impact] created a hole through which the heavier, denser items could continue forward into the building. [Accordingly, the plane's landing gear, being] one of the heaviest and most dense parts of the plane, ... flew farther than any other item... and was responsible for puncturing the wall in Ring C.[14]

Although these *Popular Mechanics* authors evidently believed that they were giving the ASCE's explanation, their account was really very different. Besides saying that the landing gear caused the hole, they, in suggesting that only the "heavier, denser items could continue forward," ignored the ASCE's statement that most of the remains of the passengers were found near the C ring.

What is important for our purposes, however, is the fact that *Popular Mechanics* brought out explicitly something that was merely implicit in the ASCE's *Pentagon Building Performance Report*: that this ASCE document, which is the official report on the damage to the Pentagon, contradicted the explanation of the hole in the C ring that was given by Pentagon spokesmen immediately after the attack. Insofar as the State Department refers readers to *Popular Mechanics*,[15] moreover, it apparently endorses the idea that the Pentagon's original explanation was false.

Why does this contradiction exist? If the whole front of the plane would have disintegrated before getting anywhere close to the C ring, why did Lee Evey say that "[t]he nose of the plane... broke through the inside of the C ring, so it was extending into A-E Drive a little bit"? Why did Donald Rumsfeld, two days after 9/11, say that "the nose is—is still in there, very close to the inner courtyard"?

Contradictory Reports from Witnesses

The contradictions, moreover, do not end there. The *Pentagon Building Performance Report*, besides contradicting Rumsfeld and Evey, also contradicted some eyewitness reports. One of these reports was by Paul K. Carlton, Jr., the surgeon general for the

US Air Force. In describing his effort to figure out what had happened, he said:

> I thought it was a terrorist bomb.... But then I saw the landing gear. It was on the ground in the alley between the B and C rings. When I saw it there, not only did I realize an airplane had struck the Pentagon but it was clear that the plane had come through the E, D, and C buildings to get there.[16]

Another witness was Navy Lt. Kevin Shaeffer, who told his story to Earl Swift of the *Virginian-Pilot*. After Shaeffer made his way out of the Pentagon following the attack by climbing through the hole in the C ring, Swift wrote:

> Shaeffer stood on a service road that circled the Pentagon between the B and C rings. A chunk of the 757's nose cone and front landing gear lay on the pavement a few feet away, resting against the B Ring wall.[17]

According to Carlton and Shaeffer, therefore, the landing gear was not ten feet short of the C ring wall. It was beyond this wall, in the service road (known as A-E Drive). According to Shaeffer, in fact, it was clear across this road, leaning up against the wall of the B ring. According to Shaeffer, moreover, part of the nose of an airplane was also there.

Conclusion

An exploration of the origin of the hole in the C ring leads, as we have seen, to several questions, such as: If the hole was caused by Flight 77's nose cone, why was this cone said by Lee Evey to be sticking out of the hole but said by Kevin Shaeffer to be resting up against the B ring wall? And if, as the ASCE's *Pentagon Building Performance Report* said, the landing gear ended up about ten feet short of the C ring, why did at least two officers report seeing it out in A-E drive? But the central question is: If the hole was *not* caused by Flight 77's nose cone, as the ASCE report implied and *Popular Mechanics* explicitly said, because this nose cone would have disintegrated long before reaching the C ring, why did Rumsfeld and Evey report that the nose cone not only created the hole but was still visible afterward? Congress and the press need to find out why this and the related contradictions exist.

21

DID A MILITARY PLANE FLY OVER WASHINGTON DURING THE PENTAGON ATTACK?

Accerording to the official story, the attack on the Pentagon was a complete surprise. No one at the Pentagon or in the military in general had known that an unidentified aircraft was headed in that direction. In response to the question of why the Pentagon was not evacuated before the attack, for example, one of its spokespersons said: "The Pentagon was simply not aware that this aircraft was coming our way."[1]

This claim of ignorance by the military was supported by the 9/11 Commission, which said that there was no warning about an unidentified aircraft heading toward Washington until 9:36, hence only "one or two minutes" before the Pentagon was struck at 9:38.[2] This short warning period, the Commission added, gave the Pentagon time only to order an unarmed military C-130H cargo plane, which was already in the air, to identify the approaching aircraft "as a Boeing 757" before it crashed into the Pentagon.[3]

Mystery Plane Spotted over Washington before the Pentagon Attack

This claim of ignorance by the military was, however, threatened from the first by reports of an unidentified airplane flying over Washington during the time of the attack on the Pentagon. At about 9:54 that morning, CNN's White House correspondent John King, reporting from Lafayette Park across from the White House, said:

> About ten minutes ago, there was a white jet circling overhead. Now, you generally don't see planes in the area over the White

House. That is restricted air space. No reason to believe that this jet was there for any nefarious purposes, but the Secret Service was very concerned, pointing up at the jet in the sky.[4]

Although King referred to this airspace as "restricted" (which is "a portion of airspace that is closed to civil aircraft at specified times"), it is actually *prohibited* airspace (which means that "civilian flying is prohibited at all times").[5] This fact suggests that the jet must have been a military plane. This possibility was raised explicitly by another CNN correspondent, Kate Snow, who at about 10:15AM reported:

> I did see a plane, about a half hour ago, circling over the Capitol. Now whether that may have been an Air Force plane, it's unclear. But that seemed to be the reason, according to security guards that I talked with, towards the evacuation of the Capitol.[6]

The plane was also reported by NBC's senior Washington correspondent, Bob Kur, who even more directly suggested that it was a government aircraft. During his description of the White House evacuation, Kur said:

> [I]n the most surreal of this morning's scenes here at the White House, a white plane, a very big jet, was flying an unusual pattern near the White House over Lafayette Park. Very slowly it made one circle and then, we have not seen it since. There was a lot of concern about what that plane might be.... [I]t's only speculation. But most people say that since flights have been cleared from US air space, and it was a totally white plane, ... that it was a government plane of some kind.[7]

ABC anchor Peter Jennings, reporting the plane in real time, with "9:41" superimposed on the screen, said:

> [T]here is a plane circling the White House at the moment. And they're clearing the grounds there.... I think probably most Americans know that there is no building in the country which is... [as] heavily defended.... [A] battery of anti-aircraft missiles [is] on the top of the White House itself.[8]

Although Jennings did not explicitly suggest that the plane belonged to the military, this suggestion was implicit in the fact that the White House's anti-aircraft missiles, which he mentioned, were not used to shoot it down.

Official Silence and Denials

These reports of an unidentified plane over Washington constituted a threat to the official story about the Pentagon attack. If the plane was indeed a military plane, as several signs suggested, and if it was there before the Pentagon was struck, then the military's claim that it had no knowledge of a plane approaching the Pentagon would be thrown into question. According to the official report on the trajectory of Flight 77, as we saw in Chapter 19, it executed a 330-degree downward spiral before crashing into the Pentagon. An NTSB report, said to be based on information from the plane's flight data recorder, stated that the execution of this spiral took 3 minutes and 2 seconds.[9] A military plane over Washington would have been in position to observe this maneuver as well as the plane's prior approach to Washington. The 9/11 Commission's claim that the military knew of an approaching aircraft only "one or two minutes" in advance would become implausible.

It would be important, therefore, to determine whether the mystery plane was indeed a military plane and, if so, whether it was over Washington before the Pentagon was attacked.

When *The 9/11 Commission Report* appeared in 2004, however, it made no mention of the reports about the plane, even though those reports were available in the CNN, NBC, and ABC transcripts from 9/11. The Commission thereby simply ignored the fact that these reports may have contradicted the Pentagon's claim of ignorance about an approaching aircraft.

In 2006, Congressman Adam Schiff (D-CA), having been made aware of the reported aircraft over Washington by one of his constituents,[10] wrote a letter to the Pentagon on behalf of this constituent's letter, which had requested information about the aircraft. A letter of reply to Schiff from the US Air Force, dated November 8, 2006, said:

> This is in reply to your inquiry on behalf of [your constituent] regarding his request for information relating to an unidentified aircraft that may have been in restricted airspace near the White House on September 11, 2001 between the hours of 9:30-10:30AM.

Air Force officials have no knowledge of the aircraft in question.[11]

Close to a year later, CNN would show that denial to be false.

CNN's Revelations of September 12, 2007

On September 12, 2007, John King, who had given the original CNN report about the mystery plane, gave a new report on CNN's *Anderson Cooper 360°*. This report differed most dramatically from the earlier one by featuring a video clip with a clear image of the airplane. Pointing out that the plane was "a four-engine jet banking slowly in the nation's most off-limits airspace," King said that "still today, no one will offer an official explanation of what we saw."[12]

King, however, made another revelation, stating: "Two government sources familiar with the incident tell CNN it was a military aircraft. They say the details are classified." Next, confirming what Congressman Adam Schiff had learned ten months earlier, King added: "Ask the Pentagon, and it insists this is not a military aircraft."[13]

But King then presented decisive evidence to the contrary. Showing two pictures side by side, King said:

> This comparison of the CNN video and an official Air Force photo suggests the mystery plane is among the military's most sensitive aircraft, an Air Force E-4B. Note the flag on the tail, the stripe around the fuselage, and the telltale bubble just behind the 747 cockpit area.[14]

Retired US Air Force Major General Don Shepperd was then shown endorsing this identification, after which King added: "The E-4B is a state-of-the-art flying command post."[15]

The E-4B

The E-4B is a militarized version of the Boeing 747-200. To see why King described it as a "flying command post," one can turn to the Strategic Air Command's page on this plane, which says:

> The E-4B serves as the National Airborne Operations Center for the president, secretary of defense and the Joint Chiefs of Staff or JCS. In case of national emergency or destruction of

ground command control centers, the aircraft provides a highly survivable, command, control and communications center to direct U.S. forces, execute emergency war orders and coordinate actions by civil authorities…. E-4B operations are directed by the JCS and executed through U.S. Strategic Command…. An advanced satellite communications system improves worldwide communications among strategic and tactical satellite systems and the airborne operations center…. To provide direct support to the president, secretary of defense and the JCS, at least one E-4B is always on alert at one of many selected bases throughout the world.[16]

An article in the *Air Force Civil Engineer*, referring to the E-4B as "a truly amazing aircraft," says that in the case of a national emergency, it would serve as "the nation's premier… command, control and communications center to direct U.S. forces [and] execute emergency war orders." Because it would be used to command US forces if the Pentagon were destroyed, it is sometimes called the "Doomsday Plane."[17]

As these descriptions make clear, the E-4B, far from being simply an ordinary military plane, has extraordinary capacities for command, control, and communication. Was it over Washington in time to have observed what was going on before the Pentagon was struck?

How Early Was the E-4B over Washington?

At the beginning of John King's 2007 report, he said that the plane "appeared overhead just before 10AM." His report ended, however, by speaking of "the giant plane over the president's house just as the smoke began to rise across the river at the Pentagon."[18] King's concluding statement, therefore, corresponded with the previously mentioned account by Peter Jennings, according to which the plane was flying over the White House by 9:41. Although King's statement might suggest that the plane did not appear over Washington until after the Pentagon was struck, his statement would surely refer to the time at which he first *noticed* the plane. The question, in any case, is whether there is any evidence that this plane was over Washington *before* the Pentagon was struck (at 9:38).

The full video, from which CNN played brief segments during its September 12, 2007, report, is 18 minutes long. At 6 minutes 20 seconds into the video, the camera, panning upward, caught the E-4B in the sky and stayed focused on it for 29 seconds. Over two minutes later, at 8 minutes and 40 seconds into the video, smoke is suddenly seen behind the White House, and the conversations of some men talking on cell phones show that they have just been informed of the strike on the Pentagon. This video shows, therefore, that the E-4B was already flying above Washington at least two minutes before the Pentagon was struck.[19]

According to another CNN report, which appeared two days after 9/11:

> Brig. Gen. Clyde Vaughn of the U.S. Army, director of military support, told reporters he was in his car on nearby Interstate 395 when the plane hit the Pentagon on Tuesday morning. Vaughn said "I was scanning the air" as he was sitting in his car. "There wasn't anything in the air, except for one airplane, and it looked like it was loitering over Georgetown, in a high, left-hand bank," he said. "That may have been the plane. I have never seen one on that (flight) pattern." ... A few minutes later, Vaughn witnessed the craft's impact.[20]

If General Vaughn thought that the Pentagon was struck by the plane that he had seen "loitering over Georgetown," he was, of course, mistaken. But his testimony provided additional evidence that the E-4B was flying over Washington some minutes before the Pentagon was struck.

Additional evidence for this view came from a report that same day (September 13) on England's Channel 4 television station, which said: "Just before the crash [of AA 77], a civilian plane was filmed over the city apparently banking hard and there were reports of a military plane circling the US capital. Moments later, the Department of Defense was hit."[21]

Still more evidence has been provided by Linda Brookhart, who was attending a National Taxpayers Conference in the Old Executive Office Building, which is right next to the White House. After the people in this building were told to evacuate, perhaps because of the plane overhead, she saw the plane and took a 35-millimeter photograph of it with her Pentax camera. She snapped this photograph, she reported, *before* the plume of smoke from the Pentagon became visible to people at the White House.[22]

Linda Brookhart's testimony and photograph, the CNN video, General Vaughn's testimony, and the Channel 4 report are, therefore, mutually supportive.

The Significance of the Official Denials

In John King's report on 9/11 about the plane above the White House, he said: "No reason to believe that this jet was there for any nefarious purposes."[23] In principle, it would be possible to maintain this view even after learning that the jet was a military plane. It could be said, for example, that the plane, while on legitimate business, just happened to appear over Washington right before the Pentagon was struck.

In 2003, in fact, Dan Verton, a former US Marine Corps intelligence officer, published a book in which he said that an E-4B, carrying both civilian and military officials, was launched from "an airfield outside of the nation's capital." It "had only just taken off," Verton wrote, when the Pentagon attack occurred. This plane was planning to "conduct a previously scheduled Defense Department exercise."[24] (This exercise would have been Global Guardian, in which three NAOC [National Airborne Operations Center] planes were participating.[25]) But once the E-4B was airborne, Verton added, it "was immediately ordered to cease the military exercise... and prepare to become the actual national airborne operations center."[26] Verton's account could, therefore, explain why an E-4B was over Washington that morning.

The fact remains, however, that the military has denied that the airplane spotted over the White House was one of its own. John King's previously quoted comment about this denial—"Ask the Pentagon, and it insists this is not a military aircraft"—could suggest that someone in the Pentagon simply made a casual, informal denial to a reporter. As we saw, however, the denial—"Air Force officials have no knowledge of the aircraft in question"— was made in a letter on USAF stationery to a member of the US Congress. If the plane was an E-4B on a perfectly legitimate training exercise, why would the military have lied about it? (The conclusion that the military has lied, and not simply made a mistake, is reinforced by Verton's statement that his source in the military, who had informed him about the E-4B's flight that morning, had also told him that he had written an after-action report about the flight.[27])

The US military, moreover, was not the only government institution that denied knowledge of the plane. John King's 2007 report ended with these words:

> [S]ix years later, the Pentagon, the Secret Service and the FAA all say they, at least for public consumption, have no explanation of the giant plane over the president's house just as the smoke began to rise across the river at the Pentagon.[28]

In making this statement, King was probably referring to information that had been provided to CNN by Congressman Schiff's constituent, mentioned earlier. Besides informing CNN, in June 2007, that it had in its own files a video of the E-4B flying over the White House,[29] this man also told CNN about letters that he had sent to the Secret Service and the FAA (as well as about the letters that he and Congressman Schiff had sent to the Pentagon).

He had, he informed CNN, sent a FOIA (Freedom of Information Act) request to the US Secret Service "for information pertaining to records of the observation by Secret Service personnel of an aircraft flying near the White House or circling above it on September 11, 2001, between 9:30AM and 10:00AM." The reply, which came from the Department of Homeland Security, stated: "A review of the Secret Service's systems of records indicated that there are no records or documents pertaining to your request in Secret Service files."[30] Insofar as this statement, which simply speaks about written records, implied that the Secret Service knew nothing about the plane, it was surely false, given John King's previously quoted statement on the morning of 9/11: "No reason to believe that this jet was there for any nefarious purposes, but the Secret Service was very concerned, pointing up at the jet in the sky."[31] The reply from the Department of Homeland Security must, therefore, be regarded as at best misleading.

Congressman Schiff's constituent also sent a FOIA request to the FAA on June 19, 2006, requesting records identifying the aircraft. On February 2, 2007, the FAA replied that it had "no identification records." This response was also sent to Schiff, who had written to the FAA on behalf of his constituent.[32]

Accordingly, when John King said that "the Pentagon, the Secret Service and the FAA all say they, at least for public consumption, have no explanation of the giant plane over the president's house," he was probably alluding to these letters to Congressman Schiff and his constituent. And if so, we can see that King's statement did not fully express the denials made by these three organizations. They did not merely say that they had "no explanation, at least for public consumption." They explicitly and formally denied, in letters responding to FOIA requests and to a US congressman, that they had any records in their files about the plane. The US Air Force went even further, saying it had "no knowledge of the aircraft" whatsoever.

Lee Hamilton and the 9/11 Commission

After CNN's John King gave his new report on the plane over Washington and pointed out that "there is no mention of it in the official report of the 9/11 Commission," he said: "Commission co-chairman Lee Hamilton says he has a vague recollection of someone mentioning a mystery plane, but staffers who looked into it never raised it as a relevant issue." Hamilton himself then said: "When you're conducting a major investigation, you get thousands of things that come at you. You can't possibly sort through them all. This never rose to the level of a discussion within the commission."[33] Hamilton thereby implied that the reports of an airplane over Washington during the period in which the Pentagon was attacked were rightly ignored by the 9/11 Commission.

The Commission, however, had defended the idea that the military did not know that an aircraft was about to strike the Pentagon. It was on this basis, presumably, that the Commission did not blame anyone at the Pentagon for not preventing 125 deaths by having the building evacuated. The Commission also said, moreover, that the Pentagon, having a warning of "one or two minutes" that an unidentified aircraft was coming its way, ordered a military plane already in the air to identify it.[34]

How then could Hamilton claim that reports of a plane over Washington were not important enough to be discussed by the Commission? The plane, Hamilton would have known, would have almost certainly been a military plane (given the fact that the airspace over Washington is off limits to nonmilitary planes at all times). And if there was a military plane over Washington at the time, there would have been no need to employ the C-130H cargo plane to identify the aircraft that was approaching the Pentagon. Also, the claim that Pentagon officials were unaware of the approaching aircraft, which spiraled downward for three minutes before crashing into the building, becomes implausible, making even more insistent the question of why the Pentagon was not evacuated.

Conclusion

Now that it is public knowledge that there was a military plane with extraordinary capabilities over Washington on 9/11 prior to the attack on the Pentagon, Congress and the press need to ask what it was doing, what it observed, why the FAA and the military gave false replies to a US congressman's enquiry about this plane, and why the 9/11 Commission failed to address the issue.

PART V

Questions about the World Trade Center

22

How Did Rudy Giuliani Know the Towers Were Going to Collapse?

O ne of the most surprising features of 9/11 was the fact that the Twin Towers of the World Trade Center completely collapsed. Because these collapses were so unexpected, it was also surprising to learn that Rudy Giuliani, then the mayor of New York City, reported that he had been told in advance that the towers were going to collapse.

Giuliani's Statement and Later Explanation

While being interviewed on 9/11 by Peter Jennings, then the anchor at ABC News, Giuliani discussed what happened after his people at the Office of Emergency Management had evacuated their command center on the 23rd floor of WTC 7 that morning:

> [W]e set up headquarters at 75 Barclay Street, which was right there with the Police Commissioner, the Fire Commissioner, the Head of Emergency Management, and we were operating out of there when we were told that the World Trade Center was gonna collapse. And it did collapse before we could actually get out of the building, so we were trapped in the building for 10, 15 minutes, and finally found an exit and got out.[1]

The South Tower, the first building to collapse, did so at 9:59AM. Giuliani said, therefore, that shortly before 9:59, he was told that "the World Trade Center was gonna collapse."

Although in the intervening years there was no public questioning of Giuliani about this remark, WNBC reported that in May 2007, he was asked about it by a small group of people with a video camera.[2] A young woman, after reminding him of what he had told Peter Jennings and of the fact that "no steel structure in history has ever collapsed due to a fire," asked: "How come people in the buildings weren't notified? And who else knew about this?" Giuliani replied: "I didn't know the towers were going to collapse." A male member of the group then reminded Giuliani that he had indeed said, during his conversation with Peter Jennings, that he had been notified in advance that the towers were going to collapse. This man then asked: "Who told you the towers were going to collapse in advance, sir?" Giuliani replied:

> I didn't realize the towers would collapse.... Our understanding was that over a long period of time, the way other buildings collapsed, the towers could collapse, meaning over a 7, 8, 9, 10-hour period. No one that I know of had any idea they would implode. That was a complete surprise.[3]

This explanation, it must be said, seems more a revision than a clarification, because Giuliani's statement to Jennings—"we were told that the World Trade Center was gonna collapse. And it did collapse before we could actually get out of the building"—did suggest that he had expected an imminent collapse.

Be that as it may, Giuliani's answer suggested that his expectation had a historical basis. Was there in fact a historical basis for an expectation that the towers would come down—whether immediately or after seven to ten hours? According to experts, it seems, there was not.

Expert Testimony and Historical Experience

In 2001, *New York Times* reporter James Glanz wrote: "[E]xperts said no... modern, steel-reinforced high-rise, had ever collapsed because of an uncontrolled fire."[4]

In 2002, Robert F. Shea, the acting administrator of FEMA's Federal Insurance and Mitigation Administration, testified to the House of Representatives' Committee on Science, which was holding hearings on the WTC collapses. Speaking on the basis of his "experience of 25 years," he said: "[T]he World Trade Center was..., frankly, ... an anomaly. No one who viewed it that day, including myself, believed that those towers would fall."[5] Since an anomaly is something that contravenes known laws, it was a good term for the collapse of the Twin Towers, because fire had never caused the total collapse of a steel-frame high-rise building.

In 1988, for example, a fire in the First Interstate Bank build-ing in Los Angeles raged for 3.5 hours. Although it gutted 5 of this building's 62 floors, it caused no significant structural damage.[6] That example by itself would suggest that there would have been no reason for anyone at the World Trade Center that morning to expect that the North and South Towers would collapse after burning only 102 and 56 minutes, respectively.

What about, however, Giuliani's later statement that he and his people had expected them to collapse "over a 7, 8, 9, 10-hour period"? In 1991, a huge fire in Philadelphia's One Meridian Plaza lasted for 18 hours and gutted 8 of the building's 38 floors. "Beams and girders sagged and twisted... under severe fire expo-sures," said the FEMA report, but "the columns continued to support their loads without obvious damage."[7] Back in 1975, moreover, there had been a fire in the World Trade Center's North Tower. It caused damage on ten floors and the effort to extinguish it was described as "like fighting a blowtorch," but the "building survived with minor damage."[8] The history of fires in steel-frame high-rise buildings, therefore, would have provided no one a basis for expecting the towers to collapse.

But the towers, of course, had been hit by airplanes. Should this fact have led someone to expect them to collapse?

These buildings, it was well known, had been designed to handle the impact of a large airliner. In 1964, when the towers were being designed, two analyses were carried out to determine how well they would stand up to being hit by one.[9]

Several people involved in building the towers had commented on this feature of their design. Leslie Robertson, who was a member of the architectural firm—Worthington, Skilling, Helle and Jackson—that designed the Twin Towers, said that they had been designed to withstand the impact of a large airliner.[10] The architect who was primarily responsible for the structural design, John Skilling, discussed in 1993 (after the WTC bombing) what would happen if one of the towers were to suffer a strike by an airliner loaded with jet fuel. Although "there would be a horrendous fire" and "a lot of people would be killed," Skilling said, "the building structure would still be there."[11] In January of 2001, Frank De Martini, who had been the on-site construction manager for the Twin Towers, said of each of them: "I believe that the building could probably sustain multiple impacts of jet liners."[12]

New York City also had historical experience to draw on. In 1945, a B-25 had struck the Empire State Building at the 79th floor, creating a hole 20 feet high. But this damage, although it caused a large fire, did not result in even a partial collapse.[13] A B-25 is, to be sure, much smaller than a Boeing 767, but the Twin Towers were also much bigger than the Empire State Building.

Expectations at Ground Zero

In conformity with this expert testimony and historical experience, firefighters and emergency medical workers on the scene reported that they had no expectation of a collapse. We have their testimony thanks to oral histories of about 500 members of the Fire Department of New York (which includes Emergency Medical Services as a special division[14]). These testimonies were recorded shortly after 9/11 and then—after a lengthy legal process[15]—made available to the public in 2005 on a *New York Times* website.[16] Here are a few examples.

Lieutenant Brendan Whelan said: "I thought maybe the floors that were burning would collapse on themselves..., I never thought the whole thing would come down."[17]

Murray Murad, an investigator with the Bureau of Investigations and Trials, said: "no one ever expected it to collapse like that."[18]

Battalion Chief Brian Dixon said that after "everything blew out on... one floor," he thought that the top of the South Tower was going to come off and fall down, but "there was never a thought that this whole thing is coming down."[19]

Emergency Medical Services Division Chief John Peruggia, speaking of the time after both buildings had been hit, said:

> Looking up at [the North Tower], you could see that... there was significant structural damage to the exterior of the building.... Now you know, ... this is not a scene where the thought

of both buildings collapsing ever entered into my mind.... We were always told by everyone, the experts, that these buildings could withstand direct hits from airplanes. That's the way they were designed.... It was hit by an airplane. That's okay. It's made to be hit by an airplane. I mean I think everyone may have believed that. We were all told years ago it was made to be hit by an airplane.[20]

Captain Charles Clarke, describing what happened after he was told by another firefighter to start running, said:

We started running.... I was kind of in disbelief that the building was actually collapsing.... I couldn't believe that the entire building was going to collapse in one heap.[21]

Captain Mark Stone, an emergency medical worker, described his thoughts at the time in the following words:

I just turned around and looked back at the Trade Center and I said, Oh my God.... Whoever in their right mind would have thought that the World Trade Center would ever fall down.... Nobody in the world, nobody ever would ever have thought these buildings were coming down.[22]

Firefighter Warren Smith, after saying that he had seen debris falling, stated: "We didn't know how much of that building was going to come down, obviously not the whole thing." He later added:

You just couldn't believe that those buildings could come down.... [I]t's like, Oh my God, what the hell happened? ... There was a little bit of a Titanic mentality because of 1993: everybody saw the damage that was done and that building didn't go down.... I didn't think those buildings would go down.... Again, there's no history of these buildings falling down.[23]

Smith's final statement—"there's no history of these buildings falling down"—can serve as a summary of the testimony of experts and firefighters at Ground Zero.

The conclusion to be drawn from these testimonies—that the collapse of the Twin Towers was completely unexpected by professionals at the scene—was even acknowledged by the 9/11 Commission, which said that, to its knowledge, "none of the [fire] chiefs present believed that a total collapse of either tower was possible."[24]

Actually, there was one fire chief who did fear a collapse. Although it did not mention this fact, the 9/11 Commission was informed by FDNY Commissioner Thomas Von Essen that Chief Ray Downey, who died in the North Tower collapse, had told him: "Boss, I think these buildings could collapse."[25] Downey's opinion had special significance, because he was an expert on building collapse, as 9/11 Commissioner Timothy Roemer pointed out.[26] One member of the FDNY, in fact, called him "the premiere collapse expert in the country."[27]

Downey, however, believed that explosives had been placed in the buildings. According to a book written by his nephew, he developed this belief as early as 9:20AM, long before the South Tower collapsed.[28] And then after the South Tower did collapse, according to one of the FDNY chaplains, Downey said that "there were bombs up there."[29]

Accordingly, Chief Downey did *not* constitute an exception to the 9/11 Commission's statement, assuming that its statement that "none of the [fire] chiefs present believed that a total collapse of either tower was possible" meant that they did not think it was possible *due to damage resulting from the airplane impact plus the fires.*

When the official report on the collapse of the Twin Towers was later issued by NIST—the National Institute of Standards and Technology—it supported the same conclusion. Referring to the North Tower, NIST's *Final Report* said:

> As far as assessments related to the structural stability of the building were concerned, the WTC 1 Command Post knew that significant damage had been done to the building.... Their fire-fighting experience led them to believe that the buildings would remain in place throughout their operations, but they did expect that there would be some localized collapse conditions in the impact zone and the fire zones. No one interviewed indicated that they thought that the buildings would completely collapse.[30]

Referring in general to the FDNY command officers in charge of planning the operations inside the towers, NIST said:

> These officers... expected that there would be localized collapse conditions on the damaged fire floors. The officers did

not expect that there would be any massive collapse conditions or complete building collapse.[31]

It would seem, therefore, that the combination of fire and structural damage would not have provided an objective basis for Giuliani's expectation, reportedly derived from some source, that the towers were going to collapse, whether immediately or after seven to ten hours. We have a contradiction, accordingly, between Giuliani and his reported source, who suggested that there was an objective basis for expecting the towers to collapse, and evidently everyone else with an informed opinion.

Dealing with the Contradiction

How did the 9/11 Commission deal with this contradiction? It failed to mention it. Although Giuliani testified before the Commission, it did not ask him about his comment to Peter Jennings.

Giuliani at the 9/11 Commission Hearing: In his testimony to the Commission, in fact, Giuliani told a different story, saying that while he was in an office at 75 Barclay Street:

> The desk started to shake, and I heard next Chief Esposito, who was the uniformed head of the police department, ... say, "The tower is down, the tower has come down." And my first thought was that one of the radio towers from the top of the World Trade Center had come down. I did not conceive of the entire tower coming down, but as he was saying that, I could see... outside a tremendous amount of debris and it first felt like an earthquake, and then it looked like a nuclear cloud. So we realized very shortly that we were in danger in the building, that the building could come down. It had been damaged. It was shaking. So the police commissioner and I, and the deputy police commissioner, we jointly decided that we had to try to get everyone out of the building.[32]

In this version of what he had experienced, Giuliani did not get any advance warning about the collapse of the Twin Towers. He could not even "conceive of [an] entire tower coming down." He simply experienced the fact that one of the towers did come down. The building he had feared might come down was the one at 75

Barclay Street. No one on the 9/11 Commission asked him about this change of story.

Thomas Kean and Lee Hamilton, in their book giving "the inside story of the 9/11 Commission," admitted that they did not do a good job of asking Giuliani questions, saying: "The questioning of Mayor Giuliani was a low point in terms of the commission's questioning of witnesses at our public hearings. We did not ask tough questions, nor did we get all of the information we needed to put on the public record."[33] The "tough questions" they had in mind, however, were limited to questions about radios and other matters related to the failure to communicate information that might have saved the lives of employees and firefighters in the towers. Those would, to be sure, have been important questions; Giuliani's failings in these and other matters related to 9/11 have been extensively discussed by other authors.[34] But the toughest questions would have involved Giuliani's reported foreknowledge that a collapse was coming.

The 9/11 Oral Histories and the Office of Emergency Management: Had the Commission investigated and reported on this issue, it could have answered, at least partially, the question as to the source of this foreknowledge. Information relevant to this question is contained in the oral histories recorded by the Fire Department of New York. Although these testimonies were not made generally available until 2005, which was after the 9/11 Commission had finished its work, it had been given access to them.[35] The Commission, moreover, evidently took full advantage of this access: Besides saying that it carried out a "review of 500 internal FDNY interview transcripts,"[36] an examination of the notes of *The 9/11 Commission Report* reveals that the FDNY oral histories were used quite extensively.[37] The Commission could have, therefore, reported on some testimonies relevant to the question of the source of Giuliani's foreknowledge of the collapses.

If the Commission had reported the testimony of Chief Albert Turi, for example, the public would have learned that he read the following statement:

I thought we would be pretty good for about three hours. Three hours is usually what the fire walls are rated for in high-rise construction…. We didn't have any indications of any structural [in]stability at that time. Then Steve Mosiello, Chief [Peter] Ganci's executive assistant, came over to the command post and he said we're getting reports from OEM [the Office of Emergency Management] that the buildings are not structurally sound, and of course that got our attention really quick, and Pete [Ganci] said, well, who are we getting these reports from? And then Steve brought an EMT person over to the command post who was I think sent as a runner to tell us this and Chief Ganci questioned him, where are we getting these reports? And his answer was… we're not sure, OEM is just reporting this.[38]

By turning then to Steven Mosiello's statement, they could have found that this "EMT person" was Emergency Medical Technician Richard Zarrillo.[39] Zarrillo himself said:

John [Perrugia] came to me and said you need to go find Chief Ganci and relay the following message: that the buildings have been compromised, we need to evacuate, they're going to collapse. I said okay…. As I was walking towards the Fire command post, I found Steve Mosiello. I said, Steve, where's the boss? I have to give him a message. He said, well, what's the message? I said the buildings are going to collapse; we need to evac[uate] everybody out. With a very confused look he said who told you that? I said I was just with John at OEM. OEM says the buildings are going to collapse; we need to get out. He escorted me over to Chief [Peter] Ganci.[40] [Steve] said, hey, Pete, we got a message that the buildings are going to collapse. His reply was who the fuck told you that? Then Steve brought me in and with Chief Ganci, Commissioner Feehan, Steve, I believe Chief Turi was initially there, I said, listen, I was just at OEM. The message I was given was that the buildings are going to collapse; we need to get our people out. At that moment, this thunderous, rolling roar came down and that's when the building came down, the first tower came down.[41]

Then, having learned from Zarrillo that he got this information from EMS Division Chief John Peruggia, the Commission could have learned that Peruggia, after reporting that he was contacted by the fire operations center while he was en route to the World Trade Center, said:

They advised me that the Office of Emergency Management had been activated. I am the person in operations who is responsible for staffing OEM or the Police Department's command and control center.... I was in a discussion with Mr. Rotanz and I believe it was a representative from the Department of Buildings, but I'm not sure. Some engineer type person, and several of us were huddled talking in the lobby and it was brought to my attention, it was believed that the structural damage that was suffered to the towers was quite significant and they were very confident that the building's stability was compromised and they felt that the North Tower was in danger of a near imminent collapse. I grabbed EMT Zarrillo, I advised him of that information. I told him he was to proceed immediately to the command post where Chief Ganci was located.... I told him "You see Chief Ganci and Chief Ganci only. Provide him with the information that the building integrity is severely compromised and they believe the building is in danger of imminent collapse."[42]

After being asked during his interview if they were talking about "just the one building or both of them," Peruggia replied:

The information we got at that time was that they felt both buildings were significantly damaged, but they felt that the north tower, which was the first one to be struck, was going to be in imminent danger of collapse.[43]

The "Mr. Rotanz" to whom Peruggia referred was Richard Rotanz, the deputy director of the Office of Emergency Management. Therefore, Zarrillo's testimony, according to which the information about the towers' expected collapse had come from the OEM, was confirmed by Peruggia.

Given the fact that neither experts nor firefighters at the scene expected the towers to collapse, with some of them even saying that the thought would not have entered their minds, the Commission certainly should have asked Richard Rotanz why he expected the towers to come down. The Commission should also have tried to identify the "engineer type person," who might have been the "representative from the Department of Buildings" mentioned by Peruggia.

The 9/11 Commission, in fact, may allude to this person in a sentence apparently referring to the episode discussed by Turi, Mosiello, Zarrillo, and Peruggia: "At about 9:57, an EMS paramedic approached the FDNY Chief of Department and advised that an engineer in front of 7 WTC had just remarked that the Twin Towers in fact were in imminent danger of a total collapse."[44] The Commission showed no sign, however, of trying to determine the identity of this engineer to find out why he had made this statement.

Conclusion

The important fact revealed in the 9/11 oral histories, in any case, is that the word that the towers were going to collapse evidently originated at the Office of Emergency Management. How was this office related to Giuliani? The director of the OEM, who at that time was Richard Sheirer, reported directly to Giuliani.[45]

So although Giuliani said that he and others at 75 Barclay Street "were told" that the towers were going to collapse, it was his own people who were doing the telling. How would they have known this, when there was a virtually universal belief that a total collapse of the towers would have been impossible, something that would not even enter one's mind? Congress and the press need to do what the 9/11 Commission failed to do: Ask Giuliani what he and his people in the OEM knew that other people did not know.

23

WERE THERE EXPLOSIONS IN THE TWIN TOWERS?

The collapse of the Twin Towers has been explained by the government, official reports, and the press as resulting from the damage inflicted by the impact of the airliners plus the ensuing fires. Any explosions within the towers are assumed to have been caused by the jet-fuel fires. The idea that there were bombs or explosives, which might have contributed to the collapses, has been denied, whether explicitly or only implicitly.

The Position of the 9/11 Commission and NIST

The 9/11 Commission Report made no mention of testimonies of explosions in the towers, except to point out that when the South Tower collapsed, some firefighters in the North Tower, not realizing what had happened, falsely "surmised that a bomb had exploded."[1]

In 2006, Lee Hamilton, the vice chairman of the 9/11 Commission, submitted to an interview with the Canadian Broadcasting Corporation, during which he was asked about the theory "that the buildings were brought down by controlled explosion, controlled demolition." Hamilton replied:

> We of course looked at that very carefully—we find no evidence of that. We find all kinds of evidence that it was the airplanes that did it.... What caused the collapse of the buildings, to summarize it, was that the super-heated jet fuel melted the steel super-structure of these buildings and caused their collapse.[2]

In stating that the jet-fuel fire melted the steel, Hamilton revealed that he did not even understand the theory presupposed by the Commission. According to this theory, the fire did not melt the steel—because an open, diffuse hydrocarbon fire would necessarily be at least 1,000 degrees (Fahrenheit) cooler than the 2,800 degrees needed to melt steel—but only weakened it sufficiently to allow it to collapse.

Hamilton's ignorance of this point reflects the fact that the Commission had virtually nothing to say about the collapse of the World Trade Center, perhaps because the primary responsibility for explaining it was assigned to the National Institute of Standards and Technology, usually called simply NIST. Of course, given the fact that NIST had published its report on the Twin Towers in 2005, one might have expected Hamilton to have absorbed its conclusions by 2006, when he participated in that interview. Be that as it may, Hamilton did share NIST's view that there was no evidence of controlled demolition.

According to NIST's *Final Report*, "the aircraft impacts and subsequent fires led to the collapses of the towers after terrorists flew jet fuel laden commercial airliners into the buildings."[3] The question of whether the collapses might have been aided by explosives, perhaps in the process known as controlled demolition, was addressed in only one sentence (although this sentence was repeated three times): "NIST found no corroborating evidence for alternative hypotheses suggesting that the WTC towers were brought down by controlled demolition using explosives planted prior to September 11, 2001."[4]

Having published its *Final Report* in 2005, NIST in 2006 put out a document entitled "Answers to Frequently Asked Questions,"[5] in which it addressed this issue more fully. In response to one of those questions—"Why did NIST not consider a 'controlled demolition' hypothesis?"—this document repeated NIST's earlier statement, namely:

> NIST found no corroborating evidence for alternative hypotheses suggesting that the WTC towers were brought down by controlled demolition using explosives planted prior to Sept. 11, 2001.

Part of its support for this statement was the following claim:

> There was no evidence (collected by NIST, or by the New York

Police Department, the Port Authority Police Department or the Fire Department of New York) of any blast or explosions in the region below the impact and fire floors.[6]

In limiting the discussion to "the region below the impact and fire floors," NIST's implicit point seemed to be that if explosions occurred on the floors that were impacted by the plane and/or on which there were fires, those explosions could be explained as resulting from those causes.

The question of whether other explosions occurred is the only question to be explored in the present chapter. This question is, of course, related to the more sweeping issue of whether the towers were brought down by controlled demolition. That more sweeping question, however, involves many considerations, only one of which is the question of whether there were explosions in the towers beyond those that might plausibly be explained as resulting from the airplane strikes and the resulting fires fed by jet fuel. As an examination of the evidence reveals, the claim that no such explosions occurred is contradicted by the testimony of many people on the scene, including firefighters, emergency medical workers, journalists, North and South Tower employees who made it out alive, and a police officer.

Testimony of Firefighters

Shortly after 9/11, as we saw in the previous chapter, 9/11 oral histories were recorded of some 500 members of the Fire Department of New York (FDNY). These testimonies were then made available to the public by the *New York Times* in 2005. Many of these testimonies—almost one-fourth of them by one count[7]—included descriptions of phenomena suggestive of explosions going off in the Twin Towers before and during their collapses that could not plausibly be explained as resulting from the impact and fire. The FDNY includes, as we have seen, emergency medical workers as well as firefighters. Beginning with the latter, we will look first at testimony about the South Tower, also known as Tower Two (WTC 2), which was the second tower to be hit, although the first one to collapse. These testimonies are simply given in alphabetical order.

South Tower: Firefighter Richard Banaciski said:

> [T]here was just an explosion. It seemed like on television [when] they blow up these buildings. It seemed like it was going all the way around like a belt, all these explosions.[8]

This description—of explosions going around the building like a belt—does not suggest that kind of random explosions that would be expected from exploding jet fuel or other after-effects of the airplane's impact and resulting fires.

Firefighter Edward Cachia said:

> As my officer and I were looking at the South Tower, it just gave. It actually gave at a lower floor, not the floor where the plane hit... [W]e originally had thought there was like an internal detonation, explosives, because it went in succession, boom, boom, boom, boom, and then the tower came down.[9]

Cachia's statement, like many of the others to follow, contradicts NIST's denial of the existence of any "evidence (collected by... the Fire Department of New York) of any blast or explosions in the region below the impact and fire floors."

Another firefighter, Craig Carlsen, said:

> [Y]ou just heard explosions coming from building two, the south tower. It seemed like it took forever, but there were about ten explosions.... We then realized the building started to come down.[10]

The South Tower was hit at 9:03 and collapsed at 9:59. The jet fuel, everyone agrees, would have burned up within about ten minutes.[11] So explosions coming just before the collapse could not have been exploding jet fuel.

Fire Marshall John Coyle said:

> The tower was—it looked to me—I thought it was exploding, actually. That's what I thought for hours afterwards, that it had exploded or... there had been some device on the plane that had exploded, because the debris from the tower had shot out far over our heads.[12]

As Coyle's statement suggests, he later decided his original interpretation—that there had been an explosion caused by some sort of explosive device—was incorrect. That same change of mind is reflected in many of the testimonies. Our concern here, however, is not with what interpretation Coyle and other witnesses ultimately came to accept, but with their report of phenomena that did suggest the occurrence of explosions—such as Coyle's statement that "debris from the tower had shot out far over our heads."

Chief Frank Cruthers said:

[T]here was what appeared to be at first an explosion. It appeared at the very top, simultaneously from all four sides, materials shot out horizontally. And then there seemed to be a momentary delay before you could see the beginning of the collapse.[13]

Although NIST wrote as if the only explosions that could not be explained as due to the airplane's impact would be those before the fire and impact floors, the same is true of those far above those floors. Certainly no jet fuel could have run up to them.

Having now made several editorial comments, I will henceforth simply quote statements without further commentary, beginning with Battalion Chief Brian Dixon, who said:

[T]he lowest floor of fire in the South Tower actually looked like someone had planted explosives around it because... it just looked like that floor blew out.... [Y]ou could actually see everything blew out on the one floor. I thought, geez, this looks like an explosion up there.[14]

Deputy Commissioner Thomas Fitzpatrick said:

[W]e saw... a puff of smoke coming from about two thirds of the way up. Some people thought it was an explosion.... It looked like sparkling around one specific layer of the building. (I assume now that that was either windows starting to collapse like tinsel or something.) Then the building started to come down. My initial reaction was that this was exactly the way it looks when they show you those implosions on TV.[15]

Assistant Commissioner Stephen Gregory said:

I thought that... I saw low-level flashes. In my conversation with Lieutenant Evangelista, never mentioning this to him, he questioned me and asked me if I saw low-level flashes in front of the building, and I agreed with him.... [A]t that time I didn't know what it was. I mean, it could have been as a result of the building collapsing, things exploding, but I saw a flash flash flash and then it looked like the building came down…. [It was at] the lower level of the building. You know like when they demolish a building, how when they blow up a building, when it falls down? That's what I thought I saw.[16]

Firefighter Timothy Julian said:

First I thought it was an explosion. I thought maybe there was a bomb on the plane, but delayed type of thing, you know secondary device…. I just heard like an explosion and then cracking type of noise, and then it sounded like a freight train, rumbling and picking up speed, and I remember I looked up, and I saw it coming down.[17]

Firefighter Joseph Meola said:

As we are looking up at the building, … it looked like the building was blowing out on all four sides. We actually heard the pops. Didn't realize it was the falling—you know, you heard the pops of the building. You thought it was just blowing out.[18]

Fire Marshall John Murray said:

[W]e were standing there watching the North Tower and not even paying attention to the South Tower. Then you look up and it's like holy shit, the building didn't come down, it shot straight out over our heads, like straight across West Street.[19]

Firefighter William Reynolds said:

I was distracted by a large explosion from the South Tower and it seemed like fire was shooting out a couple of hundred feet in each direction…. [This fire] appeared… [m]aybe twenty floors below the impact area of the plane.[20]

Firefighter Kenneth Rogers said:

[T]hen there was an explosion in the south tower…. I kept watching. Floor after floor after floor. One floor under another after another and when it hit about the fifth floor, I figured it was a bomb, because it looked like a synchronized deliberate kind of thing.[21]

Captain Dennis Tardio said:

I hear an explosion and I look up. It is as if the building is being imploded, from the top floor down, one after another, *boom, boom, boom.* I stand in amazement. I can't believe what I am seeing. This building is coming down.[22]

Firefighter Thomas Turilli said:

[A]ll of a sudden, it almost... sounded like bombs going off, like boom, boom, boom, like seven or eight.[23]

In light of all these testimonies, there can be little doubt that many members of the FDNY reported phenomena in the South Tower most naturally interpreted as explosives going off.

North Tower: There are fewer testimonies from firefighters about the North Tower because there were far fewer of them around in the moments before its collapse. There are, nonetheless, several testimonies that suggest the occurrence of explosions in this building. One of these was from Fire Marshal John Coyle, who said:

While I was down at Battery Park I finally got through on my phone to my father and said, 'I'm alive.... I just so narrowly escaped this thing.' He said, 'Where were you? You were there?' I said, 'Yeah, I was right there when it blew up.' He said, 'You were there when the planes hit?' I said, 'No, I was there when it exploded, the building exploded.' He said, 'You mean when it fell down?' I said, 'No, when it exploded.'[24]

Firefighter Christopher Fenyo said:

There was an explosion at the top of the Trade Center and a piece of Trade Center flew across the West Side Highway and hit the Financial Center.[25]

Firefighter Kevin Gorman said:

I heard the explosion, looked up, and saw like three floors explode, [and] saw the antenna coming down.[26]

Emergency Medical Workers and a Police Officer

South Tower: EMT (Emergency Medical Technician) Michael Ober said:

[W]e heard a rumble, ... we looked up in the air, and to be totally honest, at first, ... it looked to me just like an explosion. It didn't look like the building was coming down, it looked like just one floor had blown completely outside of it. I was sitting there looking at it. I... didn't think they were coming down.[27]

Paramedic Daniel Rivera, after being asked how he knew the South Tower was coming down said:

It was a frigging noise. At first I thought it was—do you ever see professional demolition where they set the charges on certain floors and then you hear 'Pop, pop, pop, pop, pop'?... I thought it was that. When I heard that frigging noise, that's when I saw the building coming down.[28]

Jay Swithers, captain of the FDNY's Bureau of Health Services, said:

I took a quick glance at the building and while I didn't see it falling, I saw a large section of it blasting out, which led me to believe it was just an explosion. I thought it was a secondary device.[29]

North Tower: Captain Karin Deshore, the commander of the FDNY's Emergency Medical Services, said:

Somewhere around the middle of the [North Tower], there was this orange and red flash coming out. Initially it was just one flash. Then this flash just kept popping all the way around the building and that building had started to explode. The popping sound, and with each popping sound it was initially an orange and then a red flash came out of the building and then it would just go all around the building on both sides as far as I could see. These popping sounds and the explosions were getting bigger, going both up and down and then all around the building.... So here these explosions are getting bigger and louder and bigger and louder and I told everybody if this building totally explodes, still unaware that the other building had collapsed, I'm going in the water.[30]

Sue Keane, a police officer for the Port Authority of New York and New Jersey, said, while discussing her experiences during the collapse of the North Tower:

[There was] another explosion. That sent me and the two fire-fighters down the stairs.... I can't tell you how many times I got banged around. Each one of those explosions picked me up and threw me…. There was another explosion, and I got thrown with two firefighters out onto the street.[31]

World Trade Center Employees

All the testimonies by employees to be quoted next were given by people who had worked in the North Tower. One of these was Genelle Guzman, the last survivor to be rescued from the rubble. When she got down to the 13th floor some 20 minutes before the North Tower came down, she said: "[I heard] a big explosion [and the] wall I was facing just opened up, and it threw me on the other side."[32]

Stationary engineer Mike Pecoraro, describing what he and his co-worker experienced after seeing lights flicker in the sixth sub-basement and hearing about a big explosion at about 8:46AM, said:

> [We went up to the C level, where there was a small machine shop, but there] was nothing there but rubble. We're talking about a 50 ton hydraulic press—gone! [We then went] to the parking garage, but found that it, too, was gone. [On the B level, we found that] a steel-and-concrete fire door that weighed about 300 pounds [was] wrinkled up like a piece of aluminum foil. [Finally, when we went up to the ground floor, the] whole lobby was soot and black, elevator doors were missing. The marble was missing off some of the walls.[33]

Anthony Saltalamacchia, a maintenance supervisor who was in his sub-basement office, reported:

> We heard a massive explosion… about 8:46AM…. Then we heard a series of other explosions…. And about, I'd say, 14 to 15 people came running and screaming into our office…. Then right after that the floor started shaking. The tile from above, which was above us, started coming down, falling on us…. A man came into the office. He was a black man, very shaky, like in shock. He had multiple wounds. His arms were bleeding. Skin was peeling off…. And as we're standing there, more explosions were happening. A lot of screaming confusion…. It was very smoky, very cloudy…. We knew we had to get out of the building…. The amount of explosions I've heard from 8:46 until the time we got out was so many, at least ten. It was just like multiple explosions to where I felt like there were

different grenades. That's what it sounded like, it was different grenades being set off in the building…. There was one major explosion, and then there was different explosions throughout that period of time until we got out.[34]

Teresa Veliz, who worked for a software development company, reported that after she got off the elevator on the 47th floor, "the whole building shook. I thought it was an earthquake." That shaking occurred at the time that the airplane struck the building. But shortly thereafter, she said, "the building shook again, this time even more violently." Then, after a terrifying experience of making her way downstairs and outside, she said:

> There were explosions going off everywhere. I was convinced that there were bombs planted all over the place and someone was sitting at a control panel pushing detonator buttons…. There was another explosion. And another. I didn't know where to run.[35]

Television Reports on 9/11

Many reports suggestive of explosions were given during live television broadcasts by various networks on 9/11. For example, a Fox News reporter, speaking before either tower had collapsed, said:

> The FBI… have roped this area off. They were taking photographs and securing this area just prior to that huge explosion that we all heard and felt.[36]

Stephen Evans, a New York–based business correspondent for the BBC, told his BBC audience:

> I was at the base of the second tower, the second tower that was hit…. There was an explosion—I didn't think it was an explosion—but the base of the building shook. I felt it shake… then when we were outside, the second explosion happened and then there was a series of explosions…. We can only wonder at the kind of damage—the kind of human damage—which was caused by those explosions—those series of explosions.[37]

While being interviewed by someone else, Evans said:

> There was another big, big explosion. In the other tower, flames coming out and this billowing grey smoke…. [S]omebody said that they saw an airliner go into one of those towers. Then an

hour later than that... we had that big explosion from much, much lower. I don't know what on earth caused that.[38]

A CBS reporter speaking to Dan Rather said:

> When you're down there, Dan, you hear smaller secondary explosions going off every 15 or 20 minutes, and so it's an extremely dangerous place to be.[39]

CNN producer Rose Arce said:

> [F]irefighters had to suspend their rescue operation and they're just watching a burning hulk of building right now. The front part of the World Trade Center has completely sheared off as well as many of the upper floors, and every few minutes you'll hear like a small sort of rumbling sound, almost like an explosion sound, and another chunk of it will come flying down into the street.[40]

Fox News interviewed a man who said:

> I was down in the basement, all of sudden we heard a loud bang. And the elevator doors blew open, some guy was burnt up, so I dragged him out, his skin was all hanging off.[41]

MSNBC Reporter Rick Sanchez, perhaps speaking to Chris Matthews, said:

> I spoke with some police officials moments ago, Chris, and they told me that they have reason to believe that one of the explosions at the World Trade Center, aside from the ones that may have been caused by the impact of the plane with the building, may have been caused by a van that was parked in the building that may have had some type of explosive device in it, so their fear is that there may have been explosive devices planted either in the building, or in the adjacent area.[42]

Pat Dawson of NBC News gave a report in which he said:

> Just moments ago I spoke to the Chief of Safety for the New York City Fire Department, Chief Albert Turi. He received word of the possibility of a secondary device, that is another bomb going off. He tried to get his men out as quickly as he could, but he said that there was another explosion which took place, and then an hour after the... first crash that took place... there was another explosion that took place in one of the towers here. He thinks that there were actually devices that were planted in the building.[43]

After the collapse of the South Tower, there were many reports of explosions: A Fox News reporter said:

> I was making my way to the foot of the World Trade Center. Suddenly while talking to an officer who was questioning me about my press credentials, we heard a very loud blast explosion. We looked up and the building literally began to collapse.[44]

CNN's Aaron Brown, looking at the towers, said:

> There has just been a huge explosion, we can see a billowing smoke rising and I'll tell you that I can't see that second tower. But here was a cascade of sparks and fire and it looks almost like a mushroom cloud explosion.[45]

On ABC News, the following exchange occurred between Peter Jennings and reporter Don Dahler:

> *Dahler*: The second building that was hit by the plane has just completely collapsed. The entire building has just collapsed as if a demolition team set off—when you see the old demolitions of these old buildings. It folded down on itself and it is not there anymore.
>
> *Jennings*: The whole side has collapsed?
>
> *Dahler*: The whole *building* has collapsed.
>
> *Jennings*: The whole *building* has collapsed?
>
> *Dahler*: The building has collapsed.[46]

At 10:13AM, a headline on CNN Live read: "BREAKING NEWS: THIRD EXPLOSION COLLAPSES WORLD TRADE CENTER IN NEW YORK."[47]

Further reports of explosions were given after the collapse of the North Tower, which occurred at 10:28. At 10:29, CNN producer Rose Arce gave this report by telephone to Aaron Brown:

> I'm about a block away, and there were several people that were hanging out the windows right below where the plane crashed. When suddenly you saw the top of the building start to shake, and people began leaping from the windows in the north side of the building... and then the entire top of the building just blew up and splinters of debris are falling on the street.[48]

MSNBC reporter Ann Thompson said:

> I tried to leave the building. But as soon as I got outside I heard a second explosion. And another rumble, and more smoke, and more dust. I ran inside the building, the chandelier shook and again black smoke filled the air. Within another five minutes we were covered again with more silt and more dust. And then a fire marshal came in and said we had to leave, because if there was a third explosion this building might not last.[49]

Some reporters and network anchors also offered reflections about the collapses of the towers. ABC's anchor, Peter Jennings, said after the collapse of the South Tower:

> Anyone who has ever watched a building being demolished on purpose knows that if you're going to do this you have to get at the under-infrastructure of the building to bring it down.[50]

After both collapses, CNN's Lou Dobbs said:

> [T]his was the result of something that was planned. This is not, it's not accidental that the first tower just happened to collapse and then the second tower just happened to collapse in exactly the same way. How they accomplished this, we don't know.[51]

A CNN reporter said:

> We've heard of secondary explosions after the aircraft impacted—whether in fact there wasn't something else at the base of the towers that in fact were the coup de grace to bring them to the ground.[52]

Newspaper and Television Accounts the Next Day

A September 12 story in London's *Guardian* said:

> [P]olice and fire officials were carrying out the first wave of evacuations when the first of the World Trade Centre towers collapsed. Some eyewitnesses reported hearing another explosion just before the structure crumbled. Police said that it looked almost like a "planned implosion."[53]

Wall Street Journal reporter John Bussey, writing about what he saw from the WSJ building, said:

I... looked up out of the office window to see what seemed like perfectly synchronized explosions coming from each floor.... One after the other, from top to bottom, with a fraction of a second between, the floors blew to pieces.[54]

A story in the *Los Angeles Times* said:

At 9:50AM, ... the first World Trade Center tower collapsed.... There were reports of an explosion right before the tower fell.... Not long afterward, ... the second tower of the World Trade Center collapsed. The top of the building exploded with smoke and dust. There were no flames, just an explosion of debris.[55]

ABC's Peter Jennings, interviewing Marlene Cruz, a carpenter who was injured in the basement of the North Tower, asked what happened to her. She said:

I was gonna go do a job. And I got on the... freight elevator. And I heard the first explosion. And the elevator blew up. The doors blew up. And it dropped. I was lucky that the elevator got caught between two floors.... I was laying on the floor about 40 minutes.... I didn't expect this bombing to occur after the first one [in 1993].... But when I heard that explosion, ... the first thing I thought was: here we go again, another bomb.[56]

How did the 9/11 Commission and NIST deal with all these testimonies?

Dealing with the Contradiction

In the preface to its final report, Thomas Kean and Lee Hamilton, the chair and vice chair of the 9/11 Commission, say that the Commission had sought "to provide the fullest possible account of the events surrounding 9/11."[57] Why, then, did it not discuss the fact that dozens of witnesses, including firefighters, emergency medical workers, police officers, journalists, and WTC employees, had reported explosions—sometimes several explosions—going off before and during the collapses?

This failure cannot be explained by supposing that the Commission did not have access to these testimonies. It could easily have obtained all the network television footage from 9/11 and the newspaper stories from the following day. And it, as we saw in the previous chapter, referred to the FDNY's 9/11 oral histories quite extensively in its notes.[58] If the 9/11 Commission knew the content of these interviews, why did it say nothing about the dozens of testimonies suggesting explosions? The Commission did, as mentioned earlier, report that, when the South Tower collapsed, some firefighters in the North Tower who could not see it "surmised that a bomb had exploded."[59] But why is the Commission's reference to this incident, when the firefighters were clearly wrong, its only reference to firefighters believing that bombs had exploded?

When Lee Hamilton was asked in 2006 about the view that explosives had brought the towers down, why did he say that the towers came down because the fire melted the steel, which is physically impossible, while claiming that the Commission found "no evidence" to support the hypothesis that explosives were responsible, when people on the Commission had to be aware of dozens of testimonies, from firefighters and emergency medical workers, supporting that hypothesis?

William Rodriguez, a janitor in the North Tower who was named a National Hero and photographed with President Bush after 9/11 for helping people escape from the building, reported that he spoke to 9/11 staff members about having heard and felt explosions after reporting to work that morning. But, he reported: "I met with the 9/11 Commission behind closed doors and they essentially discounted everything I said regarding the use of explosives to bring down the north tower."[60] Why would the Commission, given its expressed intent "to provide the fullest possible account of the events surrounding 9/11," ignore the testimony of a National Hero—even to the point of not mentioning in the endnotes of its report the fact that he had testified to the Commission's staff?

What about NIST? It also had access to the oral histories and seemed to allude to them in its *Final Report*, referring to "documents of investigative first-person interviews" that were obtained from the FDNY.[61] But, far from reporting any testimonies about explosions, it explicitly denied, as we saw, the existence of any "evidence (collected by... the Fire Department of New York) of any blast or explosions in the region below the impact and fire floors." The FDNY oral histories, however, contain several testimonies about explosions in the lower floors—and also about explosions in the upper floors, *above* the strike zone, which jet fuel could not have caused.

Conclusion

Congress and the press need to investigate this contradiction between the official reports and the testimony of firefighters, emergency medical workers, police officers, journalists, and WTC employees. They need to ask why both NIST and the 9/11 Commission ignored, and even denied the existence of, testimonial evidence that was in their possession. The press in particular needs to ask why these official reports failed to employ, and even contradicted, the firsthand evidence provided by the media on 9/11 and the following day.

24

WERE THERE EXPLOSIONS IN WTC 7?

A t about 5:20PM on 9/11, WTC 7, a 47-story building, completely collapsed in about seven seconds. There is, as of this writing, no official explanation of why this collapse occurred. *The 9/11 Commission Report* did not even mention that it happened.

The official responsibility for explaining the collapse of WTC 7 was assigned to NIST (the National Institute of Standards and Technology). In April of 2005, NIST said: "[The] WTC 7 report will be issued as a supplement to the main report; draft planned for October 2005; final for December 2005."[1] When NIST's draft report on the World Trade Center appeared in October of 2005, however, it was limited to the Twin Towers. The report on WTC 7 had been delayed until 2006. Then in August of 2006, NIST said: "It is anticipated that a draft report [on WTC 7] will be released by early 2007."[2] By December 11, 2007—over six years after WTC 7 collapsed—that draft report still had not appeared.

The Official Denial

NIST did, however, put out an "Interim Report" in 2004, which said that "fire appears to have played a key role" in the collapse, even though this report pointed out that "[n]o fire was observed or reported in the afternoon on floors 1-5, 10, or above Floor 13."[3] In other words, fires had been observed on only six of this building's 47 floors. Then in 2005, NIST put out a preliminary report, which contained its "working collapse hypothesis for WTC 7." According to this hypothesis, the "initiating event" was an "initial local failure at the lower floors… due to fire and/or debris induced structural damage to a critical column." This document then added: "NIST has seen no evidence that the collapse of WTC 7 was caused by bombs… or controlled demolition."[4]

NIST will likely, therefore, reaffirm the official theory, insofar as there has been one. That is, there has been no explanation as to why WTC 7 collapsed (even if Lee Hamilton thinks that the 9/11 Commission had a theory about this[5]). But it has been denied, whether explicitly or implicitly, that explosions played a role. The official theory, insofar as there has been one, has consisted of that denial.

Several reporters and government employees, however, gave testimony that contradicted this denial.

Reports of Explosions in WTC 7

Some of this testimony consisted of reports pointing to the occurrence of explosions in Building 7. One such report came from Peter DeMarco, a *New York Daily News* journalist, who said:

> At 5:30 [*sic*] PM there was a rumble. The building's top row of windows popped out. Then all the windows on the thirty-ninth floor popped out. Then the thirty-eighth floor. Pop! Pop! Pop! was all you heard until the building sunk into a rising cloud of gray.[6]

Another such report came from Al Jones, a reporter for WINS NYC News Radio, who said:

> People started to run away from the scene and I turned in time to see what looked like a skyscraper implosion—looked like it had been done by a demolition crew—the whole thing just collapsing down on itself and another big huge plume of gray and white smoke shooting up into the air and then more of the smoke billowing up the street here…. So that's number one, number two, and now number seven that have come down from this explosion.[7]

A New York University medical student named Daryl, who was serving as an emergency medical worker, said:

> We were watching the building actually 'cause it was on fire… and… we heard this sound that sounded like a clap of thunder…. [T]urned around—we were shocked…. [I]t looked like there was a shockwave ripping through the building and the

windows all busted out.... [A]bout a second later the bottom
floor caved out and the building followed after that.[8]

Perhaps the most extensive testimony has come from Craig Bartmer, a former NYPD police officer, who worked as a first respon-
der on 9/11. In the course of a lengthy interview, he said:

> I was real close to Building 7 when it fell down.... That didn't
> sound like just a building falling down to me.... There's a lot
> of eyewitness testimony down there of hearing explosions....
> [A]ll of a sudden the radios exploded and everyone started
> screaming "get away, get away, get away from it!" ... I looked
> up, and it was nothing I would ever imagine seeing in my life.
> The thing started pealing [*sic*] in on itself.... I started
> running... and the whole time you're hearing "boom, boom,
> boom, boom, boom."[9]

The Reports by Michael Hess and Barry Jennings

Still another report came from Michael Hess, New York City's
corporation counsel, who had gone to the Emergency Management
Center on the 23rd floor of WTC 7. During a live interview at 11:34
that morning with Frank Ucciardo of UPN 9 News, Hess said:

> I was up in the emergency management center on the twenty-
> third floor, and when all the power went out in the building,
> another gentleman and I walked down to the eighth floor where
> there was an explosion and we were trapped on the eighth floor
> with smoke, thick smoke, all around us, for about an hour and
> a half. But the New York Fire Department... just came and got
> us out.[10]

If the explosion that trapped Hess and the other gentleman had
occurred about 90 minutes before they were rescued, as Hess esti-
mated, it must have occurred before 10:00.

This conclusion can be confirmed by looking at the testimony
of the other gentleman to whom Hess referred, Barry Jennings,
who was the deputy director of the Emergency Services Department for the New York City Housing Authority. His experience
was briefly described in an Associated Press story, appearing on
9/11 itself, that said:

After the initial blast, Housing Authority worker Barry Jennings, 46, reported to a command center on the 23rd floor of 7 World Trade Center. He was with Michael Hess, the city's corporation counsel, when they felt and heard another explosion. First calling for help, they scrambled downstairs to the lobby, or what was left of it. "I looked around, the lobby was gone. It looked like hell," Jennings said.[11]

The "initial blast" referred to the crash into the North Tower,[12] which occurred at 8:46AM. According to Jennings's statement to the Associated Press, therefore, he and Hess would have arrived at the 23rd floor of WTC 7 at some time close to 9:00.

It might be assumed, therefore, that when they heard "another explosion," they were hearing the airplane crash into the South Tower, which occurred at 9:03. That assumption would be challenged, however, by Jennings's own accounts. One of those accounts was given in a program on Penn State Public Broadcasting early in 2002. In this account, Jennings said:

Well, me and Mr. Hess, the corporation counsel were on the 23rd floor. I told him, "We gotta get out of here." We started walking down the stairs. We made it to the 8th floor. Big explosion. Blew us back into the 8th floor, and I turned to Hess. I said, "this is it; we're dead. We're not gonna make it out of here." I took a fire extinguisher and I bust the window out. That's when this gentleman here heard my cries for help. This gentleman right here. And he kept saying, "Stand by. Somebody's coming to get you." They couldn't get to us for an hour because they couldn't find us.[13]

It would be hard to interpret an explosion that blew them backwards and made them fear for their lives as the airplane crash into the South Tower, about 200 yards away. It must have been an explosion in WTC 7. That this was indeed the case is confirmed by a later account, in which Jennings said:

Upon arriving into the OEMEOC [Office of Emergency Management Emergency Operating Center], we noticed that everybody was gone. I saw... smoke was still coming off the coffee. I saw half-eaten sandwiches. And after I called several individuals, one individual told me to leave and to leave right away.... So we subsequently went to the stairwell and we're going down the stairs. When we reached the 6th floor, the landing that we were standing on gave way, there was an explosion and the landing gave way. I was left there hanging. I had to climb back up, and now I had to walk back up to the 8th floor. After getting to the 8th floor everything was dark…. [B]oth buildings were still standing. Because I looked… one way, looked the other way…. When I got to the 6th floor before all this happened—there was an explosion, that's what forced us back to the 8th floor, both buildings were still standing.[14]

By reading these accounts by Jennings together with the account by Hess, we can see that they were both describing an explosion in Building 7 that occurred quite early that morning—sometime around 9:00—and trapped them for about an hour (Jennings) or an hour and a half (Hess). The quotation from Jennings in the Associated Press story about him, moreover, suggested that some big explosion had also occurred on the first floor: When he got down there, Jennings said, "the lobby was gone."[15] Jennings spoke more about this in his later statement, in which he said:

> I'm just confused about one thing…, why World Trade Center 7 went down in the first place…. I know what I heard; I heard explosions. The explanation I got was it was the fuel oil tank. I'm an old boiler guy. If it was the fuel oil tank, it would have been one side of the building. When I got [down to the] lobby [after being rescued from the eighth floor], the lobby was totally destroyed. It looked like King Kong had came through and stepped on it…. And it was so destroyed that they had to take me out through a hole in the wall.[16]

According to Jennings, therefore, the lobby had been destroyed by something that could not have simply been the explosion of WTC 7's fuel oil tank.

NIST's Treatment of the Hess–Jennings Testimony

There are two places in which the NIST documents mention Hess and Jennings (although not by name). One document has a statement saying: "At 12:10 to 12:15PM: Firefighters found individuals on Floors 7 and 8 and led them out of the building."[17] (The individual found on Floor 7 was neither Hess nor Jennings but, NIST said elsewhere, "a security officer for one of the businesses in the building."[18]) The most obvious problem with this statement is that the live interview with Hess began at 11:34, *more than a half hour earlier than the time at which NIST claims they were rescued.*

If we consider the time, the location, and the content of Hess's interview, when would the rescue have occurred? The interview took place "on Broadway about a block from City Hall," which is almost a half mile from WTC 7. So even if we allow only five minutes for the rescuers to lead Hess and Jennings out of the building and another five minutes for Hess to get to City Hall by 11:30, we can conclude that the rescuers must have found the two men no later than 11:20—almost an hour earlier than NIST claims.

A second NIST document, dealing with emergency response operations, has a longer statement about Hess and Jennings, which begins:

> With the collapse of the two towers, a New York City employee and a WTC 7 building staff person[19] became trapped inside of WTC 7. The two had gone to the OEM center on the 23rd floor and found no one there. As they went to get into an elevator to go downstairs the lights inside of WTC 7 flickered as WTC 2 collapsed. At this point, the elevator they were attempting to catch no longer worked, so they started down the staircase.[20]

According to NIST, therefore, Jennings and Hess were starting downstairs, after finding the OEM center vacated, at 9:59, when the second tower collapsed. It was this collapse, NIST suggested, that was responsible for the elevator's failure to work.

According to Jennings as reported in the Associated Press story, however, he and Hess arrived at the OEM about an hour earlier, shortly after the strike on the North Tower at 8:46. Besides contradicting Jennings's own testimony on that point, the NIST account went on to say:

> When they got to the 6th floor, WTC 1 collapsed, the lights went out in the staircase, the sprinklers came on briefly, and the staircase filled with smoke and debris. The two men went back to the 8th floor broke out a window and called for help.[21]

According to NIST, as we see, the lights went out in WTC 7 because of the collapse of WTC 1, the North Tower, which occurred at 10:28.

NIST's timeline implied that it took Hess and Jennings 29 minutes—from 9:59 to 10:28—to walk down 17 flights of stairs. Besides having this implausible implication, this timeline is also explicitly contradicted by Jennings, who said that, shortly after the explosion, he looked out the window—"looked one way, looked the other way"—and "both buildings [the Twin Towers] were still standing."[22] What Hess and Jennings called an "explosion," therefore, occurred prior to 9:59, not at 10:28.

NIST's statements about Hess and Jennings are, therefore, severely in conflict with the statements made by Hess and Jennings themselves, even though NIST, as it indicated, interviewed both men.[23]

NIST's two sets of statements about Hess and Jennings appear, moreover, to have been coordinated. In the one document, NIST stated that the two men were not rescued until 12:10. That claim meshes with NIST's claim, in the other document, that the "explosion" to which Hess and Jennings referred was really the collapse of the North Tower, which occurred at 10:28. If that had been the case and if, as Hess had publicly stated, they were trapped for 90 minutes after that, then they could not have been rescued before noon. In other words, NIST's claim that they were not rescued until 12:10 supported its claim that the "explosion" was really the North Tower collapse.

Giuliani's Treatment of the Hess–Jennings Episode

The fact that New York City's corporation counsel, Michael Hess, got trapped in WTC 7 has also been discussed by Rudy Giuliani, but in a way that supported the account given by NIST rather than that given by Hess and Jennings. In his book *Leadership*, Giuliani, referring to Hess as "my longtime friend," wrote of him:

> When he got to the 8th floor [of WTC 7], Tower 1—the North Tower—collapsed, part of it falling on top of the southern part of 7 World Trade Center. Luckily, Mike was in the northern section of the building. Unluckily, he was now trapped, as the stairs were impassable.
>
> Mike went into an office on the 8th floor, joined only by a fellow from the Housing Authority. The building was filling up

with smoke and dust from the collapsed towers, but since the men were facing north they had no way of knowing the towers had fallen.[24]

Besides saying, like NIST, that Hess and Jennings were trapped because of damage to WTC 7 caused by the collapse of the North Tower (at 10:28), Giuliani also claimed that these men were in a place from which they could not see that the Twin Towers had collapsed. According to Jennings himself, however, he *could* see in those directions and saw that both towers were still standing.

Foreknowledge of the Collapse

The testimonies about explosions in WTC 7 by Hess, Jennings, and the other people quoted above, which contradict NIST's statements, have not been widely reported. Something else that has hardly been reported is that there was little effort to put out the fires in WTC 7, because the building was expected to collapse. This fact does not, however, contradict NIST's position, because one of its documents said:

> According to the FDNY first-person interviews, ... firefighting was never started in [WTC 7]. When the Chief Officer in charge of WTC 7 got to Barclay Street and West Broadway, numerous firefighters and officers were coming out of WTC 7. These firefighters indicated that several blocks needed to be cleared around WTC 7 because they thought that the building was going to collapse.[25]

One such firefighter was Captain Ray Goldbach. In discussing events taking place in the afternoon, he said:

> There was a big discussion going on... about pulling all of our units out of 7 World Trade Center. Chief [Daniel] Nigro didn't feel it was worth taking the slightest chance of somebody else getting injured. So at that point we made a decision to take all of our units out of 7 World Trade Center because there was a potential for collapse.... Made the decision to back everybody away, took all the units and moved them all the way back toward North End Avenue, which is as far I guess west as you could get on Vesey Street, to keep them out of the way.[26]

This process of establishing a safety zone was described by many members of the FDNY. Firefighter Vincent Massa said:

> [L]ater on in the day as we were waiting for seven to come down, they kept backing us up Vesey, almost like a full block. They were concerned about seven coming down, and they kept changing us, establishing a collapse zone and backing us up.[27]

EMT Decosta Wright said:

> [B]asically they measured out how far the building was going to come, so we knew exactly where we could stand.... Five blocks. Five blocks away.... Exactly right on point, the cloud just stopped right there.[28]

As to when people were moved away from WTC 7, witnesses differed. EMT Joseph Fortis said: "They pulled us all back... almost about an hour before it... went down."[29] Chief Daniel Nigro said: "[A]pproximately an hour and a half after that order [to move away] was given, ... 7 World Trade Center collapsed completely."[30] Fire Lieutenant William Ryan said: "We found out, I guess around 3:00 o'clock, that they thought 7 was going to collapse."[31] Firefighter Kevin McGovern put it even earlier, saying: "It took about three hours [after the order] for Seven World Trade Center to actually come down."[32] Captain Robert Sohmer said that the evacuation occurred "at approximately maybe 2:00 roughly."[33] Chief Frank Fellini, one of the ones who made the decision, said that after it was made, "for the next five or six hours we kept firefighters from working anywhere near that building"[34]—which would mean that the collapse zone was established by around noon. Fellini's statement, which indicated that the belief that WTC 7 would collapse was formed quite early, corresponded with the recollection of Firefighter Christopher Patrick Murray, who said that he had "heard reports all day long of 7 World Trade possibly coming down."[35]

In any case, whenever the decision not to fight the fires in WTC 7 was made, it was not a decision with which everyone agreed—which means that the expectation of imminent collapse was not universal. For example, Chief Thomas McCarthy, describing the scene in his 9/11 oral history, said:

[The firefighters at the site] were waiting for 7 World Trade to come down…. They had… fire on three separate floors…, just burning merrily. It was pretty amazing, you know, it's the afternoon in lower Manhattan, a major high-rise is burning, and they said "we know."[36]

In stating that there was "fire on three separate floors," McCarthy was saying that, from his perspective, there was no objective basis for expecting the building to collapse. A similar statement was made by EMT Decosta Wright, who said:

I think the fourth floor was on fire…. [W]e were like, are you guys going to put that fire out? I was like, … they are going to wait for it to burn down—and it collapsed.[37]

Puzzlement about the failure to fight the fires in WTC 7 was also expressed and reported by Deputy Chief Nick Visconti, who had 34 years experience. He said: "Now, World Trade Center 7 was burning and I was thinking to myself, how come they're not trying to put this fire out?" Then, after he started implementing Chief Fellini's order to "get these people out of… 7 World Trade Center," he encountered resistance from some other chiefs. One of these chiefs "oh, that building is never coming down, that didn't get hit by a plane, why isn't somebody in there putting the fire out?"[38]

Similarly, Fire Commissioner Thomas Von Essen reported that, while walking past hundreds of firefighters who were being held away from WTC 7, he heard comments such as, "Why don't they let us in there?"[39]

Whereas some firefighters, consistently with the fact that fire had never caused a steel-frame high-rise building to collapse, did not expect WTC 7 to collapse, some senior fighters did and correctly so. The question arises, therefore, as to why the latter group had this expectation.

According to Captain Michael Currid, who was the Uniformed Fire Officers Association's sergeant at arms, he and some other FDNY officers at some point went into WTC 7, where four or five fire companies were battling its flames, and yelled up the stairwells: "Drop everything and get out!" Why did he do this?

Because, he said, "[s]omeone from the city's Office of Emergency Management" had told him that WTC 7 was "basically a lost cause and we should not lose anyone else trying to save it."[40] Accordingly, just as it was Giuliani's Office of Emergency Management (OEM) that had advance knowledge that the Twin Towers were going to collapse, it was evidently the same office that had this information about WTC 7.

Testimony about Bringing WTC 7 Down

One question that NIST should answer is how some people, such as some OEM personnel, could have known, many hours in advance, that WTC 7 would collapse. One possible answer would be that they knew this because they knew that the building had been wired to be brought down by explosives. Is there any testimony to support this view?

There has been much discussion about a statement made by Larry Silverstein, the builder and owner of WTC 7. In a PBS documentary in 2002, he said:

> I remember getting a call from the, er, fire department commander, telling me that they were not sure they were gonna be able to contain the fire, and I said, "We've had such terrible loss of life, maybe the smartest thing to do is pull it." And they made that decision to pull and then we watched the building collapse.[41]

If Silverstein's statement meant what it appears to mean—that the building was deliberately brought down—then we have a clear contradiction between his statement and NIST's preliminary report. It would, of course, be puzzling as to why Silverstein— who was hoping to receive several billion dollars in insurance money for the destruction of the World Trade Center on the assumption that the buildings had been brought down by terrorists—would have publicly admitted that one of the buildings was brought down by explosives at his own suggestion. And, indeed, a spokesperson for Silverstein has claimed that by "it," Silverstein meant not WTC 7 but "the contingent of firefighters remaining in the building."[42]

Be that as it may, the idea that this building was deliberately brought down was unequivocally expressed by Indira Singh, a senior consultant for JP Morgan Chase, who on 9/11, serving as a volunteer emergency medical worker, was in charge of setting up triage sites. In 2005, while Singh was being interviewed by Bonnie Faulkner, the producer and host of the *Guns and Butter* radio show, the following exchange occurred:

> *Singh:* [P]retty soon after midday on 9/11 we had to evacuate [the site where we had been working] because they told us Building 7 was coming down…. I do believe that they brought Building 7 down because I heard that they were going to bring it down because it was unstable because of the collateral damage. That I don't know; I can't attest to the validity of that. All I can attest to is that by noon or one o'clock, they told us we need to move from that triage site up to Pace University, a little further away, because Building 7 was gonna come down or be brought down.

> *Faulkner:* Did they actually use the word "brought down" and who was it that was telling you this?

> *Singh:* The fire department. The fire department. And they did use the words "we're gonna have to bring it down."[43]

So Indira Singh, besides supporting Chief Fellini's statement that the collapse expectation was being expressed already by about noon, also provided a possible answer to why some people had that expectation.

Revisiting the Question about Explosions

Singh's answer could, of course, be easily dismissed if there were no objective reason to believe that explosives were used. As we saw earlier, however, testimony to the occurrence of explosions in WTC 7 was given by two reporters (Peter DeMarco and Al Jones) and three New York City employees (Peter Hess, Barry Jennings, and an emergency medical worker).

There is, moreover, additional testimony that is publicly available. Most of Indira Singh's testimony as quoted above can be heard on a video entitled "Seven Is Exploding" (which is a segment from a program aired on Italian television in April of 2007). After the footage with Singh's statement about the fire department, this video then shows police officers saying:

> Keep your eye on that building, it'll be coming down.... This building is about to blow up; move it back.[44]

We then hear the sound of loud explosions, after which a firefighter says: "We gotta get back. Seven is exploding."[45]

The fact that the collapse of WTC 7 at least appeared to have been produced by explosives was expressed at the time by CBS anchor Dan Rather, who said:

> Amazing, incredible pick your word. For the third time today, it's reminiscent of those pictures we've all seen too much on television before, where a building was deliberately destroyed by well-placed dynamite to knock it down.[46]

People with greater expertise than Dan Rather, moreover, have said that the collapse not only looked like, but indeed *was*, a controlled demolition.[47]

Conclusion

Congress and the press need to ask why NIST has, by denying that there was any evidence that WTC 7 was brought down by controlled demolition, ignored the evidence, supplied by reporters and city employees, that explosions occurred in the building. They need to ask why NIST's and Rudy Giuliani's accounts of the experience of Michael Hess and Barry Jennings differ so greatly from the men's own accounts. Congress and the press also need to ask people in Giuliani's Office of Emergency Management what objective basis they had for telling the fire chiefs that WTC 7 was going to collapse. They need to ask, finally, if the contradictions discussed here are related to the repeated delays in NIST's issuance of a report on the collapse of this building.

25

DID THE WTC RUBBLE CONTAIN
EVIDENCE THAT STEEL HAD MELTED?

Another important contradiction involves the question of whether the rubble produced by the collapses of the World Trade Center buildings contained evidence that steel had been heated up to the temperatures beyond that which could have been produced by fire. In particular, was there evidence that steel had melted? Here the contradiction is between the official reports put out by the 9/11 Commission and NIST, on the one hand, and reports of numerous witnesses, several of whom were involved in the cleanup and rescue operations, on the other. We will begin with witnesses who reported the existence of what they took to be molten steel.[1]

Witness Reports of Molten Steel

Several witnesses reported the existence of molten steel. One was Leslie Robertson, a member of the engineering firm that designed the Twin Towers. According to James Williams, the president of the Structural Engineers Association of Utah, Robertson said during a speech in early October 2001: "As of 21 days after the attack, the fires were still burning and molten steel was still running."[2]

Testimony also came from Dr. Keith Eaton, the chief executive of the London-based Institution of Structural Engineers. After being given a tour of the site, he reported, he was shown slides of "molten metal, which was still red hot weeks after the event."[3]

Several firefighters gave similar testimony. The *New York Post*, in a review of the documentary *Collateral Damages*, said that firemen at Ground Zero spoke of having "encountered rivers of molten steel."[4] One such firefighter was Captain Philip Ruvolo, who said: "You'd get down below and you'd see molten steel, *molten* steel, running down the channel rails, like you're in a foundry, like lava."[5] Guy Lounsbury, a member of the New York Air National Guard, wrote in a journal he kept while spending several weeks at Ground Zero: "[M]ountains of rubble 5 or 6 stories high are all that remained of the towers.... Smoke constantly poured from the peaks. One fireman told us that there was still molten steel at the heart of the towers' remains."[6]

Some health professionals gave similar testimony. Dr. Ronald Burger of the National Center for Environmental Health, after being at Ground Zero on the day after the attacks, spoke of "[f]eeling the heat, seeing the molten steel."[7] Dr. Alison Geyh of the Johns Hopkins School of Public Health, who headed a scientific team that went to the site shortly after 9/11 at the request of the National Institute of Environmental Health Sciences, said: "Fires are still actively burning and the smoke is very intense. In some pockets now being uncovered they are finding molten steel."[8]

Some witnesses spoke specifically of seeing steel beams that were molten at the end. Herb Trimpe, an Episcopalian deacon who served as a chaplain at Ground Zero, said, "The fires burned, up to 2,000 degrees, underground for quite a while.... I talked to many contractors and they said they actually saw molten metal trapped, beams had just totally been melted because of the heat."[9] Joe O'Toole, a Bronx firefighter who worked for many months on the rescue and cleanup efforts, said of a beam that was lifted from deep below the surface: "It was dripping from the molten steel."[10] According to Greg Fuchek, vice president of a company that supplied computer equipment used to identify human remains: "[S]ometimes when a worker would pull a steel beam from the wreckage, the end of the beam would be dripping molten steel."[11] Tom Arterburn, writing in *Waste Age,* said: "[F]or about two and a half months after the attacks, ... NYDS [New York Department of Sanitation] played a major role in debris removal—everything from molten steel beams to human remains."[12]

The testimonial evidence that steel had melted is, therefore, very strong, and most of this testimony came from insiders—people involved in the cleanup operation.

A Problem

This testimony created a problem for the public story, according to which the WTC collapses were due to fire (along with external damage—the airplane impacts or, in the case of WTC 7, debris from the falling towers). The problem is that steel does not begin to melt until about 2,800°F (1,538°C), whereas an open, diffuse fire fed by hydrocarbon material, such as jet fuel, could never, even under the most ideal conditions, get much above 1,832°F (1,000°C). The existence of melted steel would, therefore, contradict the public story, by implying that there was some alternative source of energy involved in the destruction of these buildings. How did NIST and the 9/11 Commission deal with this contradiction?

Dealing with the Problem

The 9/11 Commission heard testimony about melted metal at its first public hearing. While Ken Holden, the commissioner of the New York City Department of Design and Construction, was describing the conditions faced by Ground Zero workers, he said: "Underground it was still so hot that molten metal dripped down the sides of the wall from Building 6."[13]

This testimony, however, was not mentioned in *The 9/11 Commission Report*. That omission could, to be sure, be explained by the fact that the Commission said virtually nothing whatsoever about the collapses and the resulting rubble, leaving these topics for NIST to deal with. The key question, therefore, is how NIST dealt with the evidence of molten metal.

NIST was very clear that the fire could not have melted the structural steel. Dr. Frank Gayle, a metallurgist who led NIST's team dealing with the steel forensics of the collapses, has said: "Your gut reaction would be the jet fuel is what made the fire so very intense, a lot of people figured that's what melted the steel. Indeed it didn't, the steel did not melt."[14]

There are, however, two distinct issues here. One question is whether the fire melted any structural steel. Everyone who understood the relevant scientific facts about fire and steel agreed that it did not. A quite different question is whether steel melted at all—from *any* cause. Gayle's statement suggested that it did not.

But why, then, did so many witnesses testify to the existence of melted steel?

In its *Final Report* issued in 2005, NIST, by denying that there was any evidence for pre-set explosives in the buildings,[15] implied that no steel would have melted. But it did not explicitly address the issue.

In its 2006 publication, "Answers to Frequently Asked Questions," NIST admitted that this omission led to one of the questions frequently directed to it: "Why did the NIST investigation not consider reports of molten steel in the wreckage from the WTC towers?"[16] But in responding to this question, NIST simply repeated Frank Gayle's earlier assertion, saying: "NIST investigators and [other] experts… found no evidence that would support the melting of steel in a jet-fuel ignited fire in the towers prior to collapse."[17] In other words, although the question was why NIST had failed to address the reports of molten steel in the rubble, NIST again failed to address this question. It responded instead to a different one—whether the fire could have melted any steel, a point about which there is no controversy among physical scientists. The implication was, therefore, that no steel had melted.

NIST did not, to be sure, completely rule out the possibility that some steel had melted, saying: "Under certain circumstances it is conceivable for some of the steel in the wreckage to have melted after the buildings collapsed. Any molten steel in the wreckage was more likely due to the high temperature resulting from long exposure to combustion within the pile than to short exposure to fires or explosions while the buildings were standing."[18] NIST did not, however, explain why steel melting in a hydrocarbon combustion pile, which would apparently be unprecedented, should be considered "more likely" than steel being melted by explosives.

NIST's real stance seemed to be simply to deny the existence of molten metal (except for aluminum, which melts at a much lower temperature than does steel). That this was indeed NIST's principal response to the issue was suggested by a statement made by John L. Gross, one of NIST's main scientists, while speaking at the University of Texas at Austin. Having been asked to explain the "pools of molten steel beneath the towers," Gross challenged the questioner's "premise that there was a pool of molten steel," saying: "I know of absolutely no... eyewitness who has said so."[19] As shown in the first section of this chapter, however, many eyewitnesses said so.

Sulfidized, Oxidized, Evaporated Steel

Late in 2001, three professors at Worcester Polytechnic Institute (WPI) wrote a letter to a scientific journal reporting on their analysis of a section of a steel beam retrieved from WTC 7. One of these professors, Jonathan Barnett, specializes in fire protection engineering; the other two, Ronald R. Biederman and Richard D. Sisson, Jr., are professors of materials science. Saying that "the unexpected erosion of the steel found in this beam warranted a study of microstructural changes that occurred in this steel," they offered this preliminary analysis:

> Rapid deterioration of the steel was a result of heating with oxidation in combination with intergranular melting due to the presence of sulfur. The formation of the eutectic mixture of iron oxide and iron sulfide lowers the temperature at which liquid can form in this steel. This strongly suggests that the temperatures in this region of the steel beam approached 1,000°C.[20]

Although steel normally does not melt until it reaches 1,538°C (2,800°F), the presence of a eutectic mixture involving sulfur, these professors pointed out, lowers the melting temperature significantly.

Although the full significance of these professors' technical analysis would escape most nonscientists, the threat it posed to the official account of the destruction of the buildings was brought out in *New York Times* story published in late November 2001. Reporter James Glanz wrote: "A combination of an uncontrolled fire and the structural damage might have been able to bring the building down, some engineers said. But that would not explain," he added—attributing this point to Professor Barnett—"steel members in the debris pile that appear to have been partly evaporated."[21]

The significance of the WPI analysis was further brought out in another *New York Times* story, which Glanz co-authored with

Eric Lipton. On February 2, 2002—by which time the WPI professors had extended their analysis to a section of steel from one of the Twin Towers—Glanz and Lipton wrote:

> Perhaps the deepest mystery uncovered in the investigation involves extremely thin bits of steel collected from the trade towers and from 7 World Trade Center, a 47-story high rise that also collapsed for unknown reasons. The steel apparently melted away, but no fire in any of the buildings was believed to be hot enough to melt steel outright.[22]

The reason this discovery was deemed a deep mystery was made clear by Glanz and Lipton's statement: The steel had apparently melted, even though the fires in the buildings would not have been hot enough to melt it.

A few months later, the three WPI professors provided a much more thorough analysis in an appendix to the FEMA report on the World Trade Center collapses, which appeared in May 2002. With regard to the steel from WTC 7, they summarized their analysis thus:

> 1. The thinning of the steel occurred by a high-temperature corrosion due to a combination of oxidation and sulfidation.
>
> 2. Heating of the steel into a hot corrosive environment approaching 1,000°C (1,800°F) results in the formation of a eutectic mixture of iron, oxygen, and sulfur that liquefied the steel.
>
> 3. The sulfidation attack of steel grain boundaries accelerated the corrosion and erosion of the steel.[23]

Their analysis of the section of steel from one of the towers was similar, also referring to oxidation and the "high concentration of sulfides." In their conclusion, they emphasized that the corrosion and erosion were "very unusual" and then added: "No clear explanation for the source of the sulfur has been identified."[24]

The significance of this report was made more understandable to laypeople by an article entitled "The 'Deep Mystery' of Melted Steel." Writing for a WPI publication, Joan Killough-Miller said:

> Jonathan Barnett, professor of fire protection engineering, has repeatedly reminded the public that steel—which has a melt-

ing point of 2,800 degrees Fahrenheit—may weaken and bend, but does not melt during an ordinary office fire. Yet metallurgical studies on WTC steel brought back to WPI reveal that a novel phenomenon—called a eutectic reaction—occurred at the surface, causing intergranular melting capable of turning a solid steel girder into Swiss cheese.... *The New York Times* called these findings "perhaps the deepest mystery uncovered in the investigation." The significance of the work on a sample from Building 7 and a structural column from one of the twin towers becomes apparent only when one sees these heavy chunks of damaged metal. A one-inch column has been reduced to half-inch thickness. Its edges—which are curled like a paper scroll—have been thinned to almost razor sharpness. Gaping holes—some larger than a silver dollar—let light shine through a formerly solid steel flange. This Swiss cheese appearance shocked all of the fire-wise professors, who expected to see distortion and bending—but not holes.[25]

How did the official reports deal with this "deep mystery"?

Dealing with the Contradiction

The term "mystery" here points to an outright contradiction: According to the official account of the destruction of the WTC buildings, the only source of energy that could have heated the steel was fire. And yet, according to three scientists who contributed to the FEMA report, steel recovered from WTC 7 and one of the towers revealed phenomena that could not have been produced by the fires. Given the fact that these phenomena were reported in FEMA's study and even publicized by the two *New York Times* stories, one would assume that they would have been discussed in the later official reports.

They were not, however, mentioned in *The 9/11 Commission Report*. This is perhaps not surprising, given the fact that this report, besides having very little to say about the destruction of the Twin Towers, did not even mention the fact that WTC 7 also collapsed.

What *is* surprising, however, is that NIST, which was given the task of explaining the destruction of the Twin Towers and WTC 7, also did not mention these phenomena, even though

NIST's *Final Report* had a section headed "Learning from the Recovered Steel." Why would NIST simply ignore what three WPI professors said, in an official document (the FEMA report), they had learned from some recovered steel?

This question is especially important given the fact that the phenomena reported by these professors—the oxidation and sulfidation of steel—would be expected byproducts if cutter-charges employing thermate (thermite plus sulfur) had been used to slice the steel. This fact gave rise to one of the "frequently asked questions" to which NIST responded in 2006:

> Did the NIST investigation look for evidence of the WTC towers being brought down by controlled demolition? Was the steel tested for explosives or thermite residues? The combination of thermite and sulfur (called thermate) "slices through steel like a hot knife through butter."[26]

NIST's answer: "NIST did not test for the residue of these compounds in the steel." Why?

> Analysis of the WTC steel for the elements in thermite/thermate would not necessarily have been conclusive. The metal compounds also would have been present in the construction materials making up the WTC towers, and sulfur is present in the gypsum wallboard that was prevalent in the interior partitions.[27]

But if that were a likely explanation, why did the WPI professors consider the phenomena such a mystery?

Conclusion

NIST claimed that, aside from gravity and the impact of the airplanes, the only source of energy behind the collapse of the WTC buildings was fire. NIST, accordingly, wrote as if there were no evidence of molten steel in the rubble at Ground Zero. NIST's John Gross explicitly denied knowing of any eyewitnesses who had testified to its existence. There are, however, several well-credentialed eyewitnesses who gave such testimony. Moreover, partially evaporated steel, involving sulfidation and oxidation, would be even more contradictory of the official theory. And yet the *New York Times* reported that high-level scientists, who

contributed to the FEMA report on the World Trade Center, testified that such steel was recovered from WTC 7 and one of the
towers. Congress and the press need to ask why NIST has ignored
and even contradicted such testimony.

SUMMARY AND CONCLUSION

The official story of 9/11 is riddled with internal contradictions. In this book, we have examined 25 of them:

1. With regard to President Bush's behavior in the Sarasota classroom: The story told by the White House on the first anniversary of 9/11, according to which Bush left the room immediately after being informed by Andrew Card of the second crash into the World Trade Center, was contradicted by video footage and reports of the event, which revealed that he remained much longer.

2. With regard to the time that Vice President Cheney entered the Presidential Emergency Operations Center under the White House: The 9/11 Commission's claim, according to which he did not arrive there until almost 10:00AM, was contradicted by the testimony of many people, including Secretary of Transportation Norman Mineta and even Cheney himself, according to which he arrived prior to the attack on the Pentagon.

3. With regard to Norman Mineta's report of Cheney's response to messages about an incoming flight prior to the Pentagon strike, which appeared to confirm a stand-down order: The 9/11 Commission contradicted Mineta's account by stating that Cheney did not enter the PEOC until long after the Pentagon strike and by portraying the episode described by Mineta as having occurred after 10:10.

4. With regard to the question of who gave the order to land all planes: The claim by Norman Mineta and Jane Garvey that Mineta gave the order (in the presence of Dick Cheney) was contradicted by the 9/11 Commission, which attributed the decision to Ben Sliney.

5. With regard to the time at which Cheney issued the shoot-down authorization: The 9/11 Commission's claim that Cheney

did not give it until after 10:10 was contradicted by Richard Clarke and several military officers, who reported receiving it prior to the crash of United 93.

6. With regard to the location of General Richard Myers between 9:10 and 10:00 that morning: Myers's own account, that he was in Senator Max Cleland's office on Capitol Hill, was contradicted by Richard Clarke, who said that Myers was in the Pentagon participating in Clarke's video conference.

7. With regard to where Secretary of Defense Donald Rumsfeld was between 9:10 and 9:40AM: Rumsfeld's own account, according to which he was in his office, was contradicted by Richard Clarke, who said that Rumsfeld was in the Pentagon's secure teleconferencing studio participating in Clarke's video conference.

8. With regard to whether Ted Olson received two phone calls that morning from his wife, Barbara Olson, reporting that Flight 77 had been hijacked: Olson's claim that he did is contradicted by the FBI report presented to the Moussaoui trial, according to which an attempted call from Barbara Olson to the Department of Justice was "unconnected" and hence lasted "0 seconds." Olson's claim that the calls were made from a passenger-seat phone was contradicted by American Airlines, which said that Flight 77 had no such phones.

9. With regard to the time at which the military was first notified by the FAA about American Flight 11: The 9/11 Commission's claim, that the first notification was at 8:38, was contradicted in 2002 by ABC programs, based on interviews with many of the principals involved in the military response, which said that the notification occurred at about 8:31, and by Colin Scoggins, the military liaison at the FAA's Boston Center, whose account implies that the first call to NEADS occurred prior to 8:30.

10. With regard to the time at which the military was first notified about United Flight 175: The 9/11 Commission's claim—that this notification did not come until 9:03 when the flight was crashing into the South Tower—was contradicted implicitly by the FAA's memo of May 22, 2003, and explicitly by NORAD's timeline of September 18, 2001, and several military officers, including the

NMCC's Brigadier General Montague Winfield and NORAD's Captain Michael Jellinek.

11. With regard to the time at which the military was first notified about the hijacking of American Flight 77: The 9/11 Commission's position, that the military was not notified until after the Pentagon was struck, was contradicted by NORAD's September 18 timeline, by a *New York Times* story of September 15, 2001, by the FAA's 2003 memo, and by the deputy director of the Secret Service.

12. With regard to the time at which the military was first notified about United Flight 93: The 9/11 Commission's claim, that the military did not learn about its hijacking until after it had crashed, was contradicted by NORAD's 2001 timeline, by several White House officials (including Cheney) in 2002, by Richard Clarke, and by several military officers, including Colonel Robert Marr and Generals Larry Arnold and Montague Winfield.

13. With regard to the question of whether the US military had been in position to shoot down United 93: The 9/11 Commission's claim, according to which it had not, was contradicted by Dick Cheney, Richard Clarke, Deputy Secretary of Defense Paul Wolfowitz, and several military officers, including Colonel Robert Marr, General Richard Myers, Brigadier General Montague Winfield, Major General Mike Haugen, and Lt. Anthony Kuczynski.

14. With regard to whether 9/11-type attacks had previously been envisioned: The claim by the White House, the Pentagon, and the 9/11 Commission that they had not been envisioned was contradicted by many statements from government and military officials and by several reports of military exercises based around 9/11-type scenarios.

15. With regard to whether the men said to have hijacked the airliners, especially Mohamed Atta, were really devout Muslims: The 9/11 Commission's claim that they were was contradicted by numerous reports of their sexual activities and their use of alcohol and drugs.

16. With regard to the question of where the treasure trove of evidence reportedly left by Mohamed Atta was found: The 9/11 Commission's claim, that it was found in luggage that failed to make the transfer to American Flight 11 from the Portland-to-

Boston commuter flight, was contradicted by news reports from the initial days after 9/11, according to which it was found in a Mitsubishi that Atta had left in the Logan Airport parking lot.

17. With regard to whether the presence of hijackers on the airliners was reported by passengers using cell phones to call relatives: The claim by the press and the 9/11 Commission that such calls were made was contradicted by the FBI report provided at the Moussaoui trial in 2006, which entailed that no passengers used cell phones to call relatives.

18. With regard to whether there is hard evidence of the responsibility of Osama bin Laden for the 9/11 attacks: The stance of the Bush administration and the 9/11 Commission, which have both spoken as if such evidence existed, is contradicted by the FBI, which does not list 9/11 as one of the terrorist acts for which bin Laden is wanted because, it has said, it has no hard evidence of his responsibility for 9/11.

19. With regard to whether Hani Hanjour could have flown American 77 into the Pentagon: The claim by the White House and the 9/11 Commission that he did so is contradicted by extensive evidence, reported by the mainstream press, that he did not have the skill to fly a single-engine airplane, let alone a large jet airliner, especially through the trajectory reportedly taken by American 77 in its final minutes.

20. With regard to the cause of the hole in the Pentagon's C ring: The claim by Donald Rumsfeld and Lee Evey, that it was caused by the nose of American 77, has been contradicted by the *Pentagon Building Performance Report*, which said that the front of the aircraft disintegrated upon impact, and by *Popular Mechanics*, which claimed that the hole was made instead by the plane's landing gear.

21. With regard to the identity of the plane spotted over the White House around the time of the Pentagon strike: The military's denial that it was a military plane is contradicted by CNN footage of the plane's flight, which showed, as former military officers have agreed, that it was an Air Force E-4B.

22. With regard to how Rudy Giuliani knew that the Twin Towers were going to collapse: His claim that there was a histor-

ical basis for expecting the towers to collapse was contradicted by numerous experts and evidently all the firefighters at the scene.

23. With regard to whether there were explosions in the Twin Towers beyond those that might have been caused by the fires and exploding jet fuel: The claim by NIST and the 9/11 Commission that no such explosions occurred has been contradicted by numerous firefighters, emergency medical workers, WTC employees, and by television and newspaper reports on 9/11 and the following day.

24. With regard to whether there were explosions in WTC 7 beyond those that might have been caused by the fires: The claim by NIST and the 9/11 Commission that no such explosions occurred has been contradicted by journalists, emergency medical workers, policemen, and two city employees who had been in the building.

25. With regard to whether there was evidence in the WTC rubble that steel had melted: The claim by NIST that no such evidence was found has been contradicted by many professionals at the site and by three scientists who studied steel recovered from WTC 7 and one of the towers, reporting that it showed evidence of sulfidation, oxidation, and evaporation.

Shortly after 9/11, President Bush told the American people, perhaps especially Congress and the press, that they should not "tolerate outrageous conspiracy theories concerning the attacks of 11 September."[1] Although we can probably all agree that such theories should be rejected, the meaning of the phrase "outrageous conspiracy theories about 9/11" may not be immediately self-evident.

One's first reaction might be that the term "outrageous" does not serve to distinguish some conspiracy theories about 9/11 from others, because all such theories are outrageous. However, the official account of 9/11, which Bush was advocating, is itself a conspiracy theory. A conspiracy is simply "an agreement to perform together an illegal, treacherous, or evil act."[2] A conspiracy *theory* about some event, therefore, is simply a theory that it resulted from such an agreement. According to the official account of the 9/11 attacks, they resulted from a conspiracy involving Osama bin Laden and several members of al-Qaeda. The official account is, accordingly, a conspiracy theory.

We must ask, therefore, what would make such a theory *outrageous*. What are the criteria?

Within the philosophy of science, there are two basic criteria for discriminating between good and bad theories. First, a theory should not be inconsistent with any of the relevant facts. Many critics of the official account of 9/11 have faulted it for not fulfilling this criterion. They have argued, for example, that the damage and fires resulting from the impact of two airliners cannot explain why the Twin Towers and WTC 7 collapsed.

But many journalists and politicians have felt unqualified to make judgments on such matters, which involve technical issues, such as how buildings react to being hit by planes and how steel behaves when it is heated.

The other basic criterion of good theories, however, does not require any technical expertise. It simply says that a theory must be self-consistent, devoid of any internal contradictions. If a theory contains an internal contradiction, it is an unacceptable theory. If it contained a large number of such contradictions, it would be an *outrageous* theory.

The official conspiracy theory about 9/11, containing at least 25 internal contradictions, is clearly an outrageous theory. And yet this theory has been used to justify attacks on two countries, which have caused over a million deaths, including the deaths of thousands of Americans. This theory has also been used to justify extraordinary rendition, torture, warrantless spying, the denial of habeas corpus, and a general undermining of the US Constitution.

Given the extraordinary developments that have been justified in the name of the official story about 9/11, Congress and the press need to ask if the many contradictions in this story point to its falsity.

NOTES

Abbreviations

Clarke: Richard A. Clarke, *Against All Enemies: Inside America's War on Terror*. New York: Free Press, 2004.

FAA Memo: "FAA Communications with NORAD on September 11, 2001: FAA Clarification Memo to 9/11 Independent Commission," 22 May 2003. Available in the transcript of the 9/11 Commission hearing of 23 May 2003 (www.9-11commission.gov/archive/hearing2/9-11Commission_Hearing_2003-05-23.htm) and at www.911truth.org/article.php?story= 2004081200421797.

Filson: Leslie Filson, *Air War over America: Sept. 11 Alters Face of Air Defense Mission*, Foreword by Larry K. Arnold. Public Affairs: Tyndall Air Force Base, 2003.

Freni: Pamela S. Freni, *Ground Stop: An Inside Look at the Federal Aviation Administration on September 11, 2001*. Lincoln, NE: iUniverse, 2003.

9/11CR: *The 9/11 Commission Report: Final Report of the National Commission on Terrorist Attacks upon the United States*, authorized edition. New York: W. W. Norton, 2004.

9/11 Jennings: "9/11: Interviews by Peter Jennings," ABC News, 11 September 2002 (s3.amazonaws.com/911timeline/2002/abcnews091102.html).

NORAD Response: "NORAD's Response Times," 18 September 2001 (www.standdown.net/noradseptember182001pressrelease.htm).

Oral History: 9/11 oral histories of members of the Fire Department of New York were recorded from September 2001 through January 2002; 503 of these are now available at a *New York Times* website (graphics8. nytimes.com/packages/html/nyregion/20050812_WTC_GRAPHIC/met_WT C_histories_full_01.html).

Skies 2002: "America Remembers: The Skies over America," NBC News, 11 September 2002. Available at Newsmine.org (newsmine.org/archive/9-11/air-traffic-controllers-recall-events.txt); also available as a video (www.jonhs.net/911/skies_over_america.htm).

VP Russert: "The Vice President Appears on Meet the Press with Tim Russert," MSNBC, 16 September 2001 (www.whitehouse.gov/vicepresident/news-speeches/speeches/vp20010916.html).

WP: Thomas H. Kean and Lee H. Hamilton, with Benjamin Rhodes, *Without Precedent: The Inside Story of the 9/11 Commission*. New York: Alfred A. Knopf, 2006.

PART I
Chapter 1: How Long Did Bush Remain in the Classroom?

1 Dan Balz and Bob Woodward, "America's Chaotic Road to War: Tuesday, September 11," *Washington Post* 27 January 2002 (www.washingtonpost.com/wpdyn/content/article/2006/07/18/AR20060718 01175.html). This article was the first in a six-part series, "Ten Days in September."

2 Mitch Stacy, "Florida School Where Bush Learned of the Attacks Reflects on Its Role in History," Associated Press, 19 August 2002 (s3.amazonaws.com/911timeline/2002/ap081902d.html).

3 9/11 Jennings.

4 Andrew Card, "What If You Had to Tell the President," *San Francisco Chronicle* 11 September 2002 (sfgate.com/cgi-bin/article.cgi?file=/ c/a/2002/09/11/MN911voice03.DTL&type=printable).

5 "The News with Brian Williams," NBC, 9 September 2002 (www.msnbc.com/modules/91102/interviews/card.asp).

6 "Sept. 11's Moments of Crisis: Part 1: Terror Hits the Towers," ABC News, 14 September 2002 (us-pentagon.tripod.com/cache/abcnews/ sept11_moments_1.html).

7 "9/11 Interview with Campbell Brown," NBC News, 11 September 2002 (www.msnbc.com/modules/91102/interviews/rove.asp?cp1=1).

8 9/11 Jennings.

9 Jennifer Barrs, "From a Whisper to a Tear," *Tampa Tribune* 1 September 2002 (s3.amazonaws.com/911timeline/2002/tampatri-bune090102.html). On the importance of this story, plus the fact that it has become virtually unavailable on the Internet, see Elizabeth Woodworth, "President Bush at the Florida School: New Conflicting Testimonies," 7 July 2007, 911Blogger.com (www.911blogger.com/node/9847).

10 Barrs, "From a Whisper to a Tear"; Bill Adair and Stephen Hegarty, "The Drama in Sarasota," *St. Petersburg Times* 8 September 2002 (www.sptimes.com/2002/09/08/911/The_drama_in_Sarasota.shtml).

11 Malcolm Balfour, "Tragic Lesson," *New York Post* 12 September 2002 (s3.amazonaws.com/911timeline/2002/nypost091202.html).

12 Bill Sammon, *Fighting Back: The War on Terrorism: From Inside the Bush White House* (Washington, DC: Regnery, 2002), 89–90.

13 Scot J. Paltrow, "Government Accounts of 9/11 Reveal Gaps, Inconsistencies," *Wall Street Journal* 22 March 2004 (online.wsj.com/ article/SB107991342102561383.html).

14 For both versions, see "5-Minute Video of George W. Bush on the Morning of 9/11," *The Memory Hole* 26 June 2003 (www.thememoryhole.org/911/bush-911.htm).

15 Paltrow, "Government Accounts."

16 Sandra Kay Daniels, "9/11: A Year After/Who We Are Now," *Los Angeles Times* 11 September 2002 (pqasb.pqarchiver.com/latimes/access/171354041.html?dids=171354041:171354041&FMT=ABS&FMTS=ABS:FT&type=current).

17 Balfour, "Tragic Lesson." For these stories by Daniels, I am indebted to Woodworth, "President Bush at the Florida School."

18 Barrs, "From a Whisper to a Tear."

19 Ibid.

20 Mike Riopell, "Educator's History Lesson," *Arlington Heights Daily Herald* 11 September 2006 (www.dailyherald.com/news/lakestory.asp?id=226303).

21 John Ibbitson, "Action, Not Overreaction, Prudent Course," *Globe and Mail* 12 September 2001 (www.theglobeandmail.com/special/attack/pages/where_article11.html).

22 Philip H. Melanson, *Secret Service: The Hidden History of an Enigmatic Agency* (New York: Carroll & Graf, 2002).

23 Melanson is quoted in Susan Taylor Martin, "Of Fact, Fiction: Bush on 9/11," *St. Petersburg Times* 4 July 2004 (www.sptimes.com/2004/07/04/news_pf/Worldandnation/Of_fact__fiction__Bus.shtml).

24 Tom Bayles, "The Day Before Everything Changed, President Bush Touched Locals' Lives," *Sarasota Herald-Tribune* 10 September 2002 (s3.amazonaws.com/911timeline/2002/sarasotaheraldtribune091002.html); Blakewill's statement was later quoted in Martin, "Of Fact, Fiction."

25 Clarke 4.

26 Adair and Hegarty, "The Drama in Sarasota"; Bayles, "The Day Before Everything Changed."

27 Sammon, *Fighting Back*, 25.

28 David Sanger, "2 Leaders Tell of Plot to Kill Bush in Genoa," *New York Times* 25 September 2001(query.nytimes.com/gst/fullpage.html?res=9B0DE4D9133AF935A1575AC0A9679C8B63); "Italy Tells of Threat at Genoa Summit," *Los Angeles Times* 27 September 2001 (911citizenswatch.org/?p=224).

29 CNN, 18 July 2001.

30 According to ABC News, "Vice President Dick Cheney, also [like Condoleezza Rice] in the White House bunker, said officials arranged for the evacuation of the congressional leadership, especially House Speaker Dennis Hastert, R-Ill., third in line of presidential succession." See "Sept. 11's Moments of Crisis: Part 4: Post-Attack Tremors," ABC News, 15

September 2002 (us-pentagon.tripod.com/cache/abcnews/sept11_
moments_4.html).

31 Martin, "Of Fact, Fiction."

32 9/11 Jennings.

33 9/11 Jennings.

34 Bob Woodward, *Bush at War* (New York: Simon & Schuster, 2002), 16.

35 9/11CR 39.

36 Barrs, "From a Prayer to a Tear."

37 WP 54.

38 9/11CR 39.

Chapter 2: When Did Cheney Enter the Underground Bunker?

1 VP Russert.

2 9/11CR 40.

3 9/11 Commission Hearing, 23 May 2003 (www.9-
11commission.gov/archive/hearing2/9-11Commission_Hearing_2003-05-
23.htm).

4 One objection to Mineta's timeline has been that in the earlier part of
his testimony, he said: "When I got to the White House, it was being
evacuated." Because Richard Clarke's account suggests that the evacuation
did not begin until about 9:40, just after the strike on the Pentagon (Clarke
7–8), it might be assumed that Mineta was wrong about his time of arrival.
However, during a live broadcast, CNN senior White House correspondent
John King reported at 9:52 that the evacuation had begun slowly "about 30
minutes ago" but that "in the last 10 minutes or so, the people who came
out… were told and ordered by the Secret Service to run" ("The White
House Has Been Evacuated," CNN, 11 September 2001
[transcripts.cnn.com/TRANSCRIPTS/0109/11/bn.06.html]. It is possible
that, although Clarke reported that he had suggested at about 9:10 that the
White House should be evacuated (Clarke 2), he was later unaware that the
slower evacuation had been going on for some 20 minutes prior to the
rushed evacuation.

5 Clarke 1–4.

6 Clarke 2–4. Clarke later (8) reported that he used that line to make
requests shortly after 9:30 and was "amazed at the speed of the decisions
coming from Cheney."

7 Clarke 5.

8 9/11 Jennings. The statement that this occurred "just after 9AM" was
made in "Sept. 11's Moments of Crisis: Part 2: Scramble," ABC News, 14
September 2002 (us-pentagon.tripod.com/cache/abcnews/sept11_
moments_2.html).

9 9/11 Jennings.

10 "9/11 Interview with Campbell Brown," NBC News, 11 September 2002 (www.msnbc.com/modules/91102/interviews/rove.asp?cp1=1).

11 "Clear the Skies," BBC News, 8 September 2002 (web.archive.org/web/20040701101430/http://www.mnet.co.za/CarteBlanche/Display/Display.asp?Id=2063).

12 Scott McCartney and Susan Carey, "American, United Watched and Worked In Horror as Sept. 11 Hijackings Unfolded," *Wall Street Journal* 15 October 2001 (s3.amazonaws.com/911timeline/2001/wall-streetjournal101501.html).

13 9/11CR 39–40.

14 9/11CR 464n209.

15 9/11CR 40, citing an interview with *Newsweek* of 19 November 2001. Although the Commission failed to mention it, the resulting article was Evan Thomas, "The Story of September 11," *Newsweek* 31 December 2001 (www.msnbc.msn.com/id/14738713/site/newsweek/page/0)).

16 9/11CR 40.

17 Matthew L. Wald with Kevin Sack, "'We Have Some Planes,' Hijacker Told Controller," *New York Times* 16 October 2001 (s3.amazon-aws.com/911timeline/2001/nyt101601.html).

18 Skies 2002.

19 "Clear the Skies."

20 Dan Balz and Bob Woodward, "America's Chaotic Road to War: Tuesday, September 11," *Washington Post* 27 January 2002 (www.washingtonpost.com/wpdyn/content/article/2006/07/18/AR2006071801175.html). This article was the first in a six-part series, "Ten Days in September."

21 Ibid.

22 VP Russert.

23 9/11CR 464n210. Although the Commission's note reads, "White House transcript, Vice President Cheney interview with *Newsweek*, Nov. 19, 2001," no such transcript seems to be publicly available. The reference, in any case, seems to be an article by Evan Thomas, "The Story of September 11," which appeared in the issue of *Newsweek* dated 31 December 2001 (www.msnbc.msn.com/id/14738713/site/newsweek/page/0). Evidence for this identification is provided by the fact that the 9/11 Commission elsewhere quotes Cheney as having asked, after he heard that the North Tower had been struck, "How the hell could a plane hit the World Trade Center?" (9/11CR 35). The reference cites "White House transcript, Vice President Cheney interview with *Newsweek*, Nov. 19. 2001" (462n185), and that quotation appears in Thomas's *Newsweek* article of 31 December. (Although it might seem strange that an interview carried out on November 19 would not have resulted in a story until December 31, a

statement by Condoleezza Rice quoted on the same page of the 9/11 Commission's report ("that's all we know right now, Mr. President"), which shows up in a different Evan Thomas story of 31 December, is said to have been taken from an interview that Rice had granted to *Newsweek* on November 1 (9/11CR 35, 462n184).

24 Thomas, "The Story of September 11" (see previous note).

25 Evan Thomas and Mark Hosenball, "Bush: 'We're at War,'" *Newsweek* 24 September 2001 (www.msnbc.msn.com/id/14738203/site/newsweek).

26 Cheney's speeches, news releases, and interviews are listed at www.whitehouse.gov/vicepresident/news-speeches/index.html.

27 9/11 Commission Hearing, 23 May 2003.

28 9/11CR 40.

29 See Gregor Holland, "The Mineta Testimony: 9/11 Commission Exposed," 911truthmovement.org, 1 November 2005 (www.911truthmovement.org/archives/2005/11/post.php).

30 Ibid. Mineta's interchange with Hamilton can be viewed at video.google.ca/videoplay?docid=-3722436852417384871, and his interchange with Roemer at www.911truth.org/article.php?story=20050724164122860.

31 See "9/11: Truth, Lies and Conspiracy: Interview: Lee Hamilton," CBC News, 21 August 2006 (www.cbc.ca/sunday/911hamilton.html).

32 Ibid.

33 "Interview: Norman Mineta: From Internment Camp to the Halls of Congress," Academy of Achievement, 3 June 2006 (www.achievement.org/autodoc/page/min0int-8). Part of this statement, along with Mineta's testimony to the 9/11 Commission, can be seen in an video entitled "The Lost Flight: Who Knew What and When about Flight AA77 on 9/11?" (video.google.com/videoplay?docid=7140292755378838617&hl=en).

34 "9/11 Seattle Truth Meets Norm Mineta" (www.youtube.com/v/u-5PKQTUz5o). This video is also available in Aaron Dykes, "Norman Mineta Confirms That Dick Cheney Ordered Stand Down on 9/11," Jones Report, 26 June 2007 (www.jonesreport.com/articles/260607_mineta.html). The title of Dykes's essay is misleading, however, because Mineta said nothing about a stand-down order.

Chapter Three: Was Cheney Observed...a Stand-Down Order?

1 9/11 Commission Hearing, 23 May 2003 (www.9-11commission.gov/archive/hearing2/9-11Commission_Hearing_2003-05-23.htm).

2 9/11CR 27, 34.

3 Sylvia Adcock, Brian Donovan, and Craig Gordon, "Air Attack on

Pentagon Indicates Weaknesses," *Newsday* 23 September 2001.

4 "Clear the Skies," BBC, 8 September 2002 (web.archive.org/web/20040701101430/http://www.mnet.co.za/CarteBlanche/Display/Display.asp?Id=2063).

5 "Cheney Recalls Taking Charge from Bunker," *Inside Politics*, CNN, 11 September 2002 (archives.cnn.com/2002/ALLPOLITICS/09/11/ar911.king.cheney/index.html); 9/11 Jennings; "Sept. 11's Moments of Crisis: Part 2: Scramble," ABC News, 14 September 2002 (us-pentagon.tripod.com/cache/abcnews/sept11_moments_2.html).

6 VP Russert; Skies 2002; Matthew L. Wald with Kevin Sack, "'We Have Some Planes,' Hijacker Told Controller," *New York Times* 16 October 2001 (s3.amazonaws.com/911timeline/2001/nyt101601.html); "Clear the Skies."

7 Dan Balz and Bob Woodward, "America's Chaotic Road to War: Tuesday, September 11," *Washington Post* 27 January 2002 (www.washingtonpost.com/ac2/wp-dyn/A42754-2002Jan26).

8 Evan Thomas, "The Story of September 11," *Newsweek* 31 December 2001 (www.msnbc.msn.com/id/14738713/site/newsweek/page/0).

9 9/11CR 40. This position had already been taken in "9/11 Commission Staff Statement No. 17," 17 June 2004 (www.msnbc.msn.com/id/5233007).

10 Wald and Sack, "'We Have some Planes,' Hijacker Said on Sept. 11."

11 Skies 2002; "Clear the Skies."

12 Balz and Woodward, "America's Chaotic Road to War: Tuesday, September 11."

13 See 9/11CR 464–65nn217, 219, 220, 221.

14 9/11CR 41.

15 My discussions of the incoming flight stories and the Mineta–Sliney controversy, discussed in the next chapter, are indebted to Peter Dale Scott, *The Road to 9/11: Wealth, Empire, and the Future of America* (Berkeley: University of California Press, 2007), Chs. 12–13.

Chapter 4: Did Cheney Observe the Land-All-Planes Order?

1 9/11CR 29.

2 Norman Mineta's Testimony to the Senate Committee on Commerce, Science, and Transportation, 20 September 2001 (lobby.la.psu.edu/_107th/136_Aviation%20Security/Congressional_Hearings/Testimony/S_CST_Mineta_09202001.htm).

3 Statement of Jane F. Garvey, administrator, Federal Aviation Administration, before the House Subcommittee on Aviation, 21 September 2001 (www.yale.edu/lawweb/avalon/sept_11/garvey_001.htm).

4 Clarke 4–5.

5 9/11 Commission Hearing, 23 May 2003 (www.9-11commission.gov/archive/hearing2/9-11Commission_Hearing_2003-05-23.htm). During an

interview in 2006, Mineta said that his order to Monte Belger to "ground all
the planes" was issued at "about 9:27," thereby apparently blending
together the two events that both he and Garvey had distinguished in their
2001 testimony to congressional committees, with Garvey placing the
national ground stop order at 9:26 and the order to ground all planes at
9:45 ("Interview: Norman Mineta: From Internment Camp to the Halls of
Congress," Academy of Achievement, 3 June 2006 [www.achievement.org/
autodoc/page/min0int-8]).

6 Balz and Woodward, "America's Chaotic Road to War: Tuesday,
September 11."

7 9/11CR 29.

8 Alan Levin, Marilyn Adams, and Blake Morrison, "Terror Attacks
Brought Drastic Decision: Clear the Skies," *USA Today* 2 August 2002
(www.usatoday.com/news/sept11/2002-08-12-clearskies_x.htm).

9 Joshua Green, "The Mineta Myth," Slate.com, 1 April 2002
(www.slate.com/?id=2063935). Green said that a few days before his article
was published, "Don Phillips let the cat out of the bag. Phillips told his audience he felt it necessary to make a 'historical correction,' although FAA officials had begged him to maintain the fiction. Phillips proposed, charitably,
that Mineta's order was a simple misunderstanding; that the secretary was
unaware that '[f]or at least 15 minutes before Mineta's conversation with the
FAA, controllers were bringing the planes down… at the nearest airport."
That planes were being brought down in some regions, however, does not
show that the *nationwide* order had been given. Phillips then continued: "I'm
told by very high sources that it happened this way: First, the decision was
made on a regional basis by some gutsy local FAA officials, and the FAA
command center and headquarters officials agreed that it should be spread to
the whole country. First, [the FAA] acted. Then they sought permission."
Phillips next said: "A top FAA official… then called Mineta, finding him in a
bunker with the vice president and other officials. He explained the plan,
and Mineta agreed. … Then there was a pause in the conversation. You know
what many of us do when there is a pause in the conversation. We try to fill
the dead time. The FAA official, unfortunately said something like, 'Of
course we could have let them go on to their destinations, or….' Big mistake.
Norm heard that throwaway line as saying the FAA was still considering
letting them go on to destination. He then fired off his now-famous order."
The distinction, however, was not trivial. Belger, at least as reported in the
Balz–Woodward article, was allowing pilots to have some discretion on
whether to land immediately. If Mineta replaced that order with the order that
all planes be brought down immediately, he was indeed the one who gave the
order for all planes in the nation to be brought down. So, whereas Phillips
argued that Mineta's belief that he gave the order involved a "simple misun-

derstanding" on his part, this is not necessarily the case. Green then used Phillips's account to argue that Monte Belger deserves credit for issuing the order, saying that "when the secretary issued his blunt order—'Monte, bring all the planes down!'—Monte had already done so." But whether that is true depends, apparently, on the meaning of "all." The argument as to who deserves "credit," in any case, may be a misplaced debate. Pamela Freni says: "Because of the intuition of dozens of managers, supervisors, and controllers, long before Secretary Mineta gave the command, the 'land all planes' order already permeated the system" (Freni 36).

10 Linda Schuessler, the manager of tactical operations at the FAA Command Center at Herndon, has said: "it was done collaboratively…. It wasn't one person who said, 'Yes, this has got to get done'" (David Bond, "Crisis at Herndon: 11 Airplanes Astray," *Aviation Week and Space Technology* 17 December 2001). Schuessler's account is, therefore, similar to those of Don Phillips and Pamela Freni, given in the previous note, although Freni suggested that, insofar as the order originated from any one person, that person was Linda Schuessler (Freni 65).

11 9/11CR 29.

12 Anthony Breznican, "Controller Relives Horror of '93'," *USA Today* 23 April 2006 (www.usatoday.com/life/movies/news/2006-04-23-united93-main_x.htm).

Chapter 5: When Did Cheney Issue Shootdown Authorization?

1 9/11CR 40–41. On these pages, the Commission's skepticism is muted, limited to stating that there was no documentary evidence for the call. According to *Newsweek* magazine, however, this statement was a "watered down" version of an earlier draft, which had reflected the fact that "some on the commission staff were… highly skeptical of the vice president's account." That earlier draft, which evidently expressed more clearly the belief that the vice president and the president were lying, was reportedly modified after vigorous lobbying from the White House (*Newsweek* 20 June 2004).

2 9/11CR 41.

3 "By the time the military learned about the flight, it had crashed" (9/11CR 34).

4 9/11CR 41. The movie *United 93*, which follows the timeline of *The 9/11 Commission Report*, says that the shootdown authorization was given at 10:18.

5 9/11CR 37.

6 Clarke 7.

7 Clarke 8.

8 Ibid.

9 Ibid.

10 See note 4 of Ch. 2, above.

11 Chitra Ragavan and Mark Mazzetti, "Pieces of the Puzzle: A Top-Secret Conference Call on September 11 Could Shed New Light on the Terrorist Attacks," *US News & World Report* 31 August, 2003 (www.usnews.com/usnews/news/articles/030908/8sept11.htm).

12 9/11 Jennings.

13 "'The Pentagon Goes to War': National Military Command Center," *American Morning with Paula Zahn*, CNN, 4 September 2002 (transcripts.cnn.com/TRANSCRIPTS/0209/04/ltm.11.html).

14 Filson 71.

15 Filson 68.

16 9/11 Jennings.

17 Dave Foster, "UST Grad Guides Bombers in War," *Aquin*, 4 December 2002 (www.stthomas.edu/aquin/archive/041202/anaconda.html).

18 William B. Scott, "F-16 Pilots Considered Ramming Flight 93," *Aviation Week & Space Technology* 9 September 2002 (www.aviationweek.com/aw/generic/story_generic.jsp?channel=awst&id=news/aw090971.xml).

19 Matthew L. Wald with Kevin Sack, "'We Have Some Planes,' Hijacker Told Controller," *New York Times* 16 October 2001 (s3.amazon-aws.com/911timeline/2001/nyt101601.html).

20 9/11CR 37.

21 Clarke 8.

22 9/11CR 38, 463n201, quoting "DOD transcript, Air Threat Conference Call, Sept. 11, 2001."

23 Clarke 8.

Chapter 6: Where Was General Richard Myers?

1 "Interview: General Richard B. Myers," Armed Forces Radio and Television Services (web.archive.org/web/20011118060728/http://www.dtic.mil/jcs/chairman/AFRTS_Interview.htm).

2 9/11CR 463n199, citing an interview of 17 February 2004.

3 9/11CR 38.

4 "Interview: Norman Mineta: From Internment Camp to the Halls of Congress," Academy of Achievement, 3 June 2006 (www.achievement.org/autodoc/page/min0int-8). Further evidence for the time that Clarke's conference must have begun, if his account is basically accurate, is provided by all the events that, according to Clarke, occurred prior to the moment at which he noted that it was 9:28 (Clarke 3–5).

5 Clarke 3.

6 Clarke 4.

7 Clarke 5.

8 Clarke 7–9.

9 Clarke 12.

10 This meeting is mentioned in Robert Burns, "Pentagon Attack Came Minutes after Rumsfeld Predicted: 'There Will Be Another Event,'" Associated Press, 12 September 2001 (www.dodgeglobe.com/stories/091201/nat_pentagon_attack.shtml).

11 "Rumsfeld's War," *Frontline*, PBS, 26 October 2004 (www.pbs.org/wgbh/pages/frontline/shows/pentagon/etc/script.html).

12 9/11CR 36.

13 9/11CR 36.

14 Clarke 7.

15 FAA Memo. This memo was discussed by the 9/11 Commission on 23 May 2003 (www.9-11commission.gov/archive/hearing2/9-11Commission_Hearing_2003-05-23.htm).

16 General Myers Confirmation Hearing, Senate Armed Services Committee, 13 September 2001 (emperors-clothes.com/9-11backups/mycon.htm).

17 9/11 Commission Hearing, 17 June 2004 (www.9-11commission.gov/archive/hearing12/9-11Commission_Hearing_2004-06-17.htm#two).

18 Jim Garamone, "Former Chairman Remembers 9/11 Attacks," American Forces Press Service, 8 September 2006 (www.defenselink.mil/News/NewsArticle.aspx?ID=745&4745=20060908).

19 After saying that "the Warren Commission blew it," Cleland added: "I'm not going to be part of that. I'm not going to be part of looking at information only partially. I'm not going to be part of just coming to quick conclusions. I'm not going to be part of political pressure to do this or not do that. I'm not going to be part of that" (Eric Boehlert, "The President Ought to be Ashamed: Interview with Max Cleland," Salon.com, 13 November 2003). Cleland's disagreement with the Commission's leadership was, however, not his only reason for resigning. Having lost his Senate seat in the 2002 election, he needed a job with a salary. Senate Democrats had recommended him for a Democratic slot on the board of the Export–Import Bank, and the White House sent this nomination to the Senate near the end of 2003. Being legally forbidden from holding both positions, Cleland resigned from the Commission (after which he was replaced by former Senator Bob Kerrey).

20 General Myers Confirmation Hearing.

21 "Max Cleland Speech," St. Marks Episcopal Church, Raleigh, NC 2003 (www.stmarkspeace.org/Max01.html). Although this document spelled Myers's name "Meyers," it otherwise appears to be an accurate transcription of a speech given by Cleland.

Chapter 7: Where Was Donald Rumsfeld?

1 Clarke 3.

2 See text to note 4, Chapter 6, above.

3 Clarke 7.

4 Clarke 8–9.

5 Clarke 22.

6 9/11 Commission Hearing, 23 March 2004 (www.washingtonpost.com/wp-dyn/articles/A17798-2004Mar23.html).

7 Photos are available at "9:39AM" and "Between 9:38AM and 10:00AM" under "Donald Rumsfeld" under "Day of 9/11" in Cooperative Research's "Complete 911 Timeline" (www.cooperativeresearch.org/timeline.jsp?timeline=complete_911_timeline&day_of_9/11=donaldRumsfeld).

8 See "Secretary Rumsfeld Interview with Parade Magazine," US Department of Defense, 12 October 2001 (www.defenselink.mil/transcripts/transcript.aspx?TranscriptID=3845). A supporting account is given by Torie Clarke in "Assistant Secretary Clarke Interview with WBZ Boston," 15 September 2001 (www.defenselink.mil/transcripts/transcript.aspx?transcriptid=1884).

9 9/11CR 37; the Commission cites an interview it had with Rumsfeld in December 2002, along with a Department of Defense memo and an interview with Rumsfeld's assistant, Stephen Cambone, in 2004 (9/11CR 463n193).

10 9/11CR 43.

11 "Assistant Secretary Clarke Interview with WBZ Boston."

12 "Secretary Rumsfeld Interview with John McWethy, ABC," US Department of Defense, 12 August 2002 (www.defenselink.mil/transcripts/transcript.aspx?transcriptid=3644).

13 9/11 Commission Hearing, 23 March 2004.

14 Torie Clarke, *Lipstick on a Pig: Winning in the No-Spin Era by Someone who Knows the Game* (New York: Free Press, 2006), 218–19.

15 9/11CR 43.

16 The Commission here seemed to slip. Although it claimed, as we saw in the previous chapter, that Clarke's video conference did not get started until 9:25 (9/11CR 36), it seemed here to admit implicitly that it had begun at about 9:10. Otherwise, Rumsfeld's participation, which began shortly after 10:00, would have been "in the first hour."

17 9/11 Commission Hearing, 23 March 2004.

18 9/11CR 43.

19 9/11CR 41.

20 9/11CR 43–44.

21 9/11CR 465n234.

22 "Secretary Rumsfeld Interview with John McWethy, ABC."

23 Balz and Woodward, "America's Chaotic Road to War: Tuesday, September 11."

24 "Secretary Rumsfeld Interview with the *Washington Post*," 9 January 2002 (www.defenselink.mil/transcripts/transcript.aspx?transcriptid=2602).

25 For example, Balz and Woodward wrote that after Rumsfeld had been at the crash site, helping with the rescue effort, he said, "I'm going inside," after which he "took up his post in the National Military Command Center" ("America's Chaotic Road to War"). Neither part of that statement is found in the transcript of the interview.

26 9/11CR 326 and 554n8.

27 Clarke 15.

28 9/11 Jennings.

29 "'The Pentagon Goes to War': National Military Command Center," *American Morning with Paula Zahn*, CNN, 4 September 2002 (transcripts.cnn.com/TRANSCRIPTS/0209/04/ltm.11.html).

30 "Secretary Rumsfeld Interview with John McWethy, ABC."

31 "Aircraft Piracy (Hijacking) and Destruction of Derelict Airborne Objects," CJCSI 3610.01A, 1 June 2001 (www.dtic.mil/doctrine/jel/cjcsd/cjcsi/3610_01a.pdf). The crucial passage says: "[T]he NMCC is the focal point within Department of Defense for providing assistance. In the event of a hijacking, the NMCC will be notified by the most expeditious means by the FAA. The NMCC will, with the exception of immediate responses as authorized by reference d, forward requests for DOD assistance to the Secretary of Defense for approval." As the clause about the exception indicates, not all requests do have to go to the Secretary of Defense or even his office, but many people have been led to believe otherwise.

32 9/11CR 38. Thomas Kean and Lee Hamilton, the chair and vice chair, respectively, of the 9/11 Commission, comment blandly about this episode, saying: "Rumsfeld… did not get on the Air Threat Conference until 10:39 because he had been assisting Pentagon rescue efforts" (WP 264).

33 9/11CR 38.

34 Quoted in Alexander Cockburn, *Rumsfeld: His Rise, Fall, and Catastrophic Legacy* (New York: Scribner, 2007), 2–4.

35 "Secretary Rumsfeld Interview with John McWethy, ABC."

36 "Secretary Rumsfeld Interview with Larry King, CNN," 6 December 2001 (www.defenselink.mil/transcripts/transcript.aspx?transcriptid=2603).

Chapter 8: Did Ted Olson Receive Calls from Barbara Olson?

1 Tim O'Brien, "Wife of Solicitor General Alerted Him of Hijacking from Plane," CNN, 11 September 2001, 2:06AM (archives.cnn.com/2001/US/09/11/pentagon.olson). Although this story, as now found in the CNN

archives, indicates that the story was posted at 2:06AM on September 12, reports of the story started appearing on blogs at 6:51PM on the 11th (see www.fantasticforum.com/archive_2/911/11sep01_barbaraolsonkilled.pdf and forum.dvdtalk.com/archive/index.php/t-141263.html).

2 The 9/11 Commission pointed out that this story was the sole basis for the idea that the hijackers had box cutters as well as knives (9/11CR 8).

3 *Hannity & Colmes*, Fox News, 14 September 2001.

4 "America's New War: Recovering from Tragedy," *Larry King Live*, CNN, 14 September 2001 (edition.cnn.com/TRANSCRIPTS/0109/14/lkl.00.html).

5 Theodore B. Olson, "Barbara K. Olson Memorial Lecture," 16 November 2001, Federalist Society, 15th Annual National Lawyers Convention (www.fed-soc.org/resources/id.63/default.asp).

6 Toby Harnden, "She Asked Me How to Stop the Plane," *Daily Telegraph* 5 March 2002 (s3.amazonaws.com/911timeline/2002/tele-graph030502.html).

7 See "On September 11, Final Words of Love," CNN, 10 September 2002 (archives.cnn.com/2002/US/09/03/ar911.phone.calls), which said: "Unbeknown to the hijackers, passenger and political commentator Barbara Olson, 45, was able to call her husband—Solicitor General Ted Olson—on her cellular phone."

8 The American Airlines website entitled "Onboard Technology" says: "Slide your credit card through the side of the phone and then dial 00 + country code + area or city code + number followed by the # key" (www.aa.com/content/travelInformation/duringFlight/onboardTechnology.jhtml).

9 A. K. Dewdney, a former columnist for *Scientific American*, has reported his empirical study of this issue in "The Cellphone and Airfone Calls from Flight UA93," Physics 911, 9 June 2003 (physics911.net/cell-phoneflight93.htm).

10 "Will They Allow Cell Phones on Planes?" *Travel Technologist* 19 September 2001 (www.elliott.org/technology/2001/cellpermit.htm). AT&T spokesperson Alexa Graf, explaining in 2001 that cell phone systems were not designed for calls from high altitudes, said: "On land, we have antenna sectors that point in three directions—say north, southwest, and southeast. Those signals are radiating across the land. [Insofar as] "those signals do go up, [that is] due to leakage." Quoted in Betsy Harter, "Final Contact," *Telephony's Wireless Review* 1 November 2001 (wirelessreview.com/ar/wireless_final_contact).

11 Harter, "Final Contact."

12 9/11CR 9.

13 See the National Transportation Safety Board's flight path study for AA Flight 77, 31 January 2002 (www.ntsb.gov/info/AAL77_fdr.pdf). This

study has been subjected to extensive analysis by Pilots for 9/11 Truth (pilotsfor911truth.org/pentagon.html).

14 American Airlines, "Onboard Technology" (www.aa.com/content/travelInformation/duringFlight/onboardTechnology.jhtml).

15 This exchange occurred on 6 December 2004; see Rowland Morgan and Ian Henshall, *9/11 Revealed: The Unanswered Questions* (New York: Carroll & Graf, 2005), 128-29.

16 See the submission of 17 February 2006 by "the Paradroid" on the Politik Forum (www.politikforum.de/forum/archive/index.php/t-133356-p-24.html).

17 The contradiction, besides being implicit, may also have been unintentional, because the AA representatives might have been unaware that Olson, in the final version of his story, had said that his wife had used an onboard phone.

18 9/11CR 9, 455n56.

19 9/11CR 455n57. The fact that the Commission spoke merely about what the FBI and the DOJ "believe" suggested that no records were produced to support this contention.

20 9/11CR 455n57.

21 United States v. Zacarias Moussaoui, Exhibit Number P200054 (www.vaed.uscourts.gov/notablecases/moussaoui/exhibits/prosecution/flights/P200054.html). These documents can be more easily viewed in "Detailed Account of Phone Calls From September 11th Flights" (911research.wtc7.net/planes/evidence/calldetail.html#ref1).

22 How the government could have concluded that this call was attempted by Barbara Olson was not explained.

23 Greg Gordon, "Prosecutors Play Flight 93 Cockpit Recording," KnoxNews.com, 12 April 2006 (www.knoxsingles.com/shns/story.cfm?pk=MOUSSAOUI-04-12-06&cat=WW).

24 "Did a Plane Hit the Pentagon?" Identifying Misinformation, US Department of State (usinfo.state.gov/media/Archive/2005/Jun/28-581634.html).

25 9/11CR 455n57.

26 See note 21, above. There is one trivial exception: Whereas the FBI report for the Moussaoui trial has the third call lasting 159 seconds, which would mean 2 minutes, 39 seconds, the 9/11 Commission says that the report had it lasting "2 minutes, 34 seconds." But this was probably simply a typo.

PART II
Chapter 9: When Was the Military Alerted about Flight 11?

1 NORAD Response.

2 9/11CR 31.3.

3 I learned this from Boston Center's Colin Scoggins (emails of 8 and 11 January 2007).

4 This detail is provided in Hart Seely, "Amid Crisis Simulation, 'We Were Suddenly No-Kidding Under Attack,'" Newhouse News Service, 25 January 2002 (s3.amazonaws.com/911timeline/2002/newhouse-news012502.html). Seely incorrectly identified the caller as a "military liaison." That term would designate Colin Scoggins, who did not call until a minute or so later.

5 "Moments of Crisis: Part I: Terror Hits the Towers," ABC News, 14 September 2002 (us-pentagon.tripod.com/cache/abcnews/sept11_moments_1.html).

6 9/11 Jennings.

7 The FAA official quoted in the dialogue at 9/11CR 26 was Colin Scoggins, although he was not cited by name. He was, however, mentioned by name at 9/11CR 458n101 (although his first name was incorrectly spelled "Collin").

8 Quoted in Michael Bronner, "9/11 Live: The NORAD Tapes," *Vanity Fair* September 2006, 262–85 (www.vanityfair.com/politics/features/2006/08/norad200608).

9 Email of 27 October 2006.

10 Emails from Scoggins, 11 and 12 January 2007, and 25 July 2007.

11 Email from Scoggins, 14 December 2006.

12 This, I should emphasize, is not Scoggins's own opinion but simply a deduction from his statements about his calls. He had thought his first call occurred a little later, because he had thought that he did not get to the floor that morning until about 8:35. He agrees, however, that the math appears to imply otherwise (email from Scoggins, 8 January 2007).

13 Email from Scoggins, 31 December 2006.

14 9/11CR 19. The notification of the hijacking really should have occurred by 8:26, but the supervisor, John Schipanni, disputed controller Pete Zalewski's contention that the plane had been hijacked, thereby slowing down the procedure (email from Scoggins, 8 January 2007). This dispute was reflected in the film *United 93*.

15 "A Chat with Former Boston Center Controller Robin Hordon," Pilots for 9/11 Truth, 13 December 2006 (video.google.com/videoplay?docid=-9147890225218338952&hl=en).

16 9/11CR 37.

17 Clarke 2.

18 Tom Flocco, "Rookie in the 9-11 Hot Seat?" Tomflocco.com, 17 June 2004 (tomflocco.com/fs/NMCCOpsDirector.htm).

Chapter 10: When Was the Military Alerted about Flight 175?

1 9/11CR 21.

2 9/11CR 31.

3 "Timeline in Terrorist Attacks of Sept. 11, 2001," *Washington Post* 12 September 2001 (www.washingtonpost.com/wp-srv/nation/articles/timeline.html).

4 "Officials: Government Failed to React to FAA Warning," CNN, 17 September 2001 (archives.cnn.com/2001/US/09/16/inv.hijack.warning).

5 NORAD Response.

6 William B. Scott, "Exercise Jump-Starts Response to Attacks," *Aviation Week and Space Technology* 3 June 2002 (web.archive.org/web/20020917072642/http://www.aviationnow.com/content/publication/awst/20020603/avi_stor.htm).

7 Although the F-15 can fly at 1,800 mph, this is only at very high altitudes, where the air is thin. For my calculation, I assumed that the fighters would have been traveling about half way between sea level, at which they can fly 915 mph, and 36,000 feet, at which they can fly 1,650 mph (home.att.net/~jbaugher1/f15_6.html).

8 9/11CR 23.

9 9/11CR 21–23.

10 Miller, "Military Now Notified Immediately of Unusual Air Traffic Events" (www.signonsandiego.com/news/nation/20020812-1404-attacks-faamilitary.html). The same statement was made in Steve LeBlanc, "FAA Controllers Detail Sept. 11 Events," Associated Press, 12 August 2003 (www.boston.com/news/daily/12/attacks_faa.htm).

11 Skies 2002. Otis AFB had become Otis Air National Guard Base.

12 "The Skies over America," *Dateline*, MSNBC, 9 September 2006 (www.msnbc.msn.com/id/14754701/); see footage at 4:09).

13 Skies 2002.

14 9/11 Jennings.

15 Scott Simmie, "The Scene at NORAD on Sept. 11," *Toronto Star* 9 December 2001 (911research.wtc7.net/cache/planes/defense/torontostar_russiangame.html).

16 Freni 17.

17 Freni 33.

18 Hart Seely, "Amid Crisis Simulation, 'We Were Suddenly No-Kidding Under Attack,'" Newhouse News Service, 25 January 2002 (s3.amazonaws.com/911timeline/2002/newhousenews012502.html).

19 FAA Memo. This memo was widely understood to have been

written by Laura Brown. But when it was discussed by the 9/11 Commission on May 23 (www.9-11commission.gov/archive/hearing2/9-11Commission_ Hearing_2003-05-23.htm), it was presented by Commissioner Richard Ben-Veniste as authored by "Mr. Asmus and Ms. Schuessler." However, during a telephone conversation I had with Laura Brown while she was at home on Sunday, 15 August 2004, she confirmed that she had written it. It is likely, of course, that she did so on the basis of input from these two individuals, especially Linda Schuessler, the manager of tactical operations at the FAA Command Center in Herndon.

20 9/11 Commission Hearing, 23 May 2003 (www.9-11commission.gov/archive/hearing2/9-11Commission_Hearing_2003-05-23.htm).

21 Ibid.

22 9/11CR 36.

23 In support of its claim, the Commission cited no participants. It merely wrote: "For the time of the teleconference, see FAA record, Chronology ADA-30, Sept. 11, 2001" (this chronology is available at www.gwu.edu/~nsarchiv/NSAEBB/NSAEBB165/faa1.pdf). Laura Brown has reported, incidentally, that immediately after 9/11, the FAA was required to turn over all its records from that day to the FBI—not to the NTSB, as it usually did after a major aviation disaster (telephone interview, 15 August 2004). This could perhaps help explain why so many things in this chronology are blacked out.

Chapter 11: When Was the Military Alerted about Flight 77?

1 NORAD Response.

2 See CNN's timeline (archives.cnn.com/2001/US/09/16/inv.hijack.warning).

3 NORAD Response; "Officials: Government Failed to React to FAA Warning," CNN, 17 September 2001 (archives.cnn.com/2001/US/09/16/inv.hijack.warning).

4 *Guardian* 17 October 2001; *New York Times* 17 October 2001; *Boston Globe* 23 November 2001.

5 One exception was a *Wall Street Journal* story that said: "American's operations experts received a call from the FAA saying that a second American plane, Flight 77 out of Washington-Dulles, had turned off its transponder and turned around" (Scott McCartney and Susan Carey, "American, United Watched and Worked in Horror as Sept. 11 Hijackings Unfolded," *Wall Street Journal* 15 October 2001 [s3.amazonaws.com/911timeline/ 2001/wallstreetjournal101501.html]).

6 "Timeline in Terrorist Attacks of Sept. 11, 2001," *Washington Post* 12 September 2001 (www.washingtonpost.com/wp-srv/nation/articles/timeline.html); Sylvia Adcock, Brian Donovan, and Craig Gordon, "Air Attack on Pentagon Indicates Weaknesses," *Newsday* 23 September 2001

(s3.amazonaws.com/911timeline/2001/newsday092301.html).

7 Matthew L. Wald with Kevin Sack, "'We Have Some Planes,' Hijacker Told Controller," *New York Times* 16 October 2001 (s3.amazonaws.com/911timeline/2001/nyt101601.html).

8 During the 9/11 Commission hearing at which FAA administrator Jane Garvey testified, Commissioner Richard Ben-Veniste, after saying that the FAA did not report Flight 77 to the military until 30 minutes after losing track of it, asked: "[D]id you investigate whether there was a delay by FAA in notifying NORAD with respect to Flight 77?"

9 On 23 September 2001, *Newsday* asked: "Why weren't Pentagon leaders alerted and employees evacuated?" (Adcock, Donovan, and Gordon, "Air Attack on Pentagon Indicates Weaknesses"). More recently, Steve Vogel, in *The Pentagon: A History* (New York: Random House, 2007), wrote: "The National Military Command Center learned at 9:31AM that a hijacked airplane was reported to be Washington-bound. But no steps were taken to alert Pentagon employees or evacuate the building" (429).

10 George Szamuely wrote: "F-16s can travel at 1,500 mph. If it took the F-16s half an hour to cover 150 miles, they could not have been traveling at more than 300 mph—at 20 percent capability" ("Another Look at 9/11, and Those Unscrambled Jets: Nothing Urgent," New York Press 15/2: 9–15 January 2002 [www.nypress.com/15/2/taki/bunker.cfm]). Even if we modify Szamuely's statement in light of the fact that F-16s can travel 1,500 mph only at very high altitudes (see note 7 of Chapter 10), his point still stands, because they can fly over 900 mph even at sea level (www.aerospaceweb.org/aircraft/fighter/f16).

11 Matthew Wald, "Pentagon Tracked Deadly Jet but Found No Way to Stop It," *New York Times* 15 September 2001 (query.nytimes.com/gst/fullpage.html?res=9802E5D91F38F936A2575AC0A9679C8B63).

12 As I pointed out in the previous chapter, Tom Flocco reported that Laura Brown first said that the NMCC's conference call had begun at about 8:20 or 8:25, but then, after talking to superiors, revised the time to 8:45.

13 9/11 Commission Hearing, 22 May 2003 (www.9-11commission.gov/archive/hearing2/9-11Commission_Hearing_2003-05-22.htm).

14 FAA Memo. The fact that Laura Brown is the senior career person in the FAA (which I learned during a telephone conversation on 15 August 2004) helps make it understandable that the memo would have been written by her (as discussed in note 19 of Chapter 10, above).

15 FAA Memo.

16 Telephone interview with Laura Brown on 15 August 2004.

17 The 9/11 Commission stenographer spelled this name "Tindel."

18 9/11 Commission Hearing, 23 May 2003 (www.9-11

commission.gov/archive/hearing2/9-11Commission_Hearing_2003-05-23.htm).

19 Ibid.

20 Ibid.

21 9/11CR 34. Some of the central reports that contradict the 9/11 Commission's account of AA 77 are presented in a video entitled "The Lost Flight: Who Knew What and When about Flight AA 77 on 9/11" (video.google.com/videoplay?docid=7140292755378838617&hl=en).

22 9/11 CR 34.

23 Ibid.

24 Ibid.

25 9/11CR 36.

26 Freni 20.

27 Freni 22.

28 Wald, "Pentagon Tracked Deadly Jet."

29 *Arlington County: After-Action Report on the Response to the September 11 Attack on the Pentagon*, 2002 (www.arlingtonva.us/departments/Fire/edu/about/docs/after_report.pdf), C-45.

30 9/11CR 9.

31 9/11CR 27.

32 9/11CR 24.

33 Ibid.

34 Email from Hordon, 22 December 2006.

35 9/11 Commission Hearing, 23 May 2003.

36 Michael Ellison, "'We Have Planes. Stay Quiet'—Then Silence," *Guardian* 17 October 2001 (www.guardian.co.uk/wtccrash/story/0,1300,575518,00.html).

37 Skies 2002.

38 Freni 59.

39 VP Russert.

40 Clarke 7.

41 Garth Wade, "Elmira Native Protected Ronald Reagan," *Star-Gazette* (Elmira) 5 June 2006.

42 "Spotlight on: Barbara Riggs," President's Council of Cornell Women, Spring 2006 (pccw.alumni.cornell.edu/news/newsletters/spring06/riggs.html).

43 9/11 Commission Hearing, 17 June 2004. There were, in fact, three officers in the "military cell" at Herndon that morning (Colonel John Czabaranek, Lt. Colonel Michael-Anne Cherry, and Major Kevin Bridges), and they reportedly become "immediately involved in coordinating FAA... Command Center actions with military elements." See "8:50AM" and "Before 9:03AM" in the "Complete 911 Timeline" at Cooperative Research (www.coop-

erativeresearch.org/context.jsp?item=a850phonebridges).

44 9/11 Commission Hearing, 17 June 2004.

45 Freni 21.

Chapter 12: When Was the Military Alerted about Flight 93?

1 "Officials: Government Failed to React to FAA Warning," CNN, 17 September 2001 (http://archives.cnn.com/2001/US/09/16/inv.hijack.warning).

2 NORAD Response.

3 9/11 Commission Hearing, 23 May 2007 (www.9-11commission.gov/archive/hearing2/9-11Commission_Hearing_2003-05-23.htm).

4 Ibid.

5 9/11CR 34. The statement about the beginning of the hijack is at 9/11CR 11.

6 9/11CR 34.

7 9/11CR 38.

8 9/11CR 30.

9 9/11CR 28–29.

10 9/11CR 28.

11 9/11CR 29.

12 9/11CR 29–30.

13 Clarke 7.

14 9/11 Jennings.

15 "'The Pentagon Goes to War': National Military Command Center," *American Morning with Paula Zahn*, CNN, 4 September 2002 (transcripts.cnn.com/TRANSCRIPTS/0209/04/ltm.11.html).

16 "Conversation With Major General Larry Arnold, Commander, 1st Air Force, Tyndall AFB, Florida," *Code One: An Airpower Projection Magazine* January 2002 (www.codeonemagazine.com/archives/2002/articles/jan_02/defense).

17 Filson 72.

18 9/11 Commission Hearing, 23 May 2003.

19 Ibid.

20 FAA Memo.

21 9/11CR 28.

22 9/11 Commission Hearing, 17 June 2004. For the officers in the "military cell" at Herndon that morning, see note 43 of Chapter 11, above.

23 9/11 Commission Hearing, 17 June 2004. The presence of the military liaison at FAA headquarters in Washington, D.C., was mentioned by Pamela Freni, who speaks of "the onsite Department of Defense (DoD) liaison to the FAA" (Freni 21).

24 9/11CR 41.

25 "Spotlight on: Barbara Riggs," President's Council of Cornell

Women, Spring 2006 (pccw.alumni.cornell.edu/news/newsletters/
spring06/riggs.html).

26 Jere Longman, *Among the Heroes: United 93 and the Passengers
and Crew Who Fought Back* (New York: HarperCollins, 2002), 107–10.

27 Skies 2002.

Chapter 13: Could the Military Have Shot Down Flight 93?

1 Kevin Dennehy, "I Thought It Was the Start of World War III," *Cape
Cod Times* 21 August 2002 (archive.capecodonline.com/special/terror/
ithought21.htm).

2 General Myers Confirmation Hearing, Senate Armed Services Committee,
13 September 2001 (emperors-clothes.com/9-11backups/mycon.htm).

3 Ibid.

4 This denial was reported in several articles, including Charles Lane
and Philip Pan, "Jetliner Was Diverted Toward Washington Before Crash in
Pa.," *Washington Post* 12 September 2001 (www.washingtonpost.com/
ac2/wp-dyn?pagename=article&node=& contentId=A14327-2001Sep11),
and Jonathan Silver, "Day of Terror: Outside Tiny Shanksville, a Fourth
Deadly Stroke," *Pittsburgh Post-Gazette* 12 September 2001 (www.post-
gazette.com/headlines/20010912crashnat2p2.asp).

5 Jonathan Silver, "NORAD Denies Military Shot Down Flight 93,"
Pittsburgh Post-Gazette 14 September 2001 (www.post-gazette.com/
headlines/20010914norad0914p3.asp).

6 Ibid.

7 Richard Wallace, "What Did Happen to Flight 93?" *Daily Mirror* 12
September 2002 (911research.wtc7.net/cache/planes/evidence/
mirror_whatdidhappen.html).

8 "Surprise Trip for Donald Rumsfeld," CNN, 24 December 2004
(edition.cnn.com/TRANSCRIPTS/0412/24/nfcnn.01.html). This statement
was analyzed in "Rumsfeld Says 9-11 Plane 'Shot Down' in Pennsylvania,"
WorldNetDaily.com, 27 December 2004 (www.wnd.com/news/
article.asp? ARTICLE_ID=42112).

9 Jamie McIntyre, "Pentagon: Rumsfeld Misspoke on Flight 93 Crash,"
CNN, 27 December 2004 (www.cnn.com/2004/US/12/27/rumsfeld.flt93).

10 9/11CR 13–14.

11 9/11CR 41.

12 9/11CR 45.

13 9/11CR 37.

14 Clarke 7–8.

15 Sylvia Adcock, Brian Donovan, and Craig Gordon, "Air Attack on
Pentagon Indicates Weaknesses," *Newsday* 23 September 2001
(s3.amazonaws.com/911timeline/2001/newsday092301.html).

16 Chitra Ragavan and Mark Mazzetti, "Pieces of the Puzzle: A Top-Secret Conference Call on September 11 Could Shed New Light on the Terrorist Attacks," *US News and World Report* 31 August 2003 (www.usnews.com/usnews/news/articles/030908/8sept11.htm).

17 9/11 Jennings.

18 Ibid.

19 This statement, as we saw in Chapter 7, was originally made during an interview with ABC's John McWethy.

20 Filson 68.

21 9/11 Jennings.

22 General Myers Confirmation Hearing.

23 Albert McKeon, "FAA Worker Says Hijacked Airliners Pilots Almost Collided Before Striking World Trade Center," *Telegraph* (Nashua) 13 September 2001 (www.positiontoknow.com/S-11/html/FAA%20worker%20says%20hijacked%20jeltiners%20almost%20collided%20before%20striking%20World%20Trade%20Center.htm). A largely identical article, entitled "FAA Employee: Hijacked Jets Almost Collided En Route" and attributed to the Associated Press, appeared that same day (13 September 2001) in the *Portland Press Herald* (pressherald.mainetoday.com/news/attack/010913faa.shtml). The quoted statements are found in both.

24 "Deputy Secretary Wolfowitz Interview with PBS NewsHour," PBS, 14 September 2001 (www.defenselink.mil/transcripts/transcript.aspx?transcriptid=1882).

25 "Pentagon: Air Force Was in Position to Down Hijacked Jet," Reuters, 14 September 2001 (www.topcops.com/memorial/struggle.PDF).

26 Matthew Wald, "Pentagon Tracked Deadly Jet but Found No Way to Stop It," *New York Times* 15 September 2001 (query.nytimes.com/gst/fullpage.html?res=9802E5D91F38F936A2575AC0A9679C8B63).

27 "Feds Would Have Shot Down Pa. Jet," CBS News, 16 September 2001 (www.cbsnews.com/stories/2001/09/12/archive/main311011.shtml).

28 Dave Foster, "UST Grad Guides Bombers in War," *Aquin* 4 December 2002 (www.stthomas.edu/aquin/archive/041202/anaconda.html). An E-3 Sentry is an AWACS (Airborne Warning and Control System) airplane, having advanced radar and surveillance instruments useful for directing fighters to their targets.

29 Matthew L. Wald with Kevin Sack, "'We Have Some Planes,' Hijacker Told Controller," *New York Times* 16 October 2001 (s3.amazon-aws.com/911timeline/2001/nyt101601.html).

30 Filson 73.

31 William B. Scott, "Exercise Jump-Starts Response to Attacks," *Aviation Week & Space Technology* 3 June 2002 (web.archive.org/web/20020917072642/http://www.aviationnow.com/content/publication/awst/20020603/avi_stor.htm).

32 9/11 Jennings.

33 Freni 41.

34 One exception was a report, published by the FAA on 17 September 2001, which put the time at approximately 10:04; see "Summary of Air Traffic Hijack Events" (www.oig.dot.gov/StreamFile?file=/data/pdfdocs/cc2006085.pdf), 22. Since February 2003, however, the FAA has been saying that UA 93 crashed at 10:07; see "September 11, 2001: FAA Responds" (www2.faa.gov/Sept11portraits/chronology.cfm).

35 Jonathan Silver, "Day of Terror: Outside Tiny Shanksville, a Fourth Deadly Stroke," *Pittsburgh Post-Gazette* 12 September 2001 (www.post-gazette.com/headlines/20010912crashnat2p2.asp).

36 Jonathan Silver, "What Was the Danger to City? Doomed United Flight 93 Passed Just South of Pittsburgh," *Pittsburgh Post-Gazette* 13 September 2001 (911research.wtc7.net/cache/planes/analysis/flight93/postgazette_20010913flightpath.html). The 10:06 time was also stated in another story that day in the same paper: Tom Gibb, James O'Toole, and Cindi Lash, "Investigators Locate 'Black Box' from Flight 93; Widen Search Area in Somerset Crash," *Pittsburgh Post-Gazette* 13 September 2001 (post-gazette.com/headlines/20010913somersetp3.asp).

37 Dennis Roddy, "Flight 93: Forty Lives, One Destiny," *Pittsburgh Post-Gazette* 28 October 2001 (www.post-gazette.com/headlines/20011028flt93mainstoryp7.asp).

38 William Bunch, "We Know it Crashed, But Not Why," *Philadelphia Daily News* 15 November 2001 (www.whatreallyhappened.com/flight_93_crash.html).

39 Alan Levin, Marilyn Adams, and Blake Morrison, "Terror Attacks Brought Drastic Decision: Clear the Skies," *USA Today* 12 August 2002 (www.usatoday.com/news/sept11/2002-08-12-clearskies_x.htm).

40 Won-Young Kim and Gerald R. Baum, "Seismic Observations during September 11, 2001, Terrorist Attack," Spring 2002 (www.mgs.md.gov/esic/publications/download/911pentagon.pdf).

41 NORAD Response.

42 9/11CR 30.

43 William Bunch, "Three-Minute Discrepancy in Tape: Cockpit Voice Recording Ends Before Flight 93's Official Time of Impact," *Philadelphia Daily News* 16 September 2002 (newsmine.org/archive/9-11/flight93-ua/seismologist-discrepancy.txt).

44 9/11CR 462n168.

45 Kim and Baum, "Seismic Observations."

46 Quoted in Bunch, "Three-Minute Discrepancy in Tape." Wallace at the time directed the Southern Arizona Seismic Observatory and is now at the Los Alamos National Laboratory; see "Wallace Named Strategic

Research Directorate Leader," Los Alamos National Laboratory, 4 March 2005 (www.lanl.gov/news/index.php/fuseaction/home.story/story_id/2334).
   47 9/11CR 30.
   48 Gail Sheehy, "Stewardess ID'd Hijackers Early, Transcripts Show," *New York Observer* 15 February 2004 (www.observer.com/node/48805).
   49 Bunch, "Three-Minute Discrepancy in Tape."
   50 9/11CR 13.
   51 See "Lyz Glick's Courage," *Dateline*, NBC News, 20 August 2002 (www.msnbc.msn.com/id/3080114). During an interview with Jane Pauley on this show, Lyz Glick repeated the crucial element in her testimony: that as she talked with her husband, "the first tower collapsed."
   52 Jere Longman, *Among the Heroes: United Flight 93 and the Passengers and Crew Who Fought Back* (New York: HarperCollins, 2002), 147–54.
   53 Ibid., 154, 219.
   54 9/11CR 457nn81,82.

Chapter 14: Had 9/11-Type Attacks Been Envisioned?

   1 "Remarks by the President upon Arrival," White House, 16 September 2001 (www.whitehouse.gov/news/releases/2001/09/20010916-2.html).
   2 Sylvia Adcock, Brian Donovan, and Craig Gordon, "Air Attack on Pentagon Indicates Weaknesses," *Newsday* 23 September 2001 (www.wanttoknow.info/010923newsday).
   3 "Re-examining Itself, FAA Considers Arming Pilots," CNN, 25 September 2001 (archives.cnn.com/2001/US/09/24/gen.pilots.union).
   4 White House News Release, "President Meets with Muslim Leaders," 26 September 2001 (www.whitehouse.gov/news/releases/2001/ 09/20010926-8.html).
   5 "Text: Rumsfeld on NBC's 'Meet the Press,'" 30 September 2001 (www.washingtonpost.com/wp-srv/nation/specials/attacked/transcripts/ nbctext_093001.html).
   6 "Interview: General Richard B. Myers," Armed Forces Radio and Television Service, 17 October 2001 (web.archive.org/web/20011118060728/ http:/www.dtic.mil/jcs/chairman/AFRTS_Interview.htm); quoted in Sgt. Kathleen T. Rhem, "Myers and Sept. 11: 'We Hadn't Thought About This,'" American Forces Press Service, 23 October 2001 (www.defenselink.mil/news/ newsarticle.aspx?id=44621).
   7 David E. Sanger, "Bush Was Warned Bin Laden Wanted to Hijack Planes," *New York Times* 16 May 2002 (query.nytimes.com/gst/ fullpage.html?res=9C03E2DB1139F935A25756C0A9649C8B63&sec=&s pon=&pagewanted=2); Dan Eggen and Bill Miller, "Bush Was Told of Hijacking Dangers," *Washington Post* 16 May 2002 (www.whitehouse.gov/news/releases/2002/05/20020516-13.html).

8 Ed Vulliamy, "A Bad Call?" *Guardian* 19 May 2002 (www.guardian.co.uk/september11/story/0,11209,718267,00.html).

9 "National Security Advisor Holds Press Briefing, White House, 16 May 2002 (www.whitehouse.gov/news/releases/2002/05/20020516-13.html).

10 The White House, "Press Briefing by Ari Fleischer," 16 May 2002. (www.whitehouse.gov/news/releases/2002/05/20020516-4.html)

11 "What Bush Knew Before Sept. 11," CBS News, 17 May 2002 (www.cbsnews.com/stories/2002/05/16/attack/main509294.shtml).

12 "President Discusses Response to September 11 Attacks: Remarks by the President at Presentation of Commander-in-Chief's Trophy," White House, 17 May 2002 (www.whitehouse.gov/news/releases/2002/05/20020517-1.html).

13 Stephen Braun, Bob Drogin, Mark Fineman, Lisa Getter, Greg Krikorian, and Robert J. Lopez, "Haunted by Years of Missed Warnings," *Los Angeles Times* 14 October 2001 (web.archive.org/web/20030812200356/http://www.latimes.com/news/nationworld/nation/la-101401warn,0,999276.story).

14 "Report Warned Of Suicide Hijackings," CBS News, 17 May 2002 (www.cbsnews.com/stories/2002/05/18/attack/main509488.shtml).

15 "Excerpts From Report on Intelligence Actions and the Sept. 11 Attacks," *New York Times* 25 July 2003 (www.nytimes.com/2003/07/25/national/25TTEX.html?ex=1189569600&en=87b62bfc380ea076&ei=5070).

16 "Bush, Clinton Figures Defend Terrorism Policies," CNN, 24 March 2004 (edition.cnn.com/2004/ALLPOLITICS/03/23/911.commission/index.html).

17 9/11 Commission Hearing, 8 April 2004 (www.9-11commission.gov/archive/hearing9/9-11Commission_Hearing_2004-04-08.pdf).

18 "President Addresses the Nation in Prime Time Press Conference," White House, 13 April 2004 (www.whitehouse.gov/news/releases/2004/04/20040413-20.html).

19 9/11CR 17.

20 9/11 Commission Hearing, 17 June 2004 (www.9-11commission.gov/archive/hearing12/9-11Commission_Hearing_2004-06-17.htm).

21 9/11CR 352.

22 9/11CR 18, 31.

23 9/11CR 345.

24 9/11CR 345.

25 9/11CR 345.

26 Quoted in Joby Warrick and Joe Stephens, "Before Attack, U.S. Expected Different Hit," *Washington Post* 2 October 2001 (www.washingtonpost.com/ac2/wp-dyn/A55607-2001Oct1).

27 Tom Clancy, *Debt of Honor* (New York: Putnam, 1995).

28 Bruce W. Nelan, "The Price of Fanaticism," *Time* 3 April 1995 (www.time.com/time/printout/0,8816,982759,00.html).

29 "Word for Word/Early Warnings; The Surprise Was More When Than Whether or How," *New York Times* 19 May 2002 (query.nytimes.com/gst/fullpage.html?res=9805E5DC1738F93AA25756C0A9649C8B63).

30 Dennis Ryan, "Contingency Planning: Pentagon MASCAL Exercise Simulates Scenarios in Preparing for Emergencies," MDW News Service, 3 November 2000 (www.mdw.army.mil/content/anmviewer.asp?a=290); UPI, "DOD Rehearsed Plane Hitting Pentagon," *Washington Times* 22 April 2004 (web.archive.org/web/20050211062128/http://www.washtimes.com/upi-breaking/20040422-090447-8354r.htm).

31 Matt Mientka, "Pentagon Medics Trained for Strike," *U.S. Medicine* October 2001 (www.usmedicine.com/article.cfm?articleID=272&issueID=31).

32 Steven Komarow and Tom Squitieri, "NORAD Had Drills of Jets as Weapons," *USA Today* 18 April 2004 (www.usatoday.com/news/washington/2004-04-18-norad_x.htm).

33 Gerry J. Gilmore, "NORAD-Sponsored Exercise Prepares For Worst-Case Scenarios," American Forces Press Service, 4 June 2002 (www.defenselink.mil/news/newsarticle.aspx?id=43789). For more on Amalgam Virgo 02, see www.cooperativeresearch.org/ context.jsp?item=a 01multiplehijackings.

34 Gen. Lance Lord, "A Year Ago, A Lifetime Ago," *The Beam* 13 September 2002 (www.dcmilitary.com/dcmilitary_archives/stories/091302/19212-1.shtml).

35 John J. Lumpkin, "Agency Planned Exercise on Sept. 11 Built Around a Plane Crashing into a Building," Associated Press, 21 August 2002 (911research.wtc7.net/cache/planes/defense/sfgate_exercise_082102.html); Pamela Hess, "U.S. Agencies— Strange 9/11 Coincidence," United Press International, 22 August 2002.

36 9/11 Commission Hearing, 23 May 2003 (www.9-11commission.gov/archive/hearing2/9-11Commission_Hearing_2003-05-23.htm).

37 9/11 Commission Hearing, 13 April 2004 (www.9-11commission.gov/archive/hearing10/9-11Commission_Hearing_2004-04-13.htm).

38 9/11CR 18, 45.

39 WP 257.

40 This chapter is indebted to Elizabeth Woodworth, "The Military Drills of September 11th: Why a New Investigation is Needed," *Global Research*, 27 September 2007 (www.globalresearch.ca/index.phb?context=va&aid=6906).

PART III

Chapter 15: Were Atta & Other Hijackers Devout Muslims?

1 9/11CR 160. The text says: "When Atta arrived in Germany, he appeared religious, but not fanatically so. This would change, especially as his tendency to assert leadership became increasingly pronounced." Accordingly, it seems warranted, especially when those statements are combined with the assertion that he "adopted fundamentalism" (161), to say that the Commission claimed that Atta had become fanatically religious.

2 9/11CR 154.

3 Eric Bailey, "It Was a Little Strange. Most People Want to Do Take-Offs And Landings. All They Did Was Turns," *Daily Mail* 16 September 2001 (this story is evidently no longer available on the Internet).

4 David Wedge, "Terrorists Partied with Hooker at Hub-Area Hotel," Boston Herald 10 October 2001 (web.archive.org/web/ 20011010224657/ www.bostonherald.com/attack/investigation/ausprob10102001.htm).

5 Kevin Fagan, "Agents of Terror Leave Their Mark on Sin City," *San Francisco Chronicle* 4 October 2001 (sfgate.com/cgi-bin/article.cgi?file=/ chronicle/archive/2001/10/04/MN102970.DTL).

6 "Terrorist Stag Parties," *Wall Street Journal* 10 October 2001 (www.opinionjournal.com/best/?id=95001298).

7 Jody A. Benjamin, "Suspects' Actions Don't Add Up," *South Florida Sun-Sentinel* 16 September 2001 (web.archive.org/web/20010916150533/ http://www.sun-sentinel.com/news/local/southflorida/sfl-warriors916.story).

8 Ken Thomas, "Feds Investigating Possible Terrorist-Attack Links in Florida," Associated Press, 12 September 2001 (web.archive.org/web/ 20030402060235/www.nctimes.net/news/2001/20010912/10103.html).

9 Barry Klein, Wes Allison, Kathryn Wexler, and Jeff Testerman, "FBI Seizes Records of Students at Flight Schools," *St. Petersburg Times* 13 September 2001 (www.sptimes.com/News/091301/Worldandnation/ FBI_seizes_records_of.shtml).

10 Dana Canedy with David E. Sanger, "After the Attacks: The Suspects; Hijacking Trail Leads FBI to Florida Flight School," *New York Times* 13 September 2001 (query.nytimes.com/gst/fullpage.html? res=9805E6DC1038F930A2575AC0A9679C8B63).

11 Eric Bailey, "It Was a Little Strange."

12 Neil Mackay, "The Roots of the Worst Terrorist Attack in History," *Sunday Herald* (Glasgow) 16 September 2001 (web.archive.org/web/ 20010924002816/http://www.sundayherald.com/18498).

13 Curtis Morgan, David Kidwell, and Oscar Corral, "Prelude to Terror," *Miami Herald* 22 September 2001 (web.archive.org/web/ 20010922164519/www.miami.com/herald/special/ news/worldtrade/digdocs/000518.htm).

14 Johanna McGeary and David Van Biema, "The New Breed of Terrorist," *Time* 24 September 2001 (www.time.com/time/covers/1101010924/wplot.html).

15 Evan Thomas and Mark Hosenball, "Bush: 'We're at War,'" *Newsweek* 24 September 2001 (www.msnbc.msn.com/id/14738203/site/newsweek).

16 Ibid. Although the *Time* and *Newsweek* issues were dated September 24, weekly magazines usually appear before their cover date. The articles, moreover, would have been written still earlier. Those magazines should not, therefore, be viewed as having maintained the original version of the story after the appearance of the new version in the *Washington Post* story of 16 September, discussed in the text below.

17 Nicolaas van Rijn, "Hijackers Set Down Roots, Blended In, Then Attacked," *Toronto Star* 15 September 2001 (www.vcn.bc.ca/~dastow/tst10915.txt).

18 Joel Achenbach, "'You Never Imagine' A Hijacker Next Door," *Washington Post* 16 September 2001 (www.washingtonpost.com/ac2/wp-dyn/A38026-2001Sep15?language=printer).

19 Peter Finn, "A Fanatic's Quiet Path to Terror," *Washington Post* 22 September 2001 (www.washingtonpost.com/ac2/wp-dyn?pagename=article&node=&contentId=A6745-2001Sep21&notFound=true).

20 Sydney P. Freedberg, "The Trail of the Terrorists," *St. Petersburg Times* 27 September 2001 (www.sptimes.com/News/092701/Worldandnation/The_trail_of_the_terr.shtml). This story, unlike all the others, said that the Shuckums episode occurred on September 8.

21 Carol J. Williams, John-Thor Dahlburg, and H.G. Reza, "Mainly, They Just Waited," *Los Angeles Times* 27 September 2001 (web.archive.org/web/20010927120728/http://www.latimes.com/news/natio nworld/world/la-092701atta.story).

22 John Cloud, "Atta's Odyssey," *Time* 30 September 2001 (www.time.com/time/printout/0,8816,176917,00.html). The version in which Atta drinks cranberry juice also made it to a program on Australian television, which said: "According to bar staff, Atta spends almost 4 hours at the pinball machine drinking cranberry juice, while Al-Shehhi drinks alcohol with an unidentified male companion" ("A Mission to Die For: Timeline," ABC TV (Australia), 12 November 2001 [www.abc.net.au/4corners/atta/default.htm]).

23 9/11CR 248.

24 9/11CR 161, 160. See note 1 of this chapter

25 9/11CR 253.

26 9/11CR 227–31.

27 FBI, "Hijackers Timeline," 5 December 2003 (this document does not seem to be publicly accessible). At the end of September in 2001, John

Cloud of *Time* magazine, on the basis of what the FBI was saying then, gave the following account, which agrees with the 9/11 Commission's account: "[O]n June 3, 2000, [Atta] arrived in Newark…. Within a month, Atta and Al-Shehhi signed up for flight training at Huffman Aviation International in Venice, Fla…. [T]he two men moved into a little pink house in nearby Nokomis…. On Dec. 21, Atta and Al-Shehhi got their pilot licenses. About a week later, they trained for three hours each on the Boeing 727 simulator at Simcenter Inc. at Opa-Locka Airport, outside Miami…. In January of [2001], Atta hopped a flight from Miami to Madrid…. [H]e returned to Miami International Airport on Jan. 10…. The next month, Atta and Al-Shehhi rented a single-engine Piper Warrior from a Gwinnett County, Ga., flight school…. On April 26, Broward County sheriff's deputy Josh Strambaugh stopped Atta for a traffic violation…. On June 29, Atta traveled to Las Vegas, [probably for] a planning session…. On July 9, Atta made another trip to Madrid…. [After] Atta returned to the U.S…, [h]e made another quick trip to Las Vegas but spent most of his time in Florida" (John Cloud, "Atta's Odyssey," *Time* 30 September 2001 [www.time.com/time/printout/0,8816,176917,00.html]).

28 Christy Arnold, "Search and Rescue," *Charlotte Sun* 14 September 2001 (www.sun-herald.com/NewsArchive2/091401/tp1ch11.htm?date=091401&story=tp1ch11.htm; also available at www.madcowprod.com/grapentine2.htm).

29 Elaine Allen-Emrich and Jann Baty, "Hunt for Terrorists Reaches North Port," *Charlotte Sun* 14 September 2001 (www.sun-herald.com/NewsArchive2/091401/tp4ch14.htm; also available at www.madcowprod.com/keller.htm).

30 Earle Kimel, Michael Werner, and Andy Crain, "Fourth Terrorist Suspect May Have Venice Ties, German Official Says," *Sarasota Herald-Tribune* 22 September 2001. Daniel Hopsicker reported that this article, like the other *Herald-Tribune* stories from 2001 dealing with Atta's presence in Venice in 2001, were "removed from the newspaper database Lexis-Nexis"; see Hopsicker, "'Disappearing' the News: The 'Second' Mohamed in Venice," MadCow Morning News, 3 May 2005 (www.madcowprod.com/ 05022005.html). Hopsicker has made these articles available on his website. This one is also contained and discussed in Elizabeth Woodworth, "Who Were Those Hijackers, Anyway? A Telling Story Resurrected," 911blogger.com, 30 September 2007 (www.911blogger.com/node/11781).

31 Kimel, Werner, and Crain, "Fourth Terrorist Suspect May Have Venice Ties, German Official Says."

32 Chris Grier, "Fifth Pilot Trainee Vanishes," *Sarasota Herald-Tribune* 23 September 2001 (available at www.madcowprod.com/fifthpilot.htm).

33 FBI, Press Release, "The FBI Releases 19 Photographs of Individuals Believed to Be the Hijackers of the Four Airliners that Crashed on September 11, 01," 27 September 2001 (www.fbi.gov/pressrel/pressrel01/092701hjpic.htm).

34 Daniel Hopsicker, *Welcome to Terrorland: Mohamed Atta and the 9-11 Cover-Up in Florida* (Eugene, OR: MadCow Press, 2004), 90–92, 101.

35 Ibid., 98, 283.

36 Ibid., 84, 278.

37 Ibid., 35, 276.

38 Ibid., 99–100.

39 Ibid., 91, 101.

40 Ibid., 59–61, 66.

41 Ibid., 34–35, 275.

42 Ibid., 276.

43 Ibid., 34–35, 280.

44 Ibid., 88–89.

45 Ibid., 62–63, 87; Daniel Hopsicker, "Moussaoui Trial Documents Show FBI Withheld Evidence in 9/11 Cover-Up," 4 October 2006 (madcowprod.com/10042006.html).

46 Hopsicker, *Welcome to Terrorland*, 57, 58, 62–63, 65, 77, 274, 276–77, 302–09.

47 Heather Allan, "'Lover': Amanda Keller," *Sarasota Herald-Tribune* 10 September 2006 (www.heraldtribune.com/apps/pbcs.dll/article?AID=/20060910/NEWS/609100466/1007/BUSINESS). The next line of Allan's story said: "Among other things, the government checked Atta's phone records and found the two had never called each other." In response, Hopsicker points out that the FBI's report on Atta's Nokomis-based cell phone calls does not include the months of April through May, when Atta knew Keller, even though a subpoenaed document from Verizon revealed that this cell phone remained in service until May 21, 2001; see Hopsicker, "Moussaoui Trial evidence Documents Show FBI Withheld Evidence in 9/11 Cover-Up," 4 October 2006 (madcowprod.com/10042006.html).

48 "Sources: Suspected Terrorist Leader Was Wired Funds Through Pakistan," CNN, 1 October 2001 (archives.cnn.com/2001/US/10/01/inv.pakistan.funds).

49 Larry Margasak, Associated Press, "Hot on the Hijackers' Money Trail," *Seattle Post-Intelligencer* 2 October 2001 (seattlepi.nwsource.com/attack/41025_probe02.shtml).

50 Hopsicker, *Welcome to Terrorland*, 302–09.

51 Ibid., 302–09. For Rudi Dekkers's testimony, see Hearing before the Subcommittee on Immigration and Claims of the Committee on the Judiciary, House of Representatives, 19 March 2002

(www.globalsecurity.org/security/library/congress/2002_h/hju78298_0.htm).
Dekkers claimed that after Atta and al-Shehhi made their final payments to
the school, which was apparently in late December 2000 or early January
2001, "Huffman [aviation] never heard about or from them again until
September 11th, 2001."

52 9/11CR 229–31.

53 Hopsicker, *Welcome to Terrorland*, 64. Hopsicker makes similar
statements on pages 69, 82, and 131.

54 Ibid., 68.

55 Sander Hicks, "No Easy Answer: Heroin, Al Qaeda and the Florida
Flight School," *Long Island Press* 26 February 2004 (www.mindspace.org/
liberation-news-service/archives/000599.html).

Chapter 16: Where Did Authorities Find Atta's Information?

1 9/11CR 1.

2 9/11CR 451n1.

3 FBI Director Robert S. Mueller III, "Statement for the Record," Joint
Intelligence Committee Inquiry, 26 September 2002 (www.fas.org/irp/
congress/2002_hr/092602mueller.html).

4 Richard Bernstein, Richard Frantz, Don Van Natta, Jr., and David
Johnston, "The Hijackers' Long Road to Infamy," *New York Times* 11 September
2002 (this story appears to be no longer available on the Internet).

5 9/11CR 253.

6 9/11 Commission Staff Statement No. 16, 16 June 2004
(www.msnbc.msn.com/id/5224099).

7 Thomas Kean and Lee Hamilton, the chairman and vice chairman,
respectively, of the 9/11 Commission, later reported an FBI agent's suggestion that Atta and al-Omari took the flight from Portland to avoid having
"five Arab men all arriving at Boston's Logan Airport at once for Flight 11"
(WP 245). This problem could have been avoided far less dangerously,
however, by simply having the five Arab men arrive in separate cars at
different times.

8 9/11 Commission Staff Statement No. 16.

9 Mueller, "Statement for the Record."

10 Michael Dorman, "Unraveling 9-11 was in the Bags," *Newsday* 17
April 2006 (www.newsday.com/news/nationworld/nation/
ny-uslugg274705186apr17,0,1419064,print.story).

11 9/11CR 1–2.

12 Paul Sperry, "Airline Denied Atta Paradise Wedding Suit," World-
NetDaily.com, 11 September 2002
(www.worldnetdaily.com/news/article.asp?ARTICLE_ID=28904).

13 "America Under Attack: How Could It Happen?" CNN, 12

September 2001 (transcripts.cnn.com/TRANSCRIPTS/0109/12/se.60.html).

14 Christy Arnold, "Search and Rescue," *Charlotte Sun* 14 September 2001 (www.sun-herald.com/NewsArchive2/091401/ tp1ch11.htm?date=091401&story=tp1ch11.htm; also available at www.madcowprod.com/grapentine2.htm).

15 "Two Brothers among Hijackers," CNN Report, 13 September 2001 (english.peopledaily.com.cn/200109/13/eng20010913_80131.html).

16 "Hijack Suspect Detained, Cooperating with FBI," CNN, 13 September 2001 (transcripts.cnn.com/TRANSCRIPTS/0109/13/ltm.01.html).

17 "Evidence Trails Lead to Florida," BBC News, 13 September 2001 (news.bbc.co.uk/2/hi/americas/1542153.stm).

18 "Feds Think They've Identified Some Hijackers," CNN, 13 September 2001 (edition.cnn.com/2001/US/09/12/investigation.terrorism).

19 Ibid.

20 Mike Fish, "Fla. Flight Schools May Have Trained Hijackers," 14 September 2001 (archives.cnn.com/2001/US/09/13/flight.schools).

21 "America Under Attack: List of Names of 18 Suspected Hijackers," CNN, 14 September 2001 (transcripts.cnn.com/TRANSCRIPTS/0109/14/ bn.01.html).

22 Neil Mackay, "The Roots of the Worst Terrorist Attack in History," *Sunday Herald* (Glasgow) 16 September 2001 (web.archive.org/web/ 20010924002816/http://www.sundayherald.com/18498).

23 Associated Press, "Portland Police Eye Local Ties," *Portsmouth Herald* 14 September 2001 (archive.seacoastonline.com/2001news/ 9_14maine2.htm).

24 To say that the complete transition occurred at this time is not to say that this new story was immediately accepted throughout the media. On October 5, for example, BBC News, giving a summary of what had been learned, included this item: "US investigators were reported to have found a hire car at Boston airport containing a copy of the Koran and an instruction manual on how to fly a plane" ("The Investigation and the Evidence," BBC News, 5 October 2001 [news.bbc.co.uk/2/hi/americas/1581063.stm]).

25 Joel Achenbach, "'You Never Imagine' A Hijacker Next Door," *Washington Post* 16 September 2001 (www.washingtonpost.com/ac2/wp-dyn? pagename=article&node=&contentId=A38026-2001Sep15&notFound=true).

26 "The Night Before Terror," *Portland Press Herald* 5 October 2001 (web.archive.org/web/20040404001010/http://www.portland.com/news/atta ck/011005fbi.shtml).

27 Susan Candiotti, "Source: Records Suggest Atta in NYC on Sept. 10," CNN, 22 May 2002 (archives.cnn.com/2002/US/05/22/hijack.paper.trail).

28 Ibid.

29 Greg B. Smith, "Hijacker in City Sept. 10 Used Navigation Tool to

Pinpoint WTC Site," *New York Daily News* 22 May 2002
(foi.missouri.edu/terrorbkgd/hijackerincity.html).

30 This part of an FBI chronology is reported in the *Portland Press
Herald* story of 5 October 2001, "The Night Before Terror."

31 Mueller, "Statement for the Record."

32 In a *New York Post* story of 28 May 2002, entitled "Identity Crisis"
(web.archive.org/web/20020607224610/http://www.nypost.com/news/
regionalnews/48924.htm), Murray Weiss seems to suggest that this report
was based on a case of mistaken identity involving the Mohamed Atta who
teaches medicine at Johns Hopkins University Hospital in Baltimore.
There are, however, at least three problems with his argument. First, Weiss,
speaking of the Johns Hopkins Mohamed Atta, says: "Just days before
Sept. 11, [he] visited the Big Apple for a whirlwind weekend with his new
bride." To say that this Mohamed was in Manhattan "days before" 9/11
during the "weekend" is not to say that he was there on Monday, September
10, the day before 9/11. Second, Weiss says: "[Atta and his wife] were
horrified when it was erroneously reported that the terror-attack leader was
casing the Twin Towers days before Sept. 11—even after the FBI
concluded it was just the kidney doctor, who had planned to take his wife
to Windows on the World for dinner in the north tower." But Weiss presents
no evidence that the FBI drew any such conclusion, and there appear to be
no follow-up stories by CNN and the *New York Daily News* reporting any
such retraction by the FBI. Rather, the story appears simply to have died.
Third, the case of mistaken identity mentioned by Weiss was reportedly
cleared up when the FBI visited the doctor, two days after the attacks, with
regard to "his credit-card slips from the Helmsley Hotel and the 'Les
Miserable' [*sic*] box office." If the FBI cleared up any possible confusion on
September 13, 2001, how would a "source familiar with the investigation"
have been reporting in May 2002 that the FBI had learned that Mohamed
Atta the hijacker had been in Manhattan the day before the attacks?

Chapter 17: Were Hijackers Reported on Cell Phone Calls?

1 Charles Lane and John Mintz, "Bid to Thwart Hijackers May Have
Led to Pa. Crash," *Washington Post* 13 September 2001 (www.washington-
post.com/ac2/wp-dyn/A14344-2001Sep11).

2 "Harrowing Final Phone Calls," BBC News, 13 September 2001
(news.bbc.co.uk/2/hi/americas/1543466.stm).

3 9/11CR 8.

4 Karen Gullo and John Solomon, Associated Press, "Experts, U.S.
Suspect Osama bin Laden, Accused Architect of World's Worst Terrorist
Attacks," 11 September 2001 (sfgate.com/today/suspect.shtml).

5 Kathryn Hanson, "From a Big Sister's Point of View" (www.petehan-

sonandfamily.com/doc/FROM%20A%20BIG%20SISTER.doc).

6 David Maraniss, "September 11, 2001," *Washington Post*
16 September 2001 (www.washingtonpost.com/ac2/wp-dyn/A38407-
2001Sep15).

7 9/11CR 8.

8 David Maraniss, "September 11, 2001."

9 Toby Harnden, "She Asked Me How to Stop the Plane," *Daily
Telegraph* 5 March 2002 (s3.amazonaws.com/911timeline/2002/
telegraph030502.html).

10 See "On September 11, Final Words of Love," CNN, 10 September
2002 (archives.cnn.com/2002/US/09/03/ar911.phone.calls).

11 9/11CR 9.

12 9/11CR 9.

13 Natalie Patton, "Flight Attendant Made Call on Cell Phone to
Mom in Las Vegas," *Las Vegas Review-Journal* 13 September 2001
(www.reviewjournal.com/lvrj_home/2001/Sep-13-Thu-2001/news/
16989631.html).

14 9/11CR 12.

15 Maraniss, "September 11, 2001."

16 Lane and Mintz, "Bid to Thwart Hijackers May Have Led to Pa.
Crash." It was reported that Glick had used a GTE Airfone in some other
stories, such as Dennis B. Roddy, "Flight 93: Forty Lives, One Destiny,"
Pittsburgh Post-Gazette 28 October 2001 (www.post-gazette.com/
headlines/20011028flt93mainstoryp7.asp). But it was widely believed, as
illustrated by the Lane–Mintz *Washington Post* story, that he had used a
cell phone. Two days after 9/11, for example, Evan Thomas wrote in
Newsweek: "Jeremy Glick knew that he was probably doomed. The
hijackers had told the 45 passengers and crew of United Airlines Flight
93... that they planned to blow up the plane. But Glick... was able to place
a mobile-phone call to his wife, Lyz." ("A New Date of Infamy," *Newsweek*
13 September 2001 [www.msnbc.msn.com/id/3069645]).

17 Lane and Mintz, "Bid to Thwart Hijackers May Have Led to Pa. Crash."

18 Karen Breslau, "The Final Moments of United Flight 93," *Newsweek*
22 September 2001 (www.public-action.com/911/finalmoments93).

19 Jim McKinnon, "13-Minute Call Bonds Her Forever with Hero,"
Pittsburgh Post-Gazette 22 September 2001 (www.post-gazette.com/
headlines/20010922gtenat4p4.asp).

20 Kerry Hall, "Flight Attendant Helped Fight Hijackers," *News &
Record* (Greensboro, NC) 21 September 2001 (webcache.news-record.com/
legacy/photo/tradecenter/bradshaw21.htm).

21 Maraniss, "September 11, 2001."

22 See Greg Gordon, "Widow Tells of Poignant Last Calls,"

Sacramento Bee 11 September 2002 (holtz.org/Library/Social%20Science/
History/Atomic%20Age/2000s/Sep11/Burnett%20widows%20story.htm),
and Deena L. Burnett (with Anthony F. Giombetti), *Fighting Back: Living
Beyond Ourselves* (Longwood, Florida: Advantage Inspirational Books,
2006), 61.

23 "Two Years Later…," CBS News, 10 September 2003
(www.cbsnews.com/ stories/2003/09/09/earlyshow/living/printable
572380.shtml); for the National Review letter, which appeared 20 May
2002, see http://find articles.com/p/articles/mi_m1282/is_9_54/
ai_85410322.

24 Richard Gazarik, "Felt Reaches 9/11 Just Before Crash,"
Pittsburgh Tribune-Review 8 September 2002 (www.pittsburghlive.com/
x/pittsburghtrib/s_90401.html).

25 "Flight Crew: CeeCee Lyles," *Pittsburgh Post-Gazette* 28 October
2001 (www.post-gazette.com/headlines/20011028flt93lylesbiop8.asp).

26 United States v. Zacarias Moussaoui, Exhibit Number P200054
(www.vaed.uscourts.gov/notablecases/moussaoui/exhibits/prosecution/flight
s/P200054.html). These documents can be more easily viewed in "Detailed
Account of Phone Calls From September 11th Flights"
(911research.wtc7.net/ planes/evidence/calldetail.html#ref1).

27 Ibid.

28 Greg Gordon, "Prosecutors Play Flight 93 Cockpit Recording,"
McClatchy Newspapers, KnoxNews.com, 12 April 2006
(www.knoxsingles.com/shns/story.cfm?pk=MOUSSAOUI-04-12-
06&cat=WW).

29 See note 26.

30 Gordon, "Prosecutors Play Flight 93 Cockpit Recording."

31 9/11CR 12–13.

32 Matthew Rothschild, "Enough of the 9/11 Conspiracy Theories,
Already," *The Progressive* 18 September 2006 (www.alternet.org/story/41601).

33 The question of why all these people reported, surely sincerely, that
the calls that they received were made on cell phones, if they really were
not, is a good question. But it is a question that goes beyond the purview of
this book, which is limited to pointing out contradictions. Finding out the
answer to this question should be one of the purposes of investigations by
Congress and the press.

Chapter 18: Hard Evidence of bin Laden's Responsibility?
1 9/11CR 47.
2 9/11CR 145.
3 See 9/11CR, Chap. 5, notes 1, 10, 11, 16, 32, 40, and 41. One finds
in each case: "interrogation(s) of KSM."

4 9/11CR 148, 149, 153, 154, 155, 166.

5 *Meet the Press*, NBC, 23 September 2001 (www.washingtonpost.com/wp-srv/nation/specials/attacked/transcripts/nbctext092301.html).

6 Jane Perlez and Tim Weiner, "US to Publish Terror Evidence on bin Laden," *New York Times* 24 September 2001 (query.nytimes.com/gst/fullpage.html?res=9D01EFDB143AF937A1575AC0A9679C8B63).

7 "Remarks by the President, Secretary of the Treasury O'Neill and Secretary of State Powell on Executive Order," White House, 24 September 2001 (www.whitehouse.gov/news/releases/2001/09/20010924-4.html).

8 "Daily White House Briefing by White House Press Secretary Ari Fleischer," CNN, 24 September 2001 (transcripts.cnn.com/TRAN-SCRIPTS/0109/24/se.21.html).

9 Seymour M. Hersh, "What Went Wrong: The C.I.A. and the Failure of American Intelligence," *New Yorker* 1 October 2001 (cicentre.com/Documents/DOC_Hersch_OCT_01.htm).

10 Ibid.

11 "White House Warns Taliban: 'We Will Defeat You,'" CNN, 21 September 2001 (archives.cnn.com/2001/WORLD/asiapcf/central/09/21/ret.afghan.taliban).

12 Ibid.

13 Ibid.

14 Kathy Gannon, "Taliban Willing to Talk, But Wants U.S. Respect," Associated Press, 1 November 2001 (nucnews.net/nucnews/2001nn/0111nn/011101nn.htm#300). Also available, under the title "Taliban Willing to Negotiate—Official" (english.peopledaily.com.cn/english/200111/01/eng20011101_83655.html).

15 Office of the Prime Minister, "Responsibility for the Terrorist Atrocities in the United States," BBC News, 4 October 2001 (news.bbc.co.uk/2/hi/uk_news/politics/1579043.stm).

16 Ibid., point 62.

17 "The Investigation and the Evidence," BBC News, 5 October 2001 (news.bbc.co.uk/2/hi/americas/1581063.stm).

18 Federal Bureau of Investigation, "Most Wanted Terrorists: Usama bin Laden" (www.fbi.gov/wanted/terrorists/terbinladen.htm).

19 "FBI Ten Most Wanted Fugitives: Usama bin Laden" (www.fbi.gov/wanted/topten/fugitives/laden.htm). This fact is pointed out in a story on this issue by Jeff Ferrell of KSLA 12 in Shreveport, Louisiana ("FBI and Osama," available on Google [video.google.com/videoplay?docid=-6443576002087829136] and YouTube [www.youtube.com/watch?v=fnUQczDktgI&eurl=http%3A%2F%2Fwww%2Ebrass-checktv%2Ecom%2Fpage%2F150%2Ehtml]).

20 Ed Haas, "FBI Says, 'No Hard Evidence Connecting Bin Laden to 9/11,'" *Muckraker Report* 6 June 2006 (www.teamliberty.net/id267.html).

21 Ibid.

22 This portion of INN World Report's headlines for 7 June 2006 can be viewed at muckrakerreport.com/sitebuildercontent/ sitebuilderfiles/bin_laden_fbi.mov. Haas states (email of 18 August 2007) that after INN's report, he talked to Claire Brown, who said that when she called Tomb and read the statement Haas had attributed to him, Tomb said: "That's exactly what I told Mr. Haas."

23 Ed Haas, "Fact: Osama bin Laden Has Not Been Indicted for His Involvement in 9/11," *Muckraker Report* 20 August 2006 (www.teamliberty.net/id290.html).

24 Ibid.

25 Ibid.

26 Ibid. A year later, Haas reported, he still had received no reply to his questions from anyone at the Department of Justice (email of 18 August 2007).

27 Dan Eggen, "Bin Laden, Most Wanted For Embassy Bombings?" *Washington Post* 28 August 2006 (www.washingtonpost.com/ wp-dyn/content/article/2006/08/27/AR2006082700687.html).

28 Ibid.

29 Ibid.

30 Haas, "FBI Says, 'No Hard Evidence Connecting Bin Laden to 9/11.'"

31 Eggen, "Bin Laden, Most Wanted For Embassy Bombings?"

32 Members of the Family Steering Committee for the 9/11 Independent Commission, "FSC Questions to the 9/11 Commission With Ratings of Its Performance in Providing Answers" (www.911pressfortruth.org/ file_download/11), question 21.

33 See note 3.

34 9/11CR 149, 155, 166.

35 WP 118.

36 WP 118–19.

37 WP 122–23.

38 WP 122, 119, 124.

39 WP 124.

40 WP 119.

41 One good report on this matter, a video of which is available on the Internet, is "FBI and Osama," by Jeff Ferrell of KSLA 12 in Shreveport, Louisiana. See note 19.

PART IV
Chapter 19: Could Hanjour Have Flown American 77?
   1 9/11CR 9.
   2 9/11CR 239.
   3 "List of Names of 18 Suspected Hijackers," CNN, 14 September 2001 (transcripts.cnn.com/TRANSCRIPTS/0109/14/bn.01.html).
   4 "FBI List of Individuals Identified As Suspected Hijackers," CNN, 14 September 2001, 2:00PM (archives.cnn.com/2001/US/09/14/fbi.document).
   5 "Four Planes, Four Coordinated Teams," *Washington Post* 19 September 2001 (www.washingtonpost.com/wp-srv/nation/graphics/attack/hijackers.html).
   6 Marc Fisher and Don Phillips, "On Flight 77: 'Our Plane Is Being Hijacked,'" *Washington Post* 12 September 2001 (www.washingtonpost.com/ac2/wp-dyn?pagename=article&node=&contentId=A14365-2001Sep11).
   7 John Hanchette, "Clues to Attackers Lie in Wreckage, Computer Systems," *Detroit News* 13 September 2001 (www.detnews.com/2001/nation/0109/13/a03-293072.htm).
   8 "Primary Target: The Pentagon," CBS News, 21 September 2001 (www.cbsnews.com/stories/2001/09/11/national/main310721.shtml).
   9 "'Get These Planes on the Ground': Air Traffic Controllers Recall Sept. 11," *20/20*, ABC News, 24 October 2001 (web.archive.org/web/20011024150915/http://abcnews.go.com/sections/2020/2020/2020_011024_atc_feature.html).
   10 Justin Paprocki, "Airport Owners Panic over Plummeting Profits," *Maryland Newsline* 19 September 2001 (www.newsline.umd.edu/justice/specialreports/stateofemergency/airportlosses091901.htm).
   11 Joel Furfari, "Freeway Airport Thrust into Spotlight amid Terrorist Investigation," *Greenbelt Gazette* 21 September 2001 (web.archive.org/web/20030908034933/http://www.gazette.net/200138/greenbelt/news/72196-1.html).
   12 Thomas Frank, "Tracing Trail Of Hijackers," *Newsday* 23 September 2001 (www.pentagonresearch.com/Newsday_com.htm).
   13 Amy Goldstein, Lena H. Sun, and George Lardner Jr., "Hanjour: A Study in Paradox," *Washington Post* 15 October 2001 (www.washington-post.com/ac2/wp-dyn?pagename=article&node=&contentId=A59451-2001Oct14).
   14 Jim Yardley, "A Trainee Noted for Incompetence," *New York Times* 4 May 2002 (newsmine.org/archive/9-11/suspects/flying-skills/pilot-trainee-noted-for-incompetence.txt).
   15 Ibid.
   16 "FAA Was Alerted to Sept. 11 Hijacker," CBS News, 10 May 2002

(www.cbsnews.com/stories/2002/05/10/attack/main508656.shtml).

17 Steve Fainaru and Alia Ibrahim, "Mysterious Trip to Flight 77
Cockpit: Suicide Pilot's Conversion to Radical Islam Remains Obscure,"
Washington Post 10 September 2002 (s3.amazonaws.com/911time-
line/2002/wpost091002b.html).

18 9/11CR 225–26.

19 9/11CR 242.

20 9/11CR 520n56.

21 9/11CR 530n147.

22 9/11CR 531n170.

23 With regard to Hanjour's alleged training at Congressional Air
Charters, see "August 2001: Hani Hanjour Successfully Takes Certification
Flight?" Cooperative Research (www.cooperativeresearch.org/
timeline.jsp?timeline=complete_911_timeline&the_alleged_9/11_hijacker
s=haniHanjour). With regard to a person named Eddie Shalev, research
librarian Elizabeth Woodworth, by checking the national telephone direc-
tory and doing an extensive search using Google, could find no evidence of
the existence of a flight instructor named Eddie (or, for that matter, Eddy)
Shalev (email letter of 23 August 2007). And Matthew Everett, one of the
contributors to Cooperative Research, found no such person by means of a
LexisNexis search (email of 23 August 2007). All he turned up was a story
by a journalist named Bradley Olson, who, having seen the note in *The
9/11 Commission Report* about Congressional Air Charters of Gaithersburg,
had called this flight school in 2006. Olson wrote: "A man who answered
the phone at Congressional Air Charters of Gaithersburg declined to give
his name and said the company no longer gives flight instruction." See
Bradley Olson, "Md. Was among Last Stops for Hijackers," *Baltimore Sun*
9 September 2006 (www.baltimoresun.com/ news/custom/attack/bal-
te.md.terrorist09sep09,0,5567459.story).

24 9/11CR 334.

25 *Debunking 9/11 Myths: Why Conspiracy Theories Can't Stand Up to
the Facts: An In-Depth Investigation by Popular Mechanics*, eds. David
Dunbar and Brad Reagan (New York: Hearst Books, 2006).

26 This endorsement was given in a document entitled "The Top
September 11 Conspiracy Theories" under "Identifying Misinformation" on
the US Department of State website (usinfo.state.gov/media/
misinformation.html), when that document was dated 25 October 2006.
Besides repeatedly referring readers to *Popular Mechanics'* March 2005
article, "9/11: Debunking the Myths," it had a statement at the bottom
saying: "Also, in August 2006, *Popular Mechanics* expanded its article,
referenced above, into a book, *Debunking 9/11 Myths: Why Conspiracy
Theories Can't Stand Up to the Facts*. It provides excellent additional

material debunking 9/11 conspiracy theories, including many of those mentioned above and others." By August of 2007, however, this document, now dated September 19, 2006, no longer contained the statement about the *Popular Mechanics* book. (The October 25, 2006, version can still be read at www.jackbloodforum.com/phpBB2/viewtopic.php?=&p=58499.) There is, nevertheless, a positive reference to the *Popular Mechanics* book in another document at this State Department site, "'Loose Change' Debunked" (usinfo.state.gov/ xarchives/display.html?p=pubs-english&y=2007&m=March&x= 20070330134723abretnuh0.9919245).

27 *Debunking 9/11 Myths*, 5, 7.

28 Ibid., 6.

29 Ibid., 7, 6. Marcel Bernard, the manager and chief instructor at Freeway Airport, whose reports about Hanjour's incompetence were quoted above, has also been quoted, surprisingly, as saying: "There's no doubt in my mind that once that [hijacked jet] got going, he could have pointed that plane at a building and hit it" (Thomas Frank, "Tracing Trail Of Hijackers"). However, Bernard's statement, being made less than two weeks after 9/11, may have reflected unawareness of the trajectory reportedly taken by the plane. By contrast, the *Popular Mechanics* authors, writing several years later, cited the flight data recorder and showed awareness of the 330-degree downward spiral.

30 "Pilots and Aviation Professionals Question the 9/11 Commission Report" (www.patriotsquestion911.com/pilots.html).

Chapter 20: What Caused the Hole in the C Ring?

1 *Good Morning America*, ABC, 13 September 2001.

2 Pentagon News Briefing, 15 September 2001 (www.defenselink.mil/transcripts/transcript.aspx?transcriptid=1636).

3 "On the Ground at the Pentagon on Sept. 11," *Newsweek* 28 September 2003 (www.msnbc.msn.com/id/3069699).

4 Thierry Meyssan, *Pentagate* (London: Carnot Publishing, 2002), 60.

5 Ibid., 61–63.

6 "Did a Plane Hit the Pentagon?" Identifying Misinformation, US Department of State, created 28 June 2005, updated 2 October 2006 (usinfo.state.gov/media/Archive/2005/Jun/28-581634.html).

7 *Arlington County After-Action Report on the Response to the September 11 Attack on the Pentagon*, 2002 (www.arlingtonva.us/ departments/Fire/edu/about/docs/after_report.pdf), A-8.

8 ASCE (American Society of Civil Engineers), *Pentagon Building Performance Report*, January 2003 (fire.nist.gov/bfrlpubs/build03/PDF/b03017.pdf), 28.

9 This point has been made by Sami Yli-Karjanmaa in the most

extensive critique of this report known to me, "The ASCE's Pentagon Building Performance Report: Arrogant Deception—Or an Attempt to Expose a Cover-up?" (www.kolumbus.fi/sy-k/pentagon/asce_en.htm).

10 ASCE, *Pentagon Building Performance Report*, 40.

11 Ibid., 40.

12 Ibid., 40.

13 "9/11: Debunking the Myths," *Popular Mechanics* March 2005 (www.popularmechanics.com/technology/military_law/1227842.html?page=1).

14 *Debunking 9/11 Myths*, 70.

15 "The Top September 11 Conspiracy Theories," Identifying Misinformation, US Department of State, 19 September 2006 (usinfo.state.gov/ xarchives/display.html?p=pubsenglish&y =2006&m=August&x= 20060828133846esnamfuaK0.2676355). Although, as pointed out earlier (note 26 of Chapter 19), this document no longer mentions the *Popular Mechanics* book, it repeatedly refers readers to the *Popular Mechanics* article. With regard to the Pentagon in particular, it refers readers to Part 6 of this article, which is the part that contains the claim that the hole in the C ring "was made by the jet's landing gear, not by the fuselage."

16 Quoted in Dean Murphy, *September 11: An Oral History* (New York: Doubleday, 2001), 216.

17 Earl Swift, "Inside the Pentagon on 9/11: The Call of Duty," *Virginian-Pilot* 9 September 2002 (hamptonroads.com/pilotonline/special/911/pentagon3.html).

Chapter 21: Did a Military Plane Fly Over Washington?

1 "Air Attack on Pentagon Indicates Weaknesses," *Newsday* 23 September 2001 (s3.amazonaws.com/911timeline/2001/newsday092301.html).

2 9/11CR 34.

3 9/11CR 25–26.

4 "The White House Has Been Evacuated," CNN, 11 September 2001, 9:52AM (transcripts.cnn.com/TRANSCRIPTS/0109/11/bn.06.html). The time of King's statement can be seen on the CNN footage (www.archive.org/details/cnn200109110929-1011).

5 "Pilots Notified of Restricted Airspace; Violators Face Military Action," FAA Press Release, 28 September 2001 (web.archive.org/web/20011023082620/http://www.faa.gov/apa/pr/pr.cfm?id=1415). CNN's error here would be corrected in its broadcast of 12 September 2007, discussed later in the text, which referred to the area above the White House as the "nation's most off-limits airspace" (see note 12, below).

6 "Terrorists Attacks in Both Washington D.C. and New York," CNN,

11 September 2001, 10:00AM (transcripts.cnn.com/TRANSCRIPTS/
0109/11/bn.05.html).

7 Bob Kur's statement can be heard on an audiofile (alkali.colug.org/
~kaha/whiteplane.mp3).

8 "Planes Crash into World Trade Center," ABC News, 11 September
2001, 8:53AM (www.fromthewilderness.com/timeline/2001/abcnews
091101.html). A video of this segment is available on YouTube: "ABC—
Plane Circling over White House at 9:41AM on 9/11" (video.google.ca/ video-
play?docid=-54205931111081490&q=9%2F11+pentagon+abc&total=
70&start=0&num=10&so=0&type=search&plindex=0).

9 According to the animation of Flight 77 produced by the National
Transportation Safety Board (video.google.com/videoplay?
docid=6529691284366443405&q=AA77+animation&total=4&start=0&n
um=10&so=0&type=search&plindex=0), the downward spiral began at
9:34AM and ended at 9:37:02.

10 This constituent is a man who has posted numerous statements
under the alias "Pinnacle" on the Pilots for 9/11 Truth forum devoted to
"White Jet Analysis" (z9.invisionfree.com/Pilots_For_Truth/
index.php?showtopic=483&st=0). On the basis of the photograph of the
white jet over Washington taken by Linda Brookhart (which is mentioned
later in the text), he discovered in May 2006 that it was an E-4B. On June
4, 2006, he wrote to Congressman Adam Schiff, saying:

> For nearly five years I have been aware of the fact that
> several eyewitnesses in Washington DC on September
> 11, 2001 stated they saw an unmarked white jet plane
> flying in an unusual pattern over the White House and
> near the Pentagon during the time before and after the
> Pentagon was struck by Flight 77.
>
> I was able to find two blurry images from a BBC video
> shot at the time showing a white jet aircraft in the P-56
> restricted airspace over Washington. I also was able to
> find an audio recording of an NBC news reporter
> describing this unmarked white jet circling the White
> House.
>
> Just recently I have been in contact with someone who
> was evacuated from the White House grounds on the
> morning of September 11, 2001 and who took a 35mm
> photograph that clearly shows a white four-engine jet
> aircraft, which most closely resembles a 747-400 with
> no identifying markings, flying slowly directly over the

White House in restricted airspace. This person told me
that the unknown plane turned toward the direction of
the Pentagon and flew out of sight just moments before
Flight 77 hit and caused a huge cloud of smoke.

This person gave a copy of the photograph to the FBI
but this aircraft has never been identified and is not
referred to at all in the 9/11 Commission Report....

I would very much like to know if you, as a Congressman on the Judiciary Subcommittee on Crime, Terrorism
and Homeland Security, are aware of what this aircraft
was, who was flying it, and what they were doing in the
most restricted airspace in the country as the greatest
terrorist attack in history was taking place?...

After learning about the Pilots for 9/11 Truth forum, Pinnacle reported
there (on November 27, 2006) about the photograph and a Discovery
Channel video of an E-4B, for which he had sent a request. He also
reported that he had sent letters to the FAA and the US Air Force and had
received a reply from the latter stating that it had "no knowledge" of the
white jet. At some point, he also informed Mark Gaffney about Brookhart's
photo, which Gaffney then included in an online article entitled "The 9/11
Mystery Plane" (www.rense.com/general76/missing.htm). Although John
King's 2007 CNN report did not mention Brookhart, Pinnacle, or Gaffney, it
did include Brookhart's photograph, which appears to have been taken
from Gaffney's article.

11 Letter to Congressman Adam Schiff, 8 November 2006, signed by
Lt. Col. Karen L. Cook, Deputy Chief Congressional Inquiry Division,
Office of Legislative Liaison, Department of the Air Force, the Pentagon.
The letter, incidentally, was faxed to Schiff early that morning, only a few
hours before Donald Rumsfeld resigned as secretary of defense.

12 John King segment, *Anderson Cooper 360°*, 12 September 2007
(transcripts.cnn.com/TRANSCRIPTS/0709/12/acd.01.html). The John
King segment is available on YouTube (www.youtube.com/watch?v=
h8mGvFzvwFM&watch_response) and elsewhere (anderson-cooper-
effects.blogspot.com/2007/09/mystery-plane.html).

13 Ibid.

14 Ibid. Although CNN did not give credit to any researchers for
having made this identification, its three-point comparison was remarkably
similar to that of Mark Gaffney. After learning of the plane's identity from
Pinnacle, Gaffney had written in "The 9/11 Mystery Plane" (from which
CNN had evidently obtained Linda Brookhart's photo; see note 10): "[T]he

still-shot from the docudrama matches an official photo of the E-4B, from a USAF web site.... Notice... the US flag painted on the vertical stabilizer (i.e., the tail), and the blue stripe and insignia on the fuselage. The clincher, however, is the 'bump' directly behind the bulging 747 cockpit." The "docudrama" to which Gaffney referred is *The Flight that Fought Back*, a made-for-TV movie that aired on the Discovery Channel in August 2005 (dsc.discovery.com/convergence/flight/flight.html). Gaffney had learned from Pinnacle that this film contained a three-second video of the mystery plane, taken by some other person near the White House that morning.

15 John King segment, *Anderson Cooper 360°*.

16 "E-4B," Air Force Link: The Official Web Site of the US Air Force (www.af.mil/factsheets/factsheet.asp?fsID=99).

17 James P. Zemotel, "CEs Still Have Aircrew Mission," Air Force Civil Engineer 14/2 (2006): 16–17 (72.14.253.104/search?q=cache: YFSvRWUhgNcJ:www.afcesa.af.mil/userdocuments/periodicals/cemag/AF CE_V14n02.pdf+CEs+Still+Have+Aircrew+Mission&hl=en&ct=clnk&cd =2&gl=us&client=safari).

18 John King segment, *Anderson Cooper 360°*.

19 See Mark H. Gaffney, "Why Did the World's Most Advanced Electronics Warfare Plane Circle over the White House on 9/11?" *Journal of 9/11 Studies* 13 (July 2007): 16–18 (www.journalof911studies.com/ volume/200704/911MysteryPlane.pdf). The video, entitled "White House Evacuation," is described in note 15 of Gaffney's article.

20 "Three-Star General May Be Among Pentagon Dead," CNN, 13 September 2001 (archives.cnn.com/2001/US/09/13/pentagon.terrorism). As this story explained, "Commercial aircraft that are either approaching or departing from nearby Ronald Reagan National Airport do not fly over Georgetown."

21 Mark Easton, "Aboard the Hi-jacked Planes," Channel 4 News, 13 September 2001 (s3.amazonaws.com/911timeline/2001/channel4news 091301.html).

22 Gaffney, "Why Did the World's Most Advanced Electronics Warfare Plane Circle over the White House on 9/11?"

23 "The White House Has Been Evacuated."

24 Dan Verton, *Black Ice: The Invisible Threat of Cyber-Terrorism* (New York: Osborne/McGraw-Hill, 2003), 143–44. Chapter 7 of Verton's book, in which this discussion is contained, is available online (www.webcitation.org/5QueD1mCx).

25 See Joe Dejka, "Inside StratCom on Sept. 11: Offutt Exercise Took Real-Life Twist," *Omaha World-Herald* 27 February 2002 (www.democraticunderground.com/discuss/duboard.php?az=view_all&add

ress=125x87082), and Major Margo Bjorkman, "Weather Guard and Reservists Activate," *Air Force Weather Observer* July/August 2002 (www.afweather.af.mil/ shared/media/document/AFD-061020-055.pdf), 22–24.

26 Verton, *Black Ice*, 144. Verton's claim that this E-4B, which took off at about 9:30, was planning to participate in Global Guardian is challenged by reports that Global Guardian was canceled immediately after the second tower was struck at 9:03; see the story by Bjorkman in the previous note and also Joe Dejka, "When Bush Arrived, Offutt Sensed History in the Making" *Omaha World-Herald* 8 September 2002. However, Dejka's earlier story, "Inside StratCom on Sept. 11," mentioned in the previous note, had said: "Military authorities canceled the exercise after the attacks on the World Trade Center towers and the Pentagon."

27 Dan Verton, email to Mark Gaffney, 22 September 2007. If the US Air Force has an after-action report about this flight in its files, its claim that "Air Force officials have no knowledge of the aircraft in question" can hardly be construed as simply an error, perhaps based on poor institutional memory.

28 John King segment, *Anderson Cooper 360°*.

29 Pinnacle (see note 10), having discovered that this video was listed on the CNN Image Source website, informed CNN of this fact. On June 5, 2007, he received a letter from CNN confirming that they did indeed have this video. This CNN video is crucial because, although the plane is shown in Linda Brookhart's photograph and the Discovery Channel video (plus a couple of others), only the CNN video shows that this E-4B is the plane that was flying over the White House.

30 This letter, stamped May 15, 2007, was signed by Kathy J. Lyerly, Special Agent In Charge, Freedom of Information & Privacy Acts Officer, Department of Homeland Security. (I have a copy of the letter, sent to me by Pinnacle.)

31 "The White House Has Been Evacuated," CNN News, 11 September 2001, 9:52AM (transcripts.cnn.com/TRANSCRIPTS/0109/11/bn.06.html).

32 I have a copy of this letter, which I received from Pinnacle.

33 John King segment, *Anderson Cooper 360°*.

34 9/11CR 34.

PART V

Chapter 22: How Did Giuliani Know?

1 This statement, made on 9/11 to Peter Jennings of ABC News, can be read and heard at "Who Told Giuliani the WTC Was Going to Collapse on 9/11?" *What Really Happened*, n.d. (www.whatreallyhappened.com/wtc_giuliani.html).

2 "Giuliani Confronted at New York Fundraiser," WNBC.com, 29 May 2007 (www.wnbc.com/politics/13404578/detail.html). The quotations in my text are taken directly from the video, which is available at that website (see the next note), rather than from the WNBC summary of the encounter.

3 A video of this encounter is available at video.wnbc.com/player/ ?id=112179.

4 James Glanz, "Engineers Suspect Diesel Fuel in Collapse of 7 World Trade Center," *New York Times* 29 November 2001 (www.geocities.com/streakingobject/07NYTimes7WTCwhy.html).

5 "Learning from 9/11: Understanding the Collapse of the World Trade Center," Hearing before the Committee on Science, House of Representatives, 6 March 2002 (commdocs.house.gov/committees/ science/ hsy77747.000/hsy77747_0f.htm).

6 "Interstate Bank Building Fire, Los Angeles, California," Federal Emergency Management Agency, 1988 (www.lafire.com//famous_fires/ 880504_1stInterstateFire/FEMA-TecReport/FEMA-report.htm).

7 "High-Rise Office Building Fire One Meridian Plaza Philadelphia, Pennsylvania," Federal Emergency Management Agency (www.interfire.org/res_file/pdf/Tr-049.pdf).

8 James Glanz and Eric Lipton, *City in the Sky: The Rise and Fall of the World Trade Center* (New York: Times Books, 2004); 230; Norman J. Glover, "Collapse Lessons," *Fire Engineering*, October 2002 (www.fireengineering.com/articles/article_display.html?id=163411).

9 Glanz and Lipton, *City in the Sky*, 131–32, 138–39, 366.

10 See "The Fall of the World Trade Center," *Horizon*, BBC 2, 7 March 2002 (www.bbc.co.uk/science/horizon/2001/ worldtradecentertrans.shtml).

11 Eric Nalder, "Twin Towers Engineered to Withstand Jet Collision," *Seattle Times* 27 February 1993 (archives.seattletimes.nwsource.com/ cgi-bin/texis.cgi/web/vortex/display?slug=1687698&date=19930227); partially quoted in Glanz and Lipton, *City in the Sky*, 138.

12 Quoted (from an interview for the History Channel) in Jim Dwyer and Kevin Flynn, *102 Minutes: The Untold Story of the Fight to Survive Inside the Twin Towers* (New York: Times Books, 2005), 149. Dwyer and Flynn do, to be sure, say that after the North Tower was struck, De Martini—who died, after helping others escape, when it collapsed—had become concerned that the express elevators might fall (146). But that is a far cry from expecting the building itself, with all its steel columns, to collapse.

13 Norman J. Glover, "Collapse Lessons."

14 Jim Dwyer, "Vast Archive Yields New View of 9/11," *New York Times* 13 August 2005 (www.nytimes.com/2005/08/13/nyregion/ nyregionspecial3/13records.html?_r=1&oref=slogin).

15 Early in 2002, the *New York Times* requested a copy of the oral histories under the Freedom of Information Act, but Mayor Michael Bloomberg's administration refused. So the *Times*, joined by several families of 9/11 victims, filed suit. After a long process, the city was finally ordered by the New York Court of Appeals to release the records (with some exceptions and redactions allowed). See two stories by Jim Dwyer: "City to Release Thousands of Oral Histories of 9/11 Today," *New York Times* 12 August 2005 (www.nytimes.com/2005/08/12/nyregion/12records.html?ex=1281499200&en=b245bfd8ba497f9a&ei=5088), and "Vast Archive Yields New View of 9/11."

16 For the complete set of 9/11 oral histories, see graphics8.nytimes.com/packages/html/nyregion/20050812_WTC_GRAPHIC/met_WTC_histories_full_01.html.

17 Oral History: Lieutenant Brendan Whelan, n.p.

18 Oral History: Lieutenant Murray Murad, 18.

19 Oral History: Battalion Chief Brian Dixon, 15.

20 Oral History: Chief John Peruggia, 17–18. As we will see below, Peruggia, after being told that the towers were going to collapse, did have this report passed on. In these statements, however, he was indicating that the message that the towers were going to collapse ran counter to all his prior expectations.

21 Oral History: Captain Charles Clarke, 5.

22 Oral History: Captain Mark Stone, 19, 25. James Dobson, a paramedic at St. John's Hospital who raced to the World Trade Center after the South Tower was struck, gave similar testimony, saying: "Remember, at this time, no one expected the towers to collapse. We assumed that we should get as close to the towers as possible" (quoted in "Courage and Devotion," SEIU/1199 News, November 2001 [911digitalarchive.org/webcontent/1199seiunews/courage1199.html]).

23 Oral History: Lieutenant Warren Smith, 14–15, 30–31, 32.

24 9/11CR 302.

25 9/11 Commission Hearing, 18 May 2004 (www.9-11commission.gov/archive/hearing11/9-11Commission_Hearing_2004-05-18.htm). Von Essen had already told that story in his book, *Strong of Heart: Life and Death in the Fire Department of New York* (New York: William Morrow, 2002), 22, a fact that was reported in an Associated Press review, "Former NYC Fire Commissioner Tells His Version of Sept. 11," 24 July 2002 (www.news-star.com/stories/072402/lif_5.shtml).

26 Roemer referred to Downey as "an expert—very, very respected expert on building collapse" (www.9-11commission.gov/archive/hearing11/9-11Commission_Hearing_2004-05-18.htm).

27 This statement was made by Robert Ingram, a FDNY battalion

chief, in a US Senate hearing (commerce.senate.gov/hearings/
101101Ingram.pdf).

28 Tom Downey, *The Last Men Out: Life on the Edge at Rescue 2 Fire-house* (New York: Henry Holt, 2004), 233.

29 Oral History: Father John Delendick, 5. Delendick reported that, after the top of the South Tower appeared to explode, he asked Downey whether jet fuel had blown up. "[Downey] said at that point he thought there were bombs up there because it was too even. As we've since learned, it was the jet fuel that was dropping down that caused all this. But he said it was too even."

30 NIST NCSTAR 1–8: *Federal Building and Fire Safety Investigation of the World Trade Center Disaster: The Emergency Response Operations* (wtc.nist.gov/NISTNCSTAR1-8.pdf), 72.

31 Ibid., 75–76.

32 9/11 Commission Hearing, 19 May 2004 (www.9-11commission.gov/archive/hearing11/9-11Commission_Hearing_2004-05-19.htm).

33 WP 228–231.

34 See Wayne Barrett and Dan Collins, *Grand Illusion: The Untold Story of Rudy Giuliani and 9/11* (New York: HarperCollins, 2006); for a briefer version, see Wayne Barrett, "Rudy Giuliani's Five Big Lies About 9/11," *Village Voice* 7 August 2007 (www.villagevoice.com/news/0732,barrett,77463,6.html). See also Robert Greenwald's video, "The Real Rudy: Command Center" (therealrudy.org/ ?utm_source=rgemail).

35 *New York Times* reporter Jim Dwyer wrote in 2005: "The city... initially refused access to the records to investigators from... the 9/11 Commission" but "relented when legal action was threatened" ("City to Release Thousands of Oral Histories of 9/11 Today").

36 9/11CR 554n209.

37 9/11CR Chapter 9, notes 99, 102, 109, 116, 117, 119, 124, 125, 126, 128, 134, 136, 163, 166, 167, 168, 171, 172, and 175. The FDNY interviews in question are those dated September 2001 through January 2002.

38 Oral History: Chief Albert Turi, 13–14.

39 "Richie Zarrillo came running up to me.... He said... [t]hese buildings are in imminent danger of collapse.... I ran over and grabbed Chief Ganci and said Chief, these buildings are in imminent danger of collapse.... And he said to me who would tell you something like that?... I said Richie, come over here and tell the Chief what you just told me. He got the words out of his mouth. I think it was maybe 25, 30 seconds later, maybe, the building came down.... I believe the Chief said where did he get that from? He said from OEM.... I think he told me he got it from

Peruggia" (Oral History: Fire Marshall Steven Mosiello, 8–10).

40 Chief Ganci would die later that day; see Chris Ganci, *Chief: The Life of Peter J. Ganci, A New York City Firefighter* (London: Orchard, 2003).

41 Oral History: EMT Richard Zarrillo, 5–6.

42 Oral History: Chief John Peruggia, 4, 17.

43 Ibid., 17–18.

44 9/11CR 302.

45 On Sheirer and the OEM, see Barrett and Collins, *Grand Illusion*, 13, 31–35.

Chapter 23: Were There Explosions in the Twin Towers?

1 9/11CR 306.

2 "9/11: Truth, Lies and Conspiracy: Interview: Lee Hamilton," CBC News, 21 August 2006 (www.cbc.ca/sunday/911hamilton.html). The interviewer was Evan Solomon.

3 NIST (National Institute of Standards and Technology), *Final Report on the Collapse of the World Trade Center Towers*, September 2005 (wtc.nist.gov/NISTNCSTAR1CollapseofTowers.pdf), "Abstract."

4 NIST, *Final Report*, xxxviii, 146, 176.

5 NIST, "Answers to Frequently Asked Questions," 30 August 2006 (wtc.nist.gov/pubs/factsheets/faqs_8_2006.htm).

6 Ibid., Question 2.

7 Graeme MacQueen, "118 Witnesses: The Firefighters' Testimony to Explosions in the Twin Towers," *Journal of 9/11 Studies* 2 (August 2006): 49–123 (www.journalof911studies.com/articles/ Article_5_118Witnesses_WorldTradeCenter.pdf). Although MacQueen's subtitle might suggest that he restricted himself to firefighters, many of his witnesses were emergency medical workers, who were included among the 503 members of the FDNY whose 9/11 oral histories are posted on the NYT website. By the criteria he employed, 118, and hence 23 percent, of these 503 men and women testified to phenomena suggestive of explosions.

8 Oral History: Firefighter Richard Banaciski, 3.

9 Oral History: Firefighter Edward Cachia, 5.

10 Oral History: Firefighter Craig Carlsen, 5–6.

11 Shyam Sunder, the lead investigator of the collapse of the World Trade Center carried out by NIST, said that all the jet fuel "probably burned out in less than 10 minutes" (quoted in Andy Field, "A Look Inside a Radical New Theory of the WTC Collapse," Firehouse.com, 7 February 2004 [cms.firehouse.com/content/article/article.jsp?sectionId=46&id=25807]). NIST itself said: "The initial jet fuel fires themselves lasted at most a few minutes" (*Final Report*, 179).

12 Oral History: Fire Marshal John Coyle, 7–8.

13 Oral History: Chief Frank Cruthers, 4.

14 Oral History: Battalion Chief Brian Dixon, 15. Like many others, Dixon at least professed to having come to accept the official interpretation, saying: "Then I guess in some sense of time we looked at it and realized, no, actually it just collapsed. That's what blew out the windows, not that there was an explosion there but that windows blew out." As I emphasized in the text, however, my concern here is with the phenomena these witnesses reported, not with their later interpretations of these phenomena.

15 Oral History: Deputy Commissioner Thomas Fitzpatrick, 13–14.

16 Oral History: Assistant Commissioner Stephen Gregory, 14–16.

17 Oral History: Firefighter Timothy Julian, 10.

18 Oral History: Firefighter Joseph Meola, 5.

19 Oral History: Fire Marshal John Murray, 6.

20 Oral History: Firefighter William Reynolds, 3–4.

21 Oral History: Firefighter Kenneth Rogers, 3–4.

22 Although Tardio's testimony was not included in the FDNY oral histories that are provided at the NYT website, he was quoted in Dennis Smith, *Report from Ground Zero: The Story of the Rescue Efforts at the World Trade Center* (New York: Penguin, 2002), 18.

23 Oral History: Firefighter Thomas Turilli, 4.

24 Oral History: Fire Marshal John Coyle, 15.

25 Oral History: Firefighter Christopher Fenyo, 3.

26 Oral History: Firefighter Kevin Gorman, 6.

27 Oral History: EMT Michael Ober, 4–5.

28 Oral History: Paramedic Daniel Rivera, 9.

29 Oral History: Captain Jay Swithers, 5.

30 Oral History: Captain Karin Deshore, 15–16.

31 Quoted in Susan Hagen and Mary Carouba, *Women at Ground Zero: Stories of Courage and Compassion* (Indianapolis: Alpha Books, 2002), 65–66, 68.

32 Guzman's account is contained in Mike Kelly, "Last Survivor Pulled from WTC Rebuilds Life, Recalls Horror," *The Record* (Bergen County, NJ) 10 September 2003. It can be found at What Really Happened (www.whatreallyhappened.com/wtc_mcmillan.html). Incidentally, although Kelly refers to her as "Genelle Guzman McMillan," he reports that she did not marry Roger McMillan until two months after 9/11.

33 "We Will Not Forget: A Day of Terror," *Chief Engineer* 2002 (www.chiefengineer.org/article.cfm?seqnum1=1029).

34 Patriots Question 9/11 (www.patriotsquestion911.com/survivors.html#Saltalamacchia).

35 Dean E. Murphy, *September 11: An Oral History* (New York: Doubleday, 2002), 9–15.

36 This statement can be viewed in a video by Dustin Mugford, "9/11 Revisited: Were Explosives Used?" It is available at Google (video.google.com/videoplay?docid=4194796183168750014) and YouTube (www.youtube.com/watch?v=PWgSaBT9hNU). A portion of this footage is contained in a video created by Lucus entitled "The Ultimate Con" (video.google.com/videoplay?docid=-751298171535560228). This Fox News statement and many of the other statements quoted here are contained in a compressed version, also entitled "The Ultimate Con," which is posted at www.youtube.com/watch?v=yIgoXQWiSlM. These statements as quoted here have been transcribed by Elizabeth Woodworth of Victoria, British Columbia.

37 BBC News, 11 September 2001 (www.archive.org/details/bbc200109111736-1818 [the Evans interview begins almost 11 minutes in]).

38 "The Ultimate Con" (both versions; see note 36).

39 Ibid.

40 Ibid.

41 Ibid.

42 Ibid.

43 Ibid.

44 Ibid.

45 "9/11 Revisited: Were Explosives Used?" (www.youtube.com/watch?v=PWgSaBT9hNU).

46 Ibid.

47 This headline can be seen at www.youtube.com/watch?v=mrQZE-BlNh04.

48 "9/11 Revisited: Were Explosives Used?"

49 "The Ultimate Con." Although Thompson began the report by saying "at 10:30," she was off by several minutes, because the North Tower collapsed at 10:28.

50 "The Ultimate Con."

51 Ibid.

52 Ibid.

53 "Special Report: Terrorism in the US," *Guardian* 12 September 2001 (www.guardian.co.uk/september11/story/0,11209,600839,00.html).

54 John Bussey, "Eye of the Storm: One Journey Through Desperation and Chaos," *Wall Street Journal* 12 September 2001 (online.wsj.com/public/resources/documents/040802pulitzer5.htm). Elsewhere Bussey is quoted as saying: "I heard this metallic roar, looked up and saw… individual floors, one after the other exploding outward. I thought to myself, 'My God, they're going to bring the building down.' And they, whoever they are, had set charges. In fact, the building was imploding down. I saw the explosions" (quoted in *Running Toward Danger: Stories Behind the Break-*

ing News of 9/11, by the Newseum, with Alicia Shepard and Cathy Trost, foreword by Tom Brokaw [Lanham, MD: Rowman & Littlefield, 2002], 87).

55 Geraldine Baum and Maggie Farley, "Terrorists Attack New York, Pentagon," *Los Angeles Times* 12 September 2001 (web.archive.org/web/20010912044735/http://www.latimes.com/news/nationworld/nation/la-091201main.story).

56 "The Ultimate Con."

57 9/11CR xvi.

58 See note 37 of Chapter 22.

59 9/11CR 306.

60 Greg Szymanski, "WTC Basement Blast and Injured Burn Victim Blows 'Official 9/11 Story' Sky High," Arctic Beacon.com, 24 June 2005 (www.arcticbeacon.citymaker.com/articles/article/1518131/28031.htm).

61 NIST, *Final Report*, 163.

Chapter 24: Were There Explosions in WTC 7?

1 "Schedule for Completion of Investigation," NIST & The World Trade Center: News and Events, 5 April 2005 (wtc.nist.gov/pubs/WTC%20Part%20IIC%20-%20WTC%207%20Collapse%20Final.pdf).

2 NIST, "Answers to Frequently Asked Questions," 30 August 2006 (wtc.nist.gov/pubs/factsheets/faqs_8_2006.htm), Question 14.

3 NIST, "Appendix L: Interim Report on WTC 7," June 2004. (wtc.nist.gov/progress_report_june04/appendixl.pdf), L-34, L-34.

4 NIST, "WTC 7 Collapse" (wtc.nist.gov/pubs/WTC%20Part%20IIC%20-%20WTC%207%20Collapse%20Final.pdf), 6.

5 In an interview with Evan Solomon of the Canadian Broadcast Corporation ("9/11: Truth, Lies and Conspiracy: Interview: Lee Hamilton," CBC News, 21 August 2006 [www.cbc.ca/sunday/911hamilton.html]), Hamilton said: "[W]ith regard to Building 7, we believe that it was the aftershocks of these two huge buildings in the very near vicinity collapsing."

6 Quoted in Chris Bull and Sam Erman, eds., *At Ground Zero: Young Reporters Who Were There Tell Their Stories* (New York: Thunder's Mouth Press, 2002), 97.

7 Jones's statement is in the documentary "911 Eyewitness" (video.google.com/videoplay?docid=65460757734339444) at 28:25.

8 Daryl's statement is in ibid., at 31:30.

9 "Speaking Out: An Interview with Craig Bartmer" (video.google.com/videoplay?docid=-2283625397351664218).

10 UPN9 News, WWOR-TV, September 11, 2001. The video began at 10:37AM and the interview with Hess was 57 minutes in, which would have been 11:34.

11 Associated Press, "The Scene at the Trade Towers," *Traverse City*

Record Eagle 11 September 2001 (www.record-eagle.com/2001/sep/
11scene.htm).

12 This fact was stated by Jennings in a later interview, part of which
was transcribed in "WTC 7 Eyewitness Testimony Transcribed by Rolf
Lindgren," which is included in "NIST Exploring 9/11 'Blast Events'; New
Witness Confirms Scholars Previous Findings," Scholars for 9/11 Truth, 1
July 2007 (rinf.com/alt-news/911-truth/nist-exploring-911-blast-events-for-
wtc-7-new-witness-confirms-scholars-previous-findings/693). Although the
part of the interview transcribed does not include Jennings's statement that
he and Hess went to WTC right after the strike on the North Tower, Lindgren, who had access to information from the complete interview, reported
it: After quoting Jennings's statement, "I was asked to go and man the
Office of Emergency Management [OEM] at the World Trade Center 7, on
the 23rd floor," Lindgren inserted in brackets: "This was immediately after
the North Tower was struck."

13 "Keeping Us Safe," *What's in the News*, Penn State Public Broadcasting, 1 March 2002 (is124.ce.psu.edu/Edcomm/WITNweb/
2423/script.html).

14 Jennings's statement can be heard on YouTube
(www.youtube.com/watch?v=NttM3oUrNmE). This statement is transcribed
in "WTC 7 Eyewitness Testimony Transcribed by Rolf Lindgren" (see note
12, above).

15 Associated Press, "The Scene at the Trade Towers."

16 Barry Jennings, YouTube (www.youtube.com/watch?v=
NttM3oUrNmE); transcribed in "WTC 7 Eyewitness Testimony Transcribed
by Rolf Lindgren." The accuracy of Jennings's statement about the lobby
might seem to be contradicted by the statement of Richard Sheirer, the
director of the OEM, that he tried to set up a triage center in that lobby. But
Wayne Barrett and Dan Collins, besides showing that none of Sheirer's
claims about his actions that day can be trusted, say with regard to this one
in particular: "Richard Rotanz, who was Sheirer's top deputy still at 7
WTC, was never told about the triage order. Since the building had already
been vacated as unsafe, establishing a triage area there made no sense and
was never attempted, according to sources still in the tower at that time"
(*Grand Illusion: The Untold Story of Rudy Giuliani and 9/11* [New York:
HarperCollins, 2006], 32).

17 NIST, "Appendix L: Interim Report on WTC 7" (wtc.nist.gov/
progress_report_june04/appendixl.pdf), L-18. No source for this
information is cited.

18 NIST NCSTAR 1–8, *Federal Building and Fire Safety Investigation
of the World Trade Center Disaster: The Emergency Response Operations*
(wtc.nist.gov/NISTNCSTAR1-8.pdf), Section 5.9.

19 Barry Jennings, as mentioned earlier in the text, was on 9/11 the deputy director of the New York Housing Authority's Emergency Services Department—not merely "a WTC 7 building staff person." Also Michael Hess, being New York City's corporation counsel, was not simply an ordinary "New York City employee."

20 NIST NCSTAR 1–8 (see note 18), Section 5.9.

21 Ibid.

22 Barry Jennings, YouTube (www.youtube.com/watch?v=NttM3oUrNmE); transcribed in "WTC 7 Eyewitness Testimony Transcribed by Rolf Lindgren."

23 NIST NCSTAR 1–8: 110n380.

24 Rudolph W. Giuliani, with Ken Kurson, *Leadership* (New York: Hyperion, 2002), 20.

25 NIST NCSTAR 1–8: 110.

26 Oral History: Captain Ray Goldbach, 14.

27 Oral History: Firefighter Vincent Massa, 17.

28 Oral History: EMT Decosta Wright, 12.

29 Oral History: EMT Joseph Fortis, 15.

30 Oral History: Chief Daniel Nigro, 10.

31 Oral History: Fire Lieutenant William Ryan, 15.

32 Oral History: Firefighter Kevin McGovern, 12.

33 Oral History: Captain Robert Sohmer, 5.

34 Oral History: Chief Frank Fellini, 3.

35 Oral History: Firefighter Christopher Patrick Murray, 12.

36 Oral History: Chief Thomas McCarthy, 10–11.

37 Oral History: EMT Decosta Wright, 11.

38 "WTC: This Is Their Story: Deputy Chief Nick Visconti," *Firehouse* magazine, August 2002 (www.firehouse.com/terrorist/911/magazine/gz/visconti.html).

39 Thomas von Essen, *Strong of Heart: Life and Death in the Fire Department of New York* (New York: William Morrow, 2002), 45.

40 Dean E. Murphy, *September 11: An Oral History* (New York: Doubleday, 2002), 175–76.

41 This statement, which can be seen on YouTube (www.youtube.com/watch?v=CahEva8zQas), was originally contained in a 2002 PBS documentary, *America Rebuilds*, available as a PBS Home Video (www.pbs.org/americarebuilds).

42 "9/11 Revealed? New Book Repeats False Conspiracy Theories," Identifying Misinformation, US Department of State (usinfo.state.gov/media/Archive/2005/Sep/16-241966.html). One of the issues involved in the controversy about the meaning of Silverstein's statement is whether "pull it" is slang for controlled demolition. For the view that it is not, see

"The Top September 11 Conspiracy Theories," under "Identifying Misinformation," US Department of State (usinfo.state.gov/media/misinformation.html), and *Debunking 9/11 Myths: Why Conspiracy Theories Can't Stand Up to the Facts: An In-Depth Investigation by* Popular Mechanics, ed. David Dunbar and Brad Reagan (New York: Hearst Books, 2006), 57–58. For the other view, see www.pumpitout.com/audio/pull_it_mix.mp3.

43 *Guns and Butter*, KPFA, 27 April 2005 (gunsandbutter.net/archives.php?page=13). A portion of the exchange is available in the video "Seven Is Exploding" (www.youtube.com/watch?v=58h0LjdMry0).

44 "Seven Is Exploding."

45 Ibid.

46 Rather's statement is available on YouTube (www.youtube.com/watch?v=Nvx904dAw0o).

47 Danny Jowenko, a controlled demolition expert in the Netherlands with his own firm (Jowenko Explosieve Demolitie B.V.), was asked to comment on a video of the collapse of WTC 7 without knowing what it was—he had not realized that a third building had collapsed on 9/11. After viewing it, he said: "They simply blew up columns, and the rest caved in afterwards…. This is controlled demolition." When he was asked if he was sure, he replied: "Absolutely, its been imploded. This was a hired job. A team of experts did this." When he was told that this happened on September 11, he was at first incredulous, repeatedly asking, "Are you sure?" This interview can be seen at "Controlled Demolition Expert and WTC7" (www.youtube.com/watch?v=HgoSOQ2xrbI). This 2006 video clip is an excerpt from a Dutch television program entitled "Zembla Investigates 9/11 Theories" (cgi.omroep.nl/cgi-bin/streams?/tv/vara/zembla/ bb.20060911.asf). When Jowenko was asked in 2007 whether he stood by his original statement, he replied: "Absolutely…. I looked at the drawings, the construction and it couldn't be done by fire… absolutely not" (patriotsquestion911.com/engineers.html#Jowenko). Also, Jack Keller, a well-known professor of engineering at Utah State University, has said of the demise of WTC 7: "Obviously it was the result of controlled demolition" (www.ae911truth.org/supporters.php?g=ENG). The statement that WTC 7 was "with great probability" professionally demolished has been made by two professors of structural engineering at the Swiss Federal Institute of Technology: Hugo Bachmann (patriotsquestion911.com/engineers.html# Bachmann) and Jörg Schneider (patriotsquestion911.com/engineers.html# Schneider).

Chapter 25: Evidence in Rubble that Steel Melted?

1 For the purposes of this discussion, I will ignore the issue of whether the substance described by several witnesses as "molten steel" would have more properly been called molten iron (which can result as a byproduct

when certain substances are used to melt steel).

2 James Williams, "WTC a Structural Success," *SEAU News: The Newsletter of the Structural Engineers Association of Utah* October 2001 (www.seau.org/SEAUNews-2001-10.pdf).

3 "New York Visit Reveals Extent of WTC Disaster," *Structural Engineer* 3 September 2002 (http://web.archive.org/web/20031117155808/www.istructe.org.uk/about/files/president/Tour-2002-NewYork.pdf), 6.

4 Lou Lumenick, "Unflinching Look Among the Ruins," *New York Post* 3 March 2004.

5 Ruvolo is quoted in the DVD *Collateral Damages* (www.collateral-damages.com). For just this segment plus discussion, see Steve Watson, "Firefighter Describes 'Molten Metal' at Ground Zero, Like a 'Foundry,'" Inforwars.net, 17 November 2006 (infowars.net/articles/november2006/171106molten.htm).

6 Guy Lounsbury, "Serving on 'Sacred Ground,'" *National Guard* December 2001 (findarticles.com/p/articles/mi_qa3731/is_200112/ai_n9015802).

7 Quoted in Francesca Lyman, "Messages in the Dust: What Are the Lessons of the Environmental Health Response to the Terrorist Attacks of September 11?" *National Environmental Health Association* September 2003 (www.neha.org/9-11%20report/index-The.html).

8 "Mobilizing Public Health: Turning Terror's Tide with Science," *Magazine of Johns Hopkins Public Health* Late Fall 2001 (www.jhsph.edu/Publications/Special/Welch.htm).

9 "The Chaplain's Tale," *Times-Herald Record* 8 September 2002 (archive.recordonline.com/adayinseptember/trimpe.htm).

10 Jennifer Lin, "Recovery Worker Reflects on Months Spent at Ground Zero," *Knight Ridder*, 29 May 2002 (www.whatreallyhappened.com/ground_zero_fires.html).

11 Trudy Walsh, "Handheld APP Eased Recovery Tasks," *Government Computer News* 21/27a, 11 September 2002 (www.gcn.com/21_27a/news/19930-1.html).

12 Tom Arterburn, "D-Day: NY Sanitation Workers' Challenge of a Lifetime," *Waste Age* 1 April 2002 (wasteage.com/mag/waste_dday_ny_sanitation).

13 9/11 Commission Hearing, 1 April 2003 (www.9-11commission.gov/hearings/hearing1/witness_holden.htm).

14 ABC News, 7 May 2004, quoted in Andy Field, "A Look Inside a Radical New Theory of the WTC Collapse," Firehouse.com, 7 February 2004, updated 14 June 2007 (cms.firehouse.com/content/article/article.jsp?sectionId=46&id=25807).

15 See Chapters 23 and 24, above.

16 NIST, "Answers to Frequently Asked Questions," Question 13 (wtc.nist.gov/pubs/factsheets/faqs_8_2006.htm).

17 Ibid.

18 Ibid.

19 Gross's statement can be seen in "NIST Engineer, John Gross, Denies the Existance [*sic*] of Molten Steel" (video.google.com/videoplay?docid=-7180303712325092501&hl=en). Gross is one of the thirteen members of the National Construction Safety Team listed at the beginning of NIST's *Final Report on the Collapse of the World Trade Center Towers*, September 2005 (wtc.nist.gov/NISTNCSTAR1CollapseofTowers.pdf).

20 J.R. Barnett, R. R. Biederman, and R. D. Sisson, Jr., "An Initial Microstructural Analysis of A36 Steel from WTC Building 7," *JOM* 53/12 (2001): 18 (www.tms.org/pubs/journals/JOM/0112/Biederman/Biederman-0112.html).

21 James Glanz, "Engineers Suspect Diesel Fuel in Collapse of 7 World Trade Center," *New York Times* 29 November 2001 (www.nytimes.com/2001/11/29/nyregion/29TOWE.html).

22 James Glanz and Eric Lipton, "A Search for Clues in Towers' Collapse," *New York Times* 2 February 2002 (query.nytimes.com/gst/fullpage.html?res=9C04E0DE153DF931A35751C0A9649C8B63).

23 Jonathan Barnett, Ronald R. Biederman, and Richard D. Sisson, Jr., "Limited Metallurgical Examination," FEMA, *World Trade Center Building Performance Study*, Appendix C (911research.wtc7.net/wtc/evidence/metallurgy/WTC_apndxC.htm).

24 Ibid.

25 Joan Killough-Miller, "The 'Deep Mystery' of Melted Steel," *WPI Transformations* Spring 2002 (www.wpi.edu/News/Transformations/2002Spring/steel.html).

26 NIST, "Answers to Frequently Asked Questions," Question 12.

27 Ibid.

Summary and Conclusion

1 President George W. Bush, Address to the General Assembly of the United Nations, 10 November 2001 (www.whitehouse.gov/news/releases/2001/11/20011110-3.html).

2 *The American Heritage Dictionary of the English Language* (Boston: Houghton Mifflin, 1969).

INDEX

A

AA 11. *See* American 11.

AA 77. *See* American 77.

Against All Enemies (Richard Clarke), 13, 51, 106

Air War over America, 114, 281

Amalgam Virgo, 136–38

American 11 (AA 11; Flight 11), 80–85

American 77 (AA 77; Flight 77), 94–108, 298n5, 299n8, 300n21, 323nn9,10; Hani Hanjour as pilot of, 198–206; phone calls from, 72–78, 172–73

American Society of Civil Engineers (ASCE), 209, 211–13, 322n9, 338n26

Arce, Rose, 247, 248

Arena, Kelli, 198

Arlington County After-Action Report, 103, 108, 208–09

Arnold, General Larry, 42, 44–45, 82, 98–99, 110–11, 114–15, 118, 277

Arpey, Gerard, 15

Arterburn, Tom, 267

ASCE. *See* American Society of Civil Engineers.

Atef, Mohammed, 184

Atta, Mohamed, 142–56, 157–69, 277–78, 308nn1,3, 309nnn22, 27,30, 311nn47,51, 312n7, 314n32; as devout Muslim, 142, 143–44, 147, 148, 155–56, 277; drinking alcohol, 143–48, 150, 152, 165, 277, 309n22; drinking cranberry juice, 147–48, 309n22; living in Venice (Fla.), 148–55, 161, 309–10nn27,30; sexual activities, 143, 148, 149–50, 152–56, 277; swearing, 145–46, 147; using cocaine, drugs, 150, 152, 155–56

B

Bachmann, Hugo, 336n47

Balkwill, Bill, 7

Balz, Dan, 17, 25–29, 33, 35, 38, 66–67, 288n9, 293n25

Banaciski, Richard, 240

Bardot, Rev. Bonnie, 171

Barnard, Marcel, 200–01, 321n29

Barnett, Jonathan, 270, 271

Barrett, Wayne, 334n16

Bartlett, Dan, 4

Bartmer, Craig, 255

Baum, Gerald R., 127–28

Baxter, Sheri, 200

Belger, Monte, 32–38, 107–08, 115, 286n5, 288n9

Ben–Veniste, Richard, 91–92, 96–108, 115, 137–38, 156, 297n19, 299n8

Biederman, Ronald R., 270

Binalshibh, Ramzi, 195

Bin Laden, Osama (Usama), vi, 132–33, 135, 183–196, 278, 280, 317n19, 318n23

Bingham, Mark, 174, 176, 180

Blair, Prime Minister Tony, 190, 196

Bohrer, David, 14–16, 18, 20, 113

Boston Center (FAA), 81–84, 90, 106, 112, 276, 296nn2,3

Boucher, Richard, 189

Bradshaw, Sandra and Phil, 175–76, 190

Bridges, Major Kevin, 300n43

Britton, Marion, 175–76, 180

Brokaw, Tom, 88–89, 93, 106, 117

Bronner, Michael, 90

Brookhart, Linda, 219–20, 323n10, 324n14, 326n29

Brown, Aaron, 248

Brown, Claire, 192, 318n22

Brown, Laura, 84–85, 90–92, 95–98, 102, 108, 115, 297n19, 298n23, 299nn12,14

Bukhari, Adnan and Ameer, 160–69

Bunch, William, 126, 127, 128

Burger, Dr. Ronald, 267

170–82, 219, 278, 294n7,
294n10, 295n22, 310n47,
315n16, 316n33; passenger–seat
(onboard), 73–78, 170–71, 176–
78, 182, 295nn14,17, 315n16
Pillar, Paul, 133
Pilots for 9/11 Truth, 324n10
"Pinnacle" (Congressman Schiff's
constituent), 323–25nn10,14,
326nn29,30,32
Popular Mechanics, 204–06, 211–13,
278, 320n25, 320–21nn26,29,
322n15, 326n43
Powell, Colin, 184–88, 191
Powell, Jeremy, 81
Presidential Emergency Operations
Center (PEOC), 12–20, 22–28,
30–39, 40, 47, 49, 92, 116, 121,
275
Press coverage and questions, vii–viii,
5–6, 11, 21, 39, 45, 57, 67–68,
70–71, 78, 85, 93, 108, 118, 130,
139, 155–56, 160, 169, 170–71,
179, 180, 182–85, 194, 196, 198,
206–07, 213, 223, 236–37, 252,
265, 274, 278–79, 280, 316n33

Q

al–Qaeda, 120, 135–36, 169, 182,
183–90, 193, 196, 280

R

Rancy, Brenda, 74
Rather, Dan, 247, 265
Reynolds, William, 242
Rice, Condoleezza, 8, 13–14, 16, 20,
28, 47, 132, 134, 283n30, 285n23
Riggs, Barbara, 106–07, 116
Rivera, Daniel, 244
Robertson, Leslie, 228, 266
Roddy, Dennis, 126
Rodriguez, William, 251
Roemer, Timothy, 13, 19, 22, 231,
286n30, 328n26
Rogers, Kenneth, 242
Rotanz, Richard, 235, 334n16
Rountree, Stacia, 90

Rove, Karl, 3–5, 9–11, 14–15, 20,
113, 118
Rules of engagement, 49, 51, 63–68, 122
Rumsfeld, Donald, vi, 44, 47, 50, 58–
71, 113, 120, 122, 132, 134, 139,
207, 211–13, 276, 278, 291n10,
292nn7,8,9,16, 293nn25,31,32,
302n8, 324n11
Russert, Tim (*Meet the Press*), 18, 26,
38, 132, 184–86, 281
Ruvolo, Captain Philip, 266–67, 337n5
Ryan, Lt. William, 261

S

Saltalamacchia, Anthony, 245–46
Sammon, Bill, 4
Sanchez, Rick 247
Sasseville, Lt. Col. Marc, 43–44
Schiavo, Mary, 128
Schiff, Congressman Adam, 216–17,
221–22, 323n10, 324n11
Schipanni, John, 296n14
Schneider, Jörg, 336n37
Schuessler, Linda, 289n10, 297n19
Schwartz, Arthur, 192
Scoggins, Colin, 82–85, 276,
296nn2,3,4,7,12
Scott, Col. Alan, 110, 137–38
Scott, Peter Dale, 287n15
Secret Service, 5–10, 13–14, 16, 20,
29, 40–41, 43, 49, 91, 97, 106–
08, 116–17, 125, 198, 215, 221–
22, 277, 284n4
Shaeffer, Lt. Kevin, 213
Shalev, Eddie, 204, 320n23
Shaw, John, 176, 178
Shea, Robert F., 227
al–Shehhi, Marwan, 142, 145–49,
154–55, 157, 161–64, 167–69,
300n22, 310n27, 312n51
Sheirer, Richard, 236, 334n16
Shelton, General Hugh, 46, 48, 50
Shepperd, Maj. General Don, 217
Shootdown authorization, 28, 30, 37–
38, 40–45, 49, 51, 58, 63–66,
121–26, 130, 181, 275–76, 289n4
Shuckums Bar, 144–48, 152, 165,
309n20

2/11   2 9/10
7/16 (10) 7/15